Popular Culture

A USER'S GUIDE

Susie O'Brien
McMaster University

Imre Szeman
McMaster University

THOMSON

NELSON

Australia   Canada   Mexico   Singapore   Spain   United Kingdom   United States

THOMSON

NELSON

Popular Culture: A User's Guide

by Susie O'Brien and Imre Szeman

Editorial Director and Publisher:
Evelyn Veitch

Acquisitions Editor:
Anne Williams

Marketing Manager:
Cara Yarzab

Senior Developmental Editor:
Mike Thompson

Managing Production Editor:
Susan Calvert

Copy Editor/Proofreader:
Kelli Howey

Creative Director:
Angela Cluer

Interior Design
Peter Papayanakis

Cover Design:
Angela Cluer

Cover Image:
Robin Collyer

Compositor:
Alicja Jamorski

Senior Production Coordinator:
Hedy Sellers

Permissions Coordinator:
Karen Becker

Printer:
Transcontinental

National Library of Canada Cataloguing in Publication Data

O'Brien, Susie
  Popular culture : a user's guide / Susie O'Brien, Imre Szeman.

Includes bibliographical references and index.
ISBN 0-7747-3744-1

  1. Popular culture. I. Szeman, Imre John Louis, 1968– II. Title.

CB430.O27 2003   306
C2003-903329-5

Contents

CHAPTER 3—REPRESENTATION AND THE CONSTRUCTION OF SOCIAL REALITY   57

CHAPTER 8—SUBCULTURES AND COUNTERCULTURES   237

CHAPTER 9—GLOBALIZATION AND POPULAR CULTURE   263

CHAPTER 10—WHY STUDY POPULAR CULTURE? A BRIEF HISTORY OF CULTURAL STUDIES 295

Preface: A User's Guide to the *User's Guide*

The goal of *Popular Culture: A User's Guide* is to provide readers with an introduction to the critical study of popular culture. Our aim is to give readers the analytical tools to understand the everyday texts and practices that surround them, as well as their own roles as consumers of and participants in popular culture.

Why does anyone need a guidebook to popular culture? Don't we all already know not only what is meant by popular culture, but also how to consume and use it? Guidebooks are supposed to make mysterious lands with unusual customs more familiar, or help us learn how to navigate complex tasks (like building a deck or planting a good-looking garden) with greater ease. Popular culture, on the other hand, is, well, *popular*. When it comes to watching films, listening to pop music, shopping, or sucking down cups of coffee, we believe that we know exactly what we are doing and why we are doing it. Like our native tongue, popular culture is something we know how to "speak" without resorting to lessons, audiotapes, courses, or guidebooks. So what can a user's guide tell us about popular culture that we don't already know?

In many respects, it is precisely the intimacy and familiarity with which we engage in contemporary popular culture that requires critical reflection, exploration, and analysis. After all, knowing how to speak a language because we are immersed in it does not mean that we are necessarily able to read or write it, or that we understand its syntax and structure. Reading and writing take an enormous amount of effort to get right; even once we have learned how to read, we are faced with other questions, such as how written language on a page can convey information about real and imagined worlds.

As with language, so, too, with popular culture. Because we are immersed in it, popular culture is both uniquely accessible and frustratingly opaque; it is hard to get a critical purchase on something we inhabit so completely and, most of the time, more or less unconsciously. In order to help us understand the "syntax" and "grammar" of popular culture—the unacknowledged but crucial structures that give popular culture its shape, meaning, and significance—the goal of this book is to help readers to see this familiar terrain more acutely and with greater insight. Our familiarity with popular culture tends to hide some of its most important features and its relationship to broader social, political, and economic currents. *Popular Culture: A User's Guide* will help readers to see parts of the contemporary cultural landscape that they may have been looking at all along without really perceiving.

This book aims to take readers beyond the "common sense" approach to popular culture, an approach that is defined by an odd mix of cynical knowingness and complacency. We are working from the premise that readers today possess an unprecedented level of media literacy. We are all aware, for example, that certain forms of media such as advertising operate according to particular agendas that may or may not reflect our own interests, and we also believe that we are smart enough to resist. This book seeks to create a level of awareness that goes beyond that cynical complacency, not only to make readers aware of the underlying socioeconomic structures that determine the shape of media and, by extension, consciousness, but also to recognize the myriad ways that popular culture manages to manouevre around these structures. We want to give students the tools to understand their role not just as consumers but also as agents of popular culture.

We also want to showcase the full range of activities and practices that can be considered to be part of contemporary popular cultural experience. Unlike "high culture," which is generally understood to refer to a discrete body of books or artworks that are unified by their adherence to specific aesthetic and cultural codes, the field of popular culture is diverse and uneven, comprising texts and practices ranging from commercial media to subcultural styles to the activities of everyday life (eating, shopping, drinking coffee, recreational activities, etc.).

Many books about popular culture are actually surveys or overviews of academic or theoretical *approaches* to the study of popular culture. In other words, what such books offer is a roughly historical account of a specific academic discipline (what is now often called "cultural studies") and the individuals and theories that have been important to the development of that discipline. While we certainly discuss and make use of many of the most important theories of popular culture, we have chosen to emphasize practical strategies for understanding and interpreting the popular. Working from case studies and examples, the aim of this book is to provide readers with a critical vocabulary and methods of analysis that will allow them to perform independent readings of cultural texts extending far beyond the sampling we offer here.

The specific analyses that we provide in each chapter exemplify ways of using and adapting critical and theoretical materials to addresses the issues and problems at hand. The text is organized mainly around broad themes rather than specific genres or forms of popular culture (television, music, film, etc.), and is book-ended by chapters that focus on the pre-history of contemporary popular culture (Chapter One) and on the complexities that the current historical context introduces for the study of popular culture (Chapters Nine and Ten).

There are a number of other features of this book that make it a distinctive contribution to the study of popular culture. There is, first, an emphasis throughout on the politics of popular culture—that is, on the way in which popular culture is always connected to practices and discourses related to the exercise and struggle over power and recognition in contemporary society. Second, there is an emphasis on Canadian examples and situations. Why? Even though our understanding of popular culture has been shaped and influenced by writers and thinkers from around the world, our approach to and understanding of popular culture is informed by our experiences of growing up and teaching in Canada. This does not mean, of course, that everything that we talk about or make reference to in this book has been made or created in Canada. This would be a false reflection of the experience of popular culture in Canada, which has historically always included radio and television programs from the United States and the United Kingdom (and elsewhere), and film and literature from around the world—alongside and in conjunction with home-grown programming and cultural production.

Sometimes at the expense of our own cultural producers, Canadians have been (for a variety of reasons) avid consumers of pop culture produced around the world. This book reflects this diversity of pop cultural sources, but just as importantly provides an interesting, uniquely Canadian perspective on Western pop culture that emerges out of Canada's specific structural relationship to the mythical pop cultural centre of "America." Because Canada is both outside of American pop culture and also uniquely and deeply engaged with it, we hope that this book sheds an interesting and useful light on phenomena that have thus far been examined from the perspective of too few geographic locations—for the most part, from the United States, the United Kingdom, and Australia. In the study of popular culture, what you see and do not see often depends on where you are looking from.

Finally, in order to help our readers work through the *User's Guide,* we have incorporated a number of pedagogic features. Important terms and concepts are listed in a glossary at the end of the book, and are highlighted in **bold** in the text to allow readers to cross-reference with ease. Each chapter contains one or more suggested activities and questions that are intended to get readers to think further about particular subjects and to apply them to their own experiences. In course use, these Suggested Activities may form the basis of oral or written assignments. Close-Ups in each chapter clarify key concepts, theories, or movements, and may also form the basis for further study and investigation. Each chapter ends with a brief summary of the main points discussed, followed by a list of suggestions for further reading. These titles include other introductory texts that might deal with the same material in a different way or with a different emphasis, and original works by scholars and theorists referred to in the chapter. This text also has a Website with more helpful resources and information (www.popularculture.nelson.com).

Like the writers of any guidebook, our hope is that readers use our maps and recommendations of places to visit and things to think about as a jumping-off point for the elaboration of their own maps of the landscape of popular culture. The authors would be the first to admit that not only are there plenty of things that they have not seen, but that there are places they do not yet even know exist.

Susie O'Brien
Imre Szeman
Hamilton, Ontario
February 2003

Acknowledgments

It would have been impossible to complete this book without the assistance of a number of people. First and foremost, Carolyn Veldstra and Tim Walters went above and beyond the call of duty in the amount of time and effort they put into this project. We cannot thank them enough for their work. We are also grateful to Tim Kaposy, who stepped in at short notice to help us pull things together as final deadlines loomed. To paraphrase Sandra Bernhard (an almost-forgotten icon of Nineties pop culture): Without the three of you, we'd be nothing. The other big hand of applause goes to our undergraduate and graduate students in cultural studies, on whom many of these ideas were first tested and who gave us the inspiration and impetus for this book.

At Nelson, we'd like to thank Mike Thompson for keeping us on track and leading us to complete this book faster than we could have imagined, and Anne Williams, whom we have alternately thanked and cursed for asking us to do this book in the first place (thanks, Anne). The reviewers who read parts of this book at different stages helped to make it better, and we wish to thank them for their input: Debra Clarke, Trent University; Joel Faflak, Wilfrid Laurier University; Len Findlay, University of Saskatchewan; Linda Frank, Mohawk College; Allan Gedalof, University of Western Ontario; Keith Hampson, Ryerson University; Mike Hunter, University College of Cape Breton; Daniel Keyes, Okanagan University College; Mark Lowes, University of Ottawa; Sourayan Mookerjea, University of Alberta; Deborah Parnis, Trent University; and Monique Tschofen, Ryerson University. We would also like to thank the Social Sciences and Humanities Council of Canada, grants from which provided financial assistance that helped us to complete this project.

Imre's thanks: Half of this book was written in the warm confines of the Staircase Café Theatre. Thanks to Kathy Garneau and Hugh MacLeod for enriching cultural life in Hamilton, to Tara the Soup Lady for warming my belly and sparking my imagination, and to Paul for letting me outstay my welcome day after day. (The other half was written in my office at McMaster University, which is built out of cinder blocks and lacks both heat and blinds. Though these environmental deficits actually contribute to productivity, I am not sure that they require any special acknowledgment.) Latham Hunter helped the project at an important transitional stage, while Lidia and Tony Botelho provide an important element of the "conditions of possibility" of my work in the first place. My son, Joseph, probably won't remember having to endure (among other things) being dragged to documentaries that he found utterly boring; thanks for not exacting too heavy a price in return. Finally, for putting up with obsession and depression, for giving me the time to work at the expense of her own chance to read *Gorgias* and *The Golden Ass,* and for everything else: thank you, Maria … without you, I really am nothing.

Susie's thanks: Many thanks to Jake Kennedy, whose diligent research assistance and excellent ideas helped get this project off the ground. Friends and family offered various kinds of help and inspiration: thanks especially to Duncan O'Brien for his photographs, and for his unusual insights into popular culture, almost none of which made it into the book; to my parents, who know nothing at all about popular culture; and to Marlo Edwards, whose work on gun-toting women inspired the vital inclusion in this book of a photo of Pamela Anderson as Barb Wire. Finally, my most heartfelt thanks go to Peter Mountford, whose love and generosity along with his critical insights into everything from cyber-culture to blue Pepsi informed this book in crucial ways, and to Bridget and Thomas—who, like the Industrial Revolution, pretty well wrecked popular recreation as we knew it, but made all kinds of new entertainment possible. All these people contributed to both the ideas and the ambience that made it possible to imagine and write this book.

Chapter 1

Introducing Popular Culture

APPROACHING POPULAR CULTURE

"Let's go get a coffee."

Every day, throughout North America, this phrase is uttered thousands of times, by different people—students, teachers, construction workers, lawyers, mothers, retail clerks, unemployed people, old people, young people—and in different social contexts, such as work, breaks from work, dating, interviews, therapy sessions, or hanging out. Going for a coffee is a major part of popular culture, not only in the sense that it is such a common practice, but also in that it means so much more than the literal act of tossing back a hot caffeinated beverage: in fact, "going for coffee" need not involve drinking coffee at all. So what does it mean? And what is it about coffee-drinking that makes it part of popular culture while other equally common practices—like, say, yawning, or mowing the lawn—are not? Or are they part of popular culture, too?

These are the kind of questions this book sets out to answer—not by offering a comprehensive account of what fits in the category of popular culture and what does not, but by helping us to think about the question of *why* popular culture is such a critical part of contemporary life. For this reason, it might be misleading to call this book a "user's guide" to popular culture. A standard user's guide to, say, a cell phone that you may have just received for Christmas (which happens so often in TV commercials but so seldom in real life) tells you everything there is to know about the specific object that you have in your hands, what its functions are, and what it can and cannot do. Popular culture is not like that. For one thing, popular culture is a far more difficult "thing" to pin down than a cell phone, or an Ikea desk, or Windows XP; it is constantly changing shape, shifting locations, assuming new identities and new tasks and functions. The goal of a user's guide to popular culture is to provide the users of it—that is, all of us—with a way to think about popular culture that is flexible and supple enough to also allow us to think about its changes and redefinitions. Let's face it: no one reads past the first few pages of the thick book of instructions that comes with a cell phone—you turn the phone on and figure it out as you go. Once again, popular culture is different. In this case, we *need* a guide precisely because we're already so familiar with the ways we use it that it's difficult to figure out what else we can do with it—we do not really understand its possibilities, and its limits.

What's at stake in the definition of popular culture? How can we learn to read and participate in—to *use*—the popular in a way that strengthens our understanding of our selves and the world we live in? These are large and exhausting questions—large and exhausting enough to make you want to, well, go get a coffee! That's why, although such questions are at the core of this book, the way in which we attempt to get at them is through the analysis of actual "texts" (objects that we can interpret just like a book) and "practices" (things that we do): seeing movies, listening to songs, watching TV shows, playing sports, going shopping—and drinking coffee. The purpose of this introduction is to lay out a working definition of popular culture, to outline a few key concepts that will reappear in later discussion, and to give you a diagram of the way this book is put together—a "guide to the guide"—that should help make the task of piecing the bits of popular culture together a productive one. In other words, we'll first lay out the pieces and the tools, and describe what they do. Just be forewarned: by the end of the book you will still be left with extra parts and you will likely end up with a concept of popular culture that looks different than that of your neighbours. But trust us: this is a good thing....

DEFINING POPULAR CULTURE

Like most things that form a big part of our daily lives, popular culture is familiar and obvious at first glance, but very complicated as soon as you start to think about it in any detail. Before we outline the concept of popular culture that informs this book, we suggest you take a couple of minutes to try and come up with your own working definition. When we've conducted this exercise in introductory university classes, a typical range of ideas tend to come up: popular culture consists of those things—products, texts, practices, and so on—that are enjoyed by lots and lots of people; popular culture is commercial culture (as opposed to, say, "high" culture, which people today still tend to associate with the things they imagine that rich people who own yachts like to do, like listen to opera or go to the symphony); popular culture consists of the traditional practices and beliefs or way of life of a specific group; and, finally, the most wide-ranging definition of all, that popular culture is simply the practices of everyday life.

What is interesting about these definitions is not just their range, but their differences—differences that are shaped to a large degree by the way we understand the terms "popular" and "culture." How does your definition fit with these? Does it accord more closely with some than others? What definitions of "popular" and "culture" are implied by your understanding of popular culture?

It is worth taking the time to think about different ways of understanding popular culture, though not so we can dismiss some of them in order to identify a correct definition. Like most other important social concepts—concepts such as "democracy," "progress," "justice," "civilization," and so on, that produce the shape of the societies that we live in—it does not really make sense to hope for a correct definition that would do something like solve the puzzle of all of these different meanings by establishing the essential one supposedly lurking in their midst. Rather, we want to suggest that popular culture is informed by *all* these perspectives, not just in the sense that each is partially true, but in the sense that the tension between them is fundamental to understanding the meaning of popular culture today. So before we erect a definition of popular culture that we can all feel comfortable inhabiting, we need to think about this tension. This may initially seem to be a frustratingly circuitous and unhelpful route to finding out the "facts." However, such meanderings are a critical part of the study of culture, in which the question of meaning is never self-evident, but always up for negotiation and disagreement.

What Is Culture?

When we ask our students to track the word "culture" as it is used in the media and other sources, two things tend to emerge: (1) "culture" (along with variations such as "multiculturalism") gets mentioned *a lot*, implying that it is a significant concept in our society,

ROYAL ONTARIO MUSEUM

DIOR · CHANEL · GIVENCHY

ELITE
Elegance
Couture fashion in the 1950s

Many museums now offer presentations of modern popular culture artifacts and everyday items, such as the recent "Elite Elegance: Couture Fashion in the 1950s" exhibit at Toronto's Royal Ontario Museum, which explored style in 1950s Toronto.

and one that we likely can't do without; and (2) it appears in many different, often contradictory contexts, suggesting that exactly *how* it signifies is hard to pin down. When we talk about "culture" in the sense of building opera houses, the word obviously means something different than when we talk about "Western culture" or "youth culture," "national culture," or "business culture." "Culture" in the first sense—the one that fits with opera houses, ballet, and Shakespeare, which for convenience we'll call "capital-C Culture"—focuses on what we usually think of as high-end creative production: artistic pursuits that are enjoyed by an elite minority as opposed to more accessible leisure activities, such as sports. These kinds of cultural productions are those that have over time (they are often associated with the past) assumed an especially privileged place in the collection of ideas and artifacts that comprises a cultural *tradition*. In the context of this understanding of "Culture," which is the one generally associated with university programs in humanities or the arts, the idea of "popular culture" would seem to be a contradiction in terms. After all, you go to university to learn about Stephen Daedalus, not Stephen King.

A second definition encompasses a much broader understanding of culture as a whole way of life of a society or a distinct subsection of society: along with art, it encompasses everyday rituals such as meals, work, religious observances, sports, sex, and friendship. Implicitly opposed to "nature," which we associate with biology (the things we share with the non-human world), "culture" in this context refers to the practices that define us, collectively and in distinct groups, as human. This definition of culture, or something close to it, informs the disciplines of the social sciences—particularly anthropology, which until recently tended to focus on the cultures of pre-industrial societies. When we go on vacation to experience other "cultures," it is this sense of culture that we are making reference to: a glimpse into a different way of life organized according to its own principles and around its own unique practices.

The Mass Media   Interestingly, neither the familiar humanities definition of culture nor the one employed by traditional anthropologists adequately encompasses the experience of living in a postmodern capitalist society—the experience of most of us who teach and study those subjects—which is a way of life increasingly dominated by the mass media. Not only do the mass media tend to fall outside the definitions of culture centred around elite artistic production or the practices of ordinary everyday life; they also are frequently cited as the thing that threatens to destroy "culture" in both these senses: while one set of critics laments the dumbing-down of Shakespeare to satisfy the tastes of a mass audience in the Hollywood production *William Shakespeare's Romeo and Juliet*, another warns of the corruption of "authentic" grassroots cultures by the global entertainment industry, which has made it more difficult to find cultures in our travels that are all that different from our own. While they come from different places, what these criticisms have in common is an element of nostalgia, a feeling that something has been lost, that a once-pure realm of culture has become contaminated by commerce. It is the desire to understand this world-contaminated-by-commerce that motivates the relatively new discipline of *cultural studies*, into which this book fits (and whose development as an academic field is discussed in more detail in the final chapter).

Objects of Study   To avoid the limitations of earlier definitions of "culture," cultural studies defines its object of study in very broad terms. One definition, offered in *Key*

Concepts in Communication and Cultural Studies, describes culture as "the social production and reproduction of sense, meaning and consciousness. The sphere of meaning, which unifies the spheres of production (economics) and social relations (politics)" (O'Sullivan et al. 68). This is a useful definition insofar as it manages to encompass a wide variety of "meaning-producing" practices and technologies, including both traditional definitions of culture—fine art and everyday practices—and mass media. Of course, while the incorporation of these diverse meanings into one functional frame might give us a quick snapshot of what it is that cultural studies actually *studies*—the kinds of things that it looks at and why it is that it looks at them—it is difficult to ignore the knowledge that beyond the borders of the snapshot the different conceptions of culture that are named in this definition are historically not only different, but also *contradictory*.

Rather than seeking to smooth over these contradictions, cultural studies is interested in actively teasing them out and laying them bare. It is committed to an understanding of culture that does not just expand on earlier definitions in order to include practices and objects that tended, for different reasons, to get left out (such as the novels of Stephen King), but also thinks about why and how such inclusions and exclusions occur in the first place. This means that cultural studies thinks deeply about the connections between culture and the spheres of politics and economics, and seeks to understand how that realm of activity concerned with "meanings, pleasures, and identities" (Fiske *Understanding* 1) shapes (and is shaped by) relations of power. Among the key questions that are raised by the contradictions between the different definitions of culture cited above are: How is culture produced (made by a society) and reproduced (passed on by a society into the future)? Who makes culture? For whom is it made? This brings us to the other half of the concept of "popular culture."

What/Who Defines the Popular?

Having wrestled with the complicated problem of what constitutes "culture," the meaning of "popular" seems much more straightforward, at least initially. Derived from the Latin word *popularis*, which means "of, or belonging to the people," "popular" is often used in a contemporary context to describe something that is liked by a lot of people. For example, when an authoritative source cites *Baywatch* as the most popular show on television, "boasting a peak viewership of 1.1 billion" (Hedge), we can assume, reasonably, that a lot of us are watching or have watched *Baywatch*. But when we start to look a little further into how the word "popular" is used today, it becomes obvious that it has to do with more than numbers—that the words "popular" and "the people" don't refer to absolutely everyone, but to a particular group to whom a certain quality or value is attached.

A couple of examples will serve to illustrate this. First, a number of major art museums have recently come under fire for abandoning their mandate to promote serious art in favour of "popular," blockbuster shows guaranteed to fill up the galleries (and the museum shop). A good example of this is a recent exhibit at the Guggenheim Museum in New York City on "The Art of the Motorcycle." In cases such as this, the popular audience is characterized by implicit contrast with a different audience whose members presumably possess the discriminating taste that allows them to appreciate good art. An argument can be quickly mounted in favour of the museum's decision to show more "popular" work: as a public space, the museum should respond to the preference of people in general rather than to the tastes of an overly educated minority, which is what museums have typically catered to. Since these latter tastes are often seen to be disproportionately supported by state subsidy of the arts, this argument also often concerns the appropriate allocation of tax dollars and the need for arts industries to be more market-driven. While a cultural institution can readily apply to governments for support of a show on the Group of Seven, it is harder to justify showing off BMW motorbikes in the Guggenheim's elegant confines, even if this is what the public might "really" want to see. In this case, the "popular" is evoked both as a democratic principle *and* as a judgment about who can make sense of "real" art. By including more "popular" shows, the museums invite more people inside them—but not, of course, to see the kinds of art objects they were designed to exhibit.

The second example concerns the use of the word "people" in the context of protests surrounding the 2001 Summit of the Americas, a meeting of government leaders to discuss trade liberalization (the reduction of barriers to freer trade) amongst countries in North and South America. To register widespread concern about the exclusivity of the meeting, which was restricted to government leaders and the chief executive officers of major corporations, and about the relatively scant attention paid to social justice issues during this meeting (and by these government leaders more generally), protestors organized a parallel "People's Summit." The aim of the People's Summit was to foreground the issues left off the agenda of the official meeting, in the process highlighting the failure of the political leaders to represent the legitimate interests of their constituents. In this example, the word "people" connotes something like "democratic" or "grassroots" or "ordinary," in contrast to the powerful minority running the official summit.

However, its sense gets complicated, in this case, by the refusal of the participants of the official summit and many in the media to accept the legitimacy of the protestors' claims to embody the voice of democracy. After all, as some of the leaders pointed out, *they* were the ones who were democratically elected; the protestors represented no one but themselves. In this way, the terms get flipped around so that it is the politicians who speak for "the people" against the "special interest groups" represented by the protestors: the term "people" here becomes the symbolic linchpin of a battle to gain the moral high ground over the substantive issues under debate. As with the art museum, the word "people" and its derivative "popular" are used here to convey something roughly opposite to "elite," though the *value* of those terms means something entirely different in each context.

So, we can add a couple of new elements to our understanding of the word "popular": first, it tends to carry with it connotations of value that are implicitly contrasted with the value of what it is *not*, though those values are seen differently depending on who is talking and in what context. Second, as becomes particularly evident in the latter example of the People's Summit, the question of who or what constitutes the popular is tangled up with questions of power.

With this in mind, let's return to the apparently simple usage of "popular" with which we began this section, and think about it in a little more detail. Who are the people who define the "popularity" of *Baywatch*? Are they the unenlightened masses who lack the ability to discriminate between schlock and substance? Are they discerning viewers exercising their consumer choice? Or are they engaged in an act of political activism, employing the cultural resources of *Baywatch* to construct an agenda for progressive social change? The slightly ludicrous quality of the last possibility raises a quite serious question about how we understand the popular: what kind of agency—that is, possibility for self-motivated activity or action—is involved on the part of "the people" in determining or defining something to be "popular"? This question has particular significance when we start to talk about popular culture.

What Is Popular Culture?

The most common uses of the term "popular culture" can be divided into two distinct meanings that reflect in interesting ways our understandings of the two separate words that we discussed above. The first, most familiar use of the term "popular culture" identifies it with the entertainment produced through and by commercial media (TV, film, the music industry, etc.) that have the economic and technological capacity to reach large, demographically diverse and geographically dispersed audiences. Popularity is measured, in this case, by patterns of consumption: it refers to the things we buy (or watch, or listen to, etc.). A somewhat different use of the term "popular culture" defines it in terms not of consumption, but production: popular culture is what "the people" make, or do, for themselves. This definition fits fairly closely with the anthropological definition of culture as "the practices of everyday life."

Both of these definitions differ quite clearly from the elite culture defended by those cranky art patrons who think that Marsden Hartley's paintings should never take a back seat to Harley-Davidson motorbikes. Apart from this, however, their connotations are quite different and even oppositional: "do-it-yourself" popular culture is explicitly different from the culture that is produced by large corporate entities whose interest in the everyday practices of their consumers is shaped by their need to figure out how best to sell them things. Indeed, the kind of culture produced by the commercial media is often seen as threatening the culture of everyday life by diverting people's desire for fulfillment—a desire that can ultimately be satisfied only by productive activity—into habits of passive consumption.

Folk Culture and Mass Culture   To distinguish clearly between these two different forms of cultural production, critics will sometimes use the terms *folk culture* and *mass culture*. **Folk culture** refers to those cultural products and practices that have developed over time within a particular community or socially identifiable group, and that are communicated from generation to generation and amongst people who tend to be known to one another. It tends to be seen as the direct expression of the life experiences shared by its creators and their audience (Nachbar and Lause 15; Grossberg et al. 37). **Mass culture**, on the other hand, is produced for an unknown, disparate audience. While the transmission of folk culture is generally technologically simple (e.g., face-to-face, oral communication), mass culture depends on electronic (or mechanical) media to convey its message to the largest possible audience in order to secure maximum profit, which is its ultimate goal. These terms can serve to make useful distinctions between kinds of cultural production, highlighting the differences between, say, an Inuit soapstone carving and an MTV rap video. On even a superficial examination, however, the differences start to look a little fuzzy. Inuit art has become so popular among non-Inuit that it has spawned factories in the south where carvers use power tools to create an identical series of polar bears, for which they are paid by the piece (George). Rap music, now a multi-billion dollar industry, emerged relatively recently from the black street culture of the South Bronx. In each of these cases, it is difficult to identify the precise moment when folk culture metamorphosed into mass culture. The attempt to maintain a strict division is not just tricky in a practical sense, but also, arguably, somewhat suspect ideologically.

The desire to preserve a folk culture safe from the corrupting influence of commerce is often inflected by a nostalgic desire to return to a (mythical) moment of history in which cultural and social identities were secure and cultural boundaries were clear. The power of such nostalgia for homegrown, anti-commercial culture can be seen in the huge commercial success of Martha Stewart's enterprises, which evoke feelings toward a homey, small-town America of simple values that in reality never existed. When the desire to preserve a folk culture is extended to a socially and economically disadvantaged group, as in the two examples above, the situation becomes even more complicated. While Inuit might argue that the preservation of folk culture is a matter of community survival, the unhappiness of white collectors at the move toward mass-produced art may be motivated by concerns that have little to do with indigenous autonomy and more with how the value of their own art pieces will be affected. A less crudely materialist motivation for consumer nostalgia in this case might be a well-intentioned, if racist, aesthetic investment in the image of the "noble savage" whose perseverance at the ends of a global electronic world holds up the (fantastical) possibility of a completely different world than that dominated by the values of the West.

However nominally progressive the cause that is being (or has been) promoted in the name of "the people," *folk culture* remains a term whose peculiarly heavy ideological baggage should set off alarm bells every time we hear or read it (the same alarm bells that should go off when we hear politicians invoke the mythical category of "ordinary working Americans/Canadians/Australians." Just who are these "ordinary" people?). This is not to say that we need to abandon completely the idea of folk culture and all its troublesome derivations. Like mass culture, it retains some value as a descriptive term to designate particular kinds of cultural production, especially when referring to a time before the present moment of late capitalism—a moment when, as one critic puts it, "all culture is mass culture" (Denning 258). For now, let's put aside "mass" and (particularly) "folk" cultures into the category of *concepts that are useful to know but liable to collapse under pressure,* and return to our original focus on "popular culture," a term whose ambiguity has the virtue of signifying the messy complexity of a cultural field in which authenticity and commercial value are increasingly impossible to disentangle.

Suggested Activity 1.1

Does commercialism destroy the authenticity of a cultural product or practice? Or does the authenticity of an object or practice increase its commercial value and potential? What does it mean if it is possible for us to answer both of these questions affirmatively? How does the divide between authenticity and commercial value work in the case of a practice like eco-tourism and an object like the first release of an indie band on its own label?

The Culture of Everyday Life   In order to signal this ambiguity and to avoid producing a definition of popular culture that falls too clearly on the side of celebrating the folk or denigrating the masses, we might define popular culture as something like "the communicative practices of everyday life" (where "communicative practices" comprises all those activities concerned with the production of meaning: talking, writing, social rituals such as eating, shopping, dancing, music, visual culture, sports, fashion, etc.) that are shared amongst many members of a society, including and especially those who lack social, economic, or political power. This somewhat clumsy definition accomplishes three things: (1) it signals the inclusion of mass media alongside, and even within, the practices of everyday life, without determining in advance what relationship it has to those practices; (2) it emphasizes the *meaningful* nature of popular culture—meaningful in the sense that it is important, as well as in the sense that it is concerned with the production of sense and social value; and (3) it highlights the issue of power that always and overtly dogs the production of culture in general, and popular culture in particular.

The Politics of Popular Culture

Why is power such a central issue for understanding popular culture? Culture is, as we have already tried to suggest, bound up closely with other aspects of human existence. As "the sphere of meaning which unifies the spheres of production (economics) and social relations (politics)," culture is concerned not just with individual tastes and desires, but also with the fundamental organization of society—with the distribution of material and symbolic power, which culture both reflects and influences. In the early twenty-first century, in most parts of the world the dominant economic system is **capitalism** (for more on capitalism, see Close-Up 1.1). This means that the key characteristics of capitalism, including both its wealth-generating capacity and the patterns of inequitable distribution on which that capacity depends, help to determine the shape of culture. This is particularly true for popular culture.

In fact, one could argue that capitalism doesn't just inform particular *versions* of popular culture in the sense of sustaining some dominant narratives (e.g., the story of success

Capitalism

Capitalism is the dominant economic system in the world today. It is not the only economic system that has ever been in place, nor is it likely to be the last way in which human beings organize their economies, despite some claims to the contrary.

Loosely definable as a system of private enterprise whose primary aim is the production of profit, capitalism has been developing since at least the fifteenth century, and underwrites many of the economic and cultural institutions that we take for granted today, such as private property, individual freedom, and the imperative of economic growth. Our tendency today to see these features of capitalism as not only positive but also *natural*—the products of human nature rather than consciously worked-out ideas—makes it harder to see its less desirable aspects such as social fragmentation, the unequal distribution of wealth, and the conversion of everything, including life itself, into something that can be bought or sold.

These brutal elements of capitalism were particularly evident during the heyday of European colonialism from the seventeenth to the nineteenth centuries. During this period, the exploitation of resources and enslavement of people from the non-European world helped make possible the massive accumulation of wealth enjoyed by a relatively small percentage of Europeans. This in turn fuelled the Industrial Revolution, in which both the productive and the destructive elements of capitalism were further intensified.

In capitalist economies, the means of creating, distributing, and exchanging wealth lie mainly in the hands of individuals and corporations (which in North America have the rights of individuals), rather than in public or state hands. The value of goods and labour is defined not by their social usefulness or significance, but by how much they can be exchanged for. The main goal of individuals in capitalism is to maximize the profit or the wages they receive. Proponents believe that through the dance of supply and demand goods and services are optimally and efficiently distributed throughout society. Detractors point to the growing gap between the wealthy and the poor, who often generate wealth for those at the top.

Postmodern, postindustrial, or late capitalism is distinguished by the fact that by comparison to earlier eras of capitalism there is now a far greater emphasis on the exchange of information and services (software and banking) as opposed to hard goods (steel and cars) in an economy that has become globally integrated.

through hard work) and disabling others (e.g., the triumph of the group over the individual), or by enabling certain kinds of technological innovation. *Capitalism enables the production of popular culture, period.* We will go on to define "capitalist" in more detail, and to trace the historical evolution of the relationship between capitalism and popular culture in Chapter Two. For now, it is sufficient to note that the economic and social struggle that is intrinsic to capitalism is fought, to some extent, on the terrain of popular culture.

Napster   A simple example will serve to illustrate the kind of struggle we're talking about: until the mid-1980s, the evolution of the music industry in North America was a story of skyrocketing profits. This story culminated in the introduction of the CD, which forced consumers to pay considerably more than what they had paid for vinyl LPs (with what many agreed was only a marginal improvement in sound quality), not to mention shelling out for expensive new sound systems. As promised price reductions never materialized, a quiet groundswell of annoyance with the recording industry began to grow. It seemed like a classic case of the customer getting cheated by corporations.

Enter Napster. The same digital technology that enabled the development of the CD also enabled the development of file-sharing programs that allowed people to swap music files on their PCs without paying a cent. The recording industry, predictably, began to get anxious, and launched a series of lawsuits in order to recoup their lost profits. Napster eventually settled with the industry, developing technology to monitor and restrict the downloading of songs, which would now be subject to a subscription fee. In the meantime, a host of new sites have sprung up, taking advantage of the decentralized structure of the Internet to evade the legal and technological powers of the recording industry. The story of Napster is a complicated one, with seemingly clear battle lines between "the people" and "the corporation" blurred by such issues as the rights of musicians to get paid for their work, the accessibility of technology, and its implications for the construction of the community.

"Popular culture" in this example is not simply an arena in which the disempowered exert their agency, defining themselves out from under the prevailing structures of power. Neither does it work simply to maintain those structures by co-opting dissent against the dominant ideology of consumer capitalism. It is subject, rather, to a constant struggle over pleasure, profit, and, ultimately, over the distribution of social and economic power in the world.

Power Relationships   This dimension of struggle means that it is impossible to ever fix the meaning of popular culture in terms of a collection of objects or practices, or in terms of a single group who can be said to possess them. We need to understand it, as cultural theorist Stuart Hall puts it, not as "a mere descriptive inventory—which may have the negative effect of freezing popular culture into some timeless descriptive mould—but [as] the relations of power which are constantly punctuating and dividing the domain of culture into its preferred and its residual categories" ("Notes" 234). What is true for the objects and practices of popular culture is also true for those who use/participate in them. If, as another critic, John Fiske, has claimed, "popular culture is the culture of the subordinated and disempowered" (*Understanding* 4), this does not mean that it is possible to identify, by means of a simple checklist, who's "in" and who's "out." Rather than existing in a stable form as the property of a single group, power moves between and among individuals and institutions; this movement is registered with particular acuity in the domain of popular culture. In the absence of the certainty of clear categories, we are left then with the less comfortable but more expansive framework of a series of open-ended questions. In evaluating the significance of popular culture, we always need to ask "who says what, how, to whom, with what effect and for what purpose?" (Williams qtd. in Burke 218).

This series of connected questions usefully indicates some of the areas of key concern within cultural studies. On the broadest level, these areas might be identified as *representation*, the process of making meaning from sign-systems that encompasses anything from words and images to physical structures (cars, buildings, cities) to fashion accessories; *production*, which includes the individual and corporate entities involved in the creation and distribution of cultural products, including the technologies through which they are produced and reproduced; and *consumption*, which involves the economic, technological, and physical processes by which different audiences derive meaning from cultural products.

Of course these categories—the subjects of Chapters Three, Four, and Five, respectively—can't help but bleed into one another. The texts and practices of culture are inseparable from the means of technological production or from what individual audiences do with them—nor can they be separated from non-cultural realms of existence such as economics and politics. Lest popular culture begin to sound like everything (or nothing), let's try to pin it down more firmly, by returning to our original example of drinking coffee. An examination of this practice through the lenses of representation, production, and consumption can help us to understand how popular culture operates, drawing us in as producers and consumers and working, literally, to reshape the world.

COFFEE AS POPULAR CULTURE

Coffee is a part of culture to the extent that we can ask "What does coffee *mean*?" Coffee is not, in other words, just "a liquid brown drug" (Leah Hager Cohen 10), but part of a complex set of social rituals. The significance of coffee is hugely determined by context: its meaning shifts depending on whether we are drinking it at home or in a café, from a mug or a Styrofoam cup. Its significance also varies depending on whether we are alone or with friends and on what other activities we are engaged in: a social meeting, for example, or a late-night cramming session—in which case it might really be coffee's status as a "liquid brown drug" that we are seeking.

But even then, when the physical properties of coffee are arguably more important than its symbolic properties, it is *still* more than just a drug. After all, if it were just a stimulant we were after, there are obviously other, more powerful options out there. The fact that most of us are probably inclined to reach for coffee rather than, say, amphetamines speaks to more

For both Tim Hortons and Starbucks, décor is key to producing a corporate image sugges-
tive of a particular lifestyle.

than the question of availability or a fear of being arrested for drug possession. In fact these
questions (why is caffeine legal while amphetamines are controlled and pot is illegal?) are
themselves tied up in the culture of coffee—what it means in a broader social context. To
answer them, along with the broader question of how coffee comes to be part of culture, we
need to look at coffee in the context of representation, production, and consumption.

The Representation of Coffee

To say that coffee "signifies"—that it refers to something other than its literal, physical
substance—is not to say that it has some kind of intrinsic or inherent meaning. Rather,
coffee acquires different, specific meanings as it is incorporated within different economic and social practices. It therefore makes sense to ask not just *what* does coffee
mean, but also "*how* does it acquire meaning, and under what circumstances?"

To talk about the meaning of coffee is to talk about how it operates in systems of *representation*, which translate a world of objects into one of sense, significance, and values.
So, what kind of significance or value is attached to coffee?

Suggested Activity 1.2

Take a few minutes and write down some of the meanings attached to coffee in
your life. What kinds of associations does it have and how do these change
depending on context? Strangely, this may be easier to do if you're *not* a coffee
drinker: it's easier to critically analyze a cultural practice if you're detached from it.

Something that tends to become quickly obvious when we start to come up with associations is that even something as simple as coffee signifies in multiple and different ways: for example, we might associate it with both relaxation and stimulation, both familiarity and sophistication, both social engagement and solitude. These radically different associations suggest firstly that meaning is to some extent arbitrary: there's no natural or logical meaning, only context-specific ones. It suggests secondly that meaning is qualitative or subjective, rather than objective: cultural associations fit into the category of *values* rather than *facts*. Moreover, these associations make sense only in implicit relation to a whole network of other associations to which they're connected, or from which they differ: coffee's capacity to stimulate, relax, or comfort in particular social situations derives in part from its *difference from* other liquid forms of stimulation or relaxation—beer, say, or milk—and in part through its *association with* other objects or practices—drinking containers, food, chairs, people, conversation, work, and so on. Put together, this collection of arbitrary, qualitative associations comprises what we can call a **mythology** of coffee: a widely understood if mostly unconscious network of meanings or narratives through which a specific culture makes sense of the world.

The Mythology of Drugs   We discuss the significance of mythology in more detail in Chapter Three. A key aspect to think about for now is the ways in which cultural mythologies tap into the underlying social structures of a culture, including its relations of power. To understand how this works, we can think for a moment about the cultural or *mythological* difference between coffee and some of the other drugs we cited above. Coffee, alcohol, and marijuana are all drugs (i.e., they all have mind- or body-altering properties), but they *signify* differently. The most obvious significance concerns their legality: as legal substances, coffee and alcohol fall symbolically within the realm of things our culture accepts and condones as part of social life. Marijuana (currently) does not. This different status, as cannabis activists along with many health professionals point out, is not justifiable on the basis of each drug's physical properties: marijuana is not, in other words, inherently more harmful than beer; rather, its status is determined within broader political and social structures (see Figure 1.1).

Of course, part of the mythology associated with different drugs *is* influenced by their physiological properties: the fact that caffeine is a stimulant—conducive, at least in theory, to productivity—while alcohol and marijuana are more conducive to relaxation explains in part why coffee is tolerated in most workplaces while booze and pot (even the names connote sin!) are not. While the different physiological states induced by these different drugs, and even their social effects, might be indisputable, what is less easily explained is why our society places a higher value on productivity and stimulation than on relaxation. Thinking about this question puts us in the realm not of nutrition or health, but of culture and representation.

The Production of Coffee

Clearly, the mythologies surrounding coffee, alcohol, and marijuana—mythologies that influence, as they are influenced by, their legal status—do not exist in a vacuum. Rather,

Figure 1.1 Effects of Caffeine and Marijuana

Normal   Caffeine   Marijuana

When researchers in the U.S. experimented with giving drugs to spiders, they found that caffeine had a more severe effect than marijuana, resulting in much more sparse, haphazard webs.

they are generated out of real, material processes: social, political, and economic. This becomes clear when we think about the differences in how coffee operates symbolically (i.e., what it represents) in the cultures of the North, where coffee is consumed in such large volumes, in comparison to the cultures of the South, where it is produced.

In North America, coffee is entangled in the lifestyle of postindustrial society: it is fuel, pleasure, instant gratification, relaxation. In many parts of the South, coffee is an equally integral part of life, associated not (or not only) with pleasure, but more substantially with labour and the basic conditions of life. Those social rituals that *do* exist in the South surrounding coffee are shaped by an awareness of its economic as well as its cultural significance. For example, amongst some coffee-growing cultures in Tanzania, coffee has an almost religious significance, associated with the *amagdala,* or the "life force" of the coffee grower, such that the death of a coffee tree was traditionally taken as an omen of its owner's death (Hyden qtd. in Weiss 96).

The History of Coffee in Western Culture   In the North, by contrast, coffee's role in the global economy is something that most of us, unless we're involved in the stock market or even more directly in coffee sales, are only dimly aware of. And yet its popular cultural significance is profoundly shaped by the history of its production, in conjunction with European colonialism in the seventeenth century as well as with more contemporary processes of **globalization** (see Chapter Nine). A brief discussion of this history helps to illuminate some of the ways that coffee signifies today.

The story of coffee's arrival in the West from the Middle East in the seventeenth century is part of the history of European colonialism. The importation of coffee was part of the much bigger process by which European nations sought to fuel their economies by finding new resources to develop, satisfying and promoting the desires of European consumers, and creating new markets for European manufactured goods. Coffee entered European popular culture via the eighteenth-century institution of the coffeehouse, a new meeting place described by one historian as "*the* site for the public life of the eighteenth-century middle class, a place where the bourgeoisie developed new forms of commerce and culture" (Schivelbusch 49–51.) Patronized mostly by commercial agents such as merchants and insurance brokers, coffeehouses were places for both socialization and the transaction of business. Both functions came together in the establishment of a connection between coffeehouses and newspapers. Coffeehouses such as the famous Lloyd's of London, established at the end of the seventeenth century (now more familiar as the financial institution it eventually became), often became centres of journalism, thus linking cornerstones of eighteenth-century public life—industry and print capitalism.

Coffeehouses became sites for the development of capitalist society in more direct ways, as Brad Weiss points out, through the drinking of coffee itself. As both a consumer good and a drink that promoted sobriety, coffee could be enlisted in the encouragement of good middle-class values—values such as "clear-headed rationality, alertness and restraint"—values not associated with the "rude" pleasures of ale. In short, coffee, "through the short, sudden burst of energy and concentration it supplies . . . is the original therapy for the micro-management of bourgeois personality" (Weiss 101). Coffee was thus enlisted in the reconstruction of the working day associated with the Industrial Revolution (see Chapter Two), as "coffee breaks" became a means of both marking and *making* time that is now routine in labour practices. Coffee fulfills nicely the goal of defining a break from work that is taken in order to make work more effective—a direct conversion of leisure into productivity.

Coffee and Colonialism   If it is no exaggeration to say that coffee contributed to the growth of European and North American economies over the last two hundred years, it can also be connected to the *under*development of many Southern nations. While colonialism has now formally ended (in most places, in the middle of the twentieth century), trade regulations preferential to the economies of dominant nations force developing countries to adopt agricultural practices that consign them to continued poverty. Coffee is a good example of a cash crop whose growth is encouraged in places like Central America to satisfy North American consumers. Coffee has replaced the traditional crops that once allowed the region to feed its own people, forcing them instead to import food produced and/or processed elsewhere and, in many cases, causing severe environmental degradation. While growing coffee once offered a relatively decent living to many farmers, its falling price on the world market due to overproduction means that farmers in places like Haiti are struggling to survive.

The effects of fluctuating coffee prices, so critical for producers, are barely felt at the retail end:

> In 1997, the final consumer spent $30 billion on coffee and producing countries received $12 billion or 40 per cent. At present, consumers are spending $66 billion

a year—or more than twice the 1997 figure—while producers are receiving $5.5 billion or nine percent. The value of sales has doubled, while producer incomes have fallen to less than a quarter. (Columbian treasury minister Juan Manuel Santos qtd. in Garratt)

The principal reason for the growing discrepancy between the wealth of primary producers and retailers is the growing concentration of power in the coffee industry, which is now dominated by just four companies—Nestlé, Kraft (owned by tobacco company Philip Morris, which has been newly rechristened as Altira Group, Inc.), Sara Lee, and Procter & Gamble—who are able to exercise disproportionate control over the wages received by growers and the prices paid by consumers.

These economic circumstances, circumstances that have a big impact on the day-to-day existence of coffee farmers, are remote from the experience, or at least the consciousness, of the average North American coffee drinker. While we might feel a momentary twinge as we fork over the price of a sandwich or a beer for a Styrofoam cup full of burnt beans and water, our unease is quickly forgotten as we sink into the comfy chairs of our favourite coffee bar, dimly but pleasantly aware of the hum of activity around us as we enjoy moments—or hours—of leisure away from the demands of work, home, or school. And, in fact, that enjoyment might be diminished by a too-acute awareness of the economic context in which we are drinking our coffee: part of the magic of the experience of consumption—a magic that is invoked, with variations, whether we are trying on a new dress, drinking a steaming latte, or driving a new car—is its ability to bury the crude facts of the economic transaction we have engaged in beneath the mythology surrounding the item we have just bought.

The Consumption of Coffee

We use the term "magic" deliberately to describe the experience of consumption. Karl Marx employed the phrase *commodity fetishism* to describe what happens under a capitalist system in which material objects are bought and sold: commodities come to stand in for relationships between people as symbols of meaning and value, while people and social relationships themselves become objectified (they are turned symbolically into objects). A "fetish" in pre-modern culture is an object that is believed to have magical powers or that excites erotic feeling. Commodity fetishism, then, is literally the attribution of a magical or sexual power to a commodity, assigning it a value that has no logical connection either to the human labour that produced it or to the usefulness of the object itself, but that is derived from the abstract system of exchange which determines that such-and-such an object is worth so-many dollars.

Commodities don't acquire these "magical" properties by accident, of course; rather, they are generated by sophisticated marketing campaigns that tap into prevailing social mythologies. In fact, in a commerce-driven society, the language of marketing increasingly works to *shape* mythologies, thereby defining and creating new values and desires as much as it tries to appeal to already existing ones.

We can get a sense of how this process works by looking very briefly at the mythologies evoked by two different coffee chains: Starbucks and Tim Hortons. Each works through systems of *representation* that conceal relations of economic *production* in order to enhance the consumer experience. The significant differences between the "magic" of Starbucks and Tim Hortons reflect a contemporary consumer culture that differs from earlier forms of mass culture in the way it draws on, and indeed seeks to promote, individualized **identities** (see Chapters Six and Seven) defined largely by lifestyle. The concept of lifestyle, discussed in more detail in Chapter Four, is most easily associated with Starbucks, which indeed deserves some credit for promoting it. The secret of lifestyle marketing is in the way the product falls into the background of a mythology, a mythology centred on the consumer's attitudes and practices and the identities they imply. While the attitudes or practices may have ethical or aesthetic overtones—for example, concern about the environment, a love of art—the overriding premise is one of individualism, expressed through consumer choice.

Starbucks   For a company like Starbucks, the mythological value of individualism is paramount, and it is represented not just through the diversity of blends available, but also through the careful structuring of the whole consumer experience. While it's difficult to generalize across outlets, some of the signal features of Starbucks outlets are dim, natural-looking (as opposed to fluorescent) lighting; moveable furniture, often mismatched but clearly designed with an eye not just to comfort or utility but also to style; serve-yourself cream, milk, sugar, and so on; and an aura of creativity, whether signalled by the presence of large murals featuring art or poetry or by individual paintings available for sale. The presence of other sale or display items—designer mugs, dishes, even books or CDs—emphasizes that the Starbucks experience is not about just having a cup of coffee but an act of self-expression, entry into a privileged and sophisticated world.

Begun in Seattle in 1987, Starbucks is now a truly global corporation—global in terms of its expansion throughout Western Europe and the Asian Pacific, but also in terms of the image it projects of the urbane, cosmopolitan consumer. Located mostly in large cities, in areas patronized mainly by middle- and upper-class, educated consumers (e.g., Starbucks outlets are often near, if not affiliated with, university campuses), Starbucks aligns itself with the values of style, mobility, and progressive thinking. These values emerge all the more strikingly when we compare Starbucks with Tim Hortons, a chain started in Hamilton, Ontario in 1964 and named after the late hockey player who founded it.

Tim Hortons   If the "magic" of Starbucks is associated with globalization and progress, Tim Hortons—even though it is now owned by U.S. chain Wendy's—is strongly nationalist in its flavour. (In fact, *Globe and Mail* reporter John Stackhouse titled his 2003 account of hitchhiking across Canada *Timbit Nation*, signalling the centrality of Tim Hortons to the Canadian experience.) This mythology is highlighted by such marketing strategies as the 1999 television ad featuring Canadian soldiers on a ship somewhere in the Persian Gulf, gratefully receiving a massive shipment of Tim Hortons coffee. In con-

Baskets of baked goods, prominently displayed menus with prices, and smiling, uniformed, mostly female counter staff contribute to Tim Hortons' image of comfort, value, and old-fashioned service.

trast to the foreign, slightly scary location of the Middle East (signalled in the ad by jerky camera footage of a chaotic market scene, accompanied by vaguely Arabian sounding music) Tim Hortons is a piece of home, something which presumably (like the Canadian military) "you can always count on." The soldiers in the ad are almost all men, and the servers who appear briefly to pay tribute to "our boys" overseas are all women, dressed in the familiar brown of the Tim Hortons uniform.

The world represented in the Tim Hortons ad is strikingly different from the ambience of Starbucks, evoking traditional values of the nation defended by a strong military, traditional gender roles, and clear boundaries between the familiar and comfortable and the foreign. This atmosphere is replicated in Tim Hortons restaurants, in which the comfortably padded but immovable benches, functional (and easy to clean) Formica tables, and fluorescent lighting convey an atmosphere of order and uniformity. The institutional flavour of the décor is softened somewhat by the service dynamic, in which the largely female staff deliver your coffee just the way you want it (at least within the parameters of "black," "regular," or "double-double"). Though the chain has expanded its selection of both food and beverages in recent years, the emphasis here is not on choice, and certainly not on style, so much as on comfort, embodied in the familiar combination of coffee and doughnuts. In fact, the mythology of Tim Hortons is arguably defined in obvious, even self-conscious, opposition to the snazzy ambience of Starbucks, revelling in its preservation of old-fashioned, working-class family values against the tide of globalization, speed, and the blurring of traditional identities.

Of course *both* of these mythologies are constructions—imaginary replications of the world rather than accurate reflections of it. Nevertheless, they *work*, through the dynamics of consumption—a dynamic increasingly central to the formation of popular culture—not just to sell coffee or doughnuts but also to create compelling pictures of everyday life and of human relationships that are increasingly indistinguishable from "the real thing." What's interesting about our comparison of Tim Hortons and Starbucks is not as much their differences as the similarities that are concealed beneath those differences: both are large multinational corporations that capitalize on cheap labour and resource costs in the South to generate significant profits in the North; both derive the bulk of their profits by selling coffee and sugary baked goods—products that might not do a lot for anyone's health, but which are staples in a traditional North American diet; and both are major parts of the popular cultural landscape.

SUMMARY: AND IT ALL BOILS DOWN TO . . . WHAT *IS* IN A CUP OF COFFEE?

Using coffee as an example, we might come up with a fairly depressing reading of popular culture. Dominated by practices of consumption, much of our experience of popular culture is tangled up in relations of economic exploitation—relations that are concealed by the mythologies and ideologies of capitalism, to which we are helpless, caffeine-addicted victims. Of course this is a partial picture, and one that is contradicted by the practice of coffee-drinking itself.

While there is no escaping the consumerist aspect of coffee drinking, this practice—more, perhaps, than many other aspects of commercial culture—highlights the possibilities for different kinds of consumption. For example, at a time when people are increasingly diverted by home entertainment, cafés can, at least in theory, serve as public spaces for the promotion of community, much as they did in the eighteenth century. It's easy to exaggerate this function: with its comfy chairs, free newspapers, and generally artsy aura, the image of the contemporary coffeehouse is as much a product of slick marketing as genuine community. However, it *is* possible to recall some of the positive aspects of public culture in private space, not by "seeing through" the lifestyle concept of places like Starbucks, but by taking it at its word. In other words, it's possible to sit in a Starbucks reading for hours with an empty cup in front of you, and the culture of the café (a culture Starbucks itself has actively nurtured) is such that no one's likely to ask you to leave. "Going for a coffee" need not mean actually going for a coffee—a concept places like Starbucks have successfully promoted, sometimes at the cost of their own profits.

Coffee's evolution into a highly charged commodity brings it within the realm of popular discourse, thus creating new channels of meaning and knowledge and new forms of "anti-consumerist" consumerism. The success in recent years of the Fair Trade

Federation and other co-operative ventures that seek to preserve the natural environment while ensuring that coffee producers receive a fair price for their products has been motivated by activists in conjunction with consumers themselves. The overwhelming commercial power of corporations such as Starbucks, while contributing to some extent to the growing gaps in wealth that characterize the coffee industry, has also shed a strong and sometimes harsh light on the industry, forcing it to change in productive ways. The excessive (and, some argued, unfair) focus on Starbucks as the target of protests at the 1999 World Trade Organization meeting in Seattle spoke less to the corporate sins of Starbucks per se than to its *representative* status as a model of globalization.

Mythology, then, works not just to contain, but also to spark and activate new forms of resistance, not all of which are constrained by the harness of corporate culture. Popular culture isn't just would-be poets sipping mocha lattes or commuters grabbing a box of Timbits at the drive-through; it's also the bricks through the window at Starbucks and Niketown, the creators of ads raising consumer awareness about the "real" price of coffee, and the bunches of guys who happily imbibe the "lifestyle" of the café, sitting around in animated conversation for hours without actually buying anything. The relationship between these different faces of popular culture is part of what this book will examine.

Our study of popular culture occurs at a historical moment in which

there is no human activity that is free from capitalism, commodification, and the profit motive. No space in people's everyday life remains outside these economic processes. This is most apparent in the case of culture and communication, which have become totally commercialized. By the same token, culture and communication have come to dominate the economy, with the result that, as Fredric Jameson observes, "no society has ever been saturated with signs and messages like this one." (Grossberg et al. 53)

Many contemporary cultural critics see this shift as a wholly depressing situation, representing the end of collective culture and its replacement with a society of atomized individuals who are simultaneously consumed by the drive toward self-gratification and entirely colonized by consumerist ideology. They despair over what they see as the erosion of people's ability to think critically, to produce and create things for themselves in a context where everything is supplied for them, subject to their ability to pay for it. A less bleak view, and one that we share, is that while commercial culture's grand promise to provide fulfillment and liberate individual and social potential is essentially an empty one, there are, within its intricate networks of power, all kinds of opportunities for creativity and even resistance. Through a series of concrete examples, the remainder of this book develops an idea of popular culture as a process defined by the often contradictory but sometimes collaborative interests of private and public interest, of commerce and creativity, of capitalism and community. Its ultimate goal is to provide tools that will help you to think about your own place in this compelling and sometimes invisible matrix of possibilities.

Chapter 2

The History of Popular Culture

INTRODUCTION: TAKING IT FROM THE STREETS

On January 7, 2002, a Hamilton, Ontario man and his 10-year-old son appeared in court to defend themselves against charges of playing touch football and hockey on the street. Their neighbour, Nadia Ciuriak, had become tired of retrieving balls from her garden and had asked them to stop. When they didn't, she called the police, who charged the father, Gary Kotar, with violating a municipal bylaw banning the playing of games on city streets. The case became a *cause célèbre* across Canada, as hockey fans and defenders of the right to play in public places called in to radio talk shows and wrote letters to the editor expressing their outrage. For Ciuriak, it was a matter of principle: Kotar, his son, and his friends were breaking the law. As her brother Taras put it, "It is not about hockey, it is about property rights. It's about trampling my family's garden" ("Fighting"). The case was eventually thrown out because the judge determined that the Crown couldn't prove its case that Gary Kotar had been playing a game on city property. City councillors promised to look into revising the bylaw.

This case is illuminating from a popular culture perspective for a number of reasons: first, it's about an aspect of popular culture—informal recreation—that tends to get ignored in favour of an emphasis on the commercial products of mass media; second, it features sport, whose relationship to "culture" of any kind is often questioned; finally, it concerns the critical issue of public space: who gets to use it and how? How are rights concerning the recreational use of public space balanced against laws protecting private property? These questions and issues lie at the heart of contemporary popular culture. They are, in a sense, what makes it distinct from earlier cultural forms.

Recalling traditional "grassroots" forms of recreation, a game like street hockey exists in complicated relationship with contemporary commercial sport.

We begin this chapter with the story about road hockey as a way of entering an exploration of how popular culture evolved into the form we recognize today. Beginning with a look at traditional (pre-1830) recreation, we trace some of the broad cultural changes that led to a rupture between communal enjoyments, such as "street" games, and commercial entertainment. We also look at the development of the institution of "culture" as a refined and exclusive preserve, remote from the "low," physical entertainment of the streets. And finally, in relation to the previous two developments, we look at the struggles that, beginning in the early nineteenth century, determined the shape of popular culture—struggles over work and leisure, over the emerging class structure, and over public space.

Among the questions we will be asking in this chapter are: How is contemporary popular culture different from what came before? What factors—economic, social, and political—contributed to the development of popular culture as we know it today? How is the development of popular culture tied to the broader history of the disappearance of public space? How are relationships of power, particularly class and gender, mediated through culture? Returning at the end of the chapter to the example of street hockey, we suggest that while the answers to these questions may have changed over time, the issues they touch on remain critical to an understanding of popular culture from the nineteenth century to the present day.

MAKING THE STREETS SAFE FOR COMMERCE

In 1835, a small item was added to the *English Highways Act,* imposing a fine of up to 40 shillings for playing "at Football or any other Game on any Part of the said Highways, to the Annoyance of any Passenger" (qtd. in Malcomson 141). The amendment to the act was part of a bigger movement toward the limitation and management of public space, a movement that had a major impact on the organization and practice of popular culture. As we suggested in Chapter One, the tension between democratic or popular will and corporate control—the question, in other words, of who owns/produces the space in which we live our lives—continues to be the primary force defining popular culture today. The prohibition of street-football reflects a small but significant moment in that conflict.

The reallocation of public space, which was strongly contested at every turn, occurred in conjunction with a whole series of other changes—economic, spatial, and social—that came about during the period from about 1830 to 1900, the period of the Industrial Revolution. In order to understand the magnitude of those changes, a rough snapshot of what life looked like before may be useful.

POPULAR RECREATION BEFORE 1830

Beginning around 1830 in Britain (though it is hard to pin down an exact date), popular recreation underwent some fairly rapid and dramatic changes from the forms that had existed, with few variations, since the Middle Ages. In a primarily farming economy, recreation was closely tied to work, in the form of holidays and festivals associated with particular times in the agricultural calendar and everyday social interactions that occurred as part of farm labour. Games, dances, and entertainments were largely public, in the sense that anyone could participate, and they took place on lands customarily shared (at least to some extent) by the community as a whole. Together with work, recreation tied the community together through activities whose form and meaning had been established through long tradition. Perhaps the most notable difference from popular culture today is that traditional recreation was mostly homemade, consisting of sports, games, and dancing that required little in the way of organization and equipment. Life in the towns may have involved more diverse and complex entertainment, but in general urban forms of leisure were not all that different from rural forms, with social activity strongly tied to work and both work and leisure still strongly influenced by the traditions and rhythms of the agricultural economy.

There's a danger of romanticizing this early form of popular culture, to represent it as somehow purer (since less commercialized) and more wholesome and community-minded than, say, TV or video games. It is undeniably true that pre-industrial recreation was in many ways more active than contemporary forms of entertainment, in terms of both the creativity and the physical effort demanded of its participants. It also served an important role in maintaining strong community relations, uniting workers of both sexes and all ages.

Among its less favourable aspects from a contemporary perspective were the brutally violent elements of the aptly named "blood" sports involving animals, such as bullbaiting and cockfighting, and the high level of social conformity recreation demanded. While holiday practices such as decorating and dancing around the Maypole were condemned by Protestant reformers of the time as incitements to "lasciviousness" and "ribauldrie" (qtd. in Malcomson 9), they ultimately served the conservative cause of courtship. While unsupervised trips to the woods to gather May flowers offered lots of opportunities for sexual activity, these did not translate into sexual *freedom*: when these encounters led to pregnancy, as they often did, the outcome was shame for the woman—marriage if she was lucky, but in any case a confirmation of traditional gender roles.

The Bonds of Community

The communal and strongly ritualized form of traditional popular culture reflected a highly stratified society in which leisure, like work, expressed clear distinctions between the ranks of labourers and landowners, with virtually no possibility for social mobility. However, what was in one sense a bigger gulf between socioeconomic categories than exists today was partly bridged by a tradition of patronage, in which powerful landowners tolerated and in some cases actively facilitated the recreational activities of their workers (by granting time off, for example). This occasional relaxation of social discipline served the landowners as well as the workers, partly because both groups inhabited the same small communities and also because giving workers an outlet for play made it much less likely that they would challenge the ruling class's authority. In sum, romantic images of entertainment in pre-industrial society are in some senses accurate: fun was mostly free, even when closely bound up with the economic activities of the community; it reflected a strong attachment to the natural world, and recreation fostered connections between people. On the negative side, the conservative and traditional nature of recreational activities allowed only occasional ritual challenges to social authority and tended to emphasize social solidarity over individual pleasure or inclination. For example, among the entertainments surrounding courtship, there were no alternatives for men or women who, for whatever reason, weren't interested in heterosexual coupling. Finally, traditional recreation, with its strong emphasis on blood sports, reflected the hardship and brutality of farm labourers' lives—brutality enacted most violently on animals.

CAPITALISM AND THE INDUSTRIAL REVOLUTION

The Industrial Revolution brought with it a new culture—new pleasures and identities, but also new kinds of brutality. One of the key preconditions for the development of popular culture in its contemporary form is the economic system of **capitalism**, which, throughout the eighteenth and nineteenth centuries, was dramatically altered and intensified by a series of events that came to be described as the Industrial Revolution. (For more on the development of capitalism, see Close-Up 1.1 on page 10.) Of the many social and cultural consequences of the Industrial Revolution, the banning of street football might look pretty trivial. However, this example offers one illustration of the effects of industrialism on the organization of physical space and social relations. We will look at some of these effects in more extensive detail in the section that follows.

Redefining Cultural Spaces

The 1835 ban against football in the streets was one minor event in a succession of restrictions of communal space by state or private interests happening in conjunction with changes associated with the developing capitalist economy. Among the most far-reaching of these changes were the series of Enclosure Acts that converted common grazing land to much smaller, private holdings in order to make the land more economically productive. This practice, which as its name suggests involved enclosing formerly open spaces with fences, affected popular culture in very direct ways, by placing physical constraints on certain kinds of activity. It also influenced popular culture more generally, changing the relationship between work and play and reconfiguring people's sense of community.

First and most obviously, enclosure placed an obvious restriction on the kinds of recreation that could take place. No longer was it possible, for example, to engage in the vast games of football that used to take place with unlimited players (and few rules) between villages located up to five kilometres apart. Even more modest recreations, for example the dances and wrestling matches that tended to be organized around particular times of the agricultural year such as mowing or harvesting, were gradually discontinued as the fields they were once performed or played on were closed off to the public. Beyond the significance of the loss of these specific activities was the severing of a vital link between agricultural work and recreation. By fencing off property with the aim of increasing its economic productivity, a vital connection was lost between the creative realms of work and play. More generally, the reorganization of space that resulted from enclosure changed the way people related to one another. Not only did it accentuate divisions between the landholding and labouring classes, but it also made it harder in general for people to connect with one another, resulting in the fragmentation of traditional forms of community.

Urbanization   In addition to the privatization of mostly rural land represented by enclosure, the process of **urbanization** contributed significantly to the reduction of open spaces available for recreation as land was expropriated for the building of industrial infrastructure. As fields disappeared with no new playgrounds to replace them, it became harder to find places to hold outdoor sports, festivals, and other forms of public gathering. Urbanization also affected the production of popular culture in more indirect ways. One of the most obvious changes people experienced as they moved from the country to the city was a change in their living spaces. For poor working people in particular, life in the city meant coping with crowded and unsanitary conditions. An 1844 newspaper report describes a typical slum in which:

> there are whole streets . . . which are neither flagged, paved, sewered, nor drained; where garbage and filth of every description are left on the surface to ferment and rot; where pools of stagnant water are almost constant; where the dwellings adjoining are thus necessarily caused to be of an inferior and even filthy description; thus where disease is engendered, and the health of the whole town perilled. (qtd. in Engels 49–50)

The huge influx of workers to the city meant that housing had to be built quickly and cheaply. At the same time, wealthy industrialists wanted to be spared the sights and smells of crowded working-class slums; thus, factory workers—in their small identical houses, crammed together on tiny lots—lived in more or less segregated neighbourhoods interspersed with upper- and middle-class enclaves.

But the marginalization of the poor wasn't only physical. In the complex middle-class values of the day (values that still hold sway, if you believe the ads for household cleansers), physical dirt corresponded symbolically to spiritual impurity and immorality. As convictions about the inherent character deficiencies of the poor became institutionalized, backed up by new sciences of hygiene and public health, the poor suffered from simultaneous moves to banish them from sight and to subject their behaviour to increasingly vigorous policing. These social constraints, combined with actual space constraints, powerfully reduced people's freedom and mobility.

However, the crowded conditions of working-class slums also fostered new forms of social and political solidarity. Courtyards, which functioned as sort of communal backyards, became gathering places in which people could find some respite from the isolation and loneliness that are the paradoxical byproducts of life in a crowded city. For some, "allotments" (rented gardens) provided space to grow flowers or food and recall, in however modest a way, the pleasure of outdoor life. As cities grew, however, and the demand for space increased, most of these allotments were swallowed up by development. The one other obvious location for outdoor recreation was the street, which had the advantage of more space and light than the courtyards but the disadvantage of the presence of the police, who were charged with putting a stop to recreational activities that threatened to disrupt more "legitimate" commercial activities.

The Pub as Community Space   The lack of public space, combined with the excess of official surveillance in what little space there was, contributed to the growth of what became the centre of urban community—the pub. In addition to camaraderie and beer (which, besides being cheap and satisfying, was generally safer than the drinking water), the pub supplied comforts such as heat, light, and toilets that were frequently superior to what people had at home. Indeed, the density of pubs was greatest in the poorest areas (Best 220). Pubs were often associated with particular professions, as shown in names such as "The Weaver's Arms" or "The Sailor's Dickey." In general, however, they can be seen as part of the trend in urbanization toward the separation of places of work and places of recreation.

Along with the class segregation and crowding that characterized urban life, this fragmentation of a formerly more organic existence undermined familiar forms of identity, community, and popular recreation. At the same time, it fostered new forms of sociality, as well as new forms of social freedom. The positive flipside of the anonymity that went along with life in the big city was increasing privacy from the prying eyes of the community. Moreover, the layout of the city, in which people's homes tended to be some distance from their places of work, commerce, and leisure, helped to create a new kind of mobility, both literal and symbolic. Of course, the expansion of opportunity was often more abstract than actual, particularly for women and the poor, who were prevented by a lack of economic power and an excess of social discipline from enjoying the liberation from custom and greater freedom of movement enabled by life in the city. In general, however, the process of urbanization contributed to the trend of expanding individual freedom that was to shape social life over the course of the nineteenth and twentieth centuries.

Industrialism

The term "Industrial Revolution," generally used to refer to the period in British history from approximately the mid-eighteenth to the mid-nineteenth century, describes the transition from an agricultural/small-scale commercial society to one based on organized mechanical production. While the term "industry" is often used to refer specifically to factory production as distinct from other kinds of organized work, it is also sometimes used to describe the increasing capitalization, organization, and mechanization of what were formerly thought of as non-industrial kinds of work: farming, for example, or— more significant for our purposes—culture. (We will discuss the implications of this shift in more detail in Chapter Four.) In contrast to the relative stability of earlier modes of production, industrial enterprises require major investments of capital in order to generate growth. They also require a large and disciplined workforce, trained in the performance of repetitive specialized tasks. The Industrial Revolution thus marked a significant change not only in the *mode* of production—the physical process used to generate the necessities of life—but also in the *relations* of production, or division of labour.

In the pre-industrial economy, work was not only closely integrated with other aspects of life; workers also had a strong sense of connectedness to their labour and its products. In pre-industrial agriculture, for example, workers are involved in every stage of production, from planting to harvest, and, crucially, they have at least some degree of ownership of the process, including small holdings of land. The same is true of craftspeople, who own and/or have direct control over their workshops, as well as every aspect of the production of their finished crafts. The critical difference for workers in industrial society is that their labour is detached (or, in Karl Marx's terms, alienated) from the larger process of production: rather than having any direct economic stake in the products of their labour, they receive only a small hourly wage and their activity is focused on one single fragment of the final product.

New Modes of Production   This style of work was a key part of the new production process known as **Fordism** (after Henry Ford, who pioneered it), a form of assembly-line labour that proved to be extremely efficient at churning out products, from cars to household furnishings. The factors that contributed to the high quantity and uniform quality of products, however, had a much more negative effect on the human participants in the process. Fordism worked on the principle of *mechanization,* a process that aimed to turn every facet of the economy, including human society itself, into the equivalent of an efficiently run machine. The consequences of this restructuring of labour reverberated far beyond the factory walls. Fordism is now widely understood to refer not just to a particular mode of production but also to a form of social organization based on discipline, uniformity, and atomization ("atomization" refers, basically, to a social structure defined by separate individuals rather than by a vision of the community as a whole).

The mechanization of society was accompanied by what we might term the "mathematicization" of human life. As historian Eric Hobsbawm puts it, "Arithmetic was the fundamental tool of the Industrial Revolution. Its makers saw it as a series of sums of addition and subtraction: the difference in cost between buying in the cheapest market and selling in the dearest, between cost of production and sale price, between investment and return" (*Industry* 61). As with the mechanical innovations of Fordism, the mathematic precision of the new economy extended to social relations as a whole, with relationships between employer and employee, individual and community, increasingly determined less by custom or the incalculable interactions of character and circumstance than by relations of money, or what is often called the "cash nexus."

The ideal of an economy in which human labour is enmeshed obediently and productively with machines is not so easily accomplished in reality. In order to ensure a compliant workforce, employers and legislators collaborated in the drafting of a series of new regulations and other disciplinary innovations, both in and outside the workplace, to ensure worker obedience. Perhaps the most effective form of regulation was the extremely low wages workers were paid, which meant that they had to work long hours just to earn enough to feed themselves. Workplace discipline was reinforced by such technological innovations as the punch clock, which secured the cooperation of workers in policing their own attendance at work. In instituting such forms of on-the-job discipline, employers were motivated by the (reasonable) belief that, given a choice, most people would prefer to spend their time at play rather than work. A raft of social measures sought to correct this attitude, including *master and servant laws,* which prescribed jail time for workers who violated the terms of their contracts, and *poor laws,* which "took care of" the unemployed by incarcerating them in workhouses. Poverty, once seen as a consequence of unfortunate circumstances to be remedied by the assistance of the community, came to be read as a sign of personal failure or moral weakness.

The Production of the Working Class

A more abstract but farther-reaching goal of the new laws was the radical alteration of culture, with the aim of creating a society devoted not to the goal of working hard enough to live, to put food on the table, but of feeding itself in order to work harder, to produce profits. One of the dominant **mythologies** in contemporary society is the idea that individual effort is always ultimately rewarded with economic and social success. (For a discussion of mythology, see Chapter Three.) This mythology developed in conjunction with the industrial economy. However, it was hard to sustain during the early days of the Industrial Revolution, when the fundamental inequality on which capitalism depends was so starkly evident: by definition, an economic system designed to produce a surplus requires that the majority of labourers are paid less than what their labour is actually worth, and in the early stages of industrialism this amounted to less than the barest living wage for many workers. While pre-industrial society had also been characterized by inequality, bonds of custom connected the rich and the poor—sometimes through patronage and sometimes through force, but the two groups were always in close relation with one another. Industrial society effectively broke these bonds, producing a new kind of class consciousness.

According to E. P. Thompson, one of the foremost historians of English working-class history, "class" comes about when a group of people

> as a result of common experiences (inherited or shared), feel and articulate the identity of their interests as between themselves, and as against [others] whose interests are different from (and usually opposed to) theirs. The class experience is largely determined by the productive relations into which men are born—or enter involuntarily. Class-consciousness is the way in which these experiences are handled in cultural terms: embodied in traditions, value-systems, ideas, and institutional forms. (10)

It's worth pausing on this definition in order to grasp elements of class that are often overlooked in contemporary uses of the word that either equate class simply with wealth—"low class" equals "poor"—or link it to a quality of morality or style, as in "that lady may be rich, but she's got no class." Thompson's definition is important in emphasizing that: 1) class describes a material relationship to the wealth-generating structures of society; specifically, it distinguishes capital's owners from its labourers, and 2) one's class position has a determining influence on one's identity and social orientation. To be class-conscious is to recognize the role of class in determining those aspects of one's existence—a recognition that goes against the dominant **ideology** (see Close-Up 2.1).

Working-Class Consciousness   The Industrial Revolution coincided with the expansion of working-class consciousness, which expressed itself, among other ways, in distinct cultural forms. These consist of songs, sketches, and poetry—some that were preserved in written form and many that weren't—as well as a richly interwoven set of practices (well documented in Thompson's *The Making of the English Working Class*) including

Ideology

Ideology is a term that we will make use of throughout this book. It is a concept with many shadings, but with a relatively simple idea at its core. At the most general level, ideology refers to the process by which the set of values and beliefs that bind individuals together in a society becomes "naturalized." The belief and value systems of any given society are the outcome of *history*; that is, of collective human activity that gives shape (in large and small ways) to the characteristic features of a society. Ideology names those social and political processes that directly and indirectly mask or hide this historical process by making everyday life seem natural, inevitable, and unchangeable. The claim that capitalism is the only rational form of economic organization is often ideological in this way, especially when what this claim suggests is that history was inevitably moving toward a worldwide capitalist system anyway: people did nothing to bring it about and can do nothing to stop it. This is false, and ideology is often at work in attempts to make false statements sound not only like the truth, but also like common sense.

A more restricted meaning of ideology that is related to this one has to do with the difference between how things appear to be and what they are really like. Ideology names the processes through which the real conditions in which people live are obscured by other ideas and beliefs, usually for the sake of maintaining political and social power.

sports, games, conversation, eating, and drinking that took place both in private homes and in working men's clubs. While women were included in some of these activities, on the whole working-class leisure activities, like other aspects of English culture, were strongly masculinist in character, an element that was often glossed over by early work in cultural studies that tended to cast working-class culture in overly romantic terms.

Suggested Activity 2.1

Drawing on your personal experience and general knowledge, try to answer the following questions: Is class-consciousness a significant force in the world today? Where and how is it manifested? How, if at all, is politics shaped by class concerns? (How) are hopes for radical social transformation expressed today? What role does popular culture play in promoting or subduing these hopes?

Even though it displayed the sexism of its time, one of the distinctive aspects of nineteenth-century working-class culture was its highly developed political consciousness, a sense of the urgency and possibility of radical political and economic transformation. Attempts to effect such a transformation took many forms, from the Luddite rebellions of 1811–13 in which workers smashed the machines that were replacing their labour, to the Chartist movement in the 1830s and '40s that was concerned primarily with political reform, to the less formally organized trade union movement. What most of these movements had in common was a strong sense of *collectivism*, or worker solidarity, and a demand for expanded democratic rights.

Workplace Reform In the latter half of the century, slowly and often through an uneasy alliance with employers' own desires for change, these movements achieved some important workplace reforms, including laws restricting working hours and the establishment of Saturday half-holidays. (In the first half of the century, many factory workers worked a 72-hour week, with only Sundays off—which meant nothing to working women, for whom Sunday was the only day available to do washing and other domestic tasks.) These, in combination with Bank Holidays, gradually extended to other professions and came to replace traditional holidays, resulting in a clearer, more generally shared division between work and leisure, if not exactly less time at work.

The one other significant change in the latter half of the nineteenth century that created new possibilities for popular culture was a gradual increase in wages. As with the other changes, this reform came about both because workers agitated for it and because the system demanded it: as capitalism became more efficient at producing goods, more consumers were required; hence, higher wages (see Chapter Five). The social impact of these changes—improvements, really—to working conditions was far-reaching and complex. Besides providing an obvious outlet for enjoyment and relaxation, the formalization of "free" time outside of work also influenced in subtler ways how people understood themselves and related to one another. The new distinction between spheres of work and home played a big part in establishing the almost sacred significance of the nuclear family, a development that had a particular impact on women. While she in all likelihood was still required to contribute to the household economically, the woman of the house assumed a new and arguably more difficult role as symbolic guardian of the family's moral and spiritual health. This expectation, expressed as part of a more general middle-class ideology of moral discipline, functioned in odd concert with the limited expansion of workers' freedoms: with the expansion of leisure time (and buying power) came new ideological pressures toward social conformity.

Perhaps more significantly, the extension to the poor of some limited forms of relief from the systemic deprivation they suffered arguably worked to mute demands for more substantial forms of social justice. Once arrived at, working-class consciousness remained precarious, never achieving the revolutionary expression that Marx projected. One common explanation of the decline in working-class political culture attributes it to the hegemonic success of commercial culture, a development we discuss further below. It's important not to discount the role of class solidarity, though, both as a catalyst for subsequent forms of political consciousness (discussed in more detail in Chapter Seven) and as a critical dynamic in the production of popular culture as an ongoing process of social struggle.

POPULAR RECREATION AND RESISTANCE

So, by the end of the nineteenth century, in fulfillment of one of the clichés of capitalism some of the fruits of the Industrial Revolution had begun to "trickle down" to the working classes. The benefits were hard-won, though, and had to be struggled for against the efforts of the ruling class to rein in the pleasures of their social inferiors. While the ruling classes had long been concerned with how the poor enjoyed their off-work time, these concerns took on a new urgency in the Industrial Revolution, with the flourishing of a general middle-class suspicion of leisure, directed at both the "parasitic ruling class" *and* the "reckless carousing of an irrational working class" (Bailey 76). That this disapproval was qualified by a contradictory desire among many middle-class people to *join* the leisure activities of the "parasitic ruling class" didn't make things any better for the working classes, whose own recreation became the target of stringent surveillance and discipline. These efforts at control, which ranged from outright prohibition to more subtle forms of persuasion and direction, were never entirely successful, but were met at every turn by working-class resistance to interference in their way of life.

Rational Recreation

In a bid to keep the behaviour of the "unruly masses" in check, many towns established new or enlarged police forces, charged with strictly enforcing new regulations against blood sports and street games and arresting people for such vague offences as vagrancy, trespass, and desecration of the sabbath. While strong middle-class support existed for the establishment of "a good police" and "set of laws," many of the most dedicated moral reformers also believed that "if possible, the effects of such laws should be produced, almost insensibly, and without the appearance of force: for force will hardly ever answer the end proposed in this land of liberty" (qtd. in Malcomson 97).

The move toward subtler, less overtly coercive means of social control reflected a new cultural complexity that was developing in the shadow of the Industrial Revolution. One paradoxical element of a society that in many instances produced new forms of servitude for working people was a strong emphasis on individual liberty, a critical element of capitalist ideology that took on a slightly different—and, from a ruling class perspective, less desirable—flavour in growing democracy movements. The call for individual freedom had been an important part of the middle class's rise to power, against the pillars of tradition and inheritance that had worked to sustain the dominance of the aristocracy. However, the prospect of extending the privilege to the lower classes and thus risking powerful challenges to a social order built around *their* dominance was a source of much middle-class anxiety. Though they were committed in principle to the goal of general social freedom, particularly in the domain of leisure, they were not willing to leave the working classes to determine their own forms of recreation, which might challenge the prevailing moral standards or social hierarchy.

With a primary aim, then, of keeping the lower classes out of the pub—or, worse, the trade union or Chartist halls—a significant group of concerned middle-class citizens got together to promote what they called "rational recreation." Some groups, such as the Society for the Suppression of Vice and the Lord's Day Observance Society, had a strongly Christian bent. Others—many of which were dominated by women—were more loosely organized around the aims of providing forms of public recreation in which people of different classes could mingle, with the poor benefiting from the good influence of their betters. In all cases there was a strong impulse toward diversion—that is, the sponsorship of sports and activities that would draw interest away from undesirable pastimes: drinking, traditional games, blood sports, and so on. Thus, part of the rational recreationist mandate was the promotion of so-called "counter-attractions," including trips and exhibitions organized to coincide with the old, discredited forms of pleasure.

The inspiration for this project was not entirely cynical; some middle-class people may have been moved by a genuine desire to alleviate the severe restrictions that had been imposed on workers and also to heal the fractured class relations brought about by industrialism. It was hoped—naively, maybe, and with a mix of motivations both compassionate and self-serving—that the inequalities that marked the workplace could be temporarily forgotten in forms of recreation designed to be inclusive. The main goal was not inclusivity, however, but "improvement" in the form of intellectual, moral, and spiritual development. In all the activities and organizations promoted by the rational recreationists—concerts, educational institutes, and (increasingly toward the end of the century) libraries and museums, there was a strong emphasis on encouraging intellectual as opposed to physical pursuits, the latter being regarded as base and uncivilized.

Matthew Arnold　The efforts of the rational recreationists were accompanied by an elevation of capital-C Culture as a powerful, almost mystical stimulant of moral and spiritual growth. Poet and critic Matthew Arnold (1822–88) was one of the foremost proponents of a program of education that would instill civilized virtues in the masses by exposing them to "the best that has been thought and said." Culture, which up until this time described a general process of cultivation, now encompassed a set of objects—artifacts of timeless and universal value, exposure to which would encourage the student to transcend his petty and narrow materialist (we might read "class") interests to recognize his place in the universal—or at least the national—order. The title of Arnold's most famous work of cultural criticism, *Culture and Anarchy*, gives a clear sense of the social chaos he foresaw if the guardians of culture failed in their aims. The power of Arnold's definition of Culture lies partly in its emptiness: its value can't be measured by any precise criteria, but those of discriminating tastes—like Arnold himself, presumably—know it when they see it. It worked as a powerful social ideology, one that influenced literary education until well into the twentieth century, through its contradictory gestures toward universality and hierarchy: Culture was precisely that which united everybody, but its *value* rested in its being understood by only the educated few.

Ambivalence, Appropriation, Resistance

The contradictions that characterized Arnold's definition of culture informed the project of rational recreation as a whole, a project that was only partly successful. To the extent that rational recreation was meant to bring classes together with the aim of cultivating a community defined by middle-class tastes and morals, it was an almost-total failure. In part, the failure stemmed from middle-class ambivalence about what they were attempting to do. The impulse to smooth relations between the classes was always complicated by the desire of the middle class to forget their own working-class origins and confirm their alliance with aristocracy.

This was achieved partly by the promotion of sports and leisure activities from which working classes were excluded. In the case of some sports, such as golf, cost alone was an impediment to participation. For others such as rowing—once a popular working-class activity—amateur associations drew up rules prohibiting participation from "artisans, mechanics or labourers," on the pretext that the physical nature of their labour would give them an unfair advantage (Bailey 140). Moves toward the democratization of other cultural activities such as the theatre were countered by the physical segregation of audiences through prohibitive prices at certain events or through restrictive conditions of attendance. Museums, for example, were initially closed on Sundays, which was the only day most working-class people had free. The move to extend opening hours was opposed by some on the grounds that the lower classes were not yet ready for capital-C Culture, and so could not be trusted to appreciate it in the right spirit. When museums finally did open on Sundays, to an enormously enthusiastic public, the *New York Times* warned that canes and umbrellas would have to be checked at the door "so that no chance should be given for anyone to prod a hole through a valuable painting, or to knock off any portion of a cast" (qtd. in Levine 183).

Suggested Activity 2.2

Consider the following questions: Are cultural activities still segregated today? If so, how is participation formally (or informally) restricted? To whom do restrictive conditions apply?

Middle-class nervousness about the encroachment of the lower classes on their newly won exclusive cultural terrain ironically confirmed that, in some ways, the rational recreationists were more successful than they could have hoped: working-class people not only subscribed enthusiastically to programs of self-improvement, but also, not surprisingly, showed a strong desire to run the programs themselves. A general appetite for knowledge, along with huge improvements in literacy associated with the move toward compulsory primary education, helped to blur boundaries between workers and their middle-class benefactors in ways most of the benefactors never anticipated. From the mid-1880s onward, many social clubs and mechanics' institutes (popular educational organizations) were independently run by their working-class members. Some had quite politically radical aims; many ended up focusing far more on recreation than education, in clear opposition to the vision of their founders. While the continuing need for financial sponsorship ensured that the wealthy continued to have some hand in running things, historical research suggests that the lower classes took what they wanted from the activities and societies offered them, making over rational recreation for their own purposes in ways that were often quite different from what their sponsors intended. Accepting middle-class sponsorship, in other words, did not necessarily mean accepting middle-class values (Cunningham 128).

Booze and Blood Sports   While many aspects of the rational recreationist program were appropriated by the working classes, people in general strongly resisted attempts to reform and regulate traditional forms of leisure. Drinking was notoriously hard to curb—even on the job—and blood sports and street games survived in spite of official prohibition and the promotion of alternatives. Prizefighting, or bare-knuckle boxing, is an example of one sport that flourished in spite of attempts to curb it, which ranged from fining publicans who promoted it to charging fighters themselves with assault (and occasionally homicide). The lengths to which its participants would go to maintain the sport were demonstrated in the famous international match between Sayers and Heenan in

Fight between John Jackson and Daniel Mendoza, 1795. Sports like prizefighting flourished in part because of—rather than in spite of—middle-class moralists' attempts to ban them.

1860, in which fighters were taken, in disguise, to a secret location outside the reach of mounted police, followed by supporters who left London via a special early-morning train (Bailey 37). While this and other blood sports eventually did decline, there is a lot of evidence to suggest that they persisted throughout the nineteenth century *because of,* rather than in spite of, attempts to outlaw them.

As one historian puts it, by the beginning of the twentieth century "the great majority of London workers were not Christian, provident, chaste or temperate" (Jones 471), and the favoured institutions were "not the school, the evening class, the library, the friendly society, the church or the chapel, but the pub, the sporting paper, the race course and the music hall" (Jones 479). The mass demonstrations that greeted attempts to close pubs and shops on Sunday in the 1860s offer evidence of the extent to which popular recreation had come to be regarded as a right to be defended, by force if necessary.

Popular Culture and Politics

This passionate defence of popular entertainment was a source of concern not just to the middle-class reformers, but also to two distinct groups of working-class activists—political radicals and evangelical Christians. Though their aims were, not surprisingly, very different, what these two groups had in common was a clearly defined vision of a strong and disciplined working-class society whose integrity was undermined by the corrupting influence of mass entertainment.

Pub culture was particularly suspect because of the intoxicating effect of drinking. The opportunities to get drunk increased substantially with the lifting of duty on spirits in 1825, and the deregulation of beer sales shortly afterward. Like other moves toward freer trade, this liberalization of alcohol sales had ambiguous consequences for working-class people's autonomy. For the radicals in particular, this and other aspects of popular culture were threatening not just because they were often produced through the patronage of the ruling classes but also because they consumed energies that might otherwise be directed toward more directly self-improving activities, such as education or the struggle for democracy.

The growth of popular recreation, then, was by no means a uniform or uncontroversial process. Not simply a battleground on which people sought to free themselves from the physical or ideological constraints of industrial society, popular culture was also a critical ground for struggle over exactly how that freedom could or should be pursued. The goal of working-class reformers, whose vision of freedom included the extension of democratic privilege, granting to all people the right to determine the shape of the society they lived in, never quite jibed with the more conservative view of popular culture as a necessary, if temporary, escape from the demands of working life. This conservative view, which finds echoes in the contemporary perception of popular culture as an arena in which to pursue the freedom to "be oneself," didn't challenge so much as reflect the entrepreneurial ideology of industrialism. As the most intense suffering associated with the Industrial Revolution passed, and the poor began to glimpse at least the possibility of beginning to share in its benefits, the more conservative view prevailed, assigning popular culture the role of escapist complement rather than radical antagonist to dominant social structures. The increasing commercialization of popular culture played a major role in hastening that trend.

THE PRODUCTION OF COMMERCIAL MASS CULTURE—THE BIRTH OF THE CULTURE INDUSTRY

When we talk about popular culture today, it's generally assumed to refer to the products of the mass media—TV, film, music, Internet culture, and so on. An important goal of this chapter has been to illuminate some of the currents that swirled around the birth of media culture, shaping it even as they were shaped by it. Thus, even though traditional recreation, working-class culture, and the earnest efforts of the rational recreationists were all largely eclipsed by the power of media culture, the *popularity* of media culture cannot be understood without them. Popularity, you should recall from Chapter One, is *not*, as the makers of commercial media would have it, simply a measure of how many people buy stuff; rather, it is a shifting and contested arena of power. Commercial culture was an in-your-face challenge to the Arnoldian guardians of "Culture" at the same time as it eroded the tradition and politics of the working class; however, it is in the context of the *persistence* of those alternative cultural strains—elitist attempts to defend their definition of "high" culture, and the efforts of ordinary people to shape the meaning of their own experience—that the significance of the commercial media, the most far-reaching cultural development of the last two centuries, must be measured. The concept of **hegemony** (see Close-Up 2.2) has proved most useful to cultural theorists attempting to measure the significance, in political terms, of the explosive growth of commercial culture.

It is tempting to see media culture as truly *popular* in its satisfaction of the desire and will of the people. As contemporary critics (both working-class activists and middle-class reformers) along with more recent theorists such as Stuart Hall ("Deconstructing the Popular") challenge this assumption, pointing out that the pleasures offered by what came to be known as the *culture industry* (see Chapter Four) are glossy substitutes for the satisfying kind of empowerment that would result from, say, better working conditions, stronger communities, or expanded democratic rights. This does not mean that commercial culture succeeds purely by virtue of trickery, by exploiting people's stupidity; rather, it works hegemonically, through engagement and negotiation with their real desires, which it transforms into shiny novelties—magazines, musical entertainment, films—that can be sold for profit. We will explore the concept of hegemony more fully in subsequent chapters. For now, it is important to keep it in mind as a key element in the successful development of early commercial culture.

A key assumption of this chapter has been that modern popular culture—and specifically commercial culture—emerged in the wake of the Industrial Revolution. This is something of an exaggeration: commercial forms of entertainment long pre-dated the nineteenth century—cultural producers such as publishers of pamphlets and ballads, travelling musicians, and other performers did earn a modest living from their work. The major

Hegemony

Developed by the Italian Marxist Antonio Gramsci in the 1930s, the concept of hegemony refers to the ability of dominant groups in society to exercise control over weaker groups not by means of force or domination, but by gaining their consent, so that the unequal distribution of power appears to be both legitimate and natural. In other words, hegemony operates not by forcing people against their better judgment to submit to more powerful interests, but rather by actively seeking the spontaneous cooperation of subordinate classes to maintaining social relationships that continue their subordination. Hegemony, significantly, is never total, but operates in constant struggle with newly emerging forms of oppositional consciousness. It works not by crushing those forces, but by a constant process of negotiation.

So how is popular media culture hegemonic? First, it operates in conjunction (and sometimes in tension) with institutions like the state, the law, education, and the family to legitimate the values of capitalist society—individualism, consumerism, the priority of private versus public interests, and so on. But unlike these other institutions, which sometimes resort to force, commercial culture works almost entirely through the promise, if not the fulfillment, of pleasure. That the pleasures of commercial culture are often opposed by more official institutions—the church, education, and so on—makes them that much more seductive.

shift in the nineteenth century concerned the forms and scale by which culture was turned into a profitable commodity. Products of the culture industry differed from earlier forms of culture in at least two crucial ways: first, they relied on relatively sophisticated and expensive forms of media technology in order to reach a mass audience; second, mass media was produced by a **vertically integrated** factory system, supervised by committees or boards of executives and assembled according to complex divisions of labour. This contrasts sharply with traditional cultural forms that tend to be strongly rooted in the working-class community, with performers and their material reflecting the everyday lives of their audiences. Rather than reflecting the actual experiences of any social group, mass media are designed to appeal to as many social classes or class fractions as possible in order to generate maximum profits for their producers (Naremore and Brantlinger 13).

At least two major, and several minor, factors combined to make possible the development of a mass entertainment industry. First, a large and concentrated urban population, which by the late nineteenth century enjoyed rising income levels and an increase in leisure time, ensured a captive audience for new forms of popular culture. Second, developments in technology made it possible to produce and deliver entertainment on a vast scale.

Technology

For the Canadian media theorist Marshall McLuhan, whose complex insights often get reduced to the single aphorism "the medium is the message," technology—the form, or "medium" of culture—has greater material significance than the content, or "message." While this is a fairly radical proposition that few cultural theorists accept in its totality today, it offers a useful way into understanding the impact of media technology in shaping our consciousness.

The Printing Press   To understand how technology was implicated in the creation of the media that still dominate our popular culture today—magazines, newspapers, film, and television—it is useful to recall a much earlier innovation and its effect on the way culture was produced and consumed. The printing press, invented by Johannes Gutenberg in the fifteenth century, was one of the earliest mass-production technologies. By mechanically reproducing texts that would once have been copied out by hand, the printing press radically altered the possibilities for the distribution of knowledge. This new development had far-reaching political as well as economic implications. One of the most significant changes associated with the invention of the printing press was the decentralization of the production of written information, making it accessible to a much broader segment of the population. It also made possible the creation of a vast print industry, starting with the Bible (the first widely available written text) but quickly expanding to encompass a variety of publications on different subjects, to satisfy the appetite for information (and titillation!) of an increasingly literate population. Print technology offered new opportunities for social control in the form of education and propaganda, as well as democratic empowerment as people were exposed to ideas and knowledge from different perspectives. It also affected people's understanding of their place in the world in more indirect ways.

By removing the necessity for face-to-face contact in communication, mass-printed texts such as newspapers arguably contribute to individual isolation, at the same time as they enable the creation of imaginary connections between people geographically removed from one another, linked only through their consciousness of being part of a broader audience. Thus it has been argued that the advent of print media is critical to the production of the "imagined community" of the nation (Anderson *Imagined*)—a development we discuss further in Chapter Seven. McLuhan goes further to suggest that print technology literally changes the way our minds and bodies interact with the world, reconfiguring human consciousness in a way that favours linearity, a mode of thinking that is implicated in the scientific theories and ideology of progress that fuelled the period of European history known as the Enlightenment, and the Industrial Revolution that succeeded it (Grossberg 44).

As McLuhan compellingly argued, subsequent innovations in media technology—photography, radio, film, television—have all influenced culture and consciousness in profound ways, some, paradoxically, taking us back to pre-literate tribal ways of conceiving the world, enabling the creation of the so-called "global village." Print, however, was intimately tied to the Industrial Revolution, both materially in the sense that the book was one of the first mass-produced objects, and metaphorically in that the mode of interacting with the world associated with print—linear, forward-looking, rational, mechanical—came to define a whole culture, one that is only now starting to shift.

Transportation   The Industrial Revolution was enabled by developments not just in technologies of production, but also in transportation, including the steamships that propelled voyages of discovery and colonization. The development of national rail systems had important commercial and social effects, not the least of which was to make travel much easier and more accessible for ordinary people. By the mid-nineteenth century, even working-class families were able to escape the city to spend a few days at the beach, where they stayed at resorts that offered them all kinds of commercial entertainment. Within the urban environment itself, improvements in public transit made it possible for people to travel between the suburbs and the city at night to attend the theatre and, by century's end, the cinema. Besides creating mobile audiences, better transportation fuelled the development of popular culture in other more obvious ways, by facilitating the faster, larger, and more extensive distribution of goods and services.

Suggested Activity 2.3

While the development of the railway had a huge effect on the development of culture in nineteenth century Britain, the invention of the car and the construction of vast networks of highways has arguably had an even greater effect on culture in the twentieth century. What are some of the cultural consequences of the dominance of the automobile in contemporary North American society? You should think not only of what the car makes possible in terms of transportation, but also of how the car is connected, materially and symbolically, to a whole series of contemporary ideologies and practices (including the popularity of such things as Tim Hortons drive-through coffee and doughnuts).

In fact, *technologies of delivery* arguably became even more significant than *technologies of production* in the development of mass culture. One of the most significant innovations in the delivery of information was the invention of the electrical telegraph in mid-century, which enabled the instantaneous transfer of information over distances. The telegraph, James Carey suggests, "marked the decisive separation of 'transportation' and 'communication.' Until the telegraph, these words were synonymous. The telegraph ended that identity and allowed symbols to move independently of geography and independently of and faster than transport" (213). It also turned those symbols into viable objects of exchange and, in conjunction with visual technologies such as the camera and film projector, the telegraph helped to create a culture industry founded on mass media.

Industrial technology, then, affected the domain of popular culture by changing the physical processes of production and, by extension, the kinds of objects that could be produced and the ways they were consumed. It also changed and improved means of distributing cultural goods to a vast audience. In sum, it played a key role in the commodification of culture, or its transformation into a collection of products that could be bought and sold.

Regulation, Innovation, Consolidation

Technological development doesn't take place in a vacuum. The nature of new cultural technologies, the uses to which they are put, who uses them, and who profits by them are questions that are all determined by broader political, economic, and social factors. Critical among these factors are the kinds of regulations—laws, trade agreements, unwritten social rules—that determine the circumstances in which forms of popular culture are produced and consumed. The increasingly liberal trade regulations that characterized British industrial society (developments that were not always matched by a loosening of moral and social restrictions) helped to create a climate of entrepreneurial innovation that fuelled the development of new forms of popular culture. The period is characterized by genuine rags-to-riches stories of itinerant actors, songwriters, and musicians who emerged from humble beginnings to control small-scale entertainment empires. The same environment that made their enrichment possible, however, also paved the way for the consolidation of ever-larger entertainment conglomerates, effectively shutting the door on the emergence of new independent cultural producers.

The Expansion of Mass Media   The development of print mass media offers a glimpse into how this process worked. A number of factors contributed to a growing market for printed materials over the course of the eighteenth and nineteenth centuries. Growing literacy rates—enhanced by laws such as the *Education Act* of 1870, which made public education compulsory—in combination with developments mentioned above such as increased leisure time, created a vast audience for such cheap reading matter as political pamphlets, chapbooks, and broadsheets (collections of poems or ballad lyrics). While the profit margins on these types of literature were small, there was enough demand to ensure a modest living for their publishers, whose success was guaranteed in part by their intimate familiarity with the audiences to whom they catered.

Throughout the nineteenth century, growing opportunities for print-production on a much larger scale helped to create a thriving newspaper and magazine industry that effectively destroyed the livelihood of these small-scale, independent operations. Specific regulatory changes such as the abolition of taxes on ads (1853), newspapers (1855), and paper (1861) made it increasingly feasible to sell newspapers and periodicals cheaply, while earning huge profits through advertising. Typical among these was the *Daily Mail*, established in London in 1896 and achieving an average weekly circulation of more than 200,000 in its first year. To satisfy such a large and diverse audience, the *Daily Mail*, like many other mass-produced papers, relied on sensationalism, balancing political coverage with a strong focus on sports and crime. Capitalizing on the success of the *Daily Mail*, its publisher, Edward Harmsworth (later Lord Northcliffe), quickly established *The Daily Mirror*, a tabloid initially targeted to a mostly female audience, whose stories of crime and romance were enhanced by lots of pictures. While the two papers were widely criticized, the *Mail* as "the paper for people who could not think" and the *Mirror* as "the paper for people who could not read" (Briggs 9), they were both massively successful, with the *Mirror* becoming for a time the paper with the largest circulation in the world.

The establishment of media empires in the late nineteenth century anticipates the much more significant kinds of media convergence that are in evidence today, linking not only forms of media (say, print with TV) but also form with content (for example, TV networks and sports teams; see Chapter Four). Among the costs of achieving such vast economies of scale, which can (though does not always) mean greater efficiency of delivery and higher production values, are a reduction of the diversity of opinion and a dilution of content, to satisfy as vast an audience as possible. This latter issue points to one of the most significant consequences of media consolidation in the nineteenth century: the production of a new kind of cultural literacy, based not on an intimately shared knowledge of one's own familiar surroundings but on a more general social outlook made up of ideas, beliefs, tastes, and opinions shared with a vast group of strangers. The consequences—both positive and negative—of that move toward national and, eventually, global mass culture are taken up in detail in Chapter Nine.

Pub Culture and the Music Hall   The expansion of the media industry did not, of course, diminish people's appetites for more sensual kinds of entertainment. The pub remained a cornerstone of popular recreation, forming a basis for new entertainment enterprises such as the music hall. While the deregulation of alcohol sales, mentioned above, was a welcome development for pub owners in some ways, it remained difficult to make much money in an increasingly competitive environment through the sales of food and drink alone. Pub owners thus had to resort to other innovations in order to turn their establishments into profitable commercial enterprises. While many early nineteenth-century pubs were "little more than parlours of private houses," as one historian describes them (Bailey 28), starting around the 1830s changing building regulations led to the establishment of bigger, more commercial pubs—so-called "gin palaces." Among the structural elements incorporated into these establishments were bar counters separating customers from liquor and dispensers, thus safeguarding the product and allegedly adding to an atmosphere of professionalism. A more blatantly commercial innovation

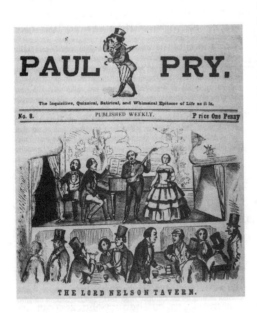

Music hall represented a transitional moment in the evolution of "homemade" popular culture into mass culture.

was the elimination of seats, which encouraged a high volume and rapid turnover of customers. Gas lamps hung outside as well as inside helped draw in customers by extending the territory of the pub into the street (Bailey 29).

The commercial activity of the pub also extended beyond the immediate business of the sale of food and alcohol. As has already been mentioned, pub owners sponsored all kinds of recreational activities, from sports to musical events. Perhaps the most substantial move to transform the institution of the pub into a form of mass culture came with the advent of music hall, in which musical and dramatic performances formed the central component of a comprehensive entertainment package, enhanced by food and drink, and enjoyed—as pub culture had not been previously—by women as well as men (the wholesome family image was no doubt complicated by the thriving trade in prostitution that its critics maintained was a key sideline of music hall). Like many early forms of mass entertainment, music hall resists easy categorization. While its commercial aspects and the presence of professional performers distinguish it from more traditional forms of do-it-yourself popular culture, it was not yet purely corporate—at least not at first.

Developed out of the more loosely organized "free and easy," in which pub patrons watched—and, more significantly, participated actively in—songs and sketches, music hall represented a bridge between those earlier forms of participatory entertainment and the kinds of mass culture we are more familiar with today, in which audiences tend to be reduced to passive spectators. In this transformation, producers of commercial entertainment found allies in a middle-class notion of culture that discouraged audience participation in public art, as part of a more general campaign against the public airing of "private" feeling—along with a whole range of other activities such as eating, spitting, nose-blowing, scratching, and farting. While certain forms of mass culture—in particular, sport—still sanctioned (as they continue to do today) some degree of public participation, thus confirming their relegation to a "lower" category of entertainment, the rules of middle-class etiquette proved to be far-reaching in their influence on a general trend to transform audiences from collective participants into passive, individual spectators (Levine 198–199). Music hall nevertheless retained many of the features of earlier forms of participatory entertainment, with audiences joining in choruses and loudly registering their approval and disapproval of performances.

Significantly, though, music hall has been linked by historians with a moment of decline in working-class democratic movements. Unlike earlier forms of pub culture, in which recreation and politics were often closely bound together with songs and skits blatantly critical of the prevailing class structure, the tone of music hall entertainment tended toward a more conservative acceptance of the dominant ideology of capitalism. Like successive forms of mass entertainment, music hall was not geared toward changing the social order; it offered, rather, a temporary escape from its constraints, a culture not of protest but of "consolation" (Jones 499).

The imbrication of music hall with prevailing economic structures was reflected not just in the transformation of its audiences, but also in the professionalization and organization of its production. In some significant ways, music hall remained rooted in the mostly working-class community that it served, with most of its performers, as well as the songs and skits they performed, coming directly out of that experience. In its ownership, however, music hall came to resemble later forms of corporate entertainment. From the opening of Charles Morton's music hall in 1851 the industry developed quickly, with the first music hall agency established in London in 1858 and others soon following. In 1860, owners of the larger halls formed the London Music Hall Proprietors' Protection Association, which helped establish standards, including common (low) wages for performers. This association, along with the tightening of building regulations, led to the closing of smaller halls and the consolidation of bigger ones. As the larger halls grew more successful, other industries grew up around them, including a thriving music hall press featuring magazines including *Era, Magnet,* and *London Entr'acte.* Music hall also forged connections with other forms of entertainment, as proprietors began to invest in multiple ventures including sport, drama, and (later) the circus, economizing through the construction of ever-larger entertainment complexes that could accommodate multiple activities. It thus played a key role in the development of popular culture as an industry.

The Film Industry   In its formative years, the culture industry was characterized both by integration of different services—production, distribution, and sales—and by strong competition, both among different kinds of entertainment, and among different providers of the same entertainment. As historian Asa Briggs has shown, both of these tendencies were powerfully illustrated in the case of the film industry, which developed in the 1890s (see further discussion in Chapter Four). First screened in music halls as part of a program that also included live performances, films came to rival, and eventually to supplant, more traditional music hall entertainment (though some entertainers, such as Charlie Chaplin, successfully made the transition from vaudeville—a form of American entertainment that resembled music hall, but without the alcohol—to cinema).

The film industry was characterized by intense rivalry, first over the technology itself (patented by Thomas Edison but contested by others) and later over control of the industry. In 1908, the ten most powerful U.S. production companies tried to establish a monopoly on the industry by setting up, with Edison's approval, the Motion Picture Patents Company, which demanded licensing fees from all film producers, distributors, and exhibitors. A group of rivals who called themselves the "Independents" fought against the Company's dominance. Their strategies included using illegal equipment and imported film stock, and moving as far away as possible from the film industry's home in New York to the then-village of Hollywood, California. When the Motion Picture Patents Company was finally forced to shut down in 1915, in response to the finding that it constituted an unfair monopoly, the Independents were in a position to do what so many industry outsiders and renegades have done since, and assumed a position of dominance (think Bill Gates in the computer industry). Thus, led by Adolph Zukor, the Independents (which eventually became Famous Players Lasky Corporation) quickly came to dominate the industry, integrating production, distribution, and exhibition, raising capital through the stock market, and establishing the Hollywood star system in the process. By 1921, Famous Players Lasky controlled more than three hundred cinemas and was itself being accused of monopolistic practices (Briggs 15–20). While the film industry was to change dramatically over the course of the twentieth century, this early struggle between independents and conglomerates, entrepreneurs and monopolistic organizations established a dominant pattern that was to characterize not just cinema, but also the entertainment industry as a whole.

One further area of competition deserves a mention. By the beginning of the twentieth century, particularly in the film industry, a trend had emerged toward U.S. dominance. This dominance was to become a subject of critical concern that emerged in the character of early twentieth-century British critiques of mass culture, in which "Americanism" was seen to be synonymous with commercial drivel—the opposite of "real" culture. At the same time, paradoxically, anxieties about American dominance prompted protectionist measures to bolster the entertainment industry at home; we will have more to say on this ambivalent response to American popular culture in Chapter Nine.

This brief survey of some diverse developments in mass culture reveals a number of general trends and implications. To recall some of the main points, it might be useful to think about four key words: *production, participation, people,* and *penetration*. First, technological and regulatory changes fuelled the development of an increasingly competitive media industry. With a few exceptions, the development of the industry was characterized by the consolidation of forces of *production* in the hands of an increasingly small number of large corporations. Second, the development of mass media changed patterns of popular cultural *participation*. People's orientation toward recreation gradually shifted from active involvement to more passive consumption and spectatorship—a development that coincided with a decline in political engagement. Products of the new commercial cultural industry—and the *people* that made them—were increasingly less likely to speak to or from their audience's own class or community, and more likely to be associated with large, corporate enterprises. Finally, by the end of the nineteenth century, commercial culture had undergone a significant shift in location and range of influence. With the rise of American dominance in the early twentieth century, particularly in the area of film, commercial culture began to reach new levels of global *penetration*, raising questions about its power to eclipse local and traditional forms of culture (see Chapter Nine).

CONTINUITIES AND CHANGES

We have looked at a number of developments occurring in the domain of popular culture that were strongly influenced by industrialization. The fragmentation—spatial, economic, and social—of an earlier way of life changed the way people related to one another and pursued work and recreation. The struggle of working-class people to define their lives, including labour and recreation, on their own terms met powerful resistance in the form of middle-class reformers and the rise of commercial culture. In general, the growth of mass media involved the intensification of commercialization and concentration of corporate control.

This movement was neither steady nor uniform, however: moves toward consolidation of corporate power were routinely challenged by competition and the flourishing of independent operators, as well as by the unionization of performers, technicians, and other employers (these tensions are discussed in more detail in Chapter Four). They were also challenged by those outside the industry—audiences and consumers whose willingness to be passively entertained existed in tension with a powerful impulse to make and do things for themselves. These tensions continue to inform the terrain of popular culture today.

The Organization and Commercialization of Sports

We began our history of popular culture by looking at street football as an apparent casualty to the movement to privatize space, and with it popular recreation. In many ways football offers a perfect example of the operation of forces of corporatization. Proceeding in tandem with the moves to ban football from the public streets were efforts to organize it into a successful commercial venture. The sponsorship of "soccer clubs" led to the establishment of organized leagues, and the eventual founding of the Football Association in 1863. Considerable effort went into the task of regularizing the rules of the game, though this was not totally successful, as demonstrated by the evolution of two games: rugby, and Association football, or soccer. (The two games differ widely both in rules of play and in culture, with the former maintaining a fairly elitist flavour in keeping with its roots in the British public school system, and the latter enjoying a strong working-class following—at least until recently, when commercial success has arguably all but severed the sport from its roots.) Professionalism—that is, the introduction of salaries for players—was legalized in 1855, and clubs began charging admission in 1870, gradually incorporating other commercial enticements such as food, drink, and other entertainment for spectators. As with music hall, a sports media industry soon developed, with Routledge's 1867 *Handbook of Football* helping to foster fan solidarity around a sport that was rapidly becoming institutionalized.

The commercialization of sport followed a similar pattern in the colonies. In Canada, as in England, industrialization (which occurred more than fifty years later in Canada) played a large role in the transformation of sport from a casual, spontaneous, and relatively inclusive activity into a regulated, formalized, and, eventually, commercial enterprise. Most obviously, urbanization placed restrictions on space as it had in England, moving sport out of fields and other open spaces into specialized athletic facilities. The introduction of fixed spatial boundaries served to transform, and eventually to formalize, rules of play. Industrialization also influenced the temporal organization of sport in at least two ways: first, the institution of long and regular working days made it necessary to establish rules limiting the duration of play (a significant development in sports such as lacrosse, in which games might once have lasted anywhere from a few minutes to several hours). Second, the marking of time into distinct periods of work and leisure made

A hardy and determined band of players resisted the general trend toward the organization and institutionalization of football (see also the photo on p. 50).

it possible to establish formal schedules of play, based on the assumption that players and spectators had regularly scheduled time off (Metcalfe 50).

The Evolution of Sport Historian Alan Metcalfe also identifies another indirect consequence of the importance of time as part of a general emphasis on quantification: the meaning of sport shifted "from the process, the contest itself, to the product, the record" (51). As a consequence, the nature of competition changed, with less emphasis on its social aspects and a greater and greater focus on winning. As in other areas of the industrial economy, sport was increasingly shaped by specialization: from a chaotic, collective endeavour in which the different tasks of the game were shared by everyone, players gradually assumed positions in accordance with their specific talents—offence, defence, goal-keeping, and so on (Guttman qtd. in Ann Hall et al. 50).

The incorporation of football into schools as part of an ideology of masculine character development was an important step in its institutionalization.

Metcalfe identifies a number of other changes associated with industrialization that contributed to the organization of sport in Canada, including the development of transportation and communications technology—the train, the telegraph, and radio and print media—that made it possible not only to arrange contests between far-flung teams, but also to broadcast schedules and results, creating a national audience for sport (52). (From the expansion of national and, eventually, international leagues, we arrive at the contemporary situation in which virtually none of the players on "local" professional teams come from the city—or even the country—in which the team is based. This development, a logical outgrowth of the forces of global capital, changes not only the organization of players, but also the relationship between players and fans, whose relationship to "their" team is an oddly contrived one, connected only arbitrarily to place.)

The evolution of "fans" is another major development in the organization and commercialization of sport. By the late 1900s, football—played according to a still unfixed set of "Canadian rules" that drew something from British rugby and something from the American game—had become a spectator sport. Ice hockey—a game that, according to at least one account, was established by Montreal football players as a form of winter training (Wise and Fisher 44)—quickly followed. Commercialization and professionalization went hand in hand, as the involvement of highly skilled, salaried players made games more exciting to watch. With ice hockey in particular, the expense involved—equipment, rink rental and maintenance—gave the game a strongly middle-class flavour, in terms of ownership if not participation or interest. Again, as with the geographical expansion of sport, its commercial intensification has even more dramatic consequences today, among them the pricing of tickets far out of the range of the average fan.

Commercialization alone was not responsible for the wresting of sports like hockey and football from the people to the elites; in fact, much in the same way as commercial media were challenged by the rational recreationists, professional sport faced strong challenges from amateur associations, connected in particular with private schools and uni-

The celebrity status and colossal salaries accorded to professional athletes, like soccer player David Beckham, are among the most visible signs of the commercialization of soccer.

versities. The leagues that were established by the universities especially maintained a strong policy against professionalism, a policy motivated as much by an elitist desire to maintain class privilege as it was by a concern for the purity of the sport. Some clubs defined their codes of amateurism according to the exclusion of particular professions and even ethnic groups (see Table 2.1). An 1873 regulation, for example, banned "labourers" and "Indians" from membership in the Montreal Pedestrian Club on the same grounds that mechanics and labourers had once been barred from rowing clubs: they were seen to enjoy a physical advantage over their more refined middle-class counterparts (Ann Hall et al. 59).

In general, nineteenth-century football and hockey amateurists (as distinct from contemporary promoters of amateur sport) were, if anything, more bound up with economic status than professionals since a strict ban on professionals meant that participation was restricted to those with plenty of time and money. Between them, however, both middle-class amateur associations and corporate owners of professional teams contributed to the creation of a culture of organized sport, a culture of spectatorship rather than participation. Indirectly, but most significantly, the propertied interests represented by both the professionals and the "gentleman amateurs" contributed to the decline of public space available for community athletic activity—a development that foreshadows the conflict over street hockey today.

As the above discussion suggests, we can read into the histories of football and ice hockey a fairly straightforward movement from the loss of public recreation space and the banning of street games to the creation of professional sport, and the conversion of players into fans. More recently, the intensification of the commercial imperative in sport has begun to wrest enjoyment of the game away from players and fans alike, as players (in exchange for hugely lucrative salaries, depending on the sport) are subject to being traded

Table 2.1 Early Definitions of "Amateur"

The Amateur Athletic Association of Canada and its successors established the following definitions of an amateur:

1884: An amateur is one who has never competed for a money prize or staked bet with or against any professional for any prize, or assisted in the practice of athletic exercises as a means of obtaining a livelihood.

1896 (add): Or who has entered any competition under a name other than his own.

1902 (add): private or public gate receipts ... who has never, directly or indirectly, received any bonus or a payment in lieu of loss of time while playing as a member of any club, or any money considerations whatever for any services as an athlete except his actual traveling and of selling or pledging his prizes.

1909 (add): promoted an athletic competition for personal gain.

(or dropped) at the whim of owners, and attendance at games is (economically) restricted to corporate executives entertaining clients. The only real winners in professional sport today, arguably, are commercial sponsors, who depend on a still-enthusiastic TV audience. And yet … when we look back to the original English battle over street football, and then forward to the road hockey case in Hamilton, the answer to the question of who controls popular culture is more complicated, and more encouraging.

Back to the Streets

Street games might, in theory, have been banned in 1835 Britain, but players were not put off that easily. In Derby in 1845, footballers responded to attempts to stop the annual Shrovetide match by throwing things at the police, including a "brick bat and bludgeon" (one or both of which hit the mayor). Pursued by police, special constables, and dragoons, players ran away to the next village—where, after a vigorous skirmish, they finally surrendered the ball (Malcomson 142). While the footballers eventually lost that contest—with greater police reinforcement in subsequent years ensuring that the tradition was eventually quashed—in other places public protests against the prohibition resulted in the setting aside of public playing fields where the game could continue without interfering with other (commercial) activities.

The Hamilton street hockey story didn't end quite so violently, and its implications are a little more complicated. As did the English footballers, Ryan Kotar and his father enjoyed a partial victory. Their case was dismissed not because the judge deemed that road hockey was *not* a crime, but because of contradictions in witnesses' testimony. The bylaw prohibiting street games still stands, in spite of a motion to Hamilton city council to rescind it. Similar bylaws exist in most Canadian municipalities, though they are rarely enforced. The tenor of Ciuriak's attack on hockey as "totally uncivilized and dangerous" (Clairmont) echoes some of the rational recreationists' charges against street football as leading not only to "moral degradation" amongst its players, but also to "injury to health, fractured limbs and (not infrequently) loss of life" (qtd. in Cunningham 78). However, the nationwide rallying of community support behind the Kotars, along with their exoneration from charges, would seem to testify to a prevailing determination to keep alive the rights of the people to enjoy themselves in public spaces. The defence of the hockey players—even by government officials in Hamilton, who promised to try to have the ban struck down—would seem to confirm the survival of grassroots, popular entertainment in spite of both attacks from moralists and the expansion of private property rights, including the conversion of sport into a corporate activity.

There are other ways of reading the story, however, that point to both its continuity with the British street football incident and its important differences from that event. First of all, although this story tended to be represented as a victory for grassroots sports—street hockey as opposed to league hockey, or the overly commercialized professional game—the distinctions between the two aren't all that clear-cut. Following the Hamilton incident, NHL players rallied in support of street hockey—as much, no doubt, out of a recognition that street hockey nurtures professional hockey fans as out of pure-hearted devotion to the game. In an article calling for the preservation of outdoor hockey rinks, columnist Roy MacGregor touted the value of "being left alone to play the game the way it is played in the imagination," in part because that kind of play nurtures the talent that goes on to win junior world championships and Olympic gold medals.

National Mythology   Victory in such international contests is substantial fodder for the national mythology of Canada—which points to another wrinkle in the story: there is no question that one of the reasons the Hamilton incident received so much press was because the sport in question was hockey—not baseball, not Frisbee, not soccer, but a sport whose restriction, according to one Hamilton city councillor, would be positively "un-Canadian" ("Game On"). As one supporter put it, "Hockey is Canada's national pas-time.... When I stumble across kids playing hockey in the street, it brings a smile to my face" (qtd. in Wente "It's Okay"). That hockey occupies a significant place in the official mythology of Canada is indisputable. However, as we discuss in more detail in subse-quent chapters (see Chapters Three and Seven in particular), national mythologies are not spontaneous expressions of citizenly love. They are, rather, contrived and partial sto-ries whose collective rhetoric conceals the stakes of *power*—both economic and social—involved in their dissemination.

It's in the interests of professional sports and its sponsors that the dream of "the game" be kept alive, by powerful images like the 1998 Labatt beer TV commercial in which Toronto commuters spontaneously join in a giant game of street hockey, and the 2002 Tim Hortons calendar that features an image of kids playing shinny. These heart-warming images are at odds with the sacrifice of public space and resources to the forces of commercialism. Corporate team owners' and sponsors' demands for tax breaks for their teams contribute to this problem, by taking funds away from public facilities such as parks and outdoor rinks. Some corporations, including Tim Hortons, *do* make finan-cial contributions to amateur sport, part of a growing trend necessitated in part by the erosion of public support due to commercialization! The underfunding of Canadian amateur hockey, particular women's hockey, in relation to the vast and increasingly U.S.–dominated entertainment complex of the NHL offers yet another contradiction in the mythology of Canada's "national game." These facts complicate the widely asserted notion that hockey is "a big part of what makes us *us*" (sportswriter Stephen Brunt qtd. in Wente "It's Okay").

Gender in Sports   As the street-hockey story attests, distinctions between grassroots and governmentality, populism and commercialism, are less clear-cut in Canada today than they were in Victorian England. The politics of the popular have also become more complicated: while it's easy to read the 1845 contest over street football in Derby as a con-test between "the people" and their political and economic rulers, the question of who constitutes "us"—the people—today is not so simple. We have already mentioned some of the gender implications of the hockey story, in relation to the underfunding of women's sport. Sports columnist Laura Robinson goes further to note an unspoken assumption of many of the defenders of street hockey players: when they say "kids," they mean "boys." She goes on to note,

> I can't recall seeing a group of girls commandeering a public street at any time to play any team sport. Boys have always understood that public space is the right space for their physical performance. The theatre of masculinity is public because we have constructed masculinity in a way that demands of men and boys constant physical proof of "who the man is," to use a basketball term.

Nowhere, arguably, is the ideology of masculinity more evident than in hockey, whose increasing violence at the professional and amateur levels has been cause for public concern. Such concern was not, significantly, voiced in relation to the street-hockey case, except by Nadia Ciuriak—a woman and an immigrant, who was demonized for, among other sins, being "un-Canadian." When she lost her case, columnist Margaret Wente notes, "the neighbourhood boys were directed to wave their hockey sticks triumphantly for the approving cameras" ("It's Okay").

The question of what, or whose, culture triumphed here is ambiguous.

SUMMARY

A crude overview of the development of popular culture from the nineteenth century to the present might yield a narrative something like the following: 1) Destruction of traditional ways of life, including popular entertainment; 2) Brief flourishing of working-class culture, in tension with middle-class promotion of capital-C, or "high" culture; 3) Triumph of commercial culture. While this chapter has acknowledged these developments, it has also attempted to show a more complex picture. First, we have attempted to demonstrate that the evolution of popular culture has not proceeded in a linear fashion, that new developments don't necessarily supersede or cancel out what came before, and that, notwithstanding the power of media culture today, other currents, including grassroots "do-it-yourself" cultural forms, persist. Second, our discussion highlights the impossibility of clearly separating out the different strands of the fabric of culture: working-class culture functioned in tension, but sometimes in cooperation, with the rational recreationists, against the narcotic effect of commercial culture. At the same time, commercial media and the guardians of capital-C Culture—different faces of the ascendant middle class—collaborated in the erosion of working-class culture. Finally, as the contemporary example of street hockey in Canada illustrates, the line between the spontaneous recreation of ordinary people and the products of the sports/entertainment industry is increasingly hard to draw.

Our "fast-forward" cut from nineteenth-century Britain to contemporary Canada also showed something else: that struggles over the meaning and value of popular culture connect to broader relations of power in complex and changing ways. The class consciousness of the nineteenth century has not disappeared; rather, it has helped to pave the way for (and occasionally served to muffle) consciousness of other unequal social relations, such as those shaped by gender, ethnicity, and—as we'll explore further in subsequent chapters—age, race, and sexuality.

This chapter has covered a lot of ground, both in time and subject matter; however, a few key points should remind you of its main themes while leading you into the discussions in subsequent chapters:

- Contemporary popular culture differs in critical ways from the cultural forms that preceded it.
- Changes associated with the Industrial Revolution in Britain, including the reconfiguration of time and space, the transformation of work (and the creation of leisure), and the fragmentation of traditional social relations, destroyed old forms of culture while making new ones possible.
- Shaped by the political currents of working-class activism, middle-class reform, and economic liberalism, popular culture both reflects and shapes ongoing struggles about freedom and democracy.
- The rise of media culture, enabled by a climate of technological innovation and economic liberalism, represents the major element in what we recognize as popular culture today. It profoundly affects, without completely overwhelming, possibilities for alternative, non-commercial, cultural expression.

SUGGESTIONS FOR FURTHER READING

Cunningham, Hugh. *Leisure in the Industrial Revolution.* London: Croom Helm, 1980.

Hobsbawm, Eric. *Industry and Empire: An Economic History of Britain Since 1750.* London: Weidenfeld and Nicolson, 1968.

Levine, Lawrence W. *Highbrow/Lowbrow: The Emergence of Cultural Hierarchy in America.* Cambridge, MA: Harvard University Press, 1988.

Malcomson, Robert W. *Popular Recreations in English Society 1700–1850.* Cambridge, UK: Cambridge University Press, 1973.

Thompson, E. P. *The Making of the English Working Class.* Harmondsworth, UK: Penguin, 1963.

Chapter *3*

Representation and the Construction of Social Reality

INTRODUCTION: CONSTRUCTING A CRISIS—THE DISCOURSE OF VIOLENT YOUTH

> Victoria is Canada's garden playground. Golfers are still on the links in January and flowers bloom all year. Its image is of a prim and proper government and tourist town. At first glance, the city is scenic, safe, and secure, but this is a tale of two cities.
>
> It may be hard to believe but there is a dangerous and violent side to Victoria, especially at night. It's when roving gangs of young people are out looking for trouble and someone to hurt. . . . In the last five years in Victoria, there has been victim after victim of violent teenagers who hang out, drink and assault. All the publicity and public outrage hasn't stopped it.
>
> —"Victoria's Secret," CTV (*W5*)

In March 2002, as part of a week's programming schedule that included no less than three specials on teen violence, CTV's *W5* aired a documentary called "Victoria's Secret" that examined the phenomenon of teenage violence in Victoria, British Columbia. In documenting the "youth gang problem," the two-part show assembled a picture of an emerging social crisis that had thus far remained hidden because of victims' fear of talking and civic boosters' reluctance to tarnish the image of the city. Together with a host of other print and television stories that appeared in the early half of 2002, "Victoria's

Secret" contributed to a developing public discourse on youth violence in Canada. As in "Victoria's Secret," other stories point to a long-simmering problem that has only recently begun to receive sustained attention.

In seeming contrast to the emphasis on the invisibility of the problem and to the "numbing indifference" of teens (Wong A30), many stories also testify to a growing atmosphere of fear. Following a shooting episode in a Toronto high school, one article—citing comments by the former vice-principal who heads the Canadian Safe Schools Network—noted that "principals lived in constant fear that their schools could be next . . . try as they might to keep students safe with video-surveillance cameras, zero-tolerance policies, hall monitors and—increasingly—uniforms or dress codes that make it easier to spot intruders" (Galt). In conjunction with the new school security measures cited in the article, a number of new and changed policies and laws—the creation of boot camps, the *Youth Criminal Justice Act* that came into effect in 2003, the *Safe Streets Act*, and so on—testify to growing public and official determination to combat the problem.

Statistics tell a somewhat different story (see Figure 3.1). Youth crime in general shows a steady rise from 1984 that peaks in 1991 then falls off. Violent crime among youth shows a slight but steady increase until 1996, then decreases until 1999. Between 1999 and 2001 (not shown on the graph) the number of youth charged with violent crimes increased by 2 percent. Countering perceptions that violent youth crime is increasing out of proportion to adult crime, the number of homicides committed by youth expressed as a percentage of all homicides remained fairly constant throughout the 1990s, at about 8 percent (John Howard Society). Consistent with a decreasing rate of homicide overall, there were 30 youths accused of homicide in 2001, the lowest level in more than 30 years ("Crime Statistics").

So what's going on? Statistics would appear to refute media claims of an unprecedented crisis of youth violence. Then again, statistics themselves, which *seem* to offer the irrefutable proof of numbers, need to be understood in context. According to critics, among the factors shaping what looks like a large escalation of youth crime between 1986 and 1992 are a significant increase in the size of the youth population; the introduction of the *Young Offenders Act* in 1984, which reclassified sixteen- and seventeen-year-olds (typically the age group most likely to commit crime) within the category of youth; changes in policing practices, including a tendency for police to charge a greater number of suspects for each crime; and, finally, increased reporting of incidents such as "minor schoolyard scuffles" that formerly would have been dealt with by schools and/or parents (John Howard Society).

We present these different accounts of youth violence, which are also different ways of representing the issue, not simply to contrast media hype with the "real" picture presented by statistics, or to illustrate the inadequacy of statistics to comprehend the complexity of the truth. Rather, we want to use the "story" of youth violence as a way into talking about **representation** and the role it plays in the construction of social reality. Questions this chapter seeks to address are: How do language and other sign systems work to signify, or to create, social meaning? How does representation map or produce

Figure 3.1 Rates of Youth *Criminal Code* Incidents, 1983–99

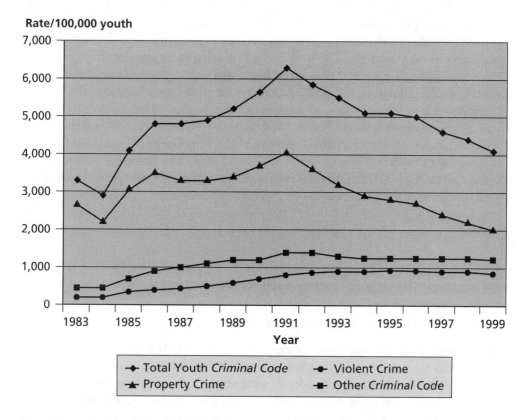

Rate/100,000 youth

Source: Statistics Canada, Juristat, Vol. 20 no. 5, Catalogue no. 85-002-XIE, July 2000.

relations of power? How do different media genres (advertising, news, entertainment) and different types of media (TV, print) help shape the production of meaning? How have processes of representation shifted historically? What is the nature and extent of media representation in contemporary global culture? And, finally, How does representation work (or fail) as a means of political resistance?

SIGNIFICATION—THE PRODUCTION OF SOCIAL SENSE

We have introduced the story of youth violence—a story we return to later in the chapter—in a way that we hope will encourage you to think *counter-intuitively* about representation. That is, rather than reading the stories and statistics as we ordinarily would—as a transparent window on the phenomenon of youth crime—we want to muddy the window, to suggest that the way these stories are represented *create* the "facts" of our social life. Before proceeding to some more examples of how this process works, let's step back and try to get a handle on it from a theoretical perspective.

Broadly speaking, representation involves "the social production of meaning through **sign** systems." Signs are the fundamental units of communication. A sign can be a word, a gesture, a facial expression, an image, a musical note, even an item of clothing—any thing that refers to something else, and is recognized as doing so by users of the sign system. Conventional wisdom has it that sign systems, or languages, evolve to communicate pre-existing realities. But even a superficial examination of different languages tells us that "reality"—at least, the way reality is organized and understood—differs from culture to culture. For example, verbs in the Native American Hopi language have no past, present, or future tenses, reflecting the fact that Hopi culture doesn't measure time in a linear sequence the way most Western cultures do. While it might be supposed that the Hopi language and culture are less evolved than European cultures, linguist Benjamin Lee Whorf advanced the controversial argument that contemporary scientific theories such as quantum physics resonate naturally with a Hopi world view. European language and culture, by contrast, remains wedded to a binary mode of thought that is incapable of imagining something existing in two states at once—past and present, or wave and particle. Language by itself isn't the determining factor here; rather, it is that language, as the central medium of culture, influences the way we perceive the world around us and our place in it.

Structuralist Theories of Representation

The suggestion that language does not simply *reflect* but actually *constructs* reality emerges from a shift that occurred in the 1960s in cultural and linguistic theory. The principles underlying that shift are clustered under the general heading of **structuralism**. Structuralist theories are concerned not with *what* words or cultural practices mean, but rather with *how* they mean, according to the structure and rules of the system from which they are generated. One of the first structuralist theorists was Swiss linguist Ferdinand de Saussure, whose **semiotic** theory has had a significant impact on the study of culture (see Close-Up 3.1).

One of the important aspects of Saussurean linguistics is the distinction it draws between *langue*, or the whole system as it exists on an abstract level, including all possible signs and conventions, and *parole*, the individual utterance or the things we do with language. Subsequent critics point out the artificiality of that separation: languages can't really be said to exist apart from their specific usage. The distinction between *langue* and *parole* is useful, however, in showing that language, in the form of *parole*, embodies all kinds of possibilities for making meaning, but that those possibilities ultimately exist with a frame—the *langue*—that places a limit on what we can intelligibly say. An obvious example of this limitation is the rules of grammar, which dictate the possibilities for word combination in a sentence.

Rules of Representation   We can build from these basic linguistic principles much broader, less clear-cut rules that determine possibilities for putting together whole narratives: for example, a convention in the Western novel that has come to shape other

Semiotics

Ferdinand de Saussure (1857–1913) was a key figure in launching a move in linguistic theory away from understanding how languages developed historically, or *diachronically*, to looking at them as structures at a single moment in time, or *synchronically*. Saussure was interested in how the individual elements of language—*signs*—worked together, according to rules of selection and combination, to produce meaning. A fundamental principle of Saussure's theory was the premise that the relationship between the two "parts" of a sign—a word (or *signifier*) and the concept it refers to (the *signified*) is not natural but arbitrary, determined by convention. Meaning is produced not by correspondence between word and world, but by differences within the system. Thus, just as the letters c-a-t are meaningless except in relation to other possible selections and combinations of letters (c-a-r, for example, or r-a-t), the word "cat" derives its meaning—an association with a particular furry animal that says "meow"—by virtue of its *difference* from a series of related words—"dog," "mouse," "lemur," "fish." Meaning here is produced by selecting particular elements from a whole *paradigm* of possibilities, and combining them in a particular order, or *syntagm*, according to rules of spelling, grammar, and sense that are specific to each language.

In formulating this theory of language (similar versions of which were being developed simultaneously by the American psychologist C. S. Peirce) Saussure argued for the necessity of a new "science" that would study "the life of signs within a society." This approach, which he termed *semiotics,* has been taken up by theorists of popular culture to read not just spoken language, but also television, film, music, fashion, and architecture.

forms of expression is the movement from chaos to order, conflict to resolution. While it is obviously possible to challenge these conventions, to depart from them entirely risks not making sense. We can see this by looking at the example of the Matt Damon and Casey Affleck movie *Gerry*. In the film, the two principal characters, both named Gerry, have parked their car somewhere in the desert and gone on a hike; now they can't find the parking lot. There is little dialogue in the film, which consists mostly of lots of shots, some as long as twenty minutes, of the two Gerrys in the desert, with no change of perspective. They never find the car. In spite of the high profile of at least one of its stars, *Gerry* never achieved commercial success, in part because its story departed so radically from the codes of mainstream Hollywood cinema that it was virtually unintelligible. While critics were diplomatic about the film, describing it as "extremely disconcerting . . .

partly because it escapes easy categorization" (Taubin), audience members at the Woodstock Film Festival, where it was first shown, reacted more straightforwardly—by walking out of the theatre.

What is interesting here is the level of emotional discomfort viewers displayed. Partly, they might have been mad simply because it wasn't a typical Matt Damon film. The extremity of people's reaction to narratives that don't make sense, however, also suggests that there is something more at stake here that has to do with representation more broadly. It is ultimately the "rules" of representation—the ways in which they are observed or broken—that shapes the stories we tell, in films and other forms of entertainment as well as in our everyday conversations; stories that allow us to figure out our place in the world.

As the example of *Gerry* suggests, the "rules" pertain not just to basic linguistic functions, but also to broader cultural processes of sense-making. Language functions not as an isolated structure within those processes, but as part of a complex social fabric that cultural theorists have sought to illuminate using structuralist principles. Anthropologist Claude Lévi-Strauss (1908–), for example, worked to uncover the general cultural structures underlying specific myths in primitive societies. A critical part of his theory derived from Saussure's argument that the process of signification, or meaning-making, works according to principles of *difference*, with a particular emphasis on **binary opposition**. In other words, things and concepts acquire meaning through what they are not, through their relation to terms that are more or less opposite and mutually exclusive. The far-reaching cultural consequences of this structuring principle become evident when we look at culturally loaded concepts—culture/nature, say, or man/woman—concepts that crucially define the values not just of "primitive" myths but of our own contemporary culture.

Mythologies

Working from a different context than Lévi-Strauss, French cultural theorist Roland Barthes (1915–1980) uses the word **mythology** in a much more generalized sense, to talk about how sign systems work **ideologically** to reproduce and legitimate particular social relationships. Barthes elaborates Saussure's theory of how meaning is encoded in signs to take account of the fact that, in addition to their *denotative*, or literal, meanings, signs also assume *connotative*, or mythological, significance. That is, they take on additional associations that are more clearly subjective, charged with a culture's dominant, often unspoken, beliefs or values. In his book *Mythologies*, Barthes examines a collection of texts, images, and practices from French mass culture, with the aim of exposing the myths that underpin their seemingly natural symbolic significance. Myth, in Barthes's sense, is a form of signification that works to express and, more or less invisibly, to justify the dominant values of a culture in a particular historical moment.

Unlike the relatively simple level of denotation, in which a word or image often corresponds to a single, obvious definition, myth generally brings into play a whole chain of associated concepts (for example: tree–nature–goodness) by which members of a culture understand certain topics and that helps to shape their collective identity. Mythological meanings are generated by the juxtaposition of images and words in particular texts, produced in particular cultural contexts. In one essay, for example, Barthes analyzes a photographic exhibit touring France in the 1960s called "The Great Family of Man." On a denotative level, the exhibit consisted of images of people of different races, wearing clothes that signal different cultural backgrounds, all engaged in simple everyday activities—giving birth, eating, singing, laughing, and so on. The denotative sign, or literal image, of people laughing in turn becomes the signifier for the humanist *myth* of universal human nature— a myth that erases historical conditions of inequality in which actual human beings live. The text uses superficial signs of difference—skin colour, dress—which it then brings together into a harmonious, seemingly *natural* whole. This process covers over the actual material and *historical* contradictions that underlie its simple message (101). Myth works, Barthes's analysis suggests, to the extent that we read it "straight," accepting unquestioningly its naturalness. The principal goal of his critical reading is to reveal the mechanism behind the myth, "to track down, in the decorative display of *what-goes-without-saying*, the ideological abuse which . . . is hidden there" (11)—to show how myths are not natural but historical, the product of particular relations of power.

Reading the Headlines

A key focus of Barthes's work is the way in which particular representational technologies—colour film, for example—work to create specific ideological effects. Before we move on to talk about visual culture, however, let's try to apply some of the principles of semiotic analysis to some simpler texts: newspaper headlines. The following headline appeared in the *Hamilton Spectator* as part of a story about the introduction of computer software programs written in Inuit languages (Akin).

FROM IGLOO TO INTERNET: FIRST NATIONS GAIN ENTRÉE TO THE ELECTRONIC AGE

These programs, the story suggested, would help facilitate government operations and education in the Canadian North. On a denotative level, the signs in this headline are easily legible, though we might struggle with the metaphor in the last half—what does it mean to "gain entry" to an age? On the connotative mythological level the headline is more complex, and its seemingly straightforward message more open to question. Meaning, as we noted above, is produced by the selection and combination of signs. Thus, "igloo" and "Internet," the main signs in the beginning part of the headline, derive their meaning in part from their juxtaposition with one another, and in part by the grammar of the phrase in which they appear. What sorts of associations do these terms have in relation to one another?

Perhaps the first thing to note is that they're both somewhat unusual words in English. "Igloo" is derived from the Inuit word for "house"; "Internet," while it has come into wide general usage, initially described the limited network of computers used by the U.S. Defense System, reflecting the military origins of the technology. "Igloo" and "Internet," then, both come out of distinct cultural and historical contexts that inform their mythological associations. Rather than evoking their specific historic origins, however, these associations tend to be much more vague, subjective perceptions of the cultures they carry: "igloo" is associated with "Inuit"—or perhaps more precisely "Eskimo," since igloos belong to a world that for the most part no longer exists, and a time when Southerners' ignorance about the cultures of the North led to the use of the generic term "eskimo" for all Northern indigenous peoples. While there's nothing obviously pejorative about "igloo," as there is about "eskimo" (generally thought to be derived from an Algonquin word meaning "eater of raw flesh"), the word does carry connotations that come from the same Southern perspective of the North: it is remote; it is cold; it is barren; it is primitive.

Contrast this with the associations summoned up by the word "Internet": connectedness, speed, modernity, globalization. The sense of the headline, which is reinforced grammatically by the use of the prepositions "from" and "to," is not only one of *opposition* and *contrast* between the two terms, but also of a hierarchical relation in which the movement from one to the other constitutes a progression, a move in the right direction. The positive connotations of the move are also signalled by the phrase "gain entrée," which implies induction into a privileged space, with the suggestion (if we want to really use our imaginations) that the Inuit have finally been brought in out of the cold and into the modern world, after waiting breathlessly on the doorstep of the frozen wasteland of the tundra through much of the twentieth century.

It might be argued that there's actually nothing ideological about the headline at all: it simply describes what happened—Internet connection arrived in the Arctic—and that it does so using the catchy alliterative words "igloo" and "Internet" to draw in readers. There's no question that headlines partly work through verbal cleverness (rhyming, alliteration, puns, etc.) that has little to do with the sense of what's being conveyed (although we might argue that the compulsion to *be* punchy, to reduce complex stories to simple tags, is itself ideological, reinforcing the primary imperative of the media which is not so much to inform the public as to sell papers). Word choice has other implications, however, for the ideological frame of the story.

The choice of the word "igloo" as a shorthand for the North, for Inuit society, characterizes that society in a way that, besides carrying certain value-laden assumptions, happens to be false: the igloo, and the hunter-gatherer lifestyle that goes with it, hardly exists anymore, a fact that can be celebrated or lamented but that contradicts the picture of the Inuit as a primitive people being catapulted into the twentieth century. Beyond announcing the introduction into the Arctic of what the sources cited in the story agree will be a useful technology, the headline places the story in a wider frame shaped by mythological assumptions about cultural difference, civilization, and the inevitable and desirable course of globalization and human progress. The issue is not whether these myths are valid or useful; it is that they are *myths*, not naturally given truths—a status that is exposed only by subjecting them to the kind of critical reading that media representations, indeed most conventional uses of language, work against.

Discourse and Power

A semiotic reading like the one we just did focuses on the way in which meaning is generated through the relationships between signs in a text. Of course, the sense of that meaning and its substance—the kind of weight it carries in the world—are determined not just by the elements in the individual text, nor even the sign system from which they are derived, but also by the broader cultural context. This includes a community of readers who share a broad collection of cultural references, and the broader system of social relations that determines not only what has meaning in a culture, but also who gets to say what, under what circumstances, and with what social effects.

French philosopher and social critic Michel Foucault (1926–84) uses the word *discourse* to describe the way speech and writing work in conjunction with specific structures and institutions to shape social reality. **Discourse**, in Foucault's specialized sense of the word, describes a distinct area of social knowledge and the linguistic practices associated with it. Along with particular subjects and ways of talking about them, discourses also define broad rules about the context of speech or writing, including who is officially permitted to speak on particular subjects and what kind of authority particular kinds of speech (and speakers) carry. Knowledge, according to this concept of discourse, is constituted through relations of power, which determine what is true, what value is accorded particular kinds of knowledge, and, by extension, what material effects that knowledge will have in the world. Knowledge, in other words, *is* power: it comes into being through the operations of power and it *exercises* power by making things happen.

Science, medicine, and law are all examples of specific discourses that emerge in the context of specific historical conditions and in connection with particular institutions. They are all broadly connected with social power, defining ways not only of talking about but also of managing human subjects, through study, treatment, incarceration, and so on. We will talk more about discourses in Chapter Six, in relation to the construction of identity. For now, the two key points to keep in mind about discourse are 1) its emphasis on the nexus of knowledge and power, which legitimates forms of social control over particular groups in society—those deemed unwell, unfit, socially maladjusted, criminal, and so on, and 2) its incorporation of forms of *representation* with forms of social *practice*, which work in reciprocal relation with one another.

REPRESENTING THE YOUTH CRISIS

Bearing in mind the concept of discourse along with Barthes's theory of mythology, we are ready to return to the example that began this chapter—the phenomenon of the youth "crisis" and its representation in the media. To understand the dynamics of that representation we need first to look at the discourses through which the concepts of youth and criminality are defined, and then to look more specifically at how they are reproduced in specific media.

The Construction of Youth

Media representations of the youth problem are shaped by a variety of separate but over-lapping discourses through which we have come to understand not just crime, but also the phenomenon of youth itself. As debates about shifting age thresholds for things like sexual consent, drivers' licences, paid employment, and subjection to the *Criminal Code* only begin to suggest, the concept of "youth" is a slippery one, with no clear biological or cultural grounding in an objective distinction between childhood and adulthood.

Historical research shows that the idea of childhood is a relatively recent one, emerging in the eighteenth century in conjunction with new ideas about education and psychological development. Almost concurrently with the Romantic mythology of childhood innocence there arose a concern about juvenile delinquency, a new social problem whose identification was closely tied to the dominant class's determination to educate, reform, and discipline the urban working class (see Chapter Two). Police, health officials, and the newly emerging fields of psychology and sociology collaborated to record, monitor, evaluate, and "treat" wayward youth, with the aim of turning them into obedient, productive members of bourgeois society.

The category "youth" emerges more clearly in sociology around the late 1920s, in conjunction with American theories of urban development—and, more specifically, urban breakdown. The commonly identified problems of urban life—alienation, rootlessness, social deprivation—get projected onto youth, a demographic category which is itself thought to be characterized by confusion and social alienation. This urban theory then becomes the model for studies of youth crime and the formation of youth gangs and subcultures (Hebdige 27). While the perspective of most social investigators tended toward sympathy with their subjects, the discipline of sociology collaborated with institutions of education and the police to construct youth as a new target for surveillance, management, and reform.

The dominant perception of youth has changed over the last half-century, largely in response to the growth of teenagers and, increasingly, children as a huge consumer market. Whether this development has contributed to the empowerment of young people is open to question (see Chapter Five for a general discussion of consumer culture). In any case, alongside an increasingly youth-centred discourse of marketing, the representation of youth continues to be shaped by sociological and legal discourses that emerged in the 1950s. The major contemporary discursive development can be seen in the identification of the "new" phenomenon of girl violence, which is a kind of spin-off from the more general category identified below.

A New Kind of Criminality?

The contemporary fascination with youth crime covers up the history of the idea of youth, specifically the timing of its emergence in conjunction with initiatives to tighten social control. Youth and crime, it would seem, have been linked together from the beginning. One of the critical elements of the current stories about violent youth, though, is an emphasis on the *newness* of the phenomenon—not just that youth are more dangerous than they were before, but also that we are seeing the development of new and terrifying forms of violent crime. To understand the construction of the "new" youth problem, it's useful to look at an earlier "new" crisis of violence that occurred in 1970s Britain, and which has been extensively analyzed by Stuart Hall, Chas Critcher, Tony Jefferson, John Clarke, and Brian Roberts.

In their book *Policing the Crisis: Mugging, the State, and Law and Order*, these writers document the emergence in 1970s Britain of a "new" category of crime—mugging. The word definitively entered British consciousness for the first time following the stabbing death of an elderly man by three men in their early twenties, an event described by a police officer and subsequently in the press as a "mugging gone wrong" (qtd. in Hall et al. 3). While the term *mugging* had never before been used to describe crime in Britain, it was familiar from its more widespread use in the United States, where it was associated not just with a particular kind of crime—violent robbery—but also with a whole range of broader themes connected to general social breakdown. Following the 1972 incident in Britain, "mugging" quickly came into routine use, appearing in media stories about crimes that actually didn't differ all that much from earlier forms of violent crime, except by virtue of the new and ominous name. Fuelling new statistical surveys (that inevitably demonstrated that "mugging" was on the rise), it became part of a broad law-and-order discourse that eventually gave rise to new and tougher criminal penalties and other forms of social control.

The story Hall et al. tell about mugging in their book is an important one—not, they acknowledge, because it tells us why muggings happen or what should be done about them, but because it places the whole issue in a broader context, looking at mugging as a social phenomenon defined not only by the crime itself, but also by society's *reaction* to that crime and the way it is represented. Hall et al. thus begin their study by looking at the emergence of "mugging" as a label that drags along with it a whole referential context, a whole narrative network overlaid with particular assumptions and values. "Mugging" picked up its symbolic baggage from the history of its usage in the United States, where it "not only dominated the whole public discussion of crime and public disorder—it had become a central *symbol* for the many tensions and problems besetting American social and political life in general" (Hall et al. 19). "Mugging" acquired this significance, they go on to say,

> because of its ability to *connote* a whole complex of social themes in which the "crisis of American society" was reflected. These themes included: the involvement of blacks and drug addicts in crime; the expansion of the black ghettoes, coupled with the growth of black social and political militancy; the threatened crisis and collapse of the cities; the crime panic and the appeal to "law and order". . .. These topics and themes were not as clearly separated as these headings imply. They tended, in public discussion, to come together into a general scenario of conflict and crisis. In an important sense the image of "mugging" came ultimately to contain and express them all. (20)

The term entered the British public vocabulary in this broad, general sense *before* it gained widespread use to describe specific crimes. In other words, "mugging" acquired significance in a *mythological* sense before being applied literally to describe concrete events. And it was in its mythological sense that mugging inspired what sociologists refer to as a "moral panic" (see Close-Up 3.2).

New Categories of Crime   In a situation that echoes the mugging crisis of 1970s Britain, the period since the mid-1990s in North America has produced what amounts to a moral panic about crime, particularly violent youth crime. A key sign and instigator of that panic is the emergence of apparently "new" categories of crime, each of which carries with it a host of anxieties about general and specific social problems. As with mugging, many of these "new" crimes really amount to the redefinition of old categories: thus, "common assault" became "swarming," "break and enter" became "home invasion," "car theft" became "carjacking," "drive-by shootings" appeared, "serial" rapes and murders became common, and the term "road rage" appeared—all justifying a push for tougher interventions (Page).

Suggested Activity 3.1

Can you think of other words or phrases that have entered (or re-entered) public discourse recently to describe "new" social phenomena? In what contexts—in relation to what issues or debates—are they employed? What kinds of symbolic baggage do these words and phrases carry? What ideological assumptions do they rest on? What sorts of social practices do they condemn or legitimate?

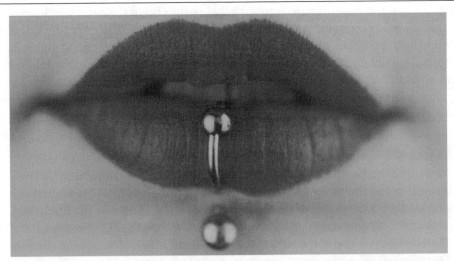

The *National Post* ran a headline in its May 8, 2002 edition that read, "Pierced girls are bad girls: study." The caption of the accompanying photo stated that "A U.S. researcher says parents, teachers and doctors should view an adolescent's desire to obtain a body piercing as a warning sign, prompting a closer inspection of the teenager's friends and pastimes."

Moral Panic

In his book on cultural responses to the 1970s subculture of mods and rockers, *Folk Devils and Moral Panics*, Stan Cohen defines moral panic this way:

> Societies appear to be subject, every now and then, to periods of moral panic. A condition, episode, person or group of persons emerges to become defined as a threat to societal values and interests; its nature is presented in a stylized and stereo-typical fashion by the mass media; the moral barricades are manned by editors, bishops, politicians and other right-thinking people; socially accredited experts pronounce their diagnoses and solutions; ways of coping are evolved or (more often) resorted to; the condition then disappears, submerges or deteriorates and becomes more visible. (28)

At its height, moral panic spreads a wide blanket over social experience, interpreting diverse and random behaviours or practices as signs of a danger. Regardless of its generally mythological origins, moral panic has real measurable effects in the form of individual behaviour, social behaviour, and governmental policy. These reactions to the perceived threat come to play an integral role in (retrospectively) defining its meaning.

These interventions extend beyond harsher penalties for crime to more general policies aimed at youth: dress and conduct codes in schools, extension and intensification of the use of identity cards, curfews (in some places), and new regulations designed to prevent youth from hanging out or loitering in public and private spaces such as malls.

Making the News

Before we turn to some specific examples of media representations of youth violence, let's take a general look at the role of the media—specifically the news—in producing social knowledge. Looking at the news media as a whole allows us to expand and contextualize critical readings of individual texts by illuminating the conditions in which those texts are produced, as well as by showing how particular meanings (particular stories) get favoured over others, and how they come to assume material significance.

Critical to an analysis of the presentation of events in the news is a recognition that the news is not a transparent window on the world; rather, it is an account assembled from a mass of chaotic data according to particular principles of selection and ordering, framed by internal, organizational constraints and broader social codes. It reflects not a single set of interests, but a limited range of interests that tend to support the preservation of existing relations of power—that is, the position of dominant social groups. This tendency should not be understood in terms of a crude conspiracy theory, which sees the news media always serving the agenda of "the state" or "big business" (though the reliance of the news, like all mainstream media, on advertising and the tendency for news production to be concentrated in the hands of fewer and fewer large corporate owners leads inevitably to a corporate capitalist bias). Even when media empires rest in the hands of outspoken defenders of the political right wing (Conrad Black, Rupert Murdoch), the relationship of news media to forces of social and economic conservatism is generally more subtle, and more mundane, than theories of direct and overt manipulation would suggest.

News-Gathering Structures   News organizations are not monolithic ideological forces; they are complex organizations in which editors and journalists generally exercise a great degree of control over the subject matter and perspective of their stories. This is not to say that writers have absolute freedom (in 2002, for example, the editor of the *Ottawa Citizen*, Russell Mills, was fired for printing a story critical of Prime Minister Jean Chrétien without seeking the approval of "head office," whose friendship with the Prime Minister was well known). In general, however, the media's reproduction of dominant ideology stems not from coercion, or even conscious cooperation; rather, it is built into established structures of news-gathering. Faced by time and resource pressures, the media rely on a steady supply of stories from reliable, accredited sources: these sources, not surprisingly, usually turn out to be dominant institutions (government, police, the courts) as well as accredited "experts" (academics, leaders of interest groups) (Hall et al. 58). As well as being, by virtue of their size and influence, the biggest news*makers* of the day, these sources also set the terms by which stories are *interpreted*, constructing them within frameworks whose dominance conceals their partiality or bias. Thus, even though the media will often consult alternative voices in order to satisfy the imperative of impartiality (generally defined in terms of showing "both sides" of a story—as though there are ever only two sides to a story!), the overall framework of the story is set by the dominant institution: its perspective determines how the issues are framed, what questions can be asked, and what *doesn't* get included in the discussion.

In reportage of the Gulf crisis that led to the war of 1990–91, for example, cultural critic Edward Said notes that discussion in the United States tended to be framed around two options: should the U.S. attack Iraq immediately following Iraq's invasion of Kuwait, or wait to see if sanctions worked? These two positions crystallized into the official boundaries of discussion when they were erected as the poles of debate between journalists Karen Elliott House and Anthony Lewis on the news/discussion show the *MacNeil/Lehrer NewsHour*. As intelligent and reasoned voices of the respected papers the *Wall Street Journal* and *The New York Times*, respectively, House and Lewis could be trusted between them to give viewers the "whole" picture, a balanced and fair assessment of the possibilities it entailed. Left unexamined in their discussion was the assumption that America *should* intervene somehow, that it "ought *to be* in the Gulf, regulating the behavior of states armies, and peoples several thousand miles away" (Said *Culture and Imperialism* 293). Consistent with the unquestioned emphasis on the United States, there was virtually no mention of the Arabs "as having something to do with the war, as its victims, for instance, or (equally convincingly) its instigators" (293). The event, rather, was circumscribed, framed in a limited way that was perceived to speak to the interests of its American audience, an audience whose character was not merely reflected, but *constituted* through the debate. That is, rather than speaking to a group whose interests were already defined around common goals and values, this news broadcast, in conjunction with ongoing CNN coverage, played a significant role in helping to *define* a consensus around which all American viewers (and to an extent Canadians, since the *MacNeil/Lehrer NewsHour* airs in Canada) could gather.

Consensus The process of assuming and building consensus is, according to Hall et al., a key aspect of news production. "'Consensual' views of society," they go on to explain, "represent society as if there are no major cultural or economic breaks, no major conflicts of interests between classes and groups. Whatever disagreements exist, it is said, there are legitimate and institutionalised means for expressing and reconciling them" (55). The ideological imperatives of consensus-building, along with the practical imperatives of news-gathering, mean that non-central, or marginalized, voices rarely get to contribute to the debate. Thus, the educated "expert"/journalist, with privileged access to government sources, becomes the voice of "all of us"—including, presumably, expatriate Iraqi-Americans and Canadians whose own "expert" views might be very different. The same rules of consensus-building apply to less elite forms of news than *MacNeil/Lehrer*, in which broadcasters assume a populist, common-sense persona that functions to unite an "us" against "them" (with "them" in this case often caricatured as the "elite" media, "special interest groups," or simply "intellectuals").

Echoes of the representation of the 1990–91 Gulf War resounded in the 2002 build-up to the war against Iraq. Once more the terms of the debate are set by dominant interests: "the honest choices now are to give up and give in, or to remove Mr. Hussein before he gets his bomb," as an editorial in *The Economist* put it ("The Case For War" 9). Once again, the news media engage in the work of consensus-building, with headlines in Canadian newspapers reading "Today We Are *All* Americans" (Wente; emphasis added), or, after the bombing of a nightclub in Bali in which most of the victims were Australians, "We Are *All* Australians Now" (Wente; emphasis added). Of course, the delineation of an inside—"we"—also entails the construction of an outside ("they," i.e., terrorists and their alleged sympathizers) without whom there would be no story. During the 2003 U.S.–led war on Iraq, the Pentagon-sanctioned practice of "embedding," in which selected reporters were attached to military units, helped to generate sympathetic coverage of the American soldiers, and thus to shore up consensus within the news audience about the justness of the war.

Media and Youth Crime

Nowhere, perhaps, is the consensus-building function of news more evident than in stories about crime. Crime is a dominant feature in news in part because it so nicely fits the general ideological criteria for what Hall et al. term "news value": it is out of the ordinary; it is dramatic in a tragic way; it is easily personalized; and it can be incorporated into a broader pattern of stories. As with all events deemed newsworthy, the media make crime stories meaningful by identifying them and placing them in a context familiar to the audience—that is, locating them "within a range of known social and cultural identifications" (Hall et al. 54). The assumption of consensus is obviously an important part of this process: the news is intelligible only to the extent that its audience shares common ideas about how society is defined and how it operates. Consensus assumes the more specific, ideologically charged significance discussed above, depending on the kind of news story being reported. Crime stories are particularly successful consensus-builders because, besides being out of the realm of the ordinary, they also fall outside the bounds of community; in fact, they play a key role in defining those boundaries. On the one side is the respectable, law-abiding community—"us"—for whom the victim becomes an innocent and sympathetic embodiment. On the other side is "them"—the accused criminals who, for reasons both ideological and pragmatic (most people charged with crimes aren't affiliated with journalists' regular "trusted sources") don't have a voice in their story. By establishing so clearly, in a way that is at once horrifying and reassuring, the borders of community, stories about crime—particularly violent crime—play a powerful role in the symbolic regulation of society.

Picturing Crime

In its construction of social reality, the news gains its substance through the power of myth. The operation of myth is evident in the photo and caption below, from a story in the *National Post* about the Ontario provincial government's proposed *Safe Streets Act* (Ibbitson). Before we analyze the text itself, we need to make a few observations about the significance of photographic representation. Unlike words, the images in photography do not translate what they signify into an arbitrary code; they are a precise *analogue*, or copy, of the objects they reproduce. This purity of reproduction encourages us

This photo appeared in the *National Post* with the headline "Harris vows to rid streets of pushy beggars, squeegees." The caption below the photo provided further information: "The Tories would amend the Highway Traffic Act to keep 'Martin' from his post at the corner of Spadina Avenue and Queen Street West."

to think of photographs as offering a truer, more authentic representation of the world than language is capable of doing; indeed, it is photography's capacity for realism that makes it such a valued part of print media.

Our inclination to trust the evidence of our eyes, for which the photographer functions as a kind of proxy, makes it hard to remember that realism, which describes a mode of representation that is taken to provide a faithful and objective picture of the world, is itself a kind of code or convention, and one with a very recent history (see Close-Up 3.3).

What makes photographic realism at once so powerful—and so deceptive—as a reproduction of reality is its capacity to capture the constant movement of things and freeze it in a single instant. In that instant, the images captured weirdly stand out as more vivid, more intense than our actual experience can ever be. This vividness contributes to photography's seeming ability to convey a world more substantial than that represented by language. The pitfalls of this vividness are twofold: first, it works by tearing objects out of their place in space and time (essentially robbing them of their historical context); second, its apparent naturalness conceals the mediating role of culture in its construction.

"Culture" here refers to the practices that make the photo make sense: first, it includes the decisions made by the photographer—what to include or exclude, how to frame the subject, what kind of lighting or other technical codes to use, and so on. The increasing ability of photographers to manipulate images digitally (as, for example, in the British

Representation and the Construction of Social Reality **73**

Realism

The history of realism is closely tied up with the development of capitalism (and popular culture) in at least three important ways: first, the emphasis in realism is on an objective reality, a world of material things, which it is the job of representation, whether textual or photographic, to capture. Connected explicitly with the discriminating power of vision, realism is part of a broader ideology of *enlightenment*, defined by rational scientific knowledge and economic liberalism. This ideology powerfully challenged traditional forms of perception, in which the seen and the unseen, the physical and spiritual, were taken to exist in conjunction with one another.

Second, the birth of realism, which critic John Berger connects with techniques of sixteenth-century oil painting, can be seen as part of a new materialist ideology. In its convention of rendering objects in almost three-dimensional substance, "oil painting," Berger suggests, "did to appearances what capital did to social relations. It reduced everything to the equality of objects. . . .. All reality was mechanically measured by its materiality" (87). The growth of art collection, not surprisingly, coincides with the rise of consumerism in general: oil painting depicts a world of objects whose visual consumption becomes an emblem of material ownership.

Finally, realism flourished in part because of the advent of the technologies of photography and film. Besides their direct commercial significance, these technologies also contributed to the development of modern capitalist society more generally, by providing tools of information-gathering to scientists, government, and corporate bodies and by providing the public with forms of mass entertainment—including and especially advertising (see Chapter Five)—that stimulate them to engage in ever higher levels of consumption.

GQ cover featuring a dramatically slimmed-down Kate Winslet) is only an extension of these cruder aesthetic technologies. Second—and harder to identify—are the multiple cultural resources viewers bring to bear in interpreting the photograph. With these cautions in mind, we are now ready to look at the photo and caption from the *National Post*.

Those "Pushy Squeegees"

On a denotative level, the photo depicts the view from inside a car, its windshield being washed by a young man in a torn T-shirt. Through the haze of the wiper fluid, a city street is visible. Separately, and even together, the images in the photo could evoke a number of different associations: they are, in semiotic terms, "polysemous." Their meaning is fixed, however, or *anchored*, by the story headline, which reads: "Harris vows to rid streets of pushy beggars, squeegees." It is the headline that gives the story its connotative significance and makes it intelligible in a particular cultural context.

Both conventional codes of reading and knowledge of the specific context make it clear that the youth cleaning the windscreen is not "Harris" (whom *National Post* readers would recognize as Mike Harris, the then-Premier of Ontario), but a "pushy squeegee." If the image alone isn't enough to convey menace and the threat of violence, the word "pushy" makes it clear that the youth in question is not providing a service, but committing an aggressive act (the squeegee being a metaphor for . . . what? a switchblade? a club?), while the phrase "rid the streets of . . ." confirms his place in the category of socially useless, even dangerous things. The caption below the photo reads, "The Tories would amend the Highway Traffic Act to keep 'Martin' from his post at the corner of Spadina Avenue and Queen Street West"; "Martin" is thus not only identified as one of the targets of the legislation, but also made representative of *all* the beggars and squeegees: men, women, and children living on—and allegedly terrorizing—the streets. The arrangement of the photo works nicely with the grammar of the sentence so that the reader identifies both with the perspective of the camera, which is inside the car, under siege along with the car's driver, *and* with Harris, who embodies the force of law and order with his reassuring vow to make the streets safe again.

We are thus made to feel both vulnerable and reassured: the threat (which is made real in the representation of this story, even if we didn't feel it before) will be taken care of. The meaning of the story and photo are further anchored through their presence in the *National Post*, a paper whose general political slant favours right-wing policies like the law-and-order initiative. The same photo and caption in a different paper—a different frame—might produce a slightly different interpretation.

In its actual context, a story like this one works to elicit public support for political programs like the *Safe Streets Act*, as well as more generally to reinforce a vision of social order in which "we" are on the inside, protected morally and legally from the onslaughts of those pushy street people. The photo reinforces the division, with the frame of the car window defining a material and ideological fortress between the driver and "Martin," a shadowy figure whose marginality is confirmed by the quotation marks surrounding his name.

Crime on TV

While the newspaper article about the *Safe Streets Act* uses image and text to turn "Martin" into the poster boy for urban disorder, the TV special "Victoria's Secret" cited at the beginning of this chapter employs the more expansive codes of television to weave representations of specific instances of violent youth crime into an elaborate narrative defining a major social issue. While photos promise to deliver a more accurate representation of the world than words, television claims a more privileged place still, in its capacity to make connections between images, in a simulation of real-life change and movement. As with photography, however, we need to resist the urge to read television representations naturalistically, and instead think about *how* they are simulated.

With television even more than photography, this means paying attention to the way its status as a form of commercial media structures its content. While the function of television clearly changes depending on whether the program being broadcast is a game show, a sitcom, or the news, a common feature of all television programming is the need to produce meaningful information out of an inherently erratic stream of programming: that is, individual television shows need to convey self-contained narratives that mark them off from the general flow of programming, and construct meaningful bridges over commercial interruptions. At the same time, the structure of commercial breaks requires that programs be broken down into manageable segments or "packages" that fit comfortably between the commercials (and it's worth remembering that, from the television industry's point of view, it's the commercials that are the meat and potatoes of the programming: the shows merely provide the hooks to bring in viewers/consumers). The tidy-package imperative, according to which information has to be marshalled into compact (i.e., ten-minute), easily digestible bits, contradicts one of TV's key selling points, which is its ability to tell stories—to place images, events, and people into a broader context.

Victoria's Not-So-Nice Secret

This is the mandate of a show like "Victoria's Secret," which seeks not just to document, but also to make sense of, the phenomenon of youth violence in Canada. The show opens *in medias res*, or "in the middle of things," with a shot of a plane landing and a stretcher being unloaded. The sense of crisis conveyed by the opening sequence is heightened by the darkness and even blurriness of the scene, which is filmed in the rain, and by a rapid series of jump-cuts from plane to ambulance to stretcher. The images are knitted together by the voiceover, which identifies the scene as the conclusion of a "mercy flight" from Victoria to Toronto. The unconscious patient on the stretcher, a teenaged boy, is "home for Christmas, but not the way he left." The dramatic events of the story are personalized in the next shot, in which the boy's mother, facing a battery of microphones, explains that her son, who is in a coma, "was very badly beaten up by three guys for no rhyme or reason; he just happened to be in the wrong place at the wrong time." The "wrong place," the voiceover resumes to tell us, is Victoria, B.C., "Canada's garden playground."

And the story, as the title suggests, is as much about this place as it is about the terrible plight of Nicholas Johnson. Specifically, it's about Victoria's "dark side," as a city besieged by roving teenaged gangs. The threatening quality of these gangs is established by words and images that from the opening shots of the program work to establish clear contrasts between safety and danger, the familiar and the unknown, light and darkness. The world of humane, civilized community and family, summoned up by phrases like "mercy" and "home for Christmas," is contrasted with—and shown to be threatened by—a chaotic underworld, in which anonymous groups of guys—gangs—roam around looking for violence. The theme of contrasts is set up by initial shots of a tourist's Victoria—a sailboat leaving a marina, golfers playing in the middle of winter, flowers, people drinking tea at the Empress hotel—accompanied by the voiceover warning ominously that, while the city is "at first glance, scenic, safe and secure . . . this is a tale of two cities. It may be hard to believe, but there is a dark side to this city. A violent and dangerous one."

Here the image changes dramatically to a scene of the reporter talking to the camera as she walks along what appears to be a dark alley, flanked by walls covered with graffiti. If the mother functions to bring us into the story, presenting a suffering human face with which the viewer is asked to identify, the reporter serves as the controlling perspective of objectivity. In the mode of a correspondent sending dispatches from a war zone, she brings alarming news of a situation that, while barely visible until now, constitutes a pervasive social problem rendered all the more threatening by its manifestation in apparently "random" and "senseless" acts of violence.

Inciting panic in its viewers, the revelation that there is "a youth gang problem in the midst of Canada's Shangri-la" also offers a kind of comfort, conveyed in the rational, authoritative voice of the reporter, that the problem has been identified, given a label. "These are legitimate gangs," a police officer confirms. "They have a hierarchy; they're wearing colours." The use of the word "legitimate" is interesting, signalling not, clearly, that the gangs are on the side of law and order, but that they fit a template, they are classifiable—and hence manageable. No longer random and unintelligible, the problem has assumed a handle we can grasp. And we are persuaded that, though we might not have been conscious of it, this is a problem whose presence we somehow recognized all along: "For too many years, gangs of young people have been allowed to terrorize the streets." This is a cause for outrage, that translates into relief that "citizens are now standing up at community meetings demanding action, searching for solutions"—solutions that are forthcoming in the form of police task forces, tougher laws, and pressure on young people to inform authorities about violence, or threats of violence, committed by their peers.

The "Inside versus Outside" Perspective   As well as being a story of contrasts, this is also, like the squeegee article, a story of insides and outsides. "Inside" represents the community, concerned citizens, the media, and us as viewers, threatened by an "outside" inhabited by dark and unruly forces, nameless young people who commit acts of violence with "no rhyme or reason." The story also invokes other "insides" and "outsides," in its characterization of Victoria as a place where things like this are not "supposed" to happen. Even the working-class suburb of Esquimault, where two of the assaults occurred, "is a far cry from the mean streets, urban decay and inner-city ghettoes normally associated with street gangs."

At the same time, then, that "Victoria's Secret" might be working to shake its urban or suburban viewers out of their complacency, suggesting that there really aren't "two cities"—we all inhabit the same big, dangerous world—it also serves to shore up boundaries, to reassure us that, unlike in the "mean streets" (of Toronto? South Central LA?), we *do* still live in a community where civilized values prevail. Problems such as poverty and racial tension, summoned up by the word "ghetto," remain "outside," not part of this story or part of Canada's garden playground though they might hover dangerously nearby, threatening to spill over if we don't monitor the borders vigilantly enough. Because the story of youth violence is perhaps above all a cautionary tale about the dangers of complacency, of not attending to signs of social disorder and not treating them seriously enough when we find them.

In looking at "Victoria's Secret" as an example of how representation constructs social reality, we are not trying to suggest that the instances of violence it documents are somehow fabricated, or that their effects are negligible. Rather, we want you to think about the process by which the media frames those instances in a particular way, incorporating them within a narrative that draws on and in turn helps to consolidate specific beliefs, emotions, and assumptions. Extending far beyond the specific crimes the show documents, these beliefs, emotions, and values inform—often unconsciously—our ideas about community, youth, law, and the society we live in. Similarly, a show like "Victoria's Secret" doesn't just inform us about events that are going on in our society; it *re-presents* those events as part of a broad vision of what society should look like. The "facts" of the story are inseparable from—indeed they are largely manufactured by—values and politics. As an authoritative force in society that holds a near-monopoly on social knowledge (in more than one sense, as control over media falls into fewer and fewer hands), the news, particularly in the area of crime, plays an effective role in constructing and delimiting public opinion. In order to recognize, and to critically challenge, the ideologies that underpin dominant constructions of the social order, it is necessary to ask, as Hall et al. do in their book on mugging, a series of questions about the news stories we watch, hear, and read: " 'What, other than what has been said about this topic, *could* be said?' 'What questions are omitted?' 'Why do the questions—which always presuppose answers of a particular kind—so often recur in this form? Why do certain other questions never appear?'" (65). In the case of the representation of youth violence, some of the missing questions might be What kinds of relationships exist between trends in youth crime and trends in adult crime? How does youth crime fit into an overall pattern of youth culture? How does society function (or not) to address the needs of youth in relation to areas such as education, job opportunities, public space, social programs, and so on? How have social views of youth changed? If you think about it, you can probably come up with other questions, other ways of framing the "youth problem."

THE POLITICS OF REPRESENTATION

As the analysis above suggests, representation has a lot to do with power. In both the organization of media and the ideological structure of language and other sign systems, representation tends to reproduce and to naturalize existing relations of social power. The example of media representation of youth violence demonstrates the function of discourse in the maintenance of social order: the simultaneous classification and marginalization of relatively powerless members of society—in this case youth—works to keep them in their place, both symbolically and materially in the form of laws and social policies.

Representing the Other: Gender and Race

Other groups for whom we can observe a clear relationship between representation and lack of social power are women and racial minorities. Indeed, it is arguable that the very premise of identity, which our signifying systems work to uphold, is predicated on their exclusion. This point can be illustrated most clearly in the case of women, in that gender is one of the most basic, if not *the* most basic, binary oppositions that underlies the process of signification. The critical thing about binary opposition, from a cultural/political perspective, is that its significance is rarely neutral: rather, it involves not just a differential but also a *hierarchical* relationship between the two terms. Thus, the associative chain that links the sign "man" with culture, reason, and consciousness and "woman" with nature, passion, and physical being doesn't just assert an absolute distinction between the opposing sets of terms; it also establishes a relation of dominance in which the first term is read as *normative* or natural, the second is characterized by difference or lack—a quality of "not-quite-ness."

This relation is not only expressed through language and culture generally; it is also reinforced by the technologies of visual culture. Psychoanalytic theory suggests that identity formation, the process of defining a "self" in relation to "others," is powerfully shaped by different kinds of looking, and that these forms of looking are gendered. It is the visual perception of others that enables both *identification*—the narcissistic projection of oneself into the place of another, based on perceived similarity—and *objectification*, the imaginary possession of another based on perceived difference. "In a world ordered by sexual imbalance," film critic Laura Mulvey suggests, "pleasure in looking has been split between active/male and passive/female" (326). Traditional Hollywood cinema perpetuates these roles, she suggests, through the production of films that enable the audience to simultaneously identify with an active (male) hero and objectify the passive heroine. This is a simplification of Mulvey's complex (and controversial) argument; the main point of her article for our purposes is that the *activity* of looking, in its contradictory narcissistic and voyeuristic aspects, is coded male, while woman, connoting "*to-be-looked-at-ness*," is consigned to the role of object of the gaze (326).

In practice, as we note in Chapter Six, the business of identity formation is a messy one, as the fantasy of mastering the other always threatens to tip over into the nightmare of *becoming* the other, of losing the power of selfhood—a power, in psychoanalytic theory, that is tied to possession of masculine agency, symbolized by the phallus. Traditional Hollywood film resolves that anxiety, offering through the combination of narrative and spectacle the simultaneous pleasures of identification and objectification: one can "be" the hero while enjoying the spectacle of the objectified heroine, with all potential contradictions or tensions miraculously resolved through the fantasy-world of the screen. The consequence for the male viewer is not just pleasure, but also a consolidation of his sense of self and power in the world; the female viewer's pleasure is more ambivalent, as she is excluded from the fantasy of complete identity and confirmed in a role of passivity and powerlessness.

Suggested Activity 3.3

Many critics have challenged Mulvey's thesis of narrative pleasure in cinema by looking, for example, at the role of women as active viewers of film images. Her thesis is also challenged by the increasingly complex ways women are represented on film. The heroine of *Barb Wire* (Pamela Anderson) is both sexy and powerful, passive object and active, aggressive agent. Can you think of other examples of women in film that disrupt the simple binary code described by Mulvey?

Popular visual culture, then, has traditionally worked to reinforce and accentuate the cultural code of masculine dominance and female subjection by spectacularizing difference and inequality. Much the same thing occurs in the representation of minorities, whose visible embodiment of difference has served, like the category of femininity, to shore up the dominant—white, masculine—code of identity. Like the female body, the non-white body, both male and female, has historically served the function of spectacle, a site for the projection of fear and desire in the form of **stereotypes** (see Chapter Seven).

Challenging Negative Representation

As the preceding discussion on media representation of youth crime suggests, negative or stereotypical representation has political consequences: it not only reflects but also reinforces the marginality of minority groups. Thus it follows that the political empowerment of subordinate groups in society—women, youth, racial minorities, gays and lesbians, the disabled, the poor, the elderly—depends in part on changing the way they are represented. General acceptance of this principle is evident in the process by which our culture self-consciously changes the words it uses, often at the instigation of educators or activist groups, to replace pejorative terms with more inclusive ones. The word "coloured," for example, has long been abandoned as a description of racial minorities, while the more recent phrase "people of colour" (which emphasizes personhood first, and race only secondarily) reflects—but also works to bring about—general acceptance of the principle of racial equality.

Representational Strategies   We can track similar shifts in popular visual culture toward more inclusive representation. In the case of racial minorities (and there are clear historical parallels in the representation of women and gays and lesbians), it is possible to identify a number of different strategies that attempt to work against dominant codes of racial representation. *Integrationist* or *assimilationist* strategies, embodied in films like *Guess Who's Coming to Dinner* (1967), serve metaphorically to invite blacks into mainstream white society on the strength of the reassuring message that "they" are "just like" us. *Affirmationist* messages work in a contrary way to emphasize essentialist black identities, but in a way that challenges the mainstream. So-called "blaxploitation" films from the 1970s (discussed in more detail in Chapter Seven) fulfill this function. More recent versions of the assimilation theme, such as that embodied in the 1980s TV series *The Cosby Show*, represent blacks succeeding in white society through their own efforts, but in a way that plays down the history and ongoing reality of discrimination, as well as politics of resistance. A related genre is the "black-and-white friendship" film (examples include *Pulp Fiction, Die Hard with a Vengeance, Lethal Weapon 1, 2, 3 & 4, White Men Can't Jump, The Shawshank Redemption, The Pelican Brief*, and *Remember the Titans*), which highlights the possibility of overcoming the barriers of race through individual tolerance and understanding.

All of these strategies—which can be plotted more or less historically, though remnants of earlier forms persist—aim toward more positive representations of blacks in the popular media. While it is tempting to frame them in terms of an evolutionary narrative toward greater equality, there are problems with each of these counter-narratives. First, as we discuss in more detail in Chapter Seven, the attempt to counter negative stereotypes with more positive ones reverses the hierarchy while leaving the codes of essential identity/difference intact. The black/white friendship movie, which avoids the stereotype altogether by constructing highly individualized relationships, is problematic in a different way. By suggesting that the problem of racial discrimination is a matter of individual morality, these films ignore the broader social and material context of race relations: it means that, while overt acts of individual racism can be universally condemned, "the more subtle, deeper forms of discursively and institutionally structured racism remain unrecognized" (Shohat and Stam 201). In more explicit social terms:

> The good news at the movies obscures the bad news in the streets and confirms the [U.S.] Supreme Court's recent decisions on busing, affirmative action and

redistricting.. . . Because black–white friendship is now understood to be the rule, there is no need for integrated schools or . . . affirmative action. The Congress and state governors can guiltlessly cut welfare, food assistance, fuel assistance . . . housing money, fellowship money, vaccine money. (DeMott 33)

The obvious criticism to make of these films, then, is that their "realistic" representation of black/white friendship glosses over the real social conditions of black people living in the United States, including disproportionate rates of mortality, poverty, and imprisonment. Serving as an emblem of already-achieved equality, these films help to legitimate neo-liberal social policies that contribute to the further marginalization of minority groups. A number of recent films, like *Do the Right Thing, Boyz N the Hood*, and *Monster's Ball* counter the upbeat message presented by these films with a more *social realist* perspective, one that emphasizes the economic and social relations of *in*equality that are concealed by the myth of tolerant individualism. Rather than focusing on exemplary characters who rise above their social circumstances (characters who always manage to be a bit richer/smarter/better-looking than everyone around them), these films offer a more complex view, one that acknowledges the role of culture and economics in shaping individual lives.

By now, however, it should be impossible for you to read the words "real" and "realism" without warning bells going off. However praiseworthy the efforts to create an accurate, rather than a simply positive, picture of a group or situation, such efforts remain troubled by the shaky "reality" of representation itself, according to which myth and ideology are not simply everywhere present, but inescapable. Under these conditions, one could argue that the only way seriously to undermine the politics of representation is to highlight the hidden conventions and codes on which they're based—much as we did in our semiotic readings of newspaper and television news reports. As Laura Mulvey puts it,

the magic of Hollywood style at its best . . . arose . . . in one important aspect, from its skilled and satisfying manipulation of visual pleasure. Unchallenged, mainstream film coded the erotic into the language of the dominant patriarchal order. In the highly developed Hollywood cinema it was only through these codes that the alienated subject . . . came near to finding a glimpse of satisfaction: through its formal beauty and its play on his own formative obsession.. . . It is said that analysing pleasure, or beauty, destroys it. (323)

That, Mulvey announces, is the intention of her article. It is also the intention of avant-garde cinema—those films, like *Paris Is Burning* or *Boys Don't Cry*, for example, that deconstruct, as they represent, dominant codes of representation.

The prospect of mainstream Hollywood films dying away, leaving in their wake only the stark, difficult, and often, as Mulvey would have it, self-consciously unpleasurable terrain of the art film is unrealistic, not to mention undesirable. We can take from her argument, however, an important point, which is that negative representations can't be undone without attending to their underlying politics, including the contexts from which they're produced.

Beyond Representation: Who's the Boss?

This points to another issue in media representation: namely, its production. For many media critics, the way minority groups are represented is secondary to who controls the production, distribution, and exhibition of those representations. The most recent report on Hollywood employment practices released by the NAACP (National Association for the Advancement of Colored People) reveals that African Americans are underrepresented in every aspect of the entertainment industry; where they participate at all it's as performers rather than producers. The consequences of this underrepresentation (using "representation" in a more directly political sense) are not just cultural, in the sense of determining whose stories get told and in what way, but also economic, since it is in production that—celebrity salaries notwithstanding—the real profit in the entertainment industry lies. Thus the 2001 Academy Awards, in which black actors took away an unprecedented share of prizes, could fairly be described as "progress but no net gain" (Kweisi Mfume qtd. in Lyman). In the words of actor/director Mario Van Peebles, "We have to be in there not just as actors, but as writers and directors—and as development executives and programmers, that's the next goal. Playing basketball's not enough any more, we've got to own our teams. Without economic power, you have no power" (qtd. in Schnellner).

As the preceding discussion suggests, representation has political consequences. In discussing the politics of representation, however, we need to go beyond the dynamics of representation itself, in order to understand the contexts in which representation occurs. The next section examines some of the ways we might go beyond the simple analysis of texts to understand representation as part of a larger process of creating popular culture.

CONTEXTS OF REPRESENTATION

We have talked a lot so far about the power of representation, particularly media representation, to construct social reality—literally, to create the world we live in, shaping our beliefs and behaviour, fears and desires. It has become commonplace to recognize the role these representations play in our lives, for good or, from the perspective of many commentators, for ill. In the words of one media critic,

> The American industrial-entertainment complex has pretty much replaced the church as the maker and enforcer of values on this continent.... We hit 18 having spent more time in front of the TV than at school. We can summon the face of Bruce Willis, the stubble and the crooked smile, more readily and vividly than our own father's. Our heads resound with the voices of strangers. (Grierson 24)

Grierson makes these observations in an article that begins by recalling the death of Reena Virk, a Victoria, B.C. teenager beaten unconscious, then drowned by a group of other teens after a party one night. Speaking at a memorial service for Reena, Budgie Basi-Reed, a family friend, drew a direct connection between what happened to Reena and the kinds of images children and teens get bombarded with in television and video games. "Violence," she notes, "has become an acceptable form of entertainment" (qtd. in Grierson 24). In the article that follows, Grierson advances what has become a familiar argument, that brutal media imagery is largely responsible for the creation of an increasingly violent society.

In the introductory section to this chapter we began by talking about the role of media in promoting the *idea* that not just violence, but youth violence, is a growing social problem. We talked about the role of representation—and, in particular, mass media representation—in creating a climate of social fear, in which dominant myths about community, morality, race, gender, and age harden into "facts" about youth violence. A critical premise of our argument is that representation plays a determining role in shaping the world we live in. We need now to take a step back from that argument, and to recognize the perils in taking it too far. Just as we need to wriggle our way out of the belief that we all like to cling to—that we as individuals possess an independent mind that somehow exists prior to language and other cultural forms—we also need to reject the equally common assumption that words and images are *all*-powerful, that their effects are clear and easily measurable. Interestingly, most of us are able to hold onto both these beliefs at once, by maintaining a dodgy distinction between our own ability to see through the snares of advertising and other forms of representation and the infinite impressionability of others, particularly children, to what they see, hear, and read. We have already tried to show, both in this chapter and the previous one, some of the weaknesses in the assumption that it's possible simply to see around or through ideology. Now we need to tackle the converse theory of mass media manipulation.

The Myth of Mass Media Manipulation

This theory is familiar to all of us in the form of arguments like Grierson's about the social effects of certain kinds of representation—particularly sex and violence. Gary Bauer, former head of the U.S. Family Research Council and one-time Republican presidential candidate, puts the argument more crudely: "If you expose children to uplifting and noble material, you're more likely to have noble citizens. If children are wallowing in sexual images and violence, that is bound to have an impact on those who are most vulnerable" (qtd. in Lacayo). While this observation seems, on first appearance, to make a certain kind of sense—the images and ideas we are exposed to *do* shape who we are—there are also some obvious problems with it.

Locating Meaning   First, the concept of "uplifting and noble material" assumes first that we all agree on what is uplifting and noble, and second that nobility and upliftingness are somehow inherent, present in some representations and absent from others. The difficulty of making that assessment is shown in the clearly arbitrary criteria by which would-be censors evaluate controversial images, particularly those that feature violence. For example, when the Republican presidential candidate Bob Dole issued his famous 1995 rant against Hollywood's "destructive messages of casual violence and even more casual sex," included amongst his list of good "family" fare was the Arnold Schwarzenegger film

True Lies. Along with its spectacular violence, the movie gained notoriety from a scene in which CIA agent Harry Tasker (Schwarzenegger), having encouraged his wife (Jamie Lee Curtis) to become a spy-posing-as-a-prostitute, poses himself as a client, then has her perform a lengthy striptease before revealing his real identity. "Uplifting and noble" this isn't! However, leaving aside perhaps the most likely reason for Dole's endorsement (Schwarzenegger is a major supporter of the Republican Party), we can surmise that the sex and violence pass the test here because the former occurs in defence of family values (Tasker puts his wife through the humiliating ordeal of the striptease as a kind of punishment or test, in response to his suspicion that she is cheating on him), and the latter is committed against obvious "bad guys"—their badness signalled, as many commentators noted, by their Middle-Eastern appearance.

The point here is not to suggest that because of its blatant misogyny and racism *True Lies* belongs in the *bad* representations bin, not the good one. Rather, this example reveals that the value and meaning of cultural texts are not qualities that reside objectively within them; they are instead determined in part by the audiences that consume them. Thus the representation of *True Lies* means differently for Bob Dole than it does for some feminist viewers (including Jamie Lee Curtis herself, who in a 2002 interview included it among roles that she now regretted taking on [Wallace]).

Representation and Social Consequences   The second problem with media theories like Bauer's is his assumption of a direct relationship between the consumption of particular images and particular social effects. Leaving aside for a moment the undefined (and undefinable) question of what constitutes noble citizenship, the assumption that viewing "good" images will lead to "good" behaviour rests on a simplistic understanding of how pedagogy, or the process of teaching and learning, operates. The meanings we take from cultural texts come from a combination of convention—ways of interpreting particular signs that are shared widely amongst members of a society—and individual subjectivity and experience. What we *do* with those interpretations is also influenced by those diverse factors.

Some studies do draw conclusive links between the consumption of violent media images and aggressive behaviour. One of the most compelling of these studies is the work done on violent video games by David Grossman, a U.S. army lieutenant and former psychologist. In his book *On Killing: The Psychological Cost of Learning to Kill in War and Society*, Grossman draws some disturbing parallels between the effects of media, particularly television and video games, on youth, and the techniques the military uses to train its soldiers to kill. In particular, Grossman points to two kinds of conditioning that work to desensitize subjects to killing. In the first form of what is called "classical" conditioning, the military trains its soldiers to find killing acceptable, and even pleasurable, by associating it with rewards. The same process is at work as "children watch vivid pictures of human suffering and death, and they learn to associate it with their favorite soft drink and candy bar, or their girlfriend's perfume or their boyfriend's touch" (26).

The second form of conditioning, what psychologists term "operant" conditioning, works by teaching subjects to perform acts habitually, without thinking. Military technology such as flight simulators and moving-target practice help to teach this kind of behaviour by offering a rapid series of stimuli that require immediate—violent—response. The same process is at work in point-and-shoot video games, Grossman notes, in which targets pop up randomly and success depends on the ability to shoot quickly and accurately—without, needless to say, imagining the consequences for the simulated victims. As evidence of the translatability of those skills to real life, Grossman presents the chilling example of the 14-year-old boy in Paducah, Kentucky who shot up a school prayer group, firing eight shots from a .22-calibre pistol and hitting eight victims, five of them in the head. (The average U.S. law enforcement officer, shooting at a distance of seven yards, has a less than one-in-five rate of actual hits.) When questioned, the killer, who had never fired a real gun before, admitted to being an avid player of video games. While this is an extreme example of the effects of simulated violence, Grossman argues for a host of more subtle and pervasive effects on children who, if they don't grow up to become killers themselves, become more or less desensitized to the effects of violence, thus creating an atmosphere of bystander tolerance for events like the beating death of Reena Virk.

Grossman's thesis is a compelling one, which seems to suggest that specific kinds of representational *content*—that is, violence—conveyed in a specific *form*—electronic media, and interactive video games in particular—produce undesirable social effects. However, in its reliance on relatively simple "behaviourist" psychological theories, his argument seriously underrates the complexity of the processes by which human beings read and respond to the world around them. Moreover, by placing the burden of proof on the representations themselves, on what they are saying and/or asking users to do, arguments such as Grierson's neglect the wider context in which users engage with this media.

Representation and Imagination This is not to say that imagination and reality are utterly distinct from one another: they aren't, which is why the realm of the imagination is such a potent place. As well as providing a storehouse of images that interpret and mediate the world for us, the imagination—culture, in general—also offers resources that help us to cope with painful aspects of reality, in ways that can be both harmful and productive for individuals and society but are rarely simply one or the other. Representations of violence, which have been around since the beginning of human civilization—though admittedly not in so graphic a form as today—offer a site for particularly complex workings-out of fear, aggression, anger, and desire. While it is frequently pointed out that youth who commit violent crimes tend to be avid consumers of violent media, what is not so frequently pointed out—and what is more difficult to measure—is the role such media might play in helping many others to work through feelings of frustration or anger, thus avoiding their explosion into actual acts of violence. As media critic Henry Jenkins puts it:

> The key issue isn't what the media are doing to our children but rather what our children are doing with the media. Eric Harris and Dylan Klebold [the Columbine murderers] weren't victims of video games. They had a complex relationship to many forms of popular culture. All of us move nomadically across the media landscape, cobbling together a personal mythology of symbols and stories, and investing those appropriated materials with various personal and subcultural

meanings. Harris and Klebold happened to be drawn toward dark and brutal images, which they invested with their personal demons, their antisocial impulses, their maladjustment, their desires to hurt those who had hurt them. (23)

Jenkins goes on to describe a Website constructed by a sixteen-year-old girl who invited submissions from across the U.S. of poems and stories based on characters from popular culture. The submissions drew on many of the same media products that had been cited in the Columbine case, particularly the film *The Basketball Diaries*, reading them not as incitements to violence, but as complicated explorations of themes such as love, friendship, and community (23).

Even when popular culture becomes the site of darker imaginings, the connection between fantasy and violence is far from clear-cut. In the atmosphere of fear following the Columbine shooting, however, social authorities were quick to establish a link, establishing "zero tolerance" policies against "violent" forms of cultural expression, ranging from making verbal threats to wearing trenchcoats. In one notorious case, a Grade 11 student in Cornwall, Ontario was jailed for more than a month in 2000 after reading aloud in class a story he had written called "Twisted" in which a bullied student plots to blow up his school. The student claimed that the piece was a work of fiction, inspired in part by the work of Stephen King. Many writers, including King himself, leapt to the student's defence, organizing a special forum/fundraiser to draw attention to the student's plight. Protesting what was clearly a violation of the boy's freedom of speech, many of his defenders were careful to distance themselves from the claim that art has no bearing on reality: a victim of bullying himself (seven of his classmates were subsequently arrested for assault), the student was clearly expressing, in the form of creative fiction, many of his own frustrations and fantasies. To draw a straight line from that expression backward to Stephen King and forward to some future act of violence is, however, to grossly oversimplify the effects of representation on individuals and society.

What Do We *Do* with Texts? The Role of the Audience in Constructing Meaning

As examples such as this suggest, we should think of representation not simply in terms of a collection of texts or images that promote irresistible messages, leading to specific kinds of desirable or undesirable behaviour. This is the assumption underlying Gary Bauer's vision, cited above, of children "*wallowing* in sexual images and violence" (authors' emphasis). This phrase paints a picture of glassy-eyed teens flaked out on the couch, washing down their Doritos and blue Pepsi with the MTV video of Christina Aguilera writhing in a boxing ring in her red thong. Besides assuming that this (hypothetical) audience's viewing practices are completely uncritical or reflective, the term "wallowing" also suggests that the *pleasure* they derive from the texts they're consuming is decadent and lazy, and should be viewed with suspicion.

The problem with that idea is demonstrated not just in the Website Jenkins describes, which showcases the creative uses to which some popular culture fans put the texts they consume (and we can all probably think of countless other examples of such creativity, in particular the fan groups for programs such as *Star Trek* that construct elaborate new, and often subversive, narratives based on the characters), but also in the documented responses of ordinary viewers, who may characterize themselves as neither hardcore fans nor creative artists. Studies on the use of cultural products, from the 1980s TV series *Dallas* to romance novels to video games, suggest that audiences *read*—rather than passively consume—cultural texts in complex ways, finding in them—often within a single text—sources of fantasy, consolation, irony, and humour.

Janice Radway explores this idea in her 1987 book *Reading the Romance: Women, Patriarchy and Popular Literature*. Countering what was then a standard feminist critique of romance fiction as reproducing the worst aspects of traditional patriarchy—passive heroines pining after dark, mysterious bad-boy heroes who abuse, then "save" them—Radway's book, which is based on an ethnographic study of actual romance readers, offers a much more complex view of the romance than a simple semiotic reading can provide. Among the elements Radway notes are a strong level of discrimination amongst romance readers, who articulate a clear sense of the difference between romances that "work" for them and those that don't. Among the most popular heroines tended to be those described by readers as "intelligent," "spunky," and "independent," even if that independence were eventually sacrificed to some extent to the conventions of the romance. Contrary to what we might expect would be the principal appeal of romance reading, some women also cited their interest in reading the books, many of which are set in remote places or times, in order to learn about history and about other cultures. Some admitted that they used the information gleaned from their reading in order to impress their husbands, who otherwise disapproved of their habit. In general, the activity of reading romances turned out to be a highly ambivalent one.

For many of the readers, married women conditioned to perform uncomplainingly the traditional wifely roles of housekeeping, cooking, and child-rearing, the romances provided a kind of escape that was both pleasurable and guilty. In Radway's words, the women's reading was both "combative" and "compensatory":

> It is combative in the sense that it enables them to refuse the other-directed social role prescribed for them by their position within the institution of marriage. In picking up a book . . . they refuse temporarily their families' otherwise constant demand that they attend to the wants of others even as they act deliberately to do something for their own private pleasure. Their activity is compensatory in that it permits them to focus on themselves and to carve out a solitary space within an arena where their self-interest is usually identified with the interests of others. (211)

The line between combat, or rebellion, and compensation, or comfort, is not a clear-cut one. Critics of the romance genre could credibly argue that, by providing temporary solace from drudgery, it merely encourages women to accept the constraints of their current lives. It serves, in other words, like the standard products of the culture industry described by Horkheimer and Adorno (see Chapter Four), to induce passivity and unthinking acceptance of the status quo. However, the desire and longing that the novels address and enhance might also help to make women aware that their needs are not being satisfied in their current situations, thereby leading them to struggle to change them. While this reading might seem overly idealistic, it successfully avoids the simplistic assumption of media effects by acknowledging that representation is not a message but a *process*, controlled in part by readers who are not just readers but also *producers* of meaning.

Encoding and Decoding

Stuart Hall describes this process of meaning-making in terms of two key operations, *encoding* and *decoding*, which are divided into multiple stages (see Figure 3.2). Focusing on television representations in particular, this model recognizes that meaning does not exist in the heads of creators, or the show itself, in a clear form that then gets distorted, either by technological constraints (a lousy satellite signal, say) or by viewer misinterpretation. Rather, meaning is created and altered at every step along the way, from the way in which producers construct a visual text, using signs and narrative forms supplied by the surrounding culture and their own position within that culture, to the way in which those encoded meanings are transmitted, via particular technologies, and then received and decoded by viewers—once again, based on the technologies of the medium as well as on their own individual and cultural storehouse of meanings.

Figure 3.2 Encoding/Decoding

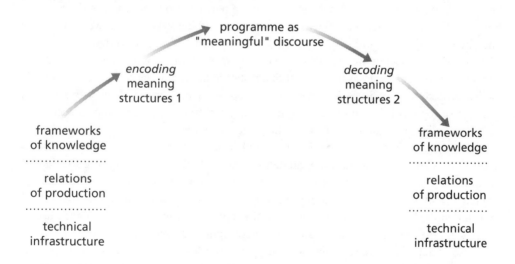

Source: Stuart Hall, "Encoding, Decoding," extracted from *Culture, Media, Language* (London: Unwin Hyman 1990). © 1990 Stuart Hall.

Representation and the Construction of Social Reality **89**

A critical point to note in Hall's theory is that, while it acknowledges a level of **agency** on the part of viewers, it does not suggest that audiences are free to take whatever meaning they wish from texts. Because the stages at which meaning is produced work interdependently with one another, the way in which messages are encoded places limitations on the way in which they are decoded. Hall identifies a continuum of possible reading positions, ranging from the *dominant-hegemonic,* in which the audience's interpretation of the text is consistent with the ideological codes in which it is produced (in other words, they subscribe to the "preferred reading"), to a *negotiated* position, in which the audience accepts the legitimacy of the preferred reading on a general level but modifies it in light of personal interests or circumstances, and finally to an *oppositional or counter-hegemonic* reading position, in which the audience understands but rejects the text's code and reads it in light of an alternative code.

Reading a Television Scene   An informal experiment, conducted in one of our introductory Popular Culture classes, highlighted the operation of these different kinds of readings. In the class, we watched a scene from the television show *NYPD Blue,* in which two of the detectives were interviewing a suspect in a murder/drug case. Employing the familiar "good cop/bad cop" TV formula in which one detective acts sympathetically toward the suspect, appearing to offer refuge from his more aggressive colleague (and, thereby, hopefully eliciting a confession), the two detectives were alternately coaxing the suspect and yelling at him. Eventually, Andy Sipowicz, playing the "bad cop," loses his temper and starts beating the suspect, a young Latino man, who falls to the floor, shielding his face with his hands. Our understanding of the scene is aided by our knowledge of Sipowicz as a talented cop, plagued with problems with alcohol and a generally bad temper. When asked to read the scene, focusing in particular on the issues of conflict and morality (Is there a "right" and "wrong" being depicted here? Whom do we as audience members identify with and why?), students came up with a variety of different answers.

A dominant-hegemonic reading—one that many students subscribed to—agreed that the morality of the scene was murky, but that it should be read in the context of "standard" police procedure: that is, Sipowicz may have gotten a bit carried away, but a certain amount of force is justified in extracting a confession from a criminal. The assumption that the audience identifies with the police, and not with the criminal, is primary in a dominant-hegemonic reading of the show. Other students read the scene according to what they identified as a more negotiated position. While not questioning the fundamental rightness of the police's position, they were uncomfortable with the violence depicted (both within the context of the story in terms of Sipowicz's apparent loss of control, and at the level of the show in terms of the representation of violence in general).

A few other students took up a counter-hegemonic/resistant reading position, which understood but rejected the premise of the unquestioned legitimacy of the police. These students focused on the status of the suspect as a member of a racial minority, and therefore as someone in particular danger of being subject to arbitrary arrest and detention. The presumption of innocence—a presumption that, they pointed out, the criminal justice system was meant to rest on in any case—becomes more highly charged in a context in which race is sometimes read as a sign of likely guilt. This reading is oppositional because it refuses the underlying principle of the show, that the police are self-evidently the "good guys," there to protect the citizens (read: "us") against the "bad guys." Rejecting the more or less black-and-white moral code of the show and replacing it with one based on various shades of grey (or, in the case of a few viewers, reversing the code altogether and rooting for the underdogs—the so-called "bad" guys) represents not a misreading but an aberrant, or atypical, form of decoding, one that may signal an explicit mode of oppositional politics.

While this example highlights the practical operation of these different kinds of readings, Hall's model can't be applied wholesale to every cultural text. Some texts are more susceptible or "open" to negotiated or oppositional readings than others, depending on such factors as the extent to which they conform to or depart from formula, and the range of audience to which they're targeted. We also need to be careful not to try and read Hall's model of encoding/decoding as offering a clear map of distinctive kinds of readings or readers. In practice, the distinction between different kinds of reading, particularly "negotiated" and "oppositional," is often murky, and readers or viewers rarely react in a uniform way to what they consume. In other words, it's possible to object to the representation of women in James Bond movies from a feminist perspective while appreciating the plots as perfect examples of the action formula.

Generally our reactions to popular culture—even of those of us who study it for a living!—are less self-conscious than that, or they are a mix of self-conscious critique and pleasure, even the wallowing kind condemned by Bauer. In addition to being shaped by our experiences and beliefs, our responses to cultural texts are powerfully influenced by the context in which we watch them. Depending on the mood we're in, our motive for watching (distraction/stimulation/intellectual engagement), the people we're watching with, and even the other kinds of texts we've consumed recently, our response to a given text will be different in different circumstances.

Suggested Activity 3.4

Try to identify the patterns in your own responses to different forms of popular culture. How, and to what extent, is pleasure moderated by critical consciousness and vice versa? How do your responses to popular cultural texts change depending on the nature of the text, the circumstances in which you are watching/reading/listening to it, or the people you are with?

REPRESENTATION IN CONTEMPORARY CULTURE

The fact that the process of making meaning is complex, individualized, and even arbitrary (based, for example, on something as trivial as whether you happen to be watching *Sex and the City* with your mother or your girlfriend) does not mean that it does not have effects. As Stuart Hall's model suggests, material practice is a critical part of the "circuit of meaning," one that determines, as it is in turn determined by, representation. As a broad indication of the connection between reading and social practice, Hall suggests that an increased instance of counter-hegemonic or oppositional readings can be taken as both symptomatic and predictive of radical shifts in the political and social landscape. In the past few years, a number of widely publicized stories about police brutality and racism (including the 1987 Rodney King beating in California, and more recently, in Toronto, the publication of a series of articles suggesting police treat blacks more harshly than whites [Shears; Rankin]) have prompted general questioning of the relationship between ideology and the administration of justice. That kind of questioning, Hall suggests, can lead not only to a shift in popular culture but also to significant political change.

Political and Ideological Context   In contrast to the trend of interrogating traditional patterns of social authority, following the events of September 11, 2001 we have also witnessed a move in the opposite direction, toward more unambiguous representations of good and evil/innocence and guilt (think, for example, of how the CIA, until recently represented as beset by corruption, has been rehabilitated in TV shows like *Alias* and *24*). These shifts mirror a more general ideological move toward increased support for practices such as racial profiling—practices that had, until recently, fallen into general disfavour because of their theoretical grounding in crude stereotyping and their practical effect of infringing the civil liberties of minority groups. Changes in political circumstances determine changes in dominant ideology, which in turn consolidate the new political order.

But the relationship between representation and reality that this example highlights goes beyond a comment on the causes/effects of particular kinds of representation. The new tolerance of the once discredited practice of racial profiling, a practice that represents an uncritical embrace of the most simplistic form of representation, suggests that the material effects of representation are not consistent over time—that is, the power of representation to influence reality changes, depending on broader circumstances.

To take a concrete, and perhaps overly simplistic, example, representation in the crude form of political propaganda is most powerful in times of economic, political, and social anxiety. It is no accident that Horkheimer and Adorno (see Chapter Four) formulated their culture industry thesis in the context of the build-up of fascism in 1940s Germany. A large part of their horror at the potential for mass media to lull people into an acceptance of brutal social regimes stemmed from the fact that audiences of Nazi propaganda *were* being lulled into such a state—to the point of accepting the slaughter of thousands of innocent people. What makes Horkheimer and Adorno's thesis particularly provocative is their argument that that media power extended to the United States, where the ideologies of industrialism and progress helped to create a mass media machine and an audience particularly receptive to its products.

Many theorists suggest that contemporary North American culture, which some see simply as the fruition of Horkheimer and Adorno's worst predictions, is characterized by the triumph of representation. That is to say, we should not be focusing concern on the content of this representation or that representation, but on the dominance of representation itself as a social, political, and economic force. French theorist Jean Baudrillard puts it this way: "Abstraction today is no longer that of the map, the double, the mirror or the concept. Simulation is ... the generation by models of a real without origin or reality: a hyperreal" (166). The phenomenon of hyperreality, of total mediatization, that characterizes contemporary culture goes beyond the paranoid fantasy of the James Bond movie *Tomorrow Never Dies*, in which one media conglomerate tries to seize control of all the world's communications industry. It resembles something more like the vision in *The Matrix*, in which people's experience of reality—even their sense of themselves— turns out to be merely a computer simulation.

Like a lot of good movies, the vision of *The Matrix* is both more and less extreme than the real-life situation it alludes to. While it would be hard to identify a real-world counterpart of the sinister conspiracy that created the matrix and enslaved people within it, *The Matrix* offered the possibility of escape, which in practice proves more difficult. One of the characteristics of the "instantaneity of communication" that characterizes postmodern popular culture is "the incursion of imagery and communication into those spaces that once were private—where the psyche previously had the chance at least to explore the 'other'; to explore, for example, alienation" (McRobbie 16). The disappearance of the mental space from which to experience a tension between the world as it is and the world as one would like it to be explains what many people who recall the Sixties lament as a lack of political idealism in contemporary generations.

Virtual Culture   The disappearance of this space also has more immediately dangerous effects. For theorists such as Thomas de Zengotita, the media are absolutely central to events like the Columbine killings—not because the killers were fans of violent movies or video games, but because they and the surrounding culture were so steeped in the culture of virtuality that the difference between the video "rehearsal" of their murder that they prepared for a class and the actual event was in some significant way immaterial. The air of unreality was not confined to the action of the shooting itself but extended to the coverage of the event, in which, de Zengotita observes, events had a generic quality, indistinguishable from coverage of hundreds of other depictions of "violence in the heartland" right down to the stock characterization of "correspondents . . . in moved-to-the breaking-point-but-professional-mode"; anchors in "grave-demeanor-reserved-forinexplicable-evil mode," and so on (56). As for the mourners themselves, de Zengotita asks, "can anyone doubt that [they], no matter how authentic their feelings, respond at some level to implicit expectations when the cameras roll? Especially since they have seen this show on TV before; now, suddenly, they are in it" (56).

The idea that representation—and the representational power of the media in particular—is all-pervasive—that we are all, somehow, watching it or "in it"—raises important questions about our ability ever to critically assess the material conditions of our existence, let alone do anything to alter them. How, and to what extent, is it possible to challenge, or at least creatively intervene in, our symbol- and image-saturated culture? The strategies of deconstruction advocated by Laura Mulvey, and taken up in different ways by avant-garde artists, filmmakers, and culture jammers, work to critique not just individual texts or ideologies, but also the codes that underwrite them, thereby robbing visual culture of some of its magic. Many critics have pointed out, however, that the ironic awareness with which we all tend to read images now has outlived its usefulness as a strategy of critique: there is no outside in postmodern culture. Perhaps the most viable response to living in a society dominated by words and images is to persistently recall the complex connections between representation in a symbolic sense and representation in a political sense: the issue is not whether popular culture offers us truth, but whether it allows us to imagine and enact a more democratic, a more truly *representative* society.

SUMMARY

In this chapter, we asked you to think counter-intuitively about representation, seeing it not as a transparent window on the world but as a thick and complex structure, embedded in while also influencing material reality. Some of the key points covered in this chapter are as follows:

- Language and other structures of representation construct rather than reflect reality.
- It is impossible to get outside representation to a "correct" view of the world.
- Representation is shaped by ideology; that is, the way we see the world is defined by particular social/cultural circumstances, particular relations of power.
- Meaning is produced intertextually, through particular discursive formations that determine what can be said by whom under what circumstances.
- While representation constructs the world, it does not do so in isolation from other cultural processes and structures, including economic processes of production and consumption and media technologies.

SUGGESTIONS FOR FURTHER READING

Barthes, Roland. *Mythologies*. Trans. Annette Lavers. London: Granada, 1973.

Berger, John. *About Looking*. New York: Pantheon, 1980.

Hall, Stuart. *Representation: Cultural Representation and Signifying Practices*. London: Sage and Open University Press, 1997.

Mirzoeff, Nicholas, ed. *The Visual Culture Reader*. London: Routledge, 1999.

Radway, Janice. *Reading the Romance: Women, Patriarchy and Popular Literature*. Chapel Hill, NC: University of North Carolina Press, 1984.

Said, Edward. *Culture and Imperialism*. London: Chatto and Windus, 1993.

Shohat, Ella, and Robert Stam. *Unthinking Eurocentrism: Multiculturalism and the Media*. London: Routledge, 1994.

Sturken, Marita, and Lisa Cartwright. *Practices of Looking: An Introduction to Visual Culture*. Oxford: Oxford University Press, 2001.

Chapter *4*

The Production of Popular Culture

INTRODUCTION: THE BUSINESS OF CULTURE

Popular culture is big business. Each and every year, trillions of dollars are spent on the production of popular culture, and trillions more on purchasing popular cultural objects (music CDs, DVDs, fashion, video games), services (cable and satellite TV, Internet providers, personal trainers), and experiences (cinema-going, musicals, tourism, restaurants, etc.). With the exception of a few recessionary dips, each year also brings an increase in the size of the contribution of popular culture to the overall economy. As just one example, video game sales in North America totalled $10 billion in 2001, greater than movie ticket sales during the same period.

While it is difficult to determine with precision the amount that the production and consumption of popular culture contributes to standard measurements of economic performance, such as **gross domestic product (GDP)**, what is certain is that the production of culture has an unprecedented significance for today's economies. For instance, the stock market boom of the 1990s was fuelled to a very large degree by a popular cultural phenomenon: the promise of new services, experiences, and consumer objects (primarily consumer electronics) associated with and generated by the rise of the Internet—new services that investors believed could result in new profits. Many of the companies whose stock valuation rose highest during the 1990s (and correspondingly fell hardest by the end of the decade) were involved in producing the equipment that allows the Internet to function: routing and switching hardware, fibre optics and other kinds of telecommunications infrastructures, and computer hardware itself. But many more were rushing to produce what can only be described as new kinds of cultural experience: new ways of dealing with personal finance, interacting with the government (as immortalized in the

NEL   The Production of Popular Culture **95**

documentary *StartUp.com*), communicating with others (MUDs, weblogs, chat rooms), and shopping (for books, groceries, plane tickets, and even, in the case of eBay.com, the ephemera that one usually finds at garage sales). These kinds of cultural experiences wouldn't be possible without the technological infrastructure provided by companies such as Oracle, Nortel, and others; at the same time, there would be no need for this infrastructure without public interest (however short lived or, in the end, limited) in the experiences and services that this infrastructure enables.

Depending on how one chooses to look at it, one could say that the *entire* economy is now dependent in surprising ways on popular culture. As we will discuss in more detail in Chapter Five, the performance of the overall economy has become dependent to an unprecedented degree on consumer spending, especially spending on supposedly "non-essential" items—the kinds of discretionary purchases that often include forms of popular cultural entertainment and other cultural experiences. But this is equally true of economic *production* itself. As a number of recent writers have pointed out, "processes of production and systems of organization can be seen... [as] assemblages of meaningful practices that construct certain ways for people to conceive of and conduct themselves at work" (du Gay 4). It would be a mistake to see production as outside of or exempt from the historical development of popular culture over the past one hundred and fifty years. The "culture of production"—that is, the guiding production philosophy of the factory or office—has become increasingly important to CEOs and management consultants intent on increasing productivity and profits through the creation of an effective work culture. The ideas that are championed in attempts to reframe work culture—for instance, the airy loft spaces and game rooms that were associated with the workspaces of the "new" Internet economy—often find their origins in popular culture; even if the links cannot be located directly in popular culture, supposedly "scientific" ideas of business management circulate in and through mass culture, and books on office management have themselves become a part of popular cultural consumption, with new fad management ideas emerging as frequently as shifts in fashion.

There is no simple way to separate the production of popular culture from the processes through which it is consumed. The aim of this chapter and the one that follows is not to suggest that production and consumption have to be treated separately; nor is it to suggest that the values and meanings generated in one don't spill over into the other in a perpetual process of osmosis across a very thin and permeable boundary. Rather, we are separating production and consumption only in order to stress the ways in which each contributes in its own way to the creation of individual and social meaning in popular culture.

Surprisingly, in the history of the academic study of culture, *neither* production nor consumption has been taken seriously enough. For the most part, cultural critics (for example, literary and art critics) have focused their interpretive and critical energies on the completed objects of culture—novels, poems, artworks, films, songs, and so on—while paying scant attention to the processes that brought these cultural forms into existence (printing presses, the invention of film camera, recording devices, etc.) as well as to the multiple uses that consumers make of culture. This has changed dramatically over the past forty years. Far more attention is now paid to the historical, social, and political contexts in which culture emerges and is read, watched, and heard. Due to the influence of various sociologies of culture, there has been relatively more attention paid to production—to the large array of processes by which culture is fashioned—than to consumption or the experience of culture. Even so, production has been considered for the most part both too generally and too abstractly: the production of culture has been seen as a small segment of economic production in general, and the culture that is produced has been treated as secondary to more primary economic and material forms and forces. To put it perhaps too simplistically, the production of steel and cars has been treated as the "real" economy, whereas the production of films and television shows has been seen as a marginal economic practice.

This chapter looks at the role of production in shaping culture in less abstract terms. While we will consider the big question of how culture is shaped by economics, we will also explore the specific economics of cultural production today in order to think through the ways in which it shapes the experience and meaning of popular culture.

"MONEY CHANGES EVERYTHING": THE PITFALLS OF THINKING ABOUT PRODUCTION

We are *all* familiar with discussing popular culture in reference to production. The entertainment section of our daily newspaper contains movie reviews, interviews with television personalities and rock stars, reports on the legal troubles of the rich and famous (e.g., Winona Ryder's recent trial on theft charges; insider trading allegations against Martha Stewart), and, perhaps, reviews of local theatrical performances and art exhibitions. Just as important, however, are stories that directly describe the economics of popular culture. Each Monday's newspaper reports the previous week's box-office grosses in full detail (e.g., for late October 2002, the top grossing movies were *Jackass: The Movie*, $22.7 million; *The Ring*, $18.8 million; and *Ghost Ship*, $11.7 million), and long newspaper and magazine articles on (among other things) the financial trials and tribulations of pop stars with their record companies (from Prince to Mariah Carey to Wilco) are regular fare. Indeed, it is often the case that we know *more* about the economics of pop culture than the "content" of pop culture itself.

For example, the release of the video game *Grand Theft Auto: Vice City* was widely reported, both as a financial story about its unprecedented success and as a (rather typical) story about the degree to which contemporary culture has continued to degenerate, reaching new lows of violence and amorality. Regardless of how popular the game will become, far fewer people will ever play it than will have heard it reported as a pop-culture phenomenon. A similar point can be made about top-ten lists of movie ticket and album sales: while even dedicated movie fans will not be able to take in all the films that circulate in and out of a top-ten list from week to week, one of the functions of the list is to inform audiences about the (financial) importance of cultural objects that they might not see immediately, but which are perhaps worthy of their attention at some point given the attention that other members of the public have bestowed on them.

Economic versus Artistic Success

Reports on contracts, financing deals, and profits and losses in the film, book, and music industry highlight the intimate connection that exists between popular culture and money. The "success" of stars, movies, pop albums, and so on—and not merely their financial success—is very often measured by the number of units sold. Directors who make movies that generate huge profits are more likely to be given the opportunity to direct future movies: one huge financial success early in a career can lead to literally dozens of chances to make future stinkers, all in the hope that the director might recapture the "magic" that led people to empty their wallets in the first place.

Just as commonly, however, financial success is taken by many consumers of popular culture as the inverse of "quality": in other words, the more *financially* successful a product might be, the less *artistically* successful it must be. The band REM's later CDs sold many more copies than their earlier ones; for early fans, the band's move from obscure club band in Athens, Georgia to heavy rotation on MuchMusic and MTV is seen as a clear sign of a decline in the quality of REM's music. Examples of this formula abound and have been applied to every aspect of popular cultural experience: the beaches of Negril, Jamaica were more interesting before resorts arrived; Queen Street West in Toronto was hip until the Gap showed up; the Haight-Ashbury district in San Francisco was a site of authentic popular culture, but is now simply a tourist trap of the first order; the writer William S. Burroughs was cool until he became a shill for Nike. This formula, which places economic success and artistic or aesthetic value in an inverse relationship, offers one common way of theorizing the impact of production on popular culture. Unfortunately, its real utility for serious cultural analysis is limited for a whole number of reasons, not least of which is that it closes off any real attention to the role played by production, by deciding on the relationship between production and popular culture in advance.

What is wrong with assuming, for example, that because a film is made in Hollywood it must necessarily be "bad" or uninteresting? After all, isn't this generally true (as anyone who saw *Jackass*, *The Ring*, and *Ghost Ship* must surely admit)? There are a number of different claims or assumptions being made in a statement like this one that need to be carefully separated out. First, one of the central assumptions lying behind this connection between money and popular culture is that if the great-unwashed masses like something, then it's impossible for it to be good. Put bluntly, such claims continue a tradition of class elitism and snobbery (discussed in Chapter Two) that presumes the intrinsic value of its own opinions while dismissing the crowds lined up for *Jackass* as little more than that: crude, uncultured people without any form of aesthetic or artistic discrimination. To take popular culture seriously means to also take seriously the whole range of reactions, interests, and values placed on the products of popular culture.

"I like his earlier work better, particularly the ones I said I didn't like at the time."

Second, such claims simply aren't true. "Hollywood" cinema—already a far too general term that applies to a vast range of products and production techniques—*has* produced films that are admired worldwide. Films that have been both critical *and* popular successes have been produced throughout the history of American cinema, including those that emerge in many ways from the belly of the beast. "Classic" Hollywood films, which were much admired, for instance, by French film critics after the Second World War, were produced on a kind of filmic factory-line whose goal was to produce as many films as cheaply as possible in order to obtain the maximum profit. The profitability of these films (from the classic Westerns of director John Ford to *film noir*), or of, say, the *Godfather* trilogy, seems to belie any easy equation between value or sophistication and money.

Third, even what is sometimes considered to be "high" art, from painting to the nineteenth-century novel, was produced in conditions in which money played an important role. Though we continue to have a romantic idea of the artist in which she is motivated by considerations other than money (which is why bio-pics of artists, such as *Frida*, always focus on the suffering and poverty that artists endure), this is largely just that: a romantic fable that tells us more about our own discomfort with the links between money and art than with the real conditions of cultural production during our own or past centuries.

Walter Benjamin

We could go on dissecting the problems of the art/money equation. The main point that we want to articulate, however, is the problem that reliance on this equation introduces into an examination of the role of production in popular culture. As the German philosopher Walter Benjamin (1892–1940) understood clearly in 1936, our discussion of cultural products continues to make use of what for him were already "a number of outmoded concepts, such as creativity and genius, eternal value and mystery" (218).

These concepts don't seem to be appropriate for describing a situation in which culture is produced in a new and very different sense than how we might imagine a nineteenth-century painter "producing" a painting (by standing in front of a canvas) or a classical composer "producing" a symphony (angrily stabbing at a piano as his long curly locks flip up and over his shoulders). As much as we might confer the status of "genius" on a film director and clap a screenwriter on the back for her great "creativity," a film is produced in a far different way and under far different circumstances than a painting or a musical composition (even in the examples we give above, we are indulging in a romantic vision of artistic creativity perpetuated by the movies). The filmic equivalent of the painter's scrawl in the bottom corner of a painting are the credits that run for minutes on end at the conclusion of a film, detailing all of the personnel required to create the finished product—set designers, sound engineers, lighting experts, assistant directors, continuity editors, technicians, accountants, and so on. The myth of the intrinsic value of "independent" films, which generally have lower budgets and are made with fewer personnel, seems to derive from the fact that in these cases it is easier to assert the filmmakers' unique voice or "genius": there are fewer intermediaries to deflect from the director's true vision. In understanding the role of production processes in the creation of contemporary popular culture, it seems essential to move away from these "outmoded concepts" that are addressed to the critical evaluation of popular culture—not because contemporary popular culture is valueless, but because a focus on value tends to obscure the complex ways in which cultural products are produced, which in turn leads us to misunderstand how production contributes to their form, shape, and broader social significance.

To summarize: we need to avoid the common connection that is made between production and value. Concentrating on how something is produced helps us to better understand the object or experience under examination. The fact that popular culture is produced for profit, and, in general, by large groups of people instead of single creative individuals, should tell us right away that understanding popular culture means to understand the process through which it is made. It doesn't tell us anything on its own, however, about how "good" or "bad" these things are. This is the wrong question to ask. The right questions would lead us to consider things such as the standard length of pop songs, the temporal structure of television programming (in which a half-hour television program means twenty-two minutes of "real" content), and the reasons why there is a disconnection between the collective labour required to produce a film, television program, or video game and the credit bestowed on those involved, which generally goes only to stars and directors. As just one example of this, the individuals who have taken credit for the *Grand Theft Auto* games that we discussed above don't even know how to program! In what sense, then, is this game an expression of *their* creativity and genius?

THE CULTURE INDUSTRY THESIS

When we think of "culture" as the kind of thing that one might experience while visiting a museum of fine arts or going to the opera (while wearing a dapper white suit and sporting a pencil-thin moustache and a monocle, of course), it seems hard to make a connection to "industry"—to the factory, work, and labour. Indeed, as we have touched on before, one of the most powerful definitions of culture that has been passed down to us positions culture as the refined, genteel *opposite* of the crude, utilitarian world of industry. One of Matthew Arnold's worries when he was writing *Culture and Anarchy* (1869) was that the Victorian faith in technological progress and the wealth created by industry was displacing culture from the centre of British society. The pursuit of human perfection through encounters with "the best that has been thought and known" was for Arnold of paramount importance; industry was a secondary, less important feature of social life. In Arnold's time, this "natural" arrangement had become (in his view) dangerously inverted: "the idea of perfection as an *inward* condition of the mind and spirit is at variance with the mechanical and material civilization in esteem with us" (23). Arnold's famous description of the "pursuit of perfection" as the "pursuit of sweetness and light" (31) is made in deliberate opposition to both the real and symbolic heaviness and dirtiness of nineteenth-century industry. The pristine, white space of art galleries, with their untouchable objects and church-like quiet, is just one of the areas where we can see the continuation of this vision of culture—even in those cases where new galleries have occupied abandoned nineteenth-century factories to take advantage of their exposed brick and massive open spaces, such as the Power Plant Gallery in Toronto, the Tate Modern in London, or the Massachusetts Museum of Contemporary Art in North Adams.

While it is easier to see popular culture as something that is necessarily produced in a way that the fine arts are not (which is part of the fascination audiences have with the television show *Popstars*), the link between *culture* and *industry* still remains mainly a figure of speech. The common use of the terms "film industry" or "record industry" points to the large productive and administrative apparatus that helps to get the band Apocalyptica's funereal heavy-metal dirges to the record stores and Steven Spielberg's latest films to the cineplex. Typically, however, these terms do not evoke images of factory workers piecing together jewel cases and etching code into CDs along an assembly line (which isn't how it's done in any case), but only, perhaps, a gentler, kinder form of production—one that takes place in office buildings and studios, and that is anchored in the productivity and creativity of the "talent." While we all understand that popular culture is mixed up with business, it nevertheless is only by stressing the connection between culture and industry that we can truly get a sense of the impact of production on popular culture.

The Frankfurt School

The social theorists Max Horkheimer (1895–1973) and Theodor Adorno (1903–1969) were the first people to use the term "culture industry" to describe the conditions in which contemporary popular culture was produced (see Close-Up 4.1). In *Dialectic of Enlightenment*, published in 1947, Horkheimer and Adorno pushed "culture" and "industry" together in an effort to create a new consciousness about the changed conditions of cultural production in contemporary societies. It was, at the time, a revolutionary new way of thinking about culture. Over the past half-century, the *cultural industry thesis* that Horkheimer and Adorno advocated has generated an enormous range of debates and discussions. It remains central to explorations of the production of culture, whether as an articulation of a thesis that remains important to understanding popular culture today, or as an extreme view about the limits of popular culture that contrary theories and viewpoints have had to contend with.

Close-Up 4.1

The Frankfurt School

The Frankfurt School is the name given to a group of innovative social theorists whose ideas remain important decades after the School was formally dissolved. Though there is no "Frankfurt School" approach to popular culture *per se* (the individual members agreed on no fixed set of ideas or concepts, and often disagreed with one another), the School's name is used to describe approaches that emphasize the production of popular culture and insist on its **ideological** constraints. Though not affiliated with the School, many contemporary critics of popular culture—especially critics that look at the influence of television on society, including Thomas Frank, Todd Gitlin, and Mark Crispin Miller—draw heavily on the general arguments made by the school.

Established in 1923 at University of Frankfurt as an independent research centre, the goal of members of the Institute for Social Research was the elaboration of a "critical theory" of society. Critical theory has since become the name for a diverse set of practices in social and cultural theory, philosophy, and literary studies. For the Frankfurt School, critical theory was meant to preserve critical reflection on the possibilities and problems of contemporary society, as a way of continuing the political work of achieving human freedom.

Members of the Frankfurt School included Horkheimer, Adorno, Herbert Marcuse, Erich Fromm, Otto Kirchheimer, and Leo Lowenthal. Some of the key texts produced by members of the school include Theodor Adorno's *Negative Dialectics* and Herbert Marcuse's *One-Dimensional Man*.

What Is the Culture Industry?

What is the culture industry? And perhaps more importantly, what kind of culture does the culture industry create?

The British communications scholar Nicholas Garnham has described the cultural industries as "institutions in our society which employ the characteristic modes of production and organization of industrial corporations to produce and disseminate symbols in the form of cultural goods and services, generally, though not exclusively, as commodities" (25). To put it in a somewhat circular fashion, the cultural industries are the industries of culture—those institutions (generally, corporations) whose product is culture. At one level, it is easy to locate such industries in contemporary society: the institutions that create films, television programs, popular music, and video games, for example, can all be seen as cultural industries.

But why stop there? While films, TV programs, and CDs may be concrete cultural products, there are numerous other institutions that "produce and disseminate symbols in the form of cultural goods and services." For example, the merchandising of sports equipment and clothing is "cultural" in this sense, as are the products of the fashion industry more generally (at all levels, from Stüssy to Harry Rosen) and all the activities and products associated with tourism. But we can even go further, and make the claim that the marketing and advertising of *all* consumer products has transformed consumer production in general into cultural industries (we will discuss this process in more detail below in the section entitled How Is Culture Shaped by Economics?). "Basic" foodstuffs such as eggs, milk, beef, chicken, and cheese are carefully marketed to consumers as part of a healthy lifestyle. The great cliché of automobile advertising is the link made between vehicles and nature: when you buy an Audi Quattro or Subaru Outback, you aren't buying an environmentally damaging mode of transportation, but the adventure of the outdoors, and an outdoors that you wouldn't be able to access *except* with these vehicles. Ads for banks and mutual funds commonly feature images of cottages, beaches, or family settings: dealing with these institutions, the images suggest, will secure you the freedom that your life otherwise so clearly lacks. The products of these industries may not be directly "cultural" in the same way as the film industry. What these examples should suggest, however, is that today the borders between cultural industries and other industries have become difficult to draw, due in part to the expansion of the field of cultural experience (such that even buying cheese has become culture in some strange way), as well as to the creation of new forms of production, such as marketing and advertising.

Garnham's definition applies to cultural *industries*; Horkheimer and Adorno spoke of a singular "culture industry," a single system that explains the function of culture in contemporary society, both those forms and kinds of culture produced by cultural industries and those that are not. There is little dispute over the fact that culture today is produced (at least in part) through an industrial process. What *is* in dispute is Horkheimer and Adorno's assertion of a single, dominant system of cultural production, and the social, political, and cultural significance that they attribute to this system. Before we can ascertain

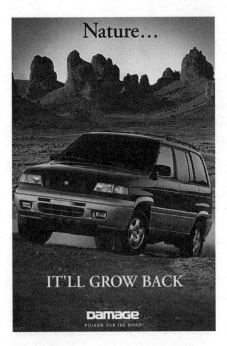

Nature…

IT'LL GROW BACK

DAMAGE
POISON FOR THE ROAD

In parodic ads like this one, the magazine *Adbusters* has drawn attention to the realities behind the images and fantasies that advertising sells to us.

how successful this thesis is in describing the production of popular culture, we need first to explore Horkheimer and Adorno's theories in greater detail.

Culture, Experience, and the Culture Industry

In order to fully grasp Horkheimer and Adorno's worries about the culture industry, it is necessary to have some sense of the larger issues explored in the *Dialectic of Enlightenment*. It is a notoriously dense and difficult book, so a brief overview cannot help but miss many of the book's nuances, especially as a good deal of the energy and effect of the book comes out of the authors' highly stylized and rhetorical mode of writing. In the introduction to *Dialectic of Enlightenment*, Horkheimer and Adorno describe their task as "nothing less than the discovery of why mankind, instead of entering into a truly human condition, is sinking into a new kind of barbarism" (xi). The legacy of Enlightenment thought that we still (to a large degree) live with sees history as a process of continual improvement and development—in a word, history is marked by progress.

The narratives of history that we encounter in classrooms, on CBC, in government documents, and on the History Channel suggest that things are constantly getting "better": once women couldn't vote, now they can; once humanity could move around the earth only slowly, now there are jet planes; once there was only semaphore, now there's the Internet. The political part of this narrative makes the claim that humanity in general is slowly increasing its degree of freedom. Horkheimer and Adorno object strongly to this "myth" of progress and to the belief in human reason that lies at its core. Far from leading to greater freedom, they see people's lives today as more restricted than ever. Humanity's faith in progress has created an inescapable system of **instrumental rationality** that limits what we understand and experience to a considerable degree, and a domination of nature that threatens the continued existence of the world (see Close-Up 4.2). The historical events that the narrative of progress would see as exceptions to the rule (in particular, the rise of Fascism in Europe) Horkheimer and Adorno see as a direct outcome of this narrative. To paraphrase Walter Benjamin, for them every document of civilization is also a document of barbarism.

The culture industry plays an important part in perpetuating the domination of human beings and nature under the guise of increasing their freedom. The subtitle of the

Instrumental Rationality

Instrumental rationality is a complex concept that has a simple idea at its core. In essence, the use of rationality or reason in an instrumental fashion suggests the use of the most efficient means to achieve the desired end. Analysis of instrumental rationality is usually associated with the German sociologist Max Weber (1864–1920), whose work had an impact on the Frankfurt School (see Close-Up 4.1) and on the shape of the *Dialectic of Enlightenment* in particular. For Weber, the rise of capitalism introduces instrumental rationality into all spheres of life—not just in economics, but also in politics, culture, and other parts of society as well. It might seem as if it is a good idea to achieve efficiency in all areas of life. However, there are drawbacks to instrumental rationality, especially when it becomes applied generally. The concept of efficiency isn't a neutral one; that is, it implies a certain set of values about the goals of human activity and human life that may in fact contradict other values that people hold dear. The Frankfurt School was critical of instrumental rationality because it eliminated the critical use of reason. Perhaps most dangerously, instrumental rationality can turn into an autonomous force. Even though human beings invented this use of rationality (indeed, they invented the concept of rationality itself), it has come to be treated as an irresistible, unchallengeable fact of nature.

Many conflicts today concern the problems of instrumental rationality. For instance, the "efficient" pursuit of profits and technological development has resulted in considerable damage to the environment. The difficulty that environmentalists have faced in changing the politics of governments and businesses has to do in part with how deeply instrumental rationality is embedded in the structure of these organizations. Similarly, the global push to privatize public services (e.g., in Canada, electricity utilities in Alberta and Ontario) has been justified in terms of greater efficiency. Those opposed to the privatization of public services oppose instrumental rationality with a different set of values, which emphasize the need to provide collective goods to everyone in society at a reasonable cost.

chapter on culture industry in the *Dialectic of Enlightenment* says it all: "Enlightenment as Mass Deception." The culture industry produces culture that is designed to deceive and mislead those engaged in it. What the culture industry creates—what we now describe as mass or popular culture—has for Horkheimer and Adorno only one real function: to reproduce incessantly the values of capitalist culture. A century earlier, Karl Marx had analyzed the exploitation of workers by capitalists in the factory system. The existence of the culture industry is one of the main reasons why over the course of a hundred years little had been done about the exploitation of labour. The culture industry deceives by making it difficult, if not impossible, to see the social limits of a life that appears to be filled with an endless degree of consumer choice, and in which one can at least engage in amusements of various kinds after the work day is done. For Horkheimer and Adorno, these choices and pleasures are false ones. Within the culture industry, "something is provided for all so that none may escape" (123), and the function of amusement is little more than "the prolongation of work" (137).

Three Points about the Production of Popular Culture In their discussion of the culture industry in *Dialectic of Enlightenment*, as well as in related work by Adorno on popular music, three main points emerge about the production of popular culture in the twentieth century.

First, what characterizes popular culture for Horkheimer and Adorno is the **standardization** of cultural production *and* of audience reaction to contemporary culture. In the age of the culture industry, culture comes packaged in a small number of predictable forms and genres and is produced by an increasingly limited number of giant corporations for consumption by a global audience. The small number of genres into which CDs are categorized at record shops (country, rock, alternative, jazz, etc.) and the similarly limited number of film genres and plots (horror, teen films, thrillers, action films, romantic comedies, etc.) are broad examples of what Horkheimer and Adorno seem to have in mind; the fact that today, just as in the 1940s, a small number of major transnational companies make the majority of films *and* music available for global consumption suggests that standardization remains a problem for contemporary cultural production (see the discussion of transnational media corporations in Chapter Nine). Standardization of cultural production is necessitated by the mass commodification of culture: there are only so many films that can be made (the number of films produced each year by Hollywood is still surprisingly low) and so many CDs that can be pressed, and the available "prime time" space on major television networks is constrained by the temporal limits imposed by the workday. We are all familiar with the effects of standardization. Indeed, one of the great complaints of cultural consumers is that there is so little that is "truly" new being produced for us to listen to, watch, and experience. Even with access to two hundred television channels, it is not an uncommon experience to flip through them over and over and still find "nothing" to watch.

This might seem paradoxical or contradictory, since one of the key features of contemporary popular culture is the importance of the "new." Spin a new disc for a few weeks and its novelty has been used up: we grow bored of it and long for something new to spend our money on. The creation of newness is linked to the perpetuation of profit: as long as the cultural industries have something "new" to offer us, the money will continue to flow in. But the creation of "newness" also presents a problem: how can any cultural producer or industry create genuinely "new" objects for culture consumers? Standardization offers a paradoxical solution to this problem by allowing producers to continue to pass off apparently new objects in old shells: the endless stream of pop love songs; *Escape from Alcatraz, Escape from New York,* and *Aliens 3*; Britney Spears, Christina

Aguilera, and Jessica Simpson; and all *ten* films dealing with the hockey-masked horror assassin, Jason (who in his latest incarnation appears in space).

Standardization is closely connected with what Adorno describes as **pseudo-individualization**. In his essay "On Popular Music," Adorno suggests that in the case of the popular music of his day, "the composition hears for the listener" (215). This is not meant to be taken literally, of course. The claim being made is that popular music (and popular culture more generally) is so standardized that not only is the audience's response predictable, but also it is in a sense "built in" to the cultural product itself. To get a sense of what Adorno has in mind, we need only think of the times when we can feel ourselves being very directly manipulated by cultural objects. The "tearjerker," a movie that leans heavily on sentimentality to hook its viewers, can bring tears to our eyes no matter how trite or predictable its plot might be; a good deal of Top 40 music at any one time seems to rely on recycling licks, hooks, and themes that we like despite ourselves (in the world of the standard pop song, humanity is engaged in the trials and tribulations of dating to the exclusion of virtually every other experience). If pop culture is so effective today at getting at our emotions and desires, it is in part because those emotions and desires have themselves been coded, created, produced, and reproduced by our experiences with popular culture to begin with.

Pseudo-individualization implies the production of a false identity: the experience of a sense of individuality and selfhood that doesn't match up to the experiential depths that these terms usually suggest. To be an "individual," as both philosophers *and* advertisers tell us, is to be separated from the crowd and in control of one's decisions and actions. Everyone is supposedly an individual in this sense—though if that's the case, then it begs the question of who exactly forms the mass or the crowd that an individual distinguishes him- or herself against. A belief in this strong sense of individuality runs deep in contemporary culture, even if almost everyone also believes that popular culture has taken away people's individuality, causing them to pursue one fad and fashion after another, year after year. For Adorno, it is precisely this belief in one's own "real" individuality that constitutes pseudo-individualization. He writes that the "standardization of song hits keeps the customer in line by doing their listening for them, as it were. Pseudo-individualization, for its part, keeps them in line by making them forget that what they listen to is already listened to for them, or 'pre-digested'" (217). Pseudo-individualization is what enables standardization to function. For instead of seeing contemporary popular culture as a landscape in which the directions we can travel are circumscribed and limited, we see (for ourselves, at least, if not for all others) a world of nearly infinite choice that emerges out of our individuality. Pseudo-individualization is the ideological screen that makes a standardized culture seem like a culture of genuine artistic expressions that we interact with in our own supposedly unique way. Standardization and pseudo-individualization pose a problem for Horkheimer and Adorno because of their political implications: they suggest we are free, when the reality is very different.

This leads into the second point they make about the production of popular culture, one that we have already anticipated. In their view, popular culture is produced only in order to reinforce and maintain the power of the status quo. Not only are the products of the cultural industries uniform and without real artistic merit, but also their aim isn't to engage the public, but to distract them from reality by drawing attention away from the contradictions and problems of contemporary society. In the case of popular music, Adorno writes that "listeners are distracted from the demands of reality by entertainment which does not demand attention either" (219). The ubiquity of standardized, mass-produced culture, the pseudo-individuation it both produces and invites, and the distraction it creates make it difficult for human beings to confront fully the enormous social and political challenges that face them. To put it bluntly, it's hard to stay focused on the problems of the environment and on the increasing corporate influence of government decision-making when there's so much good TV to watch.

As the political process itself becomes more and more beholden to the structures and systems of popular culture (the sound-bite, political advertising, the carefully staged press conference, opinion polling, etc.), it is not surprising to find that people are tuning politics out and exercising their choice in the one arena that appears to allow it: the consumption of popular culture. For Horkheimer and Adorno, the rise of popular culture seems to signal the death of the project of human emancipation. "The idea of 'fully exploiting' available technical resources and the facilities for aesthetic mass consumption is part of the economic system which refuses to exploit resources to abolish hunger" (139); this is, for them, one of the great obscenities of the production of popular culture. There is something genuinely obscene about an economic system that devotes billions of dollars to beer commercials and wrestling spectacles but that seems unwilling to intervene in the increasing polarization of wealth throughout the world, and the lack of resources to treat AIDS in those African nations that have been ravaged by the disease.

Finally, a third related point concerns the possibilities and prospects of oppositional art and culture. The vision of popular culture that emerges in Horkheimer and Adorno's work is one in which artistic and cultural resistance has all but evaporated. But how can this be? On the contrary: contemporary culture seems to be characterized by all manner of opposition to the standardization of popular culture. The limits and problems of standardized culture form a prominent theme in contemporary art, from Andy Warhol's soup cans to Roy Lichtenstein's pop art drawings, from the photos of Roy Arden to the sculptures of Jeff Koons. The same can be said of contemporary fiction and drama as well. Even within popular culture, it is possible to find criticisms of contemporary culture on television (in *The Simpsons* or *South Park*, for example) and in popular music (from Eminem to Radiohead). Contemporary culture is also home to numerous subcultural groups that oppose "the way things are." These include pop-culture subcultures (e.g., the rave scene and skateboarders), but also span the range of activist and extremist groups. There seems to be an awful lot of dissent going on in a world that is supposedly dominated and controlled through the medium of popular culture.

Perhaps this is so. At the same time, it is worth noting that all of this oppositional activity seems to have left the basic structures of capitalism in place—no matter how much they might wish to do away with it. Horkheimer and Adorno are well aware of the fact that dissidence and dissatisfaction still exist within the system of amusement and distraction that they outline. Indeed, this is to be expected by the very fact that this system limits human possibilities and expression. The amusements of popular culture might put salve on the wound of human exploitation under capitalism, but they can't heal it: the pain is still there, even if we don't always feel it.

Though the dissatisfactions that are expressed at all of the different sites suggested above are real enough, Horkheimer and Adorno believe that there is a way in which such resistance is already factored into the larger system. "Whenever Orson Welles offends against the tricks of the trade," they write, "he is forgiven because his departures from the norm are regarded as calculated mutations which serve more strongly to confirm the validity of the system" (129). Dissidence isn't a problem; indeed, it helps to offset the need to introduce "newness" into the system of standardization. Rebellion keeps the system going. "Real" art, which requires the kind of serious attention that popular culture generally doesn't, might be able to knock us out of our stupor. That this hasn't happened and seems unlikely to happen suggests that such art no longer exists: "high art," the kind that appears in museums and galleries, has also succumbed to the effects of the culture industry, becoming little more than wall decorations for rich people. In the words of Horkheimer and Adorno, "something is provided for all so that none may escape" (123).

Summarizing Horkheimer and Adorno
If we were to summarize Horkheimer and Adorno's position on popular culture, it would be that its meaning and function is determined primarily at the level of production. By understanding the ways in which popular culture is produced, in this view we also seem to be able to understand virtually *everything* there is to know about the consumption of popular culture. From this perspective, analyzing or understanding the meaning of specific cultural objects is pointless. While you might learn that *The Simpsons* is a different kind of cartoon than the old Disney cartoons that Horkheimer and Adorno discuss in *Dialectic of Enlightenment* (134–38), you would have to conclude that their general social function is, in the end, the same: the amusements that they generate impede reflection on the realities of our social and political situation.

The American artist Jeff Koons has interrogated the meaning of pop culture in provocative works, such as the sculpture *Popples* (1988).

On one level, this is a powerful point: it lends credence to the central role that popular culture plays in contemporary life. At the same time, Adorno and Horkheimer's view of popular culture is decidedly one-sided (it's all bad). Quality aside, the most superficial comparison of *The Simpsons* and, say, *Bambi* would suggest that this mode of interpretation leaves out a big part of the story of popular culture. While the culture industry thesis offers a systemic analysis of popular culture in contemporary society and draws attention to production as an important site of investigation, there are ways in which it closes off continued critical reflection and exploration—the opposite of what its formulators intended.

Some Problems with the Culture Industry Thesis

As influential as the culture industry thesis has been (and it has exerted a considerable influence, both implicitly and explicitly), Horkheimer and Adorno's analysis of popular culture has been attacked from a number of different positions. Indeed, much of what constitutes the field of cultural studies (see Chapter Ten) can be seen as a reaction to the limits of this thesis. The insistence within cultural studies on the need to consider the consumption of popular culture emerges in part as a reaction to a view that imagines what audiences and individuals do with popular culture can be determined in advance at the level of production. Taking popular culture seriously means to take seriously the ability of diverse individuals and communities to interact with popular culture in their own creative ways—within, of course, specific social, cultural, and political limits. We discuss the creative possibilities inherent in popular culture in more detail in Chapters Three, Five, and Eight.

Criticisms of the culture industry thesis can be grouped into three main categories. It is worth reviewing these criticisms (if briefly) in order to get a sense of how we might move beyond the limits of the culture industry thesis in our explorations of the production of popular culture.

First, and most commonly, Horkheimer and Adorno's cultural industry thesis has been criticized as elitist. As Keith Negus puts it, "Adorno and Horkheimer's view of cultural production has, with some justification, often been portrayed as the pessimistic lament of cultural elitists who were dismayed at what they perceived to be the homogeneity and vulgarity of 'mass' taste, and who were concerned that the potential for artistic creativity in music, literature and painting had been co-opted and corrupted by the production methods and administrative regimes of industrial capitalism" (70). The ubiquity of these criticisms alone suggests that there is something to this point. But criticisms of the elitism of the culture industry thesis actually confuse or conflate a number of points. As we suggested above, it is true that the culture industry thesis does not account for the creativity (or at least the potential creativity) of consumers of popular culture. But this does not mean that, on the contrary, Horkerheimer and Adorno leave room open for connoisseurs of "difficult" novels or abstract art. Rather, they are equally critical of the political limits of "serious" or "elite" art as well. In "The Culture Industry Reconsidered," Adorno makes a case for the "seriousness" of *both* high and low art. The problem with the culture industry for Adorno is that it attacks high *and* low culture, forcing them together in a way that strips both of their potentials to resist total social control.

What Adorno identifies as an element of certain forms of avant-garde literature and art he thus sees as residing in the "rebellious resistance" of low culture as well. In other words, it is simply *not* the case that Adorno sees only "high" art as having political potential. The problem with contemporary culture is not that it is "low," but that its political and social effectiveness has declined. If the culture industry thesis is elitist, it is because it prioritizes production to the total exclusion of consumption and not because it suggests that *Masterpiece Theatre* taken with brandy is superior to *Hockey Night in Canada* enjoyed with beer.

A second criticism is that the culture industry thesis is historically limited. Like everything else, it is a product of its times and the circumstances in which it was produced. In his introduction to an excerpt from Horkheimer and Adorno's book, Simon During points out that:

> it is worth emphasizing that when this essay was written the culture industry was less variegated than it was to become, during the 1960s in particular. Hollywood, for instance, was still 'vertically integrated' [in the mid-40s] so that the five major studios owned the production, distribution, and exhibition arms of the film business between them; television was still in its infancy; the LP and the single were unknown; the cultural market had not been broken into various demographic sectors—of which, in the 1950s, the youth segment was to become the most energetic. (29–30)

Some of the features characterizing the culture industry in the 1940s have returned: there are once again highly integrated forms of cultural production, vertical in some cases, horizontal in others (see the discussion of media convergence in Chapter Nine). Nevertheless, the fundamental point that During makes is one worth considering. The cultural industry thesis was one of the first attempts to analyze the new form of mass-produced culture that emerged by mid-century in the United States, Canada, and Europe.

As Bernie Gendron points out, while Horkheimer and Adorno have been criticized for denigrating popular music in the 1940s, the songs produced in the song mills of Tin Pan Alley *did* make use of an extremely limited melodic and lyrical palette. In the intervening years, the production of popular music has changed significantly and in complex ways in reaction to cultural and social shifts, and in accordance with the development of new technologies. No general theory of the culture industry like the one set out by Horkheimer and Adorno could sustain the wild shifts that have taken place in popular cultural production. Even if we use the cultural industry model as a rough framework for an analysis of the production of popular culture, we need to be attentive to changes in the conditions in and under which pop culture is and was produced.

Finally, critics have suggested that Horkheimer and Adorno's vision of contemporary social life is far too "totalizing." What this means is that their sense of the extent of influence of the culture industry is too widespread: like the Borg in *Star Trek: The Next*

Generation, they seem to insist that "resistance is futile." Indeed, as we saw above, Horkheimer and Adorno suggest that even resistance to the system of the culture industry is part of the system, too. The truth, however, is that popular culture is a messy and unwieldy object that can't be explained by reference to a single explanatory model.

The Relevance of the Culture Industry Thesis   In many respects, the culture industry thesis extends Karl Marx's assertion that the dominant culture at any given time is the culture of the dominant class: popular culture, then, reflects and supports the power and dominance of that class. But, as Raymond Williams has argued,

> the body of intellectual and imaginative work which each generation receives as its traditional culture is always, and necessarily, something more than the product of a single class. It is not only that a considerable part of it will have survived from much earlier periods than the immediately pre-existing form of society.... It is also that, even within a society in which a particular class is dominant, it is evidently possible both for members of other classes to contribute to the common stock, and for such contributions to be unaffected by or in opposition to the ideas and values of the dominant class. (320)

While the culture industry thesis may account for a significant degree of the production of standardized culture in contemporary society, it would be a mistake to forget the considerable remnants of "older" forms of culture (opera, classical music, art, etc.) and to minimize the anarchic energies of subcultures and counter-cultures: dominant culture is never so dominant as to form the single face of culture at any given historical moment.

None of this is to minimize the contribution of Horkheimer and Adorno to the study of popular culture. What we can conclude from our lengthy analysis of the problems and possibilities that the culture industry thesis introduces is that, while it is important to consider the role the standardized production plays in the creation of our experience of popular culture, no general theory of production describes the full experience of contemporary pop culture. One of the things that we need to realize is that contemporary cultural production is contradictory. As the film scholar Gill Branston puts it, "capitalist products have both an exchange value for their owners and shareholders, and a use value for their audiences, and sometime the two can be fairly far apart" (19). The two sections that follow will provide some sense of this complexity. The first section (How Is Culture Shaped by Economics?) will explore the development of a single consumer product, while the second (Shifting Modes of Cultural Production) will show historical shifts in production in a single segment of the culture industry: Hollywood films. The final section of this chapter (Cultural Production Today) will deal with some recent developments in the production of popular culture.

HOW IS CULTURE SHAPED BY ECONOMICS? THE INVENTION OF CRISCO

How is culture shaped by economics? This is far from an easy question to answer, especially if we break away from the "natural" assumptions about the ways in which art and economics are related. Though this may seem frustrating, the answer is that while culture *is* shaped by economics, this shaping occurs in indirect rather than (or perhaps, in addition to) direct ways. The shaping effect of economics on culture is best seen in the changes that culture undergoes over time: looking at our present circumstances will tend to lead us only to a first-level analysis of the kind we described above, in which art and money are imagined as related inversely. We also need to remember that the relationship between economics and culture is a reciprocal one: just as economics shapes culture, so culture effects and shapes the economy. The constant back and forth flow of force between culture and economics means that if we stop the process in mid-stream in order to dissect it, we get only part of the overall picture. Then again, if we look only at the larger historical frame, we tend to miss the dynamics of this interchange. The solution, of course, is to do both things simultaneously, as Susan Strasser does in her analysis of the marketing of Crisco in her book *Satisfaction Guaranteed: The Making of the American Mass Market.*

First introduced in January 1912, Crisco, a solid vegetable shortening used in a wide variety of cooking applications, has remained on the market for almost a century. By any standard, it has to be counted as one of the most successful consumer products of the twentieth century. Its success was by no means guaranteed: much of the reason why Crisco has remained on the market for so long has to do with the effective way in which it was marketed to the public. But before we discuss the specifics of a campaign that was described as setting "a new standard in modern marketing" (14), we need to ask and answer another question: in what way is a product like Crisco part of popular culture?

Although discussions of popular culture generally evoke images of popular film, television, and rock music, as we stress in Chapter One popular culture can be seen to be diffused to numerous other sites, including most consumer objects. Food items such as Crisco are no exception. As Strasser points out, "Crisco and other everyday objects function as artifacts of culture: they represent and are embedded in networks and systems of human relationship" (15). While we may not tend to conceive of the everyday objects around us as sites where we can explore the circumstances of cultural production, the story of Crisco highlights the way in which "household objects embody both the relationships and routines of private daily life and the social relations of production and distribution" (15). Analyzing the invention of Crisco as a consumer object helps us to understand the role that production played in one of the most important social shifts that underlies contemporary culture:

> During the decades around the turn of the century, branded, standardized products came to represent and embody the new networks and systems of production and distribution, the social relationships that brought people the things they used.

Household routines involved making fewer things and purchasing more; consumption became a major part of the work of the household. Formerly *customers*, purchasing the objects of daily life from familiar craftspeople and storekeepers, Americans became *consumers*. (15)

The Challenge for Procter & Gamble

The story of Crisco highlights the vagaries of the process by which consumer products were created and disseminated to a market in the midst of this shift from customers to consumers. Crisco was the solution to a problem faced by Procter & Gamble (P&G), the company that created it. P&G made use of cottonseed oil in the soaps that it produced, the best known of which was Ivory. Although it owned some of its own cottonseed processing plants, P&G's access to the raw materials it used in its soaps was affected by the influence of four other companies that made extensive use of cottonseed oil. In order to create a stronger bargaining position for the purchase of the raw materials it used in its primary product, P&G decided to come up with another consumer product that made heavy use of cottonseed oil. After years of experimentation, in 1910 P&G solved the problem of "producing an all-vegetable solid fat in commercial quantities" (5), and in 1911 Crisco was born.

In order for it to be adopted as a consumer product, Crisco faced both opportunities and challenges. By 1910, Americans were already accustomed to buying consumer objects produced in factories; Crisco would not be emerging into a society in which consumer objects were an unknown quantity. Nevertheless, since Crisco was the first product to be launched in its category, P&G had to convince consumers that they needed it. The company faced a considerable challenge—for, of course, before Crisco ever existed people had been cooking and frying with oils and animal fats. P&G was faced with the task of converting a "population accustomed to homemade products and unbranded merchandise ... into a national market for standardized, advertised, brand-named goods in general" (7). In other words, the company had to invent a need that no one yet had. And the way to accomplish this was through marketing.

Marketing Crisco

P&G had a clear goal: to get consumers to start buying Crisco in addition to or in place of animal fats and vegetable oils. How to accomplish this goal was far less clear. P&G employed a number of different, though related, strategies. Before releasing Crisco to consumers, P&G pursued extensive product testing, making it available to food researchers and home economists for recipe development. As the product become more refined Crisco was given to P&G employees, and a number of hotels and clubs in Cincinnati, P&G's home base, became early adopters of the product. The testimonials of hotel employees and of the food scientists would later be placed in ad copy for the product.

J. Walter Thompson, the advertising company that P&G commissioned to sell Crisco, experimented with different marketing campaigns (newspaper ads, store demonstrations, etc.) in different cities prior to the launch of a national campaign in January 1912. In December 1911, three to six cans of Crisco were sent "to every grocer in the United States, with a letter describing the forthcoming campaign" (10). Early on, P&G realized the importance of bringing grocers on-side by providing them with various discounts on bulk purchases, supplying them with promotional material, and so on. Crisco demonstrators toured the country, showing consumers the tasty benefits of cooking with the product, and Crisco cookbooks were made available to consumers free of charge through the mail, along with "*A Calendar of Dinners*, suggesting 365 menus with 615 recipes, [which] went through at least twenty-six editions by 1925" (12). Crisco was also amongst the first products to be designed with different market segments in mind: a specially designed container was developed for use on-board passenger trains, and a kosher version was sold in Jewish neighbourhoods.

The range of the marketing techniques that P&G engaged in as a way of getting consumers to adopt Crisco instead of lard or butter seems to smack of the kind of control of consumer response that Horkheimer and Adorno feared was the outcome of the culture industry. In order to resolve a production problem (and in so doing to create bigger profits), P&G created a product that no one really "needed"; the responses of the masses were conditioned by and through various elements of the production process (production, marketing, advertising, etc.), each of which worked to create a market for the product they had invented. However, Strasser's assessment of the situation should give us pause before we leap to this conclusion.

> The corporations that made and distributed mass-produced goods did not necessarily set out to create needs, nor did they do so in any straightforward way.... The process that makes people into consumers amalgamates changing ideas, habits, technology, demographic trends, and many other facets of culture, few of which are controlled even by the most powerful marketers, who concentrate their efforts on perceiving and taking advantage of those changes. (17)

The invention and marketing of Crisco highlights the complex cultural and social contexts within which popular culture is produced. In trying to assess the contribution that production makes to popular culture—not just the limits it imposes, but also the possibilities that it opens up—we want to make sure to attend to this complexity rather than resorting to simple narratives about the role that money plays in culture.

Suggested Activity 4.1

Can you think of other cultural products whose invention has created, rather than fulfilled, an existing need? What products have you acquired recently that you might once have had no need for, but that now seem essential?

SHIFTING MODES OF CULTURAL PRODUCTION

In the last section we looked at the production of a single consumer object (in a broad sense that includes marketing, advertising, and distribution). This section will highlight the changes in the production and distribution of one cultural form—Hollywood film— over the course of its relatively brief history. It should be obvious enough that forms and modes of production change over time. For one thing, there are technological reasons for these shifts and changes: as new technologies are introduced, the systems of production and distribution of existing forms undergo significant changes.

In the history of recorded music, numerous formats have come and gone, including record albums (of various speeds and formats), 8-tracks, and cassette tapes. The heated formal and informal discussions about the superiority of albums vs. CDs (the "warm" sounds produced by albums contrasted to the tinny-ness of CDs, etc.) seems, fifteen years later, to have been a quaint debate between audio-Luddites and technophiles that was settled in advance by the relentless march of new technological formats. In the case of film, too, the introduction of sound and colour had implications for the way in which films were produced, and the possibilities of widespread digital distribution (foreshadowed by recently introduced video-on-demand technologies and the online swapping of films through high-speed digital access) promise to change the ways in which films are both shot and screened.

Changes in production result not only from technological developments, but also from social and economic ones. Film becomes a popular cultural phenomenon in part because it arises at just the right time. By the end of the nineteenth century, leisure time had become a reality for more and more people. Prior to the invention of film, a system of public entertainments in which audience members exchanged money for cultural experiences had also become well developed. Such public entertainments included travelling orchestras, vaudeville and burlesque shows, magic shows, and amusement parks. Film arrives in a social situation in Canada and the United States, in which there are both venues in which films can be screened (e.g., vaudeville theatres) and an audience accustomed to seeing spectacles "performed" for their pleasure.

The Evolution of Hollywood

The history of Hollywood filmmaking can be divided into roughly four main eras: (1) early cinema (1895–1920), which is the period between the invention of film and its organization into an industrial system of routinized production; (2) the studio system (1920–1960), the era of classical Hollywood film production; (3) the so-called "Hollywood Renaissance" period (1965–1975), which describes the period of innovative and edgy film production that occurred between the end of the studio system and its re-organization; and (4) the blockbuster era initiated by Steven Spielberg's *Jaws* (1976), which has continued (for the most part) up to the present. Each of these eras is characterized by a different relationship among the three main elements of the film industry: *production, distribution,* and *exhibition.* The history that we offer in this section has to be understood as merely a sketch of a very complex story of a single national cinema. At different times during this history, the national cinemas of other countries have been powerfully active as well (for example, the Indian film industry today produces as many feature-length films as all the major Hollywood studios combined). However, our aim is not to offer an overview of film history in general, but to provide an example of shifting conditions and circuits of cultural production through a single, relatively well-known example.

Early Cinema   The first public film screening took place in Paris on December 28, 1895. It was organized by Auguste and Louis Lumière, who adapted Thomas Edison's Kinetoscope viewing machine, which could be viewed only by single patrons in peep-show fashion in specially designed parlours. Over the next few years the Lumière brothers screened their films around the world, in various parts of Europe and also in South Africa, Russia, India, Brazil, Mexico, Australia, and Japan. The content of early cinema has been described as "a scatter of inventions" (Williams "British" 14), which ranged from the recording of everyday events and activities (the Lumières' *actualités*, the most famous of which shows a train coming into a station from background to foreground), to early forms of short narrative films, such as Georges Méliès's *A Trip to the Moon*. The visual vocabulary of filmmaking developed as quickly as the technology of filmmaking itself. By 1916, the director D.W. Griffith had released two full-length features—*The Birth of a Nation* (1915) and *Intolerance* (1916)—which contained many of the visual elements that would come to comprise the classical Hollywood style.

In terms of cultural production, the period of early cinema was a troubled one. As with the development of any new medium, numerous players entered into various parts of the production process only to be driven out by the ferocious competition over the potential spoils. For the first few years of film exhibition, the greatest degree of control in the cinema business lay with the exhibitors. Since early films were very short, exhibitors chose films offered by numerous producers and assembled longer custom-made film programs out of the bits and pieces they had purchased. The period from 1905–07 witnessed a boom in the United States in the construction of small theatres (nickelodeons) in urban centres where a wide cross-section of the public would congregate to watch films. In order to sustain interest and keep people coming, exhibitors would change films often—sometimes on a daily basis—which produced a boom in film production as well.

As films became longer, control began to shift to film producers. In order to generate profits from longer (and, so, more expensive to make) films, producers began to evolve forms of studio production, which allowed for more precise control over the contexts of production (lighting and, later, sound) and over costs. Studio production worked like a factory for films: all of the fixed elements needed to create a film (cameras, lighting, etc.) were located in one place, at which the actors, directors, and staff involved in the film would assemble. Studio production also enabled advance planning of the production process. By 1904, films were no longer sold to exhibitors but rented to them, which allowed producers to retain control over their films and to further extend their profits by reducing the physical amount of film stock they had to produce. By the time of Griffith's films the era of "factory filmmaking," in which there were clearly defined roles for directors, cinematographers, script supervisors, and so on, was in full swing. Scripts became elaborate blueprints for the production of films, and advances in editing allowed for films to be shot in the cheapest and most efficient manner and then assembled in the correct order for exhibition.

Some of the major studios still in existence today began as chains of nickelodeons (e.g., Warner Brothers, Universal, Paramount, and Fox). These exhibitors quickly saw the advantages of producing their own films in order to ensure a steady supply for their theatres and to bypass the system of competitive bidding for films that drove profits up for producers (who would sell their films to the highest bidder) at the expense of exhibitors. Thus was born the studio system: a system in which a small number of companies became **vertically integrated**, controlling the production and distribution of films that they would then exhibit in their own theatres.

There is one other issue we need to raise with respect to film production in its early years. In early, pre-sound cinema, film technology *and* films themselves were often imported from Europe to North America. In the first years of film, France, England, and Germany were sites of film production that rivalled the United States. By 1920, the United States had established itself as the global centre of film production. There are a number of reasons for the sudden dominance of U.S. filmmaking. Most significant was the impact of the First World War (1914–18) on film production in Europe. While film production on the continent was shut down, U.S. companies rushed to fill the continued global demand for film products. For example, by 1916, 60 percent of the films shown in Argentina and 95 pecrent of the films exhibited in Australia originated in the United States. The establishment of the U.S. film industry in California helped to solidify the U.S. position through the availability of cheap land and non-unionized labour in a perfect climate for year-round production. Finally, the gains that the U.S. film industry made during the war allowed it to spend far more money on production values than its European counterparts even after the war. This continues to be the case today: there has been no wholly European–financed film made for more than US$50 million to date, an amount that is closer to the *average* cost of a U.S. feature film.

The Studio System The 1920s were a period of enormous growth in the U.S. film industry. Between 1922 and 1930 investment in the film industry rose from US$78 million to $850 million, and average film attendance doubled between 1922 and 1928 from 40 million to 80 million people per week. The studio system marks the fullest expression of the factory film system. The five major studios and the "little three" (see Table 4.1) kept all of the staff required to make a film, from actors and directors to cinematographers and stagehands, under exclusive contract to a specific studio. Films were assembled based on the available inhouse elements: scripts were assigned to the available directors, cast with those actors who were under contract but not working on other films being made by the studio, and so on. Humphrey Bogart was cast in the lead role of the film *The Maltese Falcon* only because bigger stars were busy doing other projects; such stories of studio-era Hollywood are legion.

Table 4.1 The Studio System

The Five "Majors"	• Paramount
	• MGM (Metro-Goldwyn-Mayer)
	• Fox
	• Warner Bros.
	• RKO (Radio-Keith-Orpheum)
The Little Three	• Universal
	• Columbia
	• United Artists
Independents	• Samuel Goldwyn
	• David O. Selznick
	• Hebert Biberman
"B" Movie Producers	• Roger Corman, Ed Wood, Russ Meyer

Source: Hollywood Directors. Reprinted with permission.

The studio era is also characterized by an unprecedented degree of economic and corporate integration in the film industry. Studios owned all aspects of the industry, from production to distribution to exhibition. For example, by the 1930s Paramount owned 1,210 theatres in North America, which would, of course, exhibit Paramount films exclusively. The studio era is also the period in which the major companies, in a bid to outdo one another, built opulent theatres to capture the attention of audiences. As a result of their control over the industry, independent film production in the United States dried up, with the exception of films put together by a few major producers. Independents found it difficult to get their films financed, mainly because of the difficulty in finding locations to screen their films once completed. Foreign films more or less faded from the U.S. cultural landscape. The themes of movies also narrowed considerably in comparison to cinema's early years, with the fictional drama becoming *the* genre of Hollywood filmmaking.

In 1946, Hollywood recorded its highest box office and attendance figures of all time at a figure of 98 million tickets sold per week. From this point on, however, the studio system entered a precipitous decline that was to endure for the better part of three decades. The film industry encountered two major challenges. First, in 1948 the U.S. Supreme Court ruled that the eight largest studios were guilty of violating antitrust laws enacted at the turn of the century in order to prevent the creation of monopolies or oligopolies in American business. The studios were forced to sell off major parts of their assets, in particular their theatre chains, which opened the way for independent, nonstudio productions. Second, the mid-1940s to the mid-1960s saw a shift in American movie-going habits. In part, this was the result of the movement of the middle classes after the Second World War from the cities to the suburbs, which left many large theatres devoid of the audiences needed to sustain them. In combination with the growth in television ownership (90 percent of U.S. homes owned a television by the end of the 1950s), the film industry was badly damaged: profits declined by a shocking 74 percent between 1947 and 1957. The film industry responded to these changes in ways that would begin to bear fruit only from the mid-1970s onward. Films began to be made for specific segments of the audience: children's films, movies aimed at teens, more serious dramas for adults, and so on. Foreign and "art" films, imported for distribution from abroad, were once again shown, though seldom outside of major urban centres.

Hollywood Renaissance   Before these responses to the decline of cinema-going could take hold, the decade between 1967 and 1976 saw a remarkable flowering of U.S. cinema. Eschewing the limits and standard narratives that characterized classic Hollywood cinema, a number of young directors redefined the parameters of film form and content. Often dealing with edgy narratives on contemporary themes, the films of directors such as Robert Altman, Arthur Penn, Martin Scorsese, and Francis Ford Coppola (all graduates of recently established film school programs) captured the imaginations of a society that was undergoing significant changes as a result of the Sixties counterculture and the social movements associated with this period.

   This era of filmmaking is now often lamented as a lost or squandered opportunity for the creation of serious American cinema. The lingering belief in the inherent connection between independent production and quality filmmaking (a connection that has been revived in the recent use of the term "independent" as a term of approbation) originates with the films of this era. While filmmakers were able to exercise a degree of control over their films that harkened back to the days of early cinema, films such as *Bonnie and Clyde*, *The Godfather I* and *II*, *Nashville*, and *Taxi Driver* were nevertheless still produced and distributed under the auspices of major production companies. Whatever their aesthetic successes, the remnants of the studio system continued to assert their influence on these films and their directors. Indeed, there is a way in which this era functions as a kind of laboratory in which different models for the reorganization of the film industry could be tested out. The kind of independent production that took place during this period, which brought together all of the personnel necessary to create a film on a film-by-film basis, did create the conditions for more idiosyncratic filmmaking than the old studio-based production system. At the same time, it also created a model for the mode of production that would take place in the blockbuster era that followed.

The Blockbuster Era   During the past twenty-five years, there have been numerous shifts and developments in Hollywood filmmaking—so much so that to claim that one could describe all the shifts and changes in one general category misses some important nuances. Nevertheless, the dominant idea and ideal of Hollywood film since the breakout success of *Jaws* and *Star Wars* is captured in the idea of the "blockbuster": films that shatter the barriers between market segments and draw crowds who line up around the block. Blockbuster films are crafted as events or spectacles—they are highly anticipated and carefully controlled. In order to maximize profits, distributors plan the release dates of different films to coincide with periods of high attendance (the Christmas season, early summer, etc.) *or* low attendance (which is when serious or "mature" films are released), and to minimize competition with other blockbuster movies (*Spider-Man* and *Attack of the Clones* were released on separate weekends in order to avoid impacting on each other's profits, as were *Harry Potter and the Philosopher's Stone* and *The Fellowship of the Ring*). Though no longer organized into oligopolies as during the studio system, during the blockbuster era the majors have once again come to dominate: from 1970 to 1987, films produced by the big studios generated 84 percent of box office revenues in Canada and the United States.

The production process has changed considerably from earlier eras. The big companies, such as Paramount, Warner Bros., and 20th-Century Fox, are now primarily finance and distribution companies. Like much of the rest of global economy, the production of films has been reorganized into a more flexible system. Production has become the responsibility of individual producers, financed by the old studios, who rent production space, equipment, and personnel on a short-term, film-by-film basis. There are very few stars and directors under "exclusive" contracts to production companies; everything is done on the spur of the moment during available windows of opportunity for directors, stars, and production crew.

The exhibition of films has also changed in ways that have impacted the film industry in general. Beginning with the creation of spaces such as the 18-screen Cineplex theatre in Toronto's Eaton Centre, new exhibition spaces have been designed with multiple screens on which a range of movies appealing to different market segments can be screened. Distributors wield enormous power over exhibitors. Especially for popular films, distributors can dictate the number of screens that an exhibition company must run its films on and the minimum length of time that the films have to be screened. Independent exhibitors have once again faced difficulties in competing for films against large exhibition companies, such as Cineplex Odeon and Famous Players in Canada.

Actual film screenings currently make up only one small part of the overall revenue generated through the production and distribution of films. Companies can now recoup costs in numerous ways: through the licensing of secondary screening opportunities (after the opening period but before video distribution); through distribution in the form of VHS tapes, DVDs, and cable and broadcast TV rights; through various forms of merchandising, especially in the case of children's films; and, finally, even through such mechanisms as the sale of advertising space within movies themselves in the form of product placements (Reese's Pieces in *E.T.*, FedEx and Wilson in *Castaway*, and, most significantly, Ford and others in *Die Another Day*, whose total product placement fees virtually paid for the production of the film).

Production and Meaning

This brief history of Hollywood filmmaking highlights the huge number of changes that the industry has undergone over the past century. A more detailed history would introduce further divisions and differences in the production process. One of the first things that this history should tell us is that although we might be able to watch *The Birth of a*

Nation and *The Fellowship of the Ring* at home on the same evening, they are *not* the same kind of cultural object. We refer to both as *movies* or *films*, but we should not forget that they were created under very different conditions. If we obscure this fact (which we all too often do), we risk forgetting the ways in which different systems of production create different forms of popular culture. For instance, the difference in dominant film themes and styles in each era is not simply an accident of history; nor can it be accounted for as shifts that occur on their own (that is, without influence by the productive process). At the same time, we need to be cautious about drawing direct lines of influence between style and production. Our aim in this chapter is not to argue for the reduction of theme to the logic of production practice, but to insist that we consider production when we explore the social meanings and significance of popular cultural objects.

A summary of our discussion in this section is provided in Table 4.2.

Suggested Activity 4.2

In what ways might this production history differ in the case of popular music? Unlike film, popular music combines a form of craft labour—that is, the labour of a small number of individuals practising a craft that is in some sense pre-industrial—with mass, standardized production. In addressing the question, make sure to keep this point in mind.

CULTURAL PRODUCTION TODAY

Just as production techniques and systems have changed over time in Hollywood film, they continue to evolve in significant ways in other parts of popular culture. The final section of this chapter looks at recent developments in cultural production that have an impact on the ways we examine popular culture today. As you will see right away, these developments constitute an extension of aspects of the culture industries thesis and offer important challenges to it. For example, the expansion of the Internet as a means of cultural communication and the growth of the digital production of sound and images offers cultural producers the chance to circumvent the typical channels of cultural production. But before we celebrate the birth of a new cyber-utopia, we need to be conscious of the fact that these alternative productive practices exist in a world of popular-culture production that continues to be dominated by a few major corporations. While bands with limited resources can now make their music available to people around the world through the Internet, it remains true that even a considerably weakened music industry has far greater distribution and marketing powers (and so, also, the ability to generate massive profits) than any independent band that relies on the Internet. David Bowie, Prince, Public Enemy and other major musical acts have attempted to distribute their music online with little success.

Table 4.2 Production Modes and Film Styles

Period	Production System	Theme/Style	Representative Films
Early Cinema (1895–1920s)	• Independent • International • Power divided between production and distribution	• Actualités • Varied styles • Experimental	*A Trip to the Moon* (1902); *The Birth of a Nation* (1915)
Studio System (1920s–1960s)	• Oligopolistic • Vertical integration • American	• Fictional drama • Classical Hollywood narrative (social conflict/ love stories)	*City Lights* (1931); *Stagecoach* (1939); *Strangers on a Train* (1951); *From Here to Eternity* (1953)
"Hollywood Renaissance" (1965–75)	• Independent/ corporate • "Return" of foreign film • Production	• Experimental and critical • *Cinema verité* • Documentary	*Bonnie and Clyde* (1967); *McCabe and Mrs. Miller* (1971); *Mean Streets* (1973); *The Conversation* (1974)
Blockbuster Era (1975–present)	• American • High budget • Synergy • Distribution/ cross-production • Video/TV	• Classical narrative • Special effects • Spectacle	*Jaws* (1976); *Terminator 2* (1991); *Jurassic Park* (1993); *Lord of the Rings* (*Trilogy:* 2001–2003)

Lifestyle Marketing and Market Segmentation

A recent full-page newspaper ad for Cadillac mimics the timelines that one often finds in art history books. The line begins in the dark recesses of history with an image of the Lascaux cave-paintings, which are amongst the earliest examples of human artistic expression. Next in line is the paradigmatic expression of Ancient Greek sculpture, the Venus de Milo, followed by Leonardo da Vinci's *Mona Lisa* and, closer to the present, a painting by Picasso. Bringing us up to date, at the end of the timeline are photos of three vehicles—the new Cadillac XLR, the CTS, and the Escalade XTS (a truck). The caption to this ad reads: "It seems to be humanity's destiny to find new ways to express beauty. Presenting the latest installment."

It is tempting to dismiss the artistic pretensions of this advertisement: surely, a Cadillac is not a work of art in the same sense as the paintings by Da Vinci and Picasso. But this would be to miss the real insight the ad offers into the character of contemporary popular cultural production. To an ever-increasing degree, as Celia Lury has argued in *Consumer Culture*, the production of all consumer goods has been subjected to a process of stylization. Consumer objects have become increasingly aestheticized: like art objects, it is as often as not how something "looks" that guarantees that it will sell, *not* what the object actually does or is used for. This stylization of contemporary production, Lury suggests, was achieved via a long process "through the introduction of the principles of fashion to an ever-wider range of products, often following the model developed for the product category of clothing" (61).

Product Packaging The most common place in which this stylization or aestheticization is encountered on a day-to-day basis remains product packaging, whether we think of this in terms of the enticing photographs on cereal boxes or of the first great form of aesthetic packaging: album-cover art. But the link between the stylization of production and fashion goes deeper than this. Mimicking the fashion seasons, new models of automobiles and consumer electronics, such as stereo equipment, computers, and cell phones, are "released" annually or bi-annually. Bending the supposedly immutable laws of time, the resplendent curves and shiny surfaces of *next* year's car models are available in the summer of the preceding year. Most brands of cell phones and MP3 players are designed with removable faceplates that can be changed and adapted by consumers to coordinate with their clothing or to express their artistic sensibilities. The availability at any one time of numerous models of Nike running shoes, of sleek modernist household appliances designed by architect Michael Graves for Target stores, and of trendy clothing created by designer Mossimo for Zellers all point to ways in which style and design have become essential elements of the production process, if not *the* essential element in the design of products for end-users. And no one knows this better than the shops connected to art museums, which have used the general stylization of popular culture to boost their profits through the sale of all manner of knick-knacks whose main appeal is their artistic style.

Lifestyle The increasing prominence and importance of style in popular culture production goes hand-in-hand with a redefinition of consumption as an aesthetic or artistic exercise. This shift is captured perfectly by the term "lifestyle." The idea that each of us has a lifestyle—a way of living, consuming, and being that uniquely defines us—has come to prominence only over the past several decades. Though lifestyle can be used to refer broadly to the way one lives—in the city or the country, a laid-back personality as opposed to a "work hard, play hard" mentality—the element of style emerges mainly out of what and how one consumes, and especially how one consumes popular culture (see Chapter Five for an extended discussion of this point). The idea of life being akin to a work of art has a longer heritage, with origins in the mid-nineteenth century idea of the urban *flâneur* and the figure of the dandy explored by, amongst others, the writer Oscar Wilde in *The Picture of Dorian Gray*. What has changed is that the expansion of consumption in the twentieth century has generalized the belief in lifestyle.

This has had some significant social consequences. For instance, the critic John Seabrook has suggested that as a result of lifestyle consumption the divisions between high and low culture, between "highbrow" and "lowbrow," have broken down into what he refers to as "nobrow." In perfect synchrony with lifestyle consumption, Seabrook argues that, in nobrow, "commercial culture is a source of status and currency rather than the thing that the elite define themselves against" (106). The question is no longer whether one participates in popu-lar culture; rather, it is *how* one participates in it—and, through the consumer choices that one makes or refuses to make, the kind of lifestyle that one carves out of popular culture.

At one level, we can see the relentless production and consumption of style as a perfect embodiment of the idea of pseudo-individualization that Horkheimer and Adorno describe. The idea that increasingly stylized forms of production have transformed standardized popular culture into a situation in which everyone can assume the role of the "modernist notion of artist as hero, as the advocate of radical values, challenging the consensus of public life and disturbing the complacency of domestic life" (Lury 75) seems to confirm the Frankfurt School's worries about popular culture. But things aren't quite so simple. The stylization of cultural production has extended and enhanced the power and role that popular culture plays in everyday life and in the economy. But it has also introduced surprising challenges and problems for the producers of contemporary popular culture. As Simon During suggested in his criticisms of Horkheimer and Adorno, contemporary popular culture has becoming increasingly variegated, diverse, and unruly.

In the 1950s, cultural production was, in general, geared toward the mass market as a whole. Since then, there have been greater and greater degrees of **market segmentation**, with the result being that cultural producers have to gear their products to increasingly small and specialized segments of the overall group of consumers. This trend has perhaps been most evident in television programming. In the United States, the three major networks have tried to combat declining overall audiences by adopting the techniques of their competitors: cable networks defined around specific lifestyle interests (Outdoor Life Network, Food Network, etc.) or programming to specific demographic groups (e.g., the WB network targets audiences under 35). The segmentation of the consumer market has affected producers of clothing, food, and consumer electronics as well.

As just one example, in an effort to boost its stagnant sales the Coca-Cola Corporation has unveiled an ambitious strategy to design specific beverages for up to 500 clearly defined segments of the market (e.g., children under three whose parents will allow them to drink only milk products, teens interested in skateboarding, adults who work long hours but eat healthy foods, etc.), which will be further adapted to account for national and regional differences (Stevenson).

Of course, the segmentation of the market presents producers with possibilities in addition to problems. There is the potential to tap into new markets and so to expand profits. However, the problems are significant, and go beyond, for instance, the energy and coordination required to produce thirty models of athletic shoes instead of one or two. The idea of life as style may in some sense be a false one. But inasmuch as people take it seriously, there is some evidence that they have grown more suspicious of certain forms of advertising and marketing and are resistant to being categorized even in micro-market segments. The more producers need to concentrate on style and the more (and more different) styles they have to produce, the more likely it has become that they will miss the mark when it comes to targeting their intended audiences.

In a recent interview, the heads of three of the major U.S. networks admitted that they had no idea that television programs such as *Survivor* and *The Sopranos* would be hits (Hirschberg). Their grasp on what the public "wants" is tenuous at best, and their ability as producers to dictate to audiences seems equally limited, which is attested to by the number of cancelled "sure-fire hits" that litter the television landscape each season. One of the reactions to this situation has been an increase in more invasive forms of marketing and advertising that try to grasp the moods and preferences of consumers and audiences in advance of their full cultural expression (for more on this, see our discussion of "coolhunting" in Chapter Five).

Suggested Activity 4.3

How does the re-introduction of "retro" fashions and styles contribute to lifestyle consumption? In *The Conquest of Cool*, the cultural critic Thomas Frank suggests that "retro's vision of the past as a floating style catalog from which we can choose quaint wardrobes but from which we are otherwise disconnected is, in many respects, hip consumerism's proudest achievement: it simultaneously reinforces contemporary capitalism's curious ahistorical vision and its feverish cycling of obsolescence" (227). How does this reinforce, challenge, or expand our discussion in this section?

Copyleft: Challenging Copyright

It is vain for painters or poets to endeavour to invent without materials on which the mind may work, and from which invention must originate. Nothing can come of nothing.

— Joshua Reynolds

Though it has remained a central idea of Western culture since Romanticism, artists and writers do not create authentically only when they do so autonomously—that is, when they are off on their own, away from people and the influence of the society in which they live. Such ideas of artistic autonomy might help to reinforce our belief in creative "genius"; what they fail to do is capture the complex ways in which cultural productions are always an expression of the broader social and cultural contexts out of which they originate.

This is a long way of saying that there is no such thing as absolute innovation in cultural production. Rather, as Joshua Reynolds suggested in 1797, cultural production depends on creative borrowing and adaptation; whether this is consciously done or not, it is out of such adaptation that "new" culture is produced and through such borrowing that cultures remain vibrant and alive.

Sampling   One of the clearest examples of such creative and productive "borrowing" today is in rap and hip-hop music, which often samples previously recorded songs in interesting and provocative ways. For instance, Jay-Z's anthemic "Hard Knock Life" employs the chorus of "It's the Hard-Knock Life" from the musical *Annie*; P.Diddy produced an album with samples of popular Eighties songs, including "Been Around the World," which borrows from David Bowie's "Let's Dance"; Maestro's "Stick to Yo' Vision" uses The Guess Who's "These Eyes" in a memorable fashion; and, finally, the Dream Warriors made their mark by using the distinctive notes from the theme to the 1970s Canadian game show *Definition* in their "My Definition of a Boombastic Jazz Style" (since re-used as the title music of the *Austin Powers* films). There are similar examples of re-using or borrowing in film remakes (e.g., Gus Van Sant's attempt to produce a scene-by-scene remake of Alfred Hitchcock's *Psycho*), in literary adaptations, and in the visual arts (Douglas Gordon's "Twenty-Four Hour Psycho" stretches the Hitchcock original to a full day by projecting it slowly frame by frame).

Legal Issues   Over the past decade in particular, the use of borrowed materials has begun to run into legal roadblocks. As Sven Lütticken writes, even though "some sort of appropriation of pre-existing material is ... integral to many forms of contemporary cultural practice ... these are increasingly under pressure from armies of lawyers" (89). One of the major issues in contemporary cultural production concerns the use and abuse of copyright legislation to limit and control free expression. Disputes over copyright form just one of the many disputes over **intellectual property** today, a category that includes not just copyright, but also trademarks and patents. For producers of popular culture, there is a great deal to be gained by asserting and maintaining one's copyright privileges. As cultural production has become increasingly susceptible to copying and illegal redistribution (something that might have been difficult with a painting is easy with a music CD), corporations and cultural producers alike have ever more stridently asserted their copyright in order to control all the profits generated by their products. In many cases, however, it seems that the original intent of copyright has been subverted and that the eagerness with which copyright claims have been pursued have reduced culture to mere profit-making and have made free, unfettered cultural borrowing all but impossible.

The Evolution of Copyright   The history of copyright differs from country to country. In the English-speaking world, it first developed alongside book printing as a form of state control or censorship. The Crown granted publishers the right to produce a specific book over a certain period of time, less to guarantee publishers a profit than to get access to and approve its contents. The first violations of copyright were attempts to circumvent state censorship, as in the "forbidden best-sellers" of pre-revolutionary France that the historian Robert Darnton has explored. Copyright in its contemporary sense "was stimulated by the wish to enable authors to make a decent living and hence be able to create new works" (Lütticken 94). By 1831, copyright legislation in the United States covered books, maps, engravings and etchings, and musical compositions. By limiting the reproduction of these works to the original producer of them, the goal was to boost the indigenous cultural production of the young republic and to create a self-sustaining cultural sphere.

While copyright legislation may have been developed in order to protect cultural producers, in the context of contemporary cultural production copyright seems to have become a tool of those corporations most directly involved in the culture industry. There are two kinds of copyright infringements that need to be separated in our discussion: the first involves direct infringement of existing copyright standards, while the second concerns increasingly suspect challenges to cultural appropriation, parody, and the artistic use of popular culture. The continuing debate over file-sharing services, such as Napster and KaZaA, and the illegal pirating of videos, DVDs, music CDs, and computer software occurring worldwide are examples of the first kind of dispute. There's little question that sharing music files (for example) constitutes copyright violation.

What these forms of copyright violation have highlighted, however, is the degree to which copyright works in favour of corporations rather than cultural producers and audiences. In terms of the latter, the popularity of Napster constituted a public rejection of a kind of standardized production described by Horkheimer and Adorno: tired of being sold overpriced CDs with a few songs that they desired and a bunch of "filler" material, audiences could now access only the songs that they wanted. Napster also presented consumers with a chance to sample music outside of the limited frame of popular music imposed by the marketing and distribution practices of major record labels in an effort to maximize profits. File sharing also brought to light the dirty half-secret of the contemporary music industry, which is that the artists who create the music see very little profit. While the band Metallica sued Napster in a heavily publicized case, other artists saw file sharing as an opportunity to provide their music directly to their audiences, thereby circumventing the music industry altogether.

The second form of dispute over copyright has become more prominent as of late. These are disputes over cultural appropriation of various kinds, and have come to fore as the idea of what constitutes copyright is stretched farther and farther. Copyright has now been applied to thematic *similarities*, to original music compositions that supposedly *sound like* something else (as in the case of John Fogerty, former lead singer of Creedence Clearwater Revival, sued by his former record company for songs on his solo album that sounded too much like CCR), and even to bits of lyrics. It now seems as if copyright covers the general *idea* of a product as much as the product itself. Mattel, which jealously guards its major product, Barbie, has been one of the companies to press its claim over its product the farthest. On different occasions, Mattel has sued rival producers of female toy figures on the basis that they "own" the general proportions of Barbie's surreal measurements (bust-waist-hip); blocked distribution of director Todd Haynes' film *Superstar: The Karen Carpenter Story*, which uses Barbie action figures to tell the life of the pop star who succumbed to anorexia; ended artist Mark Napier's *Distorted Barbie* project through a threatened suit; and even (though unsuccessfully) took on the band Aqua over its song "Barbie Girl."

Mattel is hardly the only corporation to engage in such practices. The Disney corporation has also sued artists for making use of its iconic images in artworks and has even effectively blocked publication of a critical biography of Walt Disney himself, on the basis that it would hurt corporate profits by damaging the image of wholesome fun that the company has built up around its brand. It seems today that almost every successful pop-culture object has been subjected to litigation. The author of the *Harry Potter* series, J.K. Rowling, has been sued (unsuccessfully) for supposedly stealing the term "Muggle," and she and her publisher have in turn pursued attempts to cash in on the Potter name, as in the case of the parodic Russian novels by Dimitri Yemetz, author of *Tanya Grotter and the Magic Double Bass*.

Who Is Popular Culture For?   The suits over the artistic re-use of popular cultural images and the use of materials for the purposes of parody or criticism raise a more general question about cultural production today: Just who and what is popular culture for? Audiences and artists seem to believe that popular culture, even if produced by large corporations, forms part of the commonly held stock of images, sounds, experiences, and ideas that make up contemporary experience, standing alongside great works of literature and masterpieces of artistic expression. Corporations seem to believe otherwise. For them, cultural production represents profits to be made—or lost, if copyright isn't enforced. The bending of copyright in the direction of corporate interests threatens the cultural commons that Reynolds describes in the quotation that begins this section. A great deal of the art made in this century, for example, has made creative use of popular culture, from Marcel Duchamp's "readymades" (the transformation of everyday objects into art) to the Surrealists through to rap and contemporary art. These possibilities now seem threatened, as does our more general access to the images of art history, which have been slowly but surely assembled into image data banks by corporations such as Microsoft, which now holds access to copyright of many artworks. The extension and expansion of copyright benefits few at the expense of many; it constitutes one of the major sites of control over popular culture in the world today.

Computer Software Copyright   One of the most successful responses to the extension of corporate control through copyright has been in the field of computer software, where the stakes over intellectual property have been perhaps the highest. The "product" created by computer software companies is in many respects immaterial: the product as such isn't

The copyleft symbol invites users of a product to make new creative and original uses of it.

the CD the program comes on but rather the program itself, which doesn't exist physically in the same way that even a film does. Software is also uniquely susceptible to being copied easily and exactly. As such, the software industry has ferociously defended the intellectual property that it has created in order to safeguard its investment both in the products and in the profits they generate. Protecting intellectual property in software has meant that companies have closed off access to the source code of their programs. No one can access this code except other companies who have paid a licensing fee in order to create programs that work in conjunction (for example) with the various incarnations of the Microsoft Windows operating system.

In response to this closed system, programmers such as Richard Stallman and Linus Torvalds have created forms of free, open-source software such as GNU and Linux. Open-source software can be used by anyone free of charge. Because the software source code is "open"—that is, accessible by everyone—not only can new programs be created to work with Linux by programmers anywhere in the world, but also the bugs (or errors) that plague most complex software programs can be pointed out and repaired in the basic code itself. With free software, the often high cost of software programs is mitigated entirely. "Copylefting" is Stallman's innovative way of using copyright against itself. Free software that is made available under a general public licence legally requires all software derived from it—"even those that carry only a tiny fragment of the original code" (Stallabrass 144)—to be copylefted; that is, made public and accessible to all.

As cultural production becomes increasingly important to the economy at large, struggles over the ownership of popular culture are likely to become more important. The *de facto* assertion of U.S. copyright regulations as the global standard through the auspices of the World Intellectual Property Organization is certain to have an impact on the ways in which popular culture is produced and distributed in the future.

Digital Production

For much of the past century, the forms of production of popular culture have effectively ruled out mass participation in many kinds of mainstream popular cultural production. Producing a film, television program, or record album "independently"—that is, outside of major production systems—was difficult, if not impossible; as we have seen above, the creation of a standard 35-mm film narrative requires the use of enormously expensive equipment, the use of equally expensive fixed capital (in the form of sound studios, sets, etc.), and, finally, a considerable investment in production personnel for the creation of even a modest film. This was true of television programming and music production as well, and was a general rule for most forms of popular cultural production. And production was just one part of the problem; even if one could make an independent film, the ability to distribute and market it to a wide audience was severely circumscribed by the degree of access one had to the "official" or standard systems of popular cultural production.

One of the major developments in popular culture over the past decade has been the introduction of new forms of production and distribution that have challenged and circumvented older modes of popular cultural production. The digital revolution in image and sound production, recording, and distribution promises to change the shape of popular culture in ways that we can only speculate about at the present time. There have been a variety of formats that have allowed cultural producers to take control of the production and distribution of their own products, from Super 8 movie cameras to four-track recorders that allowed "garage bands" to produce their own audio tapes. Forms of digital production not only permit more effective distribution of these products—whether via sound and image files shared over the Internet or through the pressing of CDs and DVDs that retain sound and image quality—but also increasingly place "small" or independent producers on par with major producers, at least in terms of the quality of sounds and images produced.

There is effectively no important difference between popular music produced within and that produced outside of the music industry (at least not in terms of sound quality), which is why the challenge of digital production has been felt most acutely to date in music. In terms of film production, however, a gap remains, due in part to the extreme visual density of 35-mm film in comparison to the highest-quality digital video and in part to the cinematic spectacle of special effects in mainstream Hollywood cinema.

The Impact of New Technologies on Popular Culture   Even so, digital production has had a decisive impact on the production of popular culture, both inside and outside the dominant forms of production. On television, "reality" television shows make use of lightweight digital cameras to record perspectives that more traditional production techniques would be unable to capture (e.g., the "helmet cam" used during some segments on *Fear Factor*). Since the popularity of *The Blair Witch Project* (1999), major studios have released a number of films shot entirely on digital video, such as Richard Linklater's *Tape* (2001) and numerous others that have incorporated digital video into standard 35-mm filmmaking (e.g., Steven Soderbergh's *Traffic* [2000]). For some filmmakers, digital video has presented an opportunity to rethink the medium of film in a wholesale way, by rejecting the limits imposed by standard production practices. Eschewing artificial lighting, sound stages, sets, and so on, filmmakers who have adopted the Dogme 95 manifesto, which calls for a return to single-camera filmmaking with an absolute minimal use of non-natural lighting and sound (it actually calls for none at all, but this has been difficult to achieve in practice), have produced a series of films celebrated for their innovation and freshness.

These uses of digital video are hardly revolutionary. But there are spaces and places in which digital video has already played an important new role. The low cost and high quality of digital video has produced an explosion in the production of documentary film, in two different senses of this term. First, digital video has revived the flagging fate of feature-length documentary productions, as has (for that matter) the ability of independent companies to distribute documentaries in DVD and VHS formats in place of film stock.

Second, digital video has been used by groups and individuals around the world to document social and political realities that mainstream media miss or deliberately avoid reporting. Video has played an important role in documenting the abuse of state power during anti-globalization demonstrations. Mainstream media outlets, including the Canadian Broadcasting Corporation, covered the demonstrations against the Free Trade Agreement of the Americas (FTAA) in Quebec City in 2001 largely from the perspective of the government officials who were meeting behind the chain-link fence separating most of Old Quebec from the rest of the city. From this perspective, the use of pepper spray, water cannons, and plastic bullets against the demonstrators was justified by the perceived threat that demonstrators posed to these officials. The tens of thousands of hours of footage shot by the demonstrators with digital video cameras offered a very different view of the demonstrations. Not only did these images highlight the numerous unprovoked attacks on peaceful demonstrators by police, but by allowing the demonstrators to articulate their own views on the FTAA they challenged the repeated assertions by the mainstream media that the protestors knew almost nothing about what they were demonstrating against.

Through its ability to bypass the systems that have defined the production of popular culture for much of the twentieth century, digital production promises to shake up the production of popular culture. Though it is unlikely to re-democratize popular culture to the extent that its most optimistic supporters suggest, it offers at least the potential for new forms of and relationships to popular culture.

SUMMARY

Beginning with an acknowledgment of the links between contemporary popular culture and economics, this chapter has concentrated on the need to examine the production of culture as a key element of an overall understanding of the function and significance of contemporary popular culture. The chapter addresses the following key points:

- Art and artistic value do not exist in an inverse relationship to money and business. The relationship between the value of a cultural object or experience and the ways in which it was created or produced is complex and needs to be examined on a case-by-case basis.
- The cultural industry thesis proposed by Max Horkheimer and Theodor Adorno to explain the situation of standardized cultural production remains a productive way to think about popular culture. However, as many critics have pointed out, there are real limits and problems with the culture industry thesis that need to be addressed in order to continue to make use of its insights for an investigation of pop culture.
- Assessing the circumstances of popular cultural production requires attention to specific histories (e.g., Crisco) as well as to long-term changes and developments (as we showed in our brief history of Hollywood film production).

- Cultural production continues to develop and change in a variety of areas. The intensification of lifestyle marketing, disputes over copyright, and the new possibilities introduced by various forms of digital production have created new and uncharted contexts for contemporary cultural production.

SUGGESTIONS FOR FURTHER READING

Dorland, Michael, ed. *The Canadian Culture Industries: Problems, Perspectives, and Policies.* Toronto: Lorimer, 1996.

Ellis, Jack C. *A History of Film.* Fourth Edition. Needham Heights, MA: Allyn & Bacon, 1995.

Hesmondhalgh, David. *The Cultural Industries.* London: Sage, 2002.

Nealon, Jeffrey T., and Caren Irr, ed. *Rethinking the Frankfurt School: Alternative Legacies of Cultural Critique.* Albany, NY: State University of New York Press, 2002.

Rosenbaum, Jonathan. *Movie Wars: How Hollywood and the Media Limit What Movies We Can See.* Chicago: A Capella Books, 2000.

Chapter 5

The Consuming Life

INTRODUCTION: BACK TO "NORMAL"

In the immediate aftermath of the events of September 11, 2001, a large number of discourses started to circulate in both political circles and amongst members of the general public. Most of these were concerned directly with the events and their political and economic consequences. In order to better understand "9-11," discussions began on the concept of terrorism, the responsibility of the West to the rest of the world (especially the degree to which it had evaded this responsibility), the "clash of civilizations" (Islam vs. the West), the role of the United States as the world's policeman (and the problems with the role), the problems and benefits of military action, the implications of the new security measures adopted in a number of countries, and so on.

Perhaps more surprisingly, what also emerged was a debate on the underlying values of Western societies and the appropriateness of these values. In the days and weeks following 9-11, political and business leaders encouraged Americans and Canadians in particular to continue to shop, travel, and spend money (see Close-Up 5.1). New Mexico Senator Pete Domenici, for instance, stated "I'm hopeful the American people will ... buy the car they planned to buy, not wait around. The terrorists will have won if consumers wait around because they're fearful." Many leaders expressed that to go out and shop was important as a means not only of sustaining the economy, but also of defending "our" fundamental cultural values.

Even if statements such as Domenici's captured something real about the economic and social practices important to the contemporary Western way of life, there was for many people something disturbing about this frank admission of the central role played in our lives by consumption and consumerism. In the immediate wake of 9-11, the public

Consumption and 9-11

If our airline [industry] goes down, the terrorists will have won.

> —Texas senator Kay Bailey Hutchison, on the need for industry-wide bailouts, in the *Dallas Morning News* (September 18, 2001)

As trivial as it may seem, every time we don't freely enjoy our recreational activities, that's a win for the terrorists.

> —Sports editor Alan Hunt, writing in the *Lompoc (California) Record* (September 30, 2001)

We cannot allow terrorism to get a victory ... by changing our way of life. That way the terrorists will have won.

> —John Fund, *Wall Street Journal* editorial page editor, on CNN's *TalkBack Live* (October 11, 2001)

I understand why some parents are worried, but we can't let the terrorists win.... More than ever, people need the kind of escapism bands like ours provide.

> —Christopher Read, saxophonist for the Frank Scott Bunnell High School Marching Band and Guard of Stratford, Connecticut, arguing in favour of his band's appearance in the Tournament of Roses Parade in Pasadena, California, on New Year's Day, in the *New York Times* (November 4, 2001)

To me, the terrorists have certainly succeeded if so few of you participate in a companywide effort to get together.

> —Martha Stewart, in an e-mail to staffers at *Martha Stewart Living Omnimedia* urging them to host staff holiday parties in their own homes following her cancellation of the company's annual Christmas bash, reported in the *New York Post* (November 18, 2001)

I want women in evening gowns. I want to see men in tuxedos. I want elegance and class. I will not let terror win.

> —Dagmar Dunlevy, president of the Hollywood Foreign Press Association, which stages the Golden Globes, on his vision for the 2002 event, reported in *Variety* (November 29, 2001)

If you don't want to let the terrorists defeat us, have that extra piece of cake and third drink.

> —Gucci designer Tom Ford in the *New York Times Magazine* (December 2, 2001)

Compiled by Christi Schuermer

stopped spending in an apparent attempt (or so the media told us) to recapture more "wholesome" values, whether this was expressed through a re-affirmation of familial relationships or connection to friends, or through a deliberate attempt to "slow down" and appreciate more greatly the days and weeks that we usually race through. Predictably, this decline in consumption caused a slowdown in the U.S. economy (something experienced to a far lesser degree in Canada after 9-11). A couple of years later, however, things are definitely "back to normal": the streets and malls are full of shoppers who are snapping up, among other things, memorabilia related to 9-11 (T-shirts, postcards, designer clothing, etc.), which appeared quickly in the stores of New York in the days and weeks after the tragedy.

Consumption Patterns

9-11 offers an example of the importance of consumption to contemporary culture, as well as the profound ambivalence that attends all forms of consumption. We consume endlessly and in multiple ways and forms, and not just when we slide money across a store counter and walk away with a bag of goodies. Consumer spending patterns are carefully monitored by both businesses and governments, since they have a direct impact on the overall state of the economy (see Close-Up 5.2). A tremor in the consumer confidence index, a measurement that tries to anticipate future consumer desires, can produce very real effects, including layoffs, business bankruptcies, and cutbacks to government programs in anticipation of declines in tax revenues.

Critiques of Consumerism   Consumption is a normal, everyday social practice around the world: in our increasingly complicated world, no one can produce everything they need (if they ever could), so the exchange of goods and services by individuals and institutions is a necessity. At the same time, consumption and consumerism are often treated as social ills. Consumerism has been associated by many critics with the rapid decline of the quality and character of social life, the result being a crass, utilitarian culture dominated by the ultimately empty pursuit of money and goods. Some of the social complexity of consumerism is captured by the fact that this uneasiness with it has become an occasion for further consumption, whether in the form of practices of consumption that express a desire for more "authentic" forms of consumption (organic food, Fair Trade coffees, holistic medicines, etc.) or through the purchase of cultural goods that criticize consumerism implicitly or explicitly (in films such as *Fight Club* and *American Beauty*, the music of bands such as Radiohead, NOFX, and Rage Against the Machine, books such as Michael Moore's *Stupid White Men* and Naomi Klein's *No Logo*, and so on).

While it is common enough to discount these criticisms by pointing out the simple contradiction produced by the sale of goods that criticize consumption (tracts against consumerism that activate further consumerism), such criticisms fail to capture adequately the full complexity of contemporary consumption. Nor do such criticisms manage to locate the ambivalence over consumption within definite geographic and social circumstances. According to the United Nations, in the year 2000 more than two

The Consumer Confidence Index

In the United States, consumer confidence is measured monthly through a survey of 5,000 representative households. The overall score is measured against a baseline of 100 established in 1985 (in September 2002, the index was 93.3). The index is based on responses to five survey questions: (1) an appraisal of the current business environment and (2) expectations about the business environment six months from the survey date; (3) appraisal of current employment conditions and (4) employment conditions six months down the road; and, finally, expectations about family income six months from the survey date.

This is a survey of subjective feelings about the economic environment. For economists and business leaders, it is important because it is such subjective reactions to economic circumstances that guide consumer behaviour much more than objective data. This is why there is often a disconnection between economic reports that pronounce the fundamental or underlying strengths of the economy (productivity levels, capital investment, etc.) and consumer behaviour that suggests otherwise (decline in stock investments, downturn in consumer spending, etc.).

and a half billion people spent less than US$2.00 per day, a figure that should act as a constant reminder of the limits of the discussions of consumption and popular culture both in this chapter and in cultural studies more generally. Around the world, the main problem that people experience with consumption is not that it has come to make their lives empty; that is, not that there is too much consumption, but that there is too little—both of the necessities of life and of a wide range of other goods.

Whether we love or loathe it, consumption has become a key aspect of social life. If we are to make sense of its social significance and its key role in contemporary popular culture, we need to begin by understanding consumption as more than exchange. Economic measurements of consumption tend to focus narrowly on the instant of exchange, the moment that money and goods change hands. However, the cultural and social dynamics of consumption extend well beyond the moment of exchange. A study of consumption has to consider what takes place before and after exchange. Why do people engage in the forms of consumption that they do? What do people do with the objects and services that they consume? What symbolic meanings are contained in consumption? How is consumption connected to our deepest emotions, desires, and fantasies? These are the questions that will be explored in this chapter.

Suggested Activity 5.1

When do you shop? Do you ever find yourself deciding to "go shopping" in order to reward yourself, to alleviate stress, to buy gifts for others, and so on? What does it mean when consumption becomes an end in itself—that is, when the point of shopping is not necessarily to purchase any specific item or service, but mostly to engage in the act of consumption?

A BRIEF HISTORY OF CONSUMER CULTURE

In our introduction to this section, we have used a number of terms more or less interchangeably: consumption, **consumerism,** and consumer culture or society. In practice, the meanings of these terms overlap considerably; however, exploring contemporary consumption necessitates that we draw some distinction between these terms. As we saw in Chapter Four, in social theory consumption has long been opposed to production. Until relatively recently, scholars have paid far more attention to the processes of production than consumption: consumption has been understood as little more than the completion of the process of production, with production privileged as the site at which the most significant social processes take place. As Karl Marx expressed famously in his preface to *A Contribution to a Critique of Political Economy* (1859), it was the "relations of production"—that is, "the economic structure of society" (45)—that for him formed the real foundation of society. How human beings organized themselves productively determined to a large degree the social experiences and cultural possibilities of their society.

Even amongst sociologists and other social scientists unsympathetic to Marx's view of society, the idea that the form in which human beings organize production (i.e., how they organize their economy) is the most important determining characteristic of society has been central to social theory throughout most of the twentieth century. The outcome of this has been that the study of consumption has only slowly emerged from the shadow of production in the analysis of popular culture.

Commodities and Desire

Consumption—all of the practices commonly associated with what happens at the end of production—came to the fore of social studies only when it became clear that a new kind of society was emerging in the twentieth century: a consumer society, a historically unique form of society in which consumption plays not only an important, but even a central role. As a general concept describing a particular form of human interaction and kind of social relationship, practices of consumption pre-date the twentieth century. It is possible, of course, to apply the concept of consumption to exchanges dating back millennia—all the way back to at least the early development of money and even possibly before that if the most common meanings of consumption are evoked.

Nevertheless, it does appear that a significant social shift takes place around the end of the nineteenth century as a result of a new focus on the consumption of commodities. **Commodities** are objects and services produced for consumption or exchange by someone other than their producers. Almost everything produced for consumption today is a commodity: we work at a specific job producing specific goods and services, whether this involves selling insurance or producing automobiles in a factory, or, in the case of professors, "producing" educated students in a university. Through the exchange of our labour for salary or wages, we are then able to purchase all of the other goods and services that we require (food, clothing, utilities, entertainment, etc.)—including, it should be added, those things that we work at producing (insurance salespeople aren't given free insurance, nor are auto workers invited to take home some of the automobiles that they produce).

Human beings have long exchanged goods that they produce for other goods: it has always been difficult to produce everything that one needs (and, certainly, everything that one wants). What has changed, then, is less the fact of exchange than the range of commodities that have become available, the ability of more and more people to engage in wider and wider forms of consumption, and the creation of new wants and desires through advertising and display. The conjunction of these and other factors has produced consumerism, the name for the dominant values and practices arising from, and providing fuel for, life in a consumer society.

The Creation of Consumer Society: Advertising, Credit, Debt

How and when did this new kind of society come into being? While the rise of consumer society is generally associated with the Industrial Revolution, it actually wasn't until relatively late in the game—the late nineteenth and early twentieth century—that people started to consume in earnest. The obvious reason behind the intensification and extensification of consumption was that the expansion of industry resulted in a massively increased amount of goods produced. Factories became bigger and more efficient, and so could produce more items more cheaply than before, which made it possible for widespread consumption. But, as the most elementary economic theory should tell us, the relationship between supply and demand doesn't work this simply or easily.

As Richard Robbins notes, the rise of consumerism can best be understood not as the natural and inevitable consequence of a burgeoning economy, but rather as a largely *manufactured* response to a specific (and continuing) crisis in the capitalist system of production. To put it simply, industry had by the end of the nineteenth century reached a level of efficiency that threatened to topple the whole economy through overproduction. The production of goods for which there are an inadequate number of buyers is clearly unsustainable and is one of the causes of economic recessions and depressions. In order to stimulate demand and so avoid a total crisis it was necessary not just to increase, but also to fundamentally change patterns of consumption in order to make buying things a more central part of everyday life. Consumerism is the answer to the inevitability of capitalist overproduction. This change in the way we consume was as much *cultural* as it was economic. That is, it wasn't enough simply to increase wages so that people could buy more with the money they earned. Rather, according to the logic advanced by Henry Ford, one of the most important products of the factory line was the consumers who were produced out of the wages that he paid his workers. In addition to automobiles, Ford created not only the kind of people that could afford to purchase them, but also the kind of people that increasingly understood their lives in reference to possibilities of consumption.

Shifting Values in Western Society   For consumerism to function correctly, what was needed was a revolution in the underlying values of Western society—a shift from thrift and the virtues of parsimony to the come-what-may *carpe diem* philosophy of the consumer. This shift is often described—particularly by critics of consumerism—as representing a decided decline in spirituality, accompanied if not actually caused by a rise in materialism. In fact, the relationship between spirituality or religion and materialism is not that simple: they cannot be considered as simply and clearly opposites, the "good" of the spiritual standing above the "bad" of materialism.

At the beginning of the twentieth century, the sociologist Max Weber argued that the materialist "spirit of capitalism" could be located (apparently paradoxically) in Protestant asceticism. While asceticism involves the rejection of worldly temptations, over time the ceaseless labour carried out to increase the glory of God became disassociated from its religious roots, leading to a situation in which "material goods . . . gained an increasing and finally an inexorable power over the lives of men as at no previous period in history" (181). The growth of materialism represented not so much an abandonment of religion as a shift in its orientation, away from guilt and self-denial toward values of self-enhancement and emancipation. This shift was enabled in part by the Enlightenment belief in progress, as well as by the actual alterations in people's material circumstances associated with the Industrial Revolution. While traditional religious doctrines, combined with the sheer difficulty of life, tended to rule out the prospect of happiness on earth in favour of an emphasis on the glories of heaven, the ideology of industrialism made secular comfort seem not only possible, but also morally good. As James Twitchell puts it, at this point "the culture of consumption . . . replaced the culture of contrition" (230). The "spiritual" redemption of materialism was accompanied by a shift away from the ideas of humility and the subordination of the self to a higher power to an emphasis on the possibility of changing and enhancing one's life through individual will. And if self-enhancement required a new stove or pair of shoes—well, so much the better, both for the individual and for the economic well-being of society as a whole.

Still, the conversion of a society organized around thrift and self-sacrifice to one committed to shopping did not come about easily. The birth of consumer society required more concerted and more creative action on the part of manufacturers and government. Richard Robbins identifies a number of key developments that together fuelled what was seen as this necessary change. The first of these were developments in retail sales, in particular the invention of the department store. Beginning in Paris, with the *Au Bon Marché* (1852) followed in 1902 by Marshall Field's in Chicago, the department store offered a whole new shopping experience: in fact, it was the department store that, more than any other development, turned shopping into an *experience* rather than simply a routine, generally boring duty. Featuring such novel attractions as coatrooms and restrooms, the department store was committed to the enhancement of consumer pleasure and comfort, inviting its mostly female patrons to leisurely browse the aisles while enjoying musical performers or drinking tea. Complementing the structural appeals of the department store was a new emphasis on service, in which sales assistants would welcome customers (the precursor to Wal-Mart greeters), offer advice, and administer general pampering. The emphasis on friendliness, however contrived, played an important role in turning an essentially economic transaction into a personal one—an important function, in an age in which the relationship between primary producers and consumers was growing ever more distant.

Advertising and Marketing Perhaps the most significant factors in boosting consumerism were innovations in advertising and marketing. In Chapter Four we looked at the example of Crisco as a product whose transformation from a simple commodity—cooking oil—to an essential part of every good housewife's cooking practice came about largely through marketing. Here we offer a more general—and much-simplified—account of the significance of developments in advertising to the growth of consumerism. Until the mid-eighteenth century, ads were mainly informational, announcing new products and providing more or less straightforward accounts of their qualities, sometimes complete with testimonials from satisfied customers or accredited experts—doctors or pharmacists, for example (this kind of advertising finds echoes today, in those ads in which a serious, white-coated commentator, whose credentials appear in print at the bottom of the screen or page, points to simple graphs or other scientific-looking data to show how this particular brand of antacid, or painkiller, or diaper outperforms the competitors). With the flourishing of competition among manufacturers, the emphasis in advertising changed from informing customers about new products to encouraging them to discriminate between a host of virtually identical brands of the same product. Part of this was achieved by innovations in packaging, beginning with the production of pre-packaged goods with labels—Ivory Soap and Quaker Oats were among the earliest such brands, promoted as early as the 1870s.

A woodcut, ca. 1880, depicting the wonders of the Au Bon Marché department store in Paris.

Over the course of the twentieth century both packaging and advertising quickly became more sophisticated, as marketers realized that the way goods were displayed and promoted was at least as important in getting people to buy them as their actual substance. Starting around the time of the First World War, marketers began to marshal the forces of psychology to help them develop more subtle and unconscious forms of persuasion. The most well-known instance of early marketing psychology was the use of so-called subliminal advertising, in which, for example, the ice cubes in a glass of Coke were engineered to look like the body of a naked woman, or the word "sex" flashed up on the screen in the middle of an ad for, say, dental floss, disappearing too quickly to be registered on anything other than an unconscious level. While advertisers have dabbled in subliminal messages, the attention paid to this kind of trickery tends to over-state its significance, ignoring the much simpler, and arguably more effective use of straightforward images with complex emotional resonances—in other words, Barthes's **mythology** (discussed in Chapter Two). The need to use mythology in advertising is obvious: the actual objects being sold are not valuable enough in and of themselves to persuade us that we actually *need* them; they therefore need to be associated with some-thing deeper, more intangible in order to evoke our desire—what Raymond Williams terms, simply, "magic."

Over the last fifty years or so, advertising has come to occupy a position of unparal-leled dominance, reflecting both the intensification of consumerism and the growth of the information economy—a development we explore in more detail in the last section of this chapter. Advertising is, as Williams puts it, "the official art of modern capitalist society: it is what 'we' put up in 'our' streets and use to fill up to half of 'our' newspapers and magazines: and it commands the services of perhaps the largest organized body of writers and artists, with their attendant managers and advisers, in the whole society" (336). As such, advertising is both a barometer and a key producer of dominant social values, chief among which is, of course, the value of consumerism itself. Underpinning the myths invoked by the specific signs in any given ad that are meant to compel an attachment to this brand over that brand is another *über* myth, that our deepest needs and desires—for love, autonomy, security, freedom, friendship—can be met by buying something. The pervasiveness of this myth, which we weirdly cling to even as we recog-nize it *as* myth, accounts for the second major development in advertising in the last few decades: the "magic" of advertising has been kicked up to a new level so that it is simul-taneously more transparent, and more powerful, than it was before.

Branding   If advertising was once about cloaking a product in a sparkly glow, disguising its mundane qualities in shimmery illusion, now it achieves its most dramatic effects by eliminating the product altogether—even to the point of announcing the product's redundancy (as in ethical ads by companies like Patagonia that actually plead with us to "buy less"). This is the hallmark of the contemporary art of **branding**, in which compa-nies vie to sell us not individual products but lifestyles that are defined by broad patterns of selective consumption. The disappearance of the actual commodity in advertising weirdly confirms the triumph of consumerism, such that "goods"—including entertainment, vacation packages, and services—are thoroughly and inextricably "knitted into the fabric of social life and cultural significance" (Jhally 80).

But the expansion and intensification of consumer society has not been stimulated by the efforts of retailers alone. As Richard Robbins notes, government policy, encouraged by corporate lobbyists, has worked in conjunction with other broad institutional changes to create a cultural climate hospitable to consumption. The introduction of MBA programs and design institutes in the early 1900s marked both the recognition and encouragement of the possibilities for the professionalization of marketing. This in turn led to the formalization of what had once been an informal, vaguely disreputable sector of the contemporary economy into a specialized profession that young people could yearn to one day join: those major advertising firms like J. Walter Thompson, Young & Rubicam, and Ogilvy & Mather that established Madison Avenue as a fixture in the collective unconscious.

There are a Hundred Imitations.

Is there more than one kind of Ivory Soap? No; but there are a hundred imitations. A dishonest grocer will give you one of these and say: "This is Ivory," or "This is just as good."

Do not accept it unless it is stamped *Ivory*. The shape of the cake and the appearance of the wrapper may be similar, but the name can not be used on any but the genuine.

There is no "free" uncombined) alkali in Ivory Soap. That is why it will not injure the finest fabric or the most delicate skin.

Ivory Soap
99⁴⁵⁄₁₀₀ Per Cent. Pure

Reprinted from *Literary Digest*, May 26, 1906.

Nineteenth-century ads were often strongly text-based, emphasizing straightforward information about products' (allegedly) unique features. Contemporary ads, by contrast, rely much more on abstract images. (See also the Diesel ad on page 151.)

Credit and Debt Around the same time, changing government policies in the United States placed increasing focus on commerce, including the eventual creation of government ministries devoted to researching and promoting its expansion. One major campaign in the U.S. and Canada was the drive to get people to buy houses. A 1920s government-issued pamphlet touted the "family values" of owning a single-detached home, backed by psychological research highlighting the importance of separate bedrooms for each child (Robbins *Global* 16). Of course the boost in home ownership could not be achieved without another major initiative—the expansion of credit. By putting limits on interest payments, making it easier to take out a mortgage or get a car loan, governments and banks have played a crucial role in fuelling consumer spending. They had the added benefit, Robbins notes, of bolstering the discipline of the workforce, which was kept in line by the fear of being unable to make credit payments.

The major cultural effect of policies making credit both easier to get and also more acceptable socially is that being in debt—a situation that was once an occasion for embarrassment—has become a way of life, such that the average household debt-to-income ratio in Canada in 2002 hovered around 95 percent. Of course, the dark side of this good-news picture for the economy as a whole is that an alarming number of individuals and families live just a hair's breadth away from bankruptcy. The ideology of consumerism, by creating not just an unquestioned right but a moral imperative out of the ownership of stuff, works to conceal, without overturning, huge discrepancies in wealth between the rich and the poor. And in the global economy, this formula applies not just to individuals, but to nations as well.

Consumerism is a value system that has rapidly (though unevenly) spread around the entire world. It is most developed in North America, Europe, Japan, and Australia (those areas commonly referred to as "the West"), but it is difficult not to see that aspects of consumerism are present globally. As discussed previously in this chapter, consumerism refers to a complex set of values and practices. What is central to consumerism is the belief that the organization of life around the purchase of commodities is in fact, for all its other problems, the optimal way to address the needs and wants of individuals, and even the best way to allocate social goods. This "belief" is often more implicit than explicit. Explicitly, people often express worries about consumption and its social, political, and environmental effects. But through the *practices* that individuals engage in— constrained as these are by the structures and institutions of consumer society—faith in the optimal efficiency of the market is restated day after day around the world. And it is not just the efficiency of market forces that is valorized in consumer society, but the underlying goals of such an economic system, too. The consumer lives what Ernest Gellner has described as a "society of perpetual growth" (Gellner 24); her central goal is to accumulate money so that she may purchase and consume ever-increasing quantities of goods and services.

Consumer Culture and Mass Culture

The history of consumer society closely mirrors the history of popular culture offered in Chapter Two. The two histories are intertwined: to a large degree, contemporary popular culture *is* consumer culture. The description of contemporary popular culture as a form of **mass culture** is one way of capturing the historical novelty of contemporary forms of consumption and its links to the popular. At the beginning of his book *Selling Culture*, the cultural critic Richard Ohmann offers a definition of mass culture that can help us to identify the distinctive features of mass and consumer culture and to see the ways in which our ideas and practices of consumption differ from those prior to the end of the nineteenth century. Ohmann describes mass culture as a system characterized by:

> voluntary experiences, produced by a relatively small number of specialists, for millions across the nation to share, in similar or identical form, either simultaneously or nearly so; with dependable frequency; mass culture shapes habitual audiences, around common needs or interests; and it is made for profit. (14)

What does this definition tell us about popular culture and consumerism? There are forms of consumption that are socially or physically necessary: food, clothing, shelter, and so on. In his discussion of mass culture, Ohmann wants to omit these in order to concentrate on forms of voluntary consumption, specifically what we have come to refer to as "entertainment."

As we will see below, the meanings that circulate around consumption cannot be limited in quite this way. We all require shelter; this requirement, though involuntary in comparison to our choices of entertainment, is explicitly connected to contemporary forms and practices of consumption through the kinds of shelter that we strive for: a big house in the suburbs, a sleek condo in a downtown high-rise, a farmhouse in the country, and so on. One of the interesting things about consumer culture, at least in those countries with relatively high standards of living, is that there is no longer anything "basic" about the necessities of life: we require clothing to keep us warm or shelter us from the sun, but, as we all know, the kinds of clothing that we choose to consume have significant social meanings and implications.

Even though Ohmann's definition is geared toward a characterization of mass cultural entertainment, it still helps us to grasp just what is unique about consumer culture. In general, we purchase the objects or services that we consume from the specialists that produce them: for the most part, we don't make our own clothing (we certainly don't make the cloth), grow our own food, or manufacture electronics in our basement. Consumption is dependent on a vast specialization of labour and industry, and on the development of an enormous set of institutions that are geared toward the production and distribution of consumable objects and services: it is no coincidence that the history of the modern corporation parallels the rise of consumer culture (see Close-Up 5.3). There continues to exist a wide range of hand-made goods, home-baked foods, and so on, but these exceptions merely prove the rule of specialized production.

Further, the things we consume, from T-shirts to soft drinks to televisions, are consumed by millions of others around the world in virtually the same form, with only slight variations from country to country. McDonald's, for instance, has famously modified parts of its standard fast-food menu to account for local tastes or prohibitions against certain food items. On the whole, though, one of the appeals of McDonald's is in fact the almost global standardization of its menu: consumers can expect a Big Mac to taste the same in St. John's as it does in Santa Cruz. Contemporary consumption is premised on such uniformity. It makes little sense to prefer to buy Nikes in one store over another on the assumption that the shoes that one can purchase in one location are "better made" than in the other (though they may of course be priced differently).

Simultaneity, dependable frequency and the creation of habitual audiences are important for understanding the ways in which most forms of popular entertainment are offered up to us for consumption. Television schedules are standardized across nations (*The Sopranos* doesn't appear on a different night in Toronto than it does in Edmonton), NFL football games and *Hockey Night in Canada* take place at predictable (and scheduled) times, and new videos and DVDs miraculously appear on video store shelves across

Corporations

Though it might seem as if corporations have been with us forever, they are relatively recent inventions; it is more recently still that they assumed the legal status they hold in most Western countries today.

Corporations first emerged in the seventeenth century through the establishment of chartered corporations, which were given specific missions outlined by an act of government. Such chartered corporations were granted the exclusive right to engage in colonial ventures over a specifically defined geographic space. The economic logic of these corporate bodies was to allow for huge pools of capital to be accumulated in order to carry out ventures that would have been impossible for small groups to carry out independently. The United States was initially settled by a corporation, the Massachusetts Bay Company, as was a large part of Canada under the auspices of the Hudson's Bay Company.

Early corporations were chartered to fulfill some form of public mission. In the United States after independence, corporations were involved in building bridges, in constructing roads, and in other activities that now fall to governments. Once corporations began to be involved in raising capital for the creation of private wealth, it became necessary to define their status more formally in legal terms. In a landmark case in 1886, corporations in the United States were defined as "persons" as a result of the application of the 14th amendment to the U.S. Constitution, which was originally designed to protect recently emancipated slaves, to a case involving a dispute over differences in tax rates for individuals and corporations. The 14th amendment states that "no state shall deprive any person of life, liberty or property": once defined as "persons," corporations gained the same rights and protections as individuals. Though corporations have slightly different status in different countries, the trend globally has been toward the U.S. model of corporate rights. This nineteenth-century quirk in legal jurisprudence has bolstered the strength of corporations immeasurably: corporations have repeatedly appealed to their rights as individuals to strike down laws that attempt to limit or regulate their activities.

North America at midnight each and every Monday (or, in the worst-case scenario, Tuesday morning). Finally, what links everything together is profit. Today, consumption almost always involves the exchange of money and almost always occurs in a situation in which it contributes to the creation of profit.

Identifying these general features of consumer society does not mean that it is impossible to find contrary examples or situations. It is not to suggest, as theorists of consumer culture sometimes have, that there are no forms of exchange, social relationships, or cultural experiences that are not part of consumerism. Education, religious participation, and forms of "self-produced" entertainment (playing your guitar for your friends) are just some examples of experiences that fall somewhat outside the guiding values of consumer society, even if they are informed by those values (as when education becomes merely a way to secure a high-paying job so that one can buy a big-screen TV). Rather, what we want to draw attention to is that our particular forms of consumption are a recent historical "invention." Only recently did we turn to others to the extent to which we do today to feed, clothe, and entertain us.

It is this fundamental shift in the character of consumption that in turn produces a need to explore the new and complex social and cultural meanings generated by consumer society. We will do this by turning now to look at three important ways in which consumption produces the cultural meanings that are an important part of contemporary culture: consumption as a means of producing and reinforcing social and cultural distinctions and differences; the connections between consumption and individual identity and agency; and the political meaning of contemporary forms of consumption, which includes the impact of consumption on social spaces that we now inhabit. Many of the issues raised in this chapter overlap with the explorations of identity (Chapter Six) and representation (Chapter Three).

CONSUMPTION AS DISTINCTION

As we've already noted, the practice of consumption is not exhausted in the moment of exchange; nor is what is exchanged "used up" or destroyed through consumption, even if this is one of the typical meanings associated with "consuming." To consume food means that the food gets "used up" and broken down. But in its social and cultural meanings, exchange is only one part of a larger system of meaning produced in and through consumption. *What* we choose to consume and *how* we consume are already pregnant with social significance. The ability or lack of ability to consume certain objects and services, or even to consume at all (in the case of extreme poverty or social and geographic isolation), has profound consequences that most of us implicitly understand. For example, we might choose to purchase an automobile that is more expensive than we can really afford because of what we imagine that it enables us to do (climb effortlessly over boulders to the top of a butte where we can survey the endless desert stretching in front of us), and what that particular make and model symbolizes. Automobiles offer mobility and convenience; they can symbolize youthfulness or hipness, comfort or a concern with safety, economic status or thrift. In the end, however, all automobiles perform the same function—moving people around. The existence of a vast number of brands and models, colours and option packages, and so on suggests that other forces of meaning are at work in an individual's choice of vehicle—forces that may seem more important than (in this example) fiscal responsibility or concern over the environment (in which case the best option would be not to purchase a car at all). *What* we choose to consume in this case highlights certain values (mobility, convenience) at the expense of others; *how* we do so—what kind of vehicle, what colour, what features we add or subtract—immediately brings to light other values or symbolic associations (for example, the importance of youthfulness in our culture) that are involved in all forms of consumption.

Consumption and Agency

There is one important category in this scenario that needs to be addressed in further detail before we proceed. It is perhaps the central concept at issue in contemporary analyses of consumer culture, and indeed it is essential to consumerism itself. This is the category of **agency**, the ability of individuals to act as self-conscious, willful social "agents" or actors and to exert their will through involvement in social practices, relationships, and decision-making. This concept is discussed in more detail in Chapter Six. Certainly, debates over the ultimate social significance of consumer culture often revolve around questions about the degree to which individuals are able to express their free will or agency in their day-to-day decision making, as opposed to their actions and decisions being relatively determined, decided on in advance as a result of the structures and institutions within which they live.

Analyses of consumerism and consumer practices will differ depending on the degree of real choice that we imagine individuals have in contemporary society. For instance, we are free to vote for whom we want; on the other hand, that freedom is limited by the degree to which political parties in North America tend to express small variations on the same political theme. We can see this same "non-choice" in our automobile example. You are able to choose the colour and make of your car. What is more difficult to "choose" in most North American cities and towns is to go without an automobile: mass transit systems are under-funded, and low-density development has made it difficult to go (for instance) from a suburban home to work at a light industrial park, and from there back home or to shop for food at a supermarket located on a retail strip.

Going beyond these examples, what feels to each of us like free choices are also heavily determined by our social and cultural backgrounds. Our choices define and are defined by the social categories within which we *want* to situate ourselves and in which we are already situated. There are certain ways in which we have to act and dress in order to "belong" or participate in certain social or career circles. We might in some sense "choose" to belong to these groups; nevertheless, it is important to put aside the idea that there is some kind of *absolute*, unconstrained agency or free choice in consumer society (or any society, for that matter). There is a reason that demographical studies of consumer choice capture patterns of consumption linked to income levels, geographic region, and so on. All of the consumers in an area may be freely choosing to buy one brand of clothing over another, one brand of beer over another. And yet, when grouped together, these individual "free" choices point to similarities in consumer choices that cannot be written off as mere coincidence. There is also a reason why television programs are developed in order to "deliver" certain target audiences to advertisers interested in selling their products to (say) 19- to 25-year-olds. No one is twisting the arms of young adults to tune in to these shows, but hopefully they do anyway, so satisfying both the hopes of TV executives and of advertisers.

Understanding the meanings of contemporary consumption involves a comprehension of both the structures and institutions of consumption that define and shape our choices *and* the way in which these choices in turn shape and define these structures and institutions. It is common to understand social structures and institutions as necessarily imposing constraints or limits on behaviour. Attending high school, for example, places limits on what you do and where you can go during the day on weekdays. But if schooling limits some behaviours and choices, it also enables a whole range of others (through education, exposure to peers and extracurricular activities, etc.) and does so in ways that cannot be easily controlled or predicted. The structures of consumption both enable individual consumption and provide restrictions on it in a continuously shifting way: our choices are structured, but this does not mean that they are determined in advance. While realizing that agency and structure always go together, we will look first at some of the structures that consumption produces and reproduces, and then will consider in the next section the individual and collective meanings that we make through our use of the things that we consume.

Taste and Distinction

It is obvious to most of us that the things we own have a meaning above and beyond the simple possession of them. Few if any of us have a sense of how much monetary value all of the things around us are worth taken together. But what we do know is that many of the objects we surround ourselves with mean something to us: they may remind us of the person who gave it to us, or they in some way express our individuality—who we are and what we like. The furniture we own, the objects that we place on our walls, the music we collect and listen to, the books that we display on our shelves—all of these objects externalize our own sense of ourselves, whether explicitly or implicitly. What they also do, however, is connect us with others through the subtle forms of distinction they produce. For example, if we like the music of Belle and Sebastian and Sonic Youth, seeing these CDs in other people's homes will indicate a connection between them and us; conversely, seeing a rack comprised only of Celine Dion and Bryan Adams CDs will suggest something very different.

Sociocultural Differentiation   One of the most important ways in which contemporary consumption functions is that it produces systems of sociocultural differentiation. To put this more plainly, what we "choose" to consume *includes* us in some groups and *excludes* us from others. Once again, to a certain degree, what we can consume (or not consume) has always functioned as a form of social **distinction**. At an earlier point in European history, only the nobility could afford to consume large quantities of meat flavoured with exotic spices from abroad; peasants, craftspeople, and city dwellers had to make do with bread and beer.

In comparison to contemporary forms and modes of social distinction through consumption, even up to the end of the nineteenth century there was a relatively minimal degree of social differentiation signalled by the consumption of different kinds of commodities. Shops in the late nineteenth century had a limited number of consumer items, few of which were readily identifiable by brand name: coffee, sugar, and other food items came out of barrels rather than in the clearly distinguished packages of a specific brand. To a considerable degree distinction through consumption is a relatively recent phenomenon, first described by the sociologist Thorstein Veblen (1857–1929) in 1899 and more fully theorized and systemized by the French sociologist Pierre Bourdieu (1930–2002) in the 1970s.

Thorstein Veblen   Veblen's famous analysis of **conspicuous consumption** explored the uses to which "excess" consumption was already being put by the end of the nineteenth century. "Wasted" or excess consumption was the result of a widespread increase in incomes and consequent expansion of consumption that occurred at the end of that century. For Veblen, "wasted" consumption wasn't illegitimate, useless, or purposeless. What he was trying to capture by using this term were forms of consumption beyond those that "serve human life or human well-being on the whole" (203). Consumption at the turn of the century was becoming "conspicuous"—obvious, noticeable, visible—in order to signal or symbolize class differences and distinctions. As Veblen points out, there are a number of possible categories that could be used to symbolize social differences: moral and intellectual qualities, physical or aesthetic differences, and so on. In the United States and Canada, all of these categories were being subsumed by displays of money. But one needn't be rich to be able to render one's forms of consumption visible to other classes. Veblen insisted that there existed conspicuous forms of consumption all the way down to the very poorest groups. A difference between the very rich and the poor and middle-class rested in the creation of the category of "taste." Veblen writes that

In contrast to earlier print ads, contemporary ads, such as this magazine ad for Diesel clothing, rely more on abstract visual signs—to the point where it's sometimes difficult to tell what product is being advertised!

> The growth of punctilious [precise or demanding] discrimination as to qualitative excellence in eating, drinking, etc., presently affects not only the manner of life, but also the training and intellectual activity of the gentleman of

leisure. He is no longer the successful, aggressive male.... In order to avoid stulti-fication he must also cultivate his tastes, for it now becomes incumbent on him to discriminate with some nicety between the noble and ignoble in consumable goods. (190)

Pierre Bourdieu   In many ways, Pierre Bourdieu's research and writing takes up the same themes as Veblen. Bourdieu, too, is interested in the social uses of consumption as a form of class or group distinction or discrimination. For Bourdieu, whenever we con-sume—be it images, types of food, music, or art—we are engaging in complex forms of social differentiation, discrimination, and display whether we realize it or not. We may be aware of being involved in this social "game of distinction," as we most definitely are when we dress up for a job interview (for instance). But for Bourdieu, we participate in this game of social distinction even when we make decisions that seem to express per-sonal or individual choices. The sum meaning of consumption for Bourdieu *is* this game of distinction. "Taste," the faculty that Veblen believed the rich had to cultivate in order to be able to make accurate distinctions between better and worse forms of consumables, is now something that we all exercise.

But even in our expressions of our likes and dislikes through consumption, Bourdieu believes there is a form of social meaning at work. He writes: "Taste is the basis of all that one has—people and things—and all that one is for others, whereby one classifies one-self and is classified by others" (45). Taste appears to us as something that is individual; it is not only social, but also a site at which social power is produced and maintained.

Suggested Activity 5.2

Reflect on your own consumption and the purchases that your peer group makes. What forms of distinction can you see yourself engaged in? How is social distinc-tion represented in popular culture? Think, for example, of the importance of forms of display in music video and in contemporary Pygmalion narratives, such as in films like *Pretty Woman*, *Maid in Manhattan*, *Sweet Home Alabama,* and *Real Women Have Curves*. What is required besides money to move from the lower to the upper classes?

Consumption and Power

In his exhaustively researched book *Distinction* (1979), Bourdieu and his research associ-ates perform a number of experiments in which they ask respondents from different eco-nomic levels of society (expressed through their job titles) to rank and identify films, pieces of classical music, and photographs based on their likes or dislikes. Astonishingly, there was a remarkably strong correspondence between the choices individuals made and the socioeconomic groups to which they belonged. There was, for example, a link between supposedly "difficult" music and art and members of higher-income groups, while blue-collar workers "liked" more melodic forms of classical music, narrative films vs. more experimental films, and so on. The grounds of this difference in taste between socioeconomic groups have most often been thought to be based on either education or innate ability. Bourdieu saw things differently. He argued that differences in consumption express *only* the way in which consumption has been used to create and reinforce pre-existing class divisions. There is no "taste" that is more correct or accurate than any other. Rather, by virtue of their socioeconomic status, groups in power have been able to transform *their* tastes into the legitimate ones by which others are measured. In this way, consumption has placed barriers to class mobility, for, in addition to one's economic status, one has to also have correct ideas about what to consume and how to consume it. This is the lesson of innumerable movies about class, from *My Fair Lady* to *Trading Places* to *Pretty Woman* and *The Princess Diaries* (see the analysis of *Working Girl*, Chapter Six). In each of those movies, it is only when the protagonist has learned the proper dispositions about the kinds of consumption that are legitimate or appropriate (along with a set of practices and bodily dispositions: holding tea cups correctly, etc.) that they can join a different social class or group.

There are two things that Veblen and Bourdieu's theories tell us about contemporary consumption. First, the idea that we consume "freely"—that is, that our choices are somehow entirely our own and are disconnected from larger social structures—is an illusion. Of course, subjectively, it certainly *feels* as if our choices are free. Nevertheless, "objectively and subjectively aesthetic stances adopted in matters like cosmetics, clothing or home decoration are opportunities to experience or assert one's position in social space, as a rank to be upheld or a distance to be kept" (Bourdieu 57). Second, these theories tell us that one of the primary social meanings of consumption is social distinction and differentiation. Juliet Schor writes that

> Bourdieu argues that class status is gained, lost, and reproduced in part through everyday acts of consumer behaviour. Being dressed incorrectly or displaying "vulgar" manners can cost a person a management or professional job. Conversely, one can gain entry into social circles, or build lucrative business contracts, by revealing appropriate tastes, manners, and culture. Thus, consumption practices become important in maintaining the basic structures of power and inequality which characterize our world. (457)

Bourdieu has claimed that "there is no way out of the game of culture." For this reason, he has sometimes been criticized for theorizing consumption in a way that stresses structure(s) at the expense of agency. Is it always the case that our choices necessitate the adoption of a position in social space? How then do societies changes and develop? While Bourdieu does have his own theory of the relationship between structure and agency, at their most extreme his views can start to seem like those of the Frankfurt School that we discussed in Chapter Five. We need not take Bourdieu or Veblen as being totally correct about consumption in order to find a great deal that is useful in their descriptions of the symbolic meaning of consumption. Indeed, one of the things that Bourdieu asserts in *Distinction* is important to our discussion in the next section of this chapter. For Bourdieu, there is no more or less legitimate form of consumption: whatever difference there might be between watching the opera on PBS or watching *Blind Date* lies not in the intrinsic value of one television program over the other, but in the way that these choices are mobilized socially. The next section will explore why it is important to see the meaning of consumption as being produced through the uses to which agents put the things they consume.

CONSUMPTION, DESIRE, AND PLEASURE

It is extremely easy to dismiss consumption as wasteful, pointless, without purpose, and so on. As we suggested at the outset of this chapter, consumption is both a normal part of contemporary societies and yet also a social practice accompanied by feelings of ambivalence, guilt, and uncertainty. When social critics write about the ills and traumas associated with consumer society, the image they project is of a present peopled by indistinguishable drones mystified by the electronic buzz of advertising, grimly doing their duty by dragging themselves through malls and dutifully filling up shopping bags with slick-looking black leather shoes, wafer-thin cell phones, and flavoured popcorn bought by the bucket—none of which they need! In a nutshell, many critics portray consumer society as a form of Technicolor totalitarianism—the grey dreariness of life in the Soviet Union, only lit up by neon lights and the smiling faces of Gap employees.

Not only do these views miss much of what takes place in consumption, they also presume what consumption means without ever investigating or considering that its meanings may be multiple and vary from place to place. Is contemporary life really so grim and empty? Not at all! Or, at the very least, since life is experienced very differently depending on "an individual's participation in consumption or their practical freedom to exercise choice" (Lury 6), the landscape of consumer culture can't simply be equated with a gulag of the soul. Through consumer culture, individuals enact their desires and develop new ones; consumption is also a source of enormous amounts of pleasure—especially the consumption of entertainment, whether this involves reading Jonathan Franzen's *The Corrections* or watching any one of Adam Sandler's sublime comedies.

Of course, it is possible to point out (as we will in the next section) that there are rather serious consequences of this kind of pleasure and this system of desire. And it is also possible to assert that the desires and pleasures of consumer culture are not ones that are particularly worth having, or are at best degraded remainders of more lofty and serious feelings and dispositions—the ones that a small subset of humanity experienced at some point in the past while the vast majority of people were engaged in endless labour in terrible conditions.

A more effective rejoinder that doesn't rely on positions that are difficult to substantiate, or arguments that re-enact the legitimation of tastes that Bourdieu criticizes, insists on consumerism as a system that is inscribed in our most intimate pleasures and desires.

Richard Ohmann paints the following picture of the consumer in mass culture at the beginning of *Selling Culture*:

> The advertiser can sell Bill Black an image of himself as a carefree male ... because he has already learned from a million other commercials to fill vacancies in his life through commodities, because advertisers have long since inscribed that nexus on his mind, because *they* have to expand sales to cope with the productive capacity that manufacturers have achieved partly by making Bill's job mechanical, which in turn makes him long for autonomy and market-free social relations, which desire has over decades been fixed to an image of the home as a place of care and refuge, which image drew him into a marriage with impossible hopes, and the burden of these hopes on his wife, along with her own ad-inflated aspirations to be superwoman, has made her resentful and no fun to be with.... And so on and on. (12–13)

In this system, there is no space for "real" or "authentic" desires. And this is probably right: all of us are now born into a culture that is consumerist through and through in such a way that renders appeals to "authentic" desires or pleasures as suspect as our desire for pure, unconstrained agency. Still, what such accounts are never able to explain is why consumer culture "fails" so frequently and why advertisers have to constantly re-evaluate their audiences and re-consider the ways in which they might reach them.

To put this slightly differently: "if consumption was simply a reflex of production, what need would there be for design, advertising or marketing expertise?" (du Gay et al. 85). One of the errors in thinking about consumer culture is to assume that it is total in the way that Ohmann suggests here—that there is no excess, slippage, or contradiction that breaks up the smooth operation of consumerism, or at least produces other forms and moments of social interaction and meaning. To question the absolute power of consumerist ideology does not require a return to "real" or "authentic" desires; rather, what it means is that we need to consider the ways in which individuals create social and individual meaning through consumption—however problematically, however incompletely.

Making Meaning in Use

In the words of the authors of *Doing Cultural Studies*, consumption needs to be understood to some degree, and in conjunction with our discussion of structure above, as a process of "appropriation and resistance," "an ongoing cycle of *commodification*—where producers make new products or different versions of old products as a result of consumers' activities—and *appropriation*—where consumers make those products meaningful, sometimes making them achieve a new 'register' of meaning that affects production in some way" (du Gay et al. 103). Consumers don't passively accept the meanings that supposedly come pre-packaged with the things that they consume—or at least they don't *always* do so. Rather, consumers help to *make* culture in a variety of complex and contradictory ways. First, consumers engage in a process of distinction and discrimination through the things that they choose to consume or not to consume. The landscape of consumer society is littered with products and services that didn't hit their mark: it is estimated that more than 80 percent of consumer items introduced each year fail. Second, consumers produce meaning at the intersection of the wide range of experiences, practices, and relationships that they are or have been engaged in. The unpredictable connection of these elements creates new possibilities and meanings that can fall outside of the structures of consumption.

It is possible to overstate the agency that individuals engage through their practices of consumption. Cultural studies has at times gone too far in creating a "vision of consumption practices as inherently democratic and implicitly subversive" (du Gay et al. 104). Nevertheless, the fundamental point of insisting on even the possibility of consumer activity (as opposed to passivity) can be substantiated by looking at actual practices of consumption as they occur in specific social situations. (The discussion of McDonald's in Chapter Nine is one example.) To decide that we know the meaning of every situation of consumption from the outset doesn't help us to understand either the ways in which consumption has changed over time or the politics of consumption—that is, the larger social issues that we need to consider whenever we investigate consumption.

THE POLITICS OF CONSUMPTION

The most common critical responses to consumer culture have been *normative*: consumer culture has been assessed on the basis of its supposed innate value. Put most simply: is it good or bad for us? Thumbs up or thumbs down? Bran Flakes or Frosted Flakes? For all the boosters who celebrate consumers and consumption as engines for economic growth and the spread of democracy, others decry consumerism and consumption more generally as innate social evils. On the one hand there are those

> who say that TV (for instance) educates and amuses people, democratically opens up the range of possibilities available to them, puts them in touch with the whole society or even the whole global village, makes them informed citizens, helps them to improve their material lives, and so keeps the economy going; and on the other, those who say TV creates illusions, destroys literacy and the English language, isolates people from one another, puts them in debt by making them want things they don't really need, and turns them into political zombies. (Ohmann 11–12)

The former position tends to be held implicitly, except at times when—as in the post–9-11 crisis—consumers need to be reminded again of the duty and joy of shopping. The latter position is part of a long tradition of normative critiques of mass culture dating back to Matthew Arnold's worries in *Culture and Anarchy* (1869), about the eclipse of an interest in spiritual values through the "vulgar" pursuit of material wealth during the rapid industrialization of Britain in the nineteenth century.

Writing in the 1920s, Samuel Strauss spoke directly about the problems of what he referred to as "consumptionism," "a philosophy of life that committed human beings to the production of more and more things—'more this year than last year, more next year than this'—and that emphasized the 'standard of living' above all other values" (cited in R. Robbins 3). The decline of all other values at the expense of consumer values was criticized in the 1950s by former advertising executive Vance Packard, who drew attention to the psychological tricks of advertising that led to overconsumption. Every new publishing season brings a raft of critiques of consumer culture more or less along these same lines (such as *Bowling Alone: The Collapse and Revival of American Community*). Consumerism seems to be a perpetual problem, and a problem that a century of both scholarly and public criticism seems to have done little about.

Shopping and Women

Debates about whether consumerism is a force for good or ill have frequently centred on the subject of shopping and gender. Specifically, many critics have explored the question of whether shopping, an activity claimed—whether justifiably or not—as primarily the domain of women, has worked to enslave or empower them. From the time when critiques of consumerism and shopping first began to appear with regularity toward the end of the nineteenth century, they were often framed in terms of gender. All of the negative qualities connected with shopping—its association with leisure and frivolity, as opposed to work; its emphasis on outward appearances at the expense of deeper, spiritual values; and, worst of all, its erosion of shoppers' powers of discrimination as they succumbed to mindless acts of consumption—were traditionally coded feminine, in opposition to the masculine world of work, substance, and rationality. These generalized attacks on shopping as a threat to masculine values were accompanied by more specific attacks on the relatively new and alarming figure of the woman shopper.

As we noted in Chapter Two, an important aspect of the bourgeois ideology that grew up around the Industrial Revolution was its delineation of separate spheres of home and work—the public world, or the world of men, and the domestic space of women. Though women, particularly working-class women, crossed these boundaries all the time, the ideology of separate spheres served to create a mythological distinction between the feminine ideal—the "angel in the house"—and her evil sister, embodied in the figure of that notorious homewrecker, the prostitute. The advent of the department store—a kind of domestic space outside the home—confused the clear-cut divisions between public and private space, granting women a new and (from a masculine perspective) threatening kind of freedom that itself heralded the corruption of that sacred space, the English home.

Feminist Perspectives   But women were equally critical of the induction of their sisters into consumer culture, if for entirely different reasons. Charlotte Perkins Gilman, a nineteenth-century advocate of women's liberation, lamented what she saw as the enslavement of women to a new cult of consumerism, in which they functioned as "priestesses." Excluded from the public realm of "true industry and true art" (60), women were relegated to the world of false things in which their only role was both a passive and a destructive one as "a limitless demander of things to use up" (60). Sue Thornham places Gilman's argument at the beginning of a long tradition of feminist criticism of shopping as an activity that works, paradoxically, to keep women in their place even as it allows them an illusory freedom in the form of temporary escape from the home. Just as Gilman described women as "priestesses" of a new "temple of consumption," later writers extend the religious metaphor in their construction of shopping as a form of mass ritual, in which women's active participation conceals their passive subjection.

For example, Betty Friedan, writing in 1965, observed that "like a primitive culture which sacrificed little girls to its tribal gods, we sacrifice our girls to the feminine mystique, grooming them ever more efficiently through the sexual sell to become consumers of the things to whose profitable sale our nation is dedicated" (qtd. in Thornham 126). The image of girls as sacrificial victims to the religion of shopping (and its associated cults of beauty and fashion) anticipates a more radical critique of the role of women in consumer society. Not only are women cast in the position of relatively passive consumers in contrast to the active realm of masculine production, but also they are themselves commodities, "disinvested" of their bodies and "reclothed in a form that makes [them] suitable for exchange among men" (Irigaray qtd. in Thornham).

For many critics, then, consumerism is a social force whose largely negative effects have a particularly strong impact on women. From a masculinist Victorian perspective, shopping represents self-indulgence, frivolity, materialism, and irrationality. Because these are seen to be qualities to which women in particular are susceptible, succumbing to the lure of consumerism risks not only corrupting women's already precarious moral characters, but also emasculating society as a whole. From a feminist perspective, by contrast, shopping reinforces women's exclusion from the realm of production, where real social power lies. More troubling still, in its embodiment of the economic relations that characterize capitalist society in general, shopping confirms the status of women as *objects* of exchange: things to be looked at and possessed, whose commodification is only accentuated by their active participation in the process.

In opposition to these negative perspectives on women and shopping, another group of critics makes the counter argument that far from enslaving women, shopping actually empowers them. One strand of this argument proceeds from the same premise that so troubled nineteenth-century male critics, but takes the opposite view: shopping is an activity—the first significant activity—that allowed women to leave the home and enter the public sphere. According to this argument, the contemporary shopping mall functions in a similar way to the early department store, by blurring the boundaries of the private and the public, of work and leisure:

> The consumer is allowed to wander in and out of private space to look at, handle and try out products that she does not own. In a department store it is possible to wander through privately owned space, holding or wearing someone else's property as if it were your own, without asking to do so, often without even having to go through the usual social intercourse appropriate to being a guest in someone's place. Boundaries between public and private become ambiguous. (Ferrier qtd. in Fiske 23)

Moreover, as shoppers women could for the first time exercise a degree of control and decision-making power in the economic realm—power that had until then been confined to their roles as household managers. Shopping, in these terms, can be viewed as a kind of *work*, in the way that women's traditional labour in the home is not. Commenting on the construction of her house as a place of comfort for its inhabitants "where no one ever runs out of the necessaries: stamps, Aspirin, pudding, tweezers, blankets," newspaper columnist Heather Mallick notes, "It isn't leisure that produced this. It was hard graft, thoughtful travelling and selection, judicious studying of bank balances.... And it is work that does good" (Mallick). Shopping's ability to fulfill what Mallick identifies as women's desire to be good, or at least to be seen to be good, by satisfying the needs of their loved ones might make it seem like a further entrenchment in their traditional roles rather than a way of moving outside them.

However, a number of critics argue that this general analysis of shopping's function doesn't pay sufficient attention to the complexity and ambiguity of shoppers' actual practices. While anthropologist Daniel Miller, on the basis of an intensive study of women shoppers on a North London street, largely concurs with Mallick's characterization of shopping as a way for women to consolidate relationships or express love, he refutes the easy equation of women's love with disempowerment under patriarchy, in part by highlighting the active and self-conscious nature of his interview subjects' shopping habits. Mallick, moreover, highlights the ambiguity of women's position as shoppers by her sly distinction between "being good and *being seen to be* good" (emphasis added). The activity of shopping might be largely constrained both by the material structures and by the ideologies of patriarchal society, but within those structures individuals have considerable leeway in how they perform their role as consumers.

Performance   The concept of *performance*, which will be discussed in greater detail in Chapter Six, highlights the distinction between the role of the consumer as an ideal subject of capitalist ideology and the enactment of that role by individual consumers. The image of the feminine consumer, an image that both reflects and is a critical part of the image of her as "woman," is not natural, or given, but constructed within a particular context according to particular economic relations. While it might be impossible ever to escape or refuse the image entirely, it *is* possible, feminist theorists such as Luce Irigaray and Judith Butler suggest, to inhabit it self-consciously, to perform it in a playful or excessive way that undercuts the authority of the system it represents. In the realm of shopping, this kind of subversive performance might entail the cultivation of a style that mimics ironically the image of traditional femininity. Or it might involve the combination of different styles to create a visually jarring effect that draws attention to the constructedness of style as "fashion" rather than a natural accentuation of female beauty. In either case, the emphasis in the theory of performance is on the agency of a shopper, who does not just passively inhabit, but rather participates actively in the construction of her role as consumer/embodiment of a social ideal.

That construction cannot be understood solely in economic terms either. As we discuss further below, the things we buy aren't solely commodities but also are bits of culture, resources from which we fashion meanings and pleasures that often challenge the commercial system that sold them. Women have traditionally shown particular ingenuity at subverting the profit-making goals of the retail industry—for example, by buying cheap knock-offs or even sewing their own versions of the high-fashion items displayed in shops or magazines, or by creating their own styles through the recycled resources of vintage shops (see McRobbie).

The *Flâneur* John Fiske extends the argument about women's agency as consumers by drawing out the ambiguity of the concept of "looking," which is central to both the activity of shopping and, as we have seen in Chapter Three, the structuring of gender relations. As Laura Mulvey noted in her psychoanalytic analysis of Hollywood cinema, one of the ways the gender hierarchy operates is through an economy of sight, in which women connote "to-be-looked-at-ness." Accentuated in film, this relation also operates in public space. In the nineteenth century, one of the figures that became emblematic of the new urban culture was the *flâneur*, the connoisseur of the city and all its pleasures, whose principal activities consisted of just walking around and *looking*.

First described by the French poet Charles Baudelaire, the *flâneur* is a "passionate spectator" who enacts the dream of a restless romantic: "to be away from home and yet to feel oneself everywhere at home; to see the world, to be at the centre of the world, and yet to remain hidden from the world—impartial natures which the tongue can but clumsily define. The spectator is a prince who everywhere rejoices in his incognito."

For the contemporary theorist Walter Benjamin, the *flâneur* is the quintessential figure of modernity. He is also, quite clearly, male. The feminine counterpart of the *flâneur*—the *flâneuse*—is, as Janet Wolff and Elizabeth Wilson have noted, the prostitute, whose freedom to look is constrained by her status as commodity. However, the economy of spectatorship is complicated by the figure of the female shopper who, while she doesn't stop being an object of the male gaze, also engages in active looking. As she window-shops, tries on dresses, or picks up produce, the customer consumes a whole raft of images, some of which she may choose to purchase and incorporate into her own self-construction. While it can be argued that the self-image she shops for is heavily determined by patriarchal culture, as embodied especially in the advertising industry, the element of *choice* here is important. Moreover, the idea that women simply buy obediently into dominant myths of femininity—essentially seeing themselves through male eyes and constructing themselves accordingly—is too reductive an account of what Mulvey calls the pleasures of looking. As Fiske suggests,

> The pleasure of the look is not just the pleasure of looking good for the male, but rather of controlling how one looks and therefore of controlling the look of others upon oneself. Looking makes meanings; it is therefore a means of entering social relations, of inserting oneself into the social order in general, and of controlling one's immediate social relations in particular. Commodities are the resources of

the woman (or man) who is exercising some control over her look, her social relations, and her relation to the social order. (35)

Caroline Evans and Minna Thornton further question the essentialist reading of gendered looking, suggesting that "fashion, unlike cinema, generates images of women for women, a system of representations that one might suppose to be cut to the measure of a *female* desire" (10). While this may be true, it would be a mistake, as Evans and Thornton acknowledge, to see fashion as a zone of women's emancipation: female desire is not generated outside of culture, and thus it is necessarily shaped in part by ideology, an ideology that remains strongly patriarchal.

Having surveyed the arguments for and against shopping as it pertains to women in particular, we can conclude that it is neither wholly disempowering nor wholly empowering. In the nineteenth century certainly, and perhaps even today, shopping is a way for those who lack economic power as *producers*—particularly women, but we can also include other groups, such as youth or the unemployed—to exercise some, albeit limited, control as *consumers*. Indeed, Judith Williamson suggests that in our contemporary culture, which is generally unsympathetic to labour rights, consumption is one of the *only* viable ways for people to control their environments and produce their own identities (231). This somewhat depressing proposition is itself perhaps inadequate, however, to describe the complexities of shopping that, as we have suggested above, emerge most clearly in the case of *women* shoppers. One of the ways women complicate the case against consumerism is by messing up the categories on which such critiques are founded. As Sue Thornham notes, citing the work of theorist Janice Winship on the ideology of women's magazines,

> The "split" within capitalist society between production/consumption; work/leisure; work/personal life; work/everyday life is one which operates . . . only for men. It depends on a concept of the labourer who is a "free" individual able to sell his labour—separable from himself—freely. Women, however, live out the relations of capitalism "through their femininity." (Winship qtd. in Thornham 135)

As they play a role that combines elements of consumer, producer, and commodity, women achieve benefits from shopping that are, at best, ambiguous. However, by challenging the traditional oppositions between public and private, subject and object, and masculine and feminine on the level of both economics and pleasure, they refute essentialist arguments about female—or consumer—passivity.

As the example of women and shopping shows, the "yay or nay" approach to consumerism is not a viable way of understanding it. Though such approaches are perhaps inevitable, it is important to recognize that at least to some degree criticisms of consumer culture are themselves part of the process of distinction that Bourdieu analyzes: critics assert their own aesthetic values by dismissing lowbrow television (*Married with Children, COPS*) and praising their more meritorious cousins (*The Sopranos, Buffy the Vampire Slayer*). As critics like Thornham have shown, these distinctions have gender, as well as class, implications.

The Consequences of Consumption

Another way of approaching consumer culture frames the implications of consumerism in a somewhat different way. This is to ask: What are the consequences of consumer society? What is the price of the pleasures we can and do derive from making meanings through our practices of consumption? A response to this question can take various forms, ranging from the philosophical to the empirical. Philosophically, the capitalist system that gives rise to and perpetuates consumerism has long been seen as a fundamentally alienating system: it is a system in which the pleasures of consumption are purchased for most at the cost of engaging in forms of labour that are antithetical to our real interests and that have become more and more specialized and narrow.

Empirically, a number of critics have drawn attention to the impact of Western consumerism on other peoples and on the environment. Richard Robbins has explored in detail the global consequences of consumerism through his examination of the development of the sugar and beef industries (194–220). The Western appetite for sugar led to the expansion of the plantation economy in the eighteenth and nineteenth centuries, and, correspondingly, to the untold suffering of millions who were displaced from their homelands to serve as slaves on these plantations. The modern beef industry, to take another example, has had an environmentally devastating impact around the world, leading to environmental degradation through the deforestation that often accompanies large-scale ranching, the pollution of groundwater and the atmosphere by waste products, and the spread of disease both to human beings and to wild animal populations.

What is perhaps more telling is that we can see the same stories of human and environmental damage if we consider virtually *any* aspect of contemporary consumption, from the use of automobiles (depletion of both non-renewable resources and the ozone layer, combined with increased human health risks due to smog and increased UV radiations) to the purchase of hip, funky clothing (almost all of which is produced in degrading sweatshop factories, a form of labour that approximates slavery even if workers "freely" choose to work in them).

While this chapter has argued that it is important to take consumerism seriously in order to understand contemporary popular culture, it is just as important to understand the global impact of our "society of perpetual growth." When perpetual growth takes place in a world of limited natural and human resources, serious and inevitable problems will arise. Finding answers to these problems generated by consumption is one of the major challenges of this century. The greatest challenge is to try to understand how to mobilize the pleasures and possibilities of consumption, and the way in which consumption can be a place of individual and collective agency, in a manner that also addresses the sometimes terrible consequences of consumption.

A Different Kind of Consumer Culture

In "Towards a New Politics of Consumption," the sociologist Juliet Schor proposes a model for thinking past the either/or way in which consumption has typically been

Workers in the cocoa fields of Ivory Coast are paid less than 50 cents a day—if they are paid at all.

addressed. Her proposal is to reorient rather than do away with consumption (which is, as we will see in the final section of this chapter, one of the common critical reactions to consumerism: the belief that the only solution is to do away with it altogether), by addressing one of the key, if under-theorized, aspects of consumption.

Contemporary modes of consumption put untold stresses and strains on individuals. Schor believes that there is already an enormous amount of discontent with consumerism; what is lacking is a way to conceptualize it. Social well-being in a consumer society has always been linked to income levels. The assumption is that the more money you have, the more you can spend and the more satisfied with life you will be. (This is why politicians always employ the rhetoric of tax cuts to try to win votes.) What is lacking is a market for "alternatives to status or positional goods" (457): there is a market for things, but not for public goods or more time. In turn, since it is difficult to express one's desires for these kinds of goods in a society where achievement is measured almost solely by monetary wealth, consumer society "underproduces" goods that people find important: a clean environment (since environmental costs are not included in the price of goods), leisure (it is harder to choose more free time over higher incomes in virtually every employment sector), and all manner of public goods (since mass transit is so poor we are forced to use private cars, which in turn leads to a further decline in mass transit since it is used less and less).

A new politics of consumption would try to create a language and a political framework in which it is possible to create an economy of "less work and less stuff" (459). Schor believes that there is a strong demand for such an economy, even if it is difficult to see this because we can participate only in the forms of consumption currently "on offer" (459). She makes seven suggestions, all of which are important to our discussion here.

The first involves the revival of a discussion of the minimal social needs for every individual in society to be fully able to participate in it. Second is a focus on "quality of life" rather than "quantity of stuff," which in turn is related to the third, the need for more ecologically sustainable forms of consumption. Addressing minimal social needs has to be accompanied by more democratic consumption practices, that is (fourth), a way of "de-cooling" high-end products and changing the rules of the game of distinction. Fifth and sixth, a "vast consumer policy agenda" has to put pressure on the development of government policy, including the creation of policy to control the "cultural environment" (ad-free zones, diversity in retailing, etc.).

Seventh is a point that is absolutely crucial to any politics of consumption. Schor points out what Marx insisted on almost a century and a half ago: "Everything we consume has been produced. So a new politics of consumption must take into account the labor, environmental, and other conditions under which products are made, and argue for high standards" (461). *This* constitutes the real agenda for rethinking our consuming lives—lives whose frantic pace, absurdities, and wasted efforts, all in the name of accumulating more stuff faster and faster, are in turn threatening to consume us. The forms that our criticisms take, however, rely all too frequently on the use and abuse of a set of concepts that seem unable to push us out of the dangerous orbit that we've assumed around the planet Consumption; we will look at these concepts below. If we continue our present trajectory, the future explorers who find our remains will only come across a tape with a single sentence recorded on it: "We had compulsions that made us confuse shopping with creativity..." (Coupland 11).

Authenticity and Co-optation: "The Merchants of Cool"

Rachel Dretzin and Barak Goodman's *Frontline* documentary "The Merchants of Cool" (2001) explores the hyper-commodified world of contemporary youth culture. Narrated by PBS correspondent Douglas Rushkoff, who appears in the documentary as a lonely adult figure wandering through the landscape of youth pop culture, the documentary explores a whole range of contemporary marketing and advertising practices that extend their way deep into the lives of one of consumer culture's most cherished subjects—youth.

The current generation of teenagers is the wealthiest in history. The documentary claims that in the United States in 2000 teenagers spent $100 billion themselves and influenced the spending of another $50 billion. Since teens generally don't have to pay for the necessities of life, the vast majority of spending went toward forms of what Veblen described as "conspicuous consumption"—CDs, movie passes, soft drinks and fast food, fashion, and video games. For companies involved in producing the objects that teenagers consume, there is fierce competition to secure these discretionary dollars.

Dretzin and Goodman explore the forms that this competition has taken, as well as the impact that it has had on youth culture and contemporary popular culture more generally, in order to come to some conclusions about the degree to which the values of industry have infiltrated the last remaining cracks and gaps in consumer society.

Defining "Cool" According to Goodman, teens today respond "most reliably" to "this maddeningly elusive thing called cool." Increasingly, "cool" has been understood as standing in opposition to the mainstream consumer products: something that everyone likes cannot possibly be cool. This has created a paradoxical situation for companies that produce consumer products, especially for those that target teens. In order to ensure sales of their products, they need to appeal to what teens find cool; as soon as they begin to flood the market with their products, a product that started out cool quickly becomes yet another mass-produced object intended primarily to separate teens from their money.

"The Merchants of Cool" showcases the ways in which companies have tried to search out what youth think is cool in order to capitalize on it; it also shows the transformation of something cool (and thus supposedly *transgressive,* or opposed to the dominant values of consumer culture) into a form of mainstream consumer culture. In the first instance, they focus on a variety of marketing techniques that employ forms of ethnography. "Cool hunters" are marketers who search out what youth think is cool before it becomes part of the culture at large (or even of youth culture at large). Such cool hunters visit high schools and try to track down "early adopters"—teens who are willing to take a chance in wearing radical clothing, listening to music that might be unpopular with their peers, and decorating their bodies and styling their hair in original ways. They then compile this information into reports that are purchased by large companies, which in turn use the information to try to anticipate the kinds of products and styles that teens will purchase.

The filmmakers paint a picture of a present in which marketers, by entering into the lives of teens more and more intrusively, have shortened the time between the expression of an authentic agency with respect to popular culture (teens making their own forms of cool, or re-working parts of existing consumer forms) and the time at which this expression becomes commodified, turned into an experience or object to be bought and sold to as many people as possible. Rushkoff, the narrator, suggests that what is being witnessed in youth culture today is the intensification and extensification of a longer historical narrative of consumer culture. The fundamental "engine" of consumerism (what drives it onward and upward) that the film identifies involves the co-optation by businesses of genuine, authentic forms of cultural expression.

The worry of the filmmakers is that co-optation of authentic forms of popular expression now occurs so rapidly that youth culture no longer has any room to breathe or to develop and grow. And what this in turn implies is that consumer culture is now in danger of becoming total, with structure coming to overwhelm the few remaining sites of agency.

We are all familiar with the narrative offered in this documentary. When our favourite indie band signs to a major label or achieves unexpectedly widespread sales, or when a reputable film star begins appearing in mass-culture schlock (many fans have wondered why Robert De Niro would ever agree to star in *Showtime* or *Meet the Parents*), we can't help but feel as though they have somehow "sold out," trading their artistic authenticity for the comfort of cold hard cash. This narrative seems to work particularly well in discussions of popular music.

Music Scene Fashion Narratives   Punk in England and grunge in Seattle emerged out of local situations and music subcultures in response to specific social and political contexts. In both cases, punk and grunge style—comments on consumer culture's fascination with fashion (punks ripped and defaced their clothing, reassembling items with staples and safety pins; grunge musicians adopted working-class clothing, specifically the iconic lumberjack shirt)—quickly crossed over to the mainstream, or at the very least were transposed to other cultural and subcultural settings. British soccer star David Beckham saw fit to wear a version of the mohawk in the qualifying rounds leading up to the 2002 World Cup; in North America, youth living outside the Pacific Northwest quickly started wearing lumberjack shirts and listening to Nirvana and other examples of the Seattle sound. The narrativization of these kinds of cultural movements implies an early, non-commodified, non-consumer moment of authenticity, followed by an inexorable process of commercial and cultural assimilation of apparently threatening or oppositional discourses into mainstream culture.

But while this may be a familiar narrative about the dynamics of contemporary consumption, it is one that passes over a number of issues that we have tried to emphasize here. First, there is a way in which (as with so many other examples of cultural criticism directed toward consumption) this narrative translates into political stasis: since genuine expressions are fated to be assimilated into mainstream discourses, it's pointless to even *try* to make your own forms of popular culture. And, since being popular means being co-opted, it is more or less structurally impossible to spread (say) an anti-consumerist message as widely as possible, as many bands have wanted to do.

More significantly, this narrative assumes the solidity of two categories that should be seen as both more porous and more incomplete than the "co-optation thesis" implies. The claim that the products of youth culture are *ever* authentic in the first place—or at least, authentic in the way that "The Merchants of Cool" implies, outside of consumer culture and in opposition to it—positions youth culture in an impossible place. Punk didn't come suddenly out of nowhere: it was itself already part of a pop-culture discourse and has to be seen as "inside" rather than "outside" of consumer culture. (How else would one ever have the idea that you could cause a social/cultural revolution by playing your guitar?) Finally, the co-optation thesis displays little faith in the uses to which people put consumer objects. Co-opted culture is imagined as a culture bereft of agency, a position that we explored above in the section on desire and pleasure.

Counterculture Narratives   One of the most important challenges to the view that consumer culture involves the co-optation of real, genuine, or authentic forms of culture is found in Thomas Frank's analysis of the supposed co-optation of the politics of the 1960s into consumer culture, a transformation that turned Sixties hippies into Eighties yuppies. In *The Conquest of Cool*, he focuses on the supposed absorption of the energies of the Sixties counterculture into the language of advertising. He writes that "at the heart of every interpretation of the counterculture is a very particular—and very questionable—understanding of corporate ideology and of business practice ... business was the monolithic bad guy who had caused America to become a place of puritanical conformity and empty consumerism" (7).

But an examination of Fifties and Sixties business culture gives us a very different vision of things: in many cases, business saw the counterculture not as an enemy, but as a symbolic ally in their own efforts to modify and update business practices. The bureaucratized, overly rationalized business environment of the Fifties was producing fewer and fewer gains. The solution was to adopt a model of flexibility and creativity that mirrored the values inherent in the counterculture. Indeed, Frank even suggests that advertisers adopted a critical position on mainstream culture before the Sixties radicals. Like the hippies themselves, advertisers and businesses were responding to the fact that "the mass culture critique was, if not populist, enormously popular ... by the middle of the 1950s, talk of conformity, of consumerism, and of the banality of mass-produced culture were routine elements of middle-class American life" (11).

What Frank's analysis shows us is that the standard co-optation model, which places the values of the dominant culture and the counterculture (or youth culture) into strict opposition, offers a far too simplistic understanding of both. The popularity of this model, its presence as a cultural commonplace that we all turn to all the time to explain changes in popular culture, has correspondingly skewed our own understanding of it, reinforcing both the overwhelming power and solidity of the structures of consumer culture (the forces of co-optation) and the uncritical presence of those authentic experiences or expressions which are then co-opted.

SUMMARY

This chapter has argued that our experiences of contemporary popular culture (and, indeed, contemporary experience more generally) take place within a consumer culture—a culture that is defined by a belief in perpetual growth and which is characterized by commodity exchange. In order to understand popular culture, it is essential to understand the limits and possibilities imposed by contemporary consumption. Key points to remember include the following:

- Consumer culture is historically unique and comes into existence fully only in the past century or so. Prior to this, exchange was less commodified and people were more directly and explicitly involved in the production of the things that they consumed.
- What and how we consume has broader social meaning and significance than the act of consumption itself might suggest.

- Though choice is one of the major characteristics that we associate with consumers, choices and individual decisions about consumption are guided by larger social structures. One of the most important of these in terms of contemporary consumption is the way in which consumption symbolically governs social and class distinctions.
- Examinations of consumption need to attend to the way in which meaning is produced at specific sites and in specific circumstances. Even though choice is governed by social structures, it remains important to attend to the ways in which individuals express agency through consumption.
- It is also important to be attuned to the costs of consumption and to explore the impacts that the forms of consumption that underlie Western popular culture have on the rest of the world.

SUGGESTIONS FOR FURTHER READING

Bocock, Robert. *Consumption.* New York: Routledge, 1994.

Clark, David B., Marcus Doel, and Kate M.K. Housiaux, eds. *The Consumption Reader.* New York: Routledge, 2003.

Gottdiener, Mark. *New Forms of Consumption.* Lanham, MD: Rowman and Littlefield, 2000.

McCracken, Grant. *Culture and Consumption.* Bloomington: Indiana University Press, 1988.

Scanlan, Jennifer. *The Gender and Consumer Culture Reader.* New York: New York University Press, 2000.

Schor, Juliet B. *Do Americans Buy Too Much?* Boston: Beacon Press, 2000.

———. *The Overspent American: The Unexpected Decline of Leisure.* New York: Basic Books, 1998.

Schor, Juliet B., and Douglas Holt. *The Consumer Society Reader.* New York: The New Press, 2000.

Chapter 6

Identity and the Body

INTRODUCTION: IDENTITY—A NECESSARY FICTION?

In 2002, FOX introduced a new series called *John Doe*, in which the main character suffers from a profound identity crisis. He has awakened on a tropical island, naked and in the fetal position, with no idea who he is. Bizarrely, he turns out to possess an extraordinary breadth of knowledge about everything from advanced statistics to the history of Seattle's building codes. Much of the show's interest derives from Doe's use of his amazing mental ability to help the police solve crimes. However, the action/adventure formula is complicated by his more serious existential dilemma: in the words of one reviewer, "he knows everything—except himself" (Gilbert). His extraordinary talent at piecing together stories that help the police solve difficult cases springs partly from his anguished need to solve his own "case": to assemble the narrative that will give him coherence, a self. There is nothing really remarkable about this premise; in fact, it is arguably a cliché. The fact that it *works* as a cliché, however—that the story of a haunted individual on a quest to find himself is so familiar—highlights the centrality of identity in Western society. In the following two chapters we examine the concept of identity, framing our discussion around some key questions: What is identity? Why is it so important in contemporary society? What is at stake in the representation and production of identities, individual and collective?

That something *is* at stake is clear to see from the many kinds of popular culture that derive at least part of their meaning from the significance of identity. From magazine ads that appeal to our sense of ourselves as unique individuals, to subcultural styles that allow us to create resistant identities (see Chapter Eight), popular culture testifies to the centrality of identity in producing meaning and pleasure in our everyday lives. In this chapter we explore conflicting ideas about identity that can be summed up under two general approaches: **essentialist** vs. **social constructivist**. Essentialist theories posit identity as a fundamental, unchanging core of meaning that precedes and transcends culture and politics. Identity derives its sense and legitimacy, according to these theories, through its grounding in nature and/or history, where "history" is seen as an unbroken line of development whose truth is unquestionable. Social constructivist theories, on the other hand, emphasize the cultural and political circumstances in which identities are produced. Social constructivism takes issue with the essentialist premise of identity as something inherent within an individual or group, foregrounding instead the complex *process* through which narratives of identity express broader social relations, including and especially relations of power. Those relations remain invisible to the extent that identities are naturalized or essentialized—that is, represented as outside or prior to particular historical circumstances.

Over the course of the last century, developments in the field of psychology, political theory, and philosophy have highlighted some of the logical and practical problems with essentialism, while offering variations on constructivist models of identity. These models inform much of the discussion in this chapter, which explores the role of social and political forces in constructing narratives of identity. To see identity as a form of narrative or story—something made up, rather than given—does not lead us to suggest it is insubstantial or dispensable. Rather, this chapter demonstrates the symbolic and material weight of identity, both as an ideological force that inserts us into particular roles we may or may not have chosen in a social script we do not ultimately control, and as a platform for self-expression that may allow us limited forms of rewriting. The fluid and contradictory nature of human experience further means that we cannot be defined by any simple mechanism of identity—or even multiple identities (e.g., sister, friend, student, musician, bartender); there will always be parts of us, conscious and unconscious, that exceed the narratives that at various times work to explain or confine us.

A critical issue in debates about the significance and limits of identity is the role of our bodies in determining who we are. The assumption that has prevailed in Western thought since the time of René Descartes (1596–1650)—that mind and, by extension, self and identity were fundamentally distinct from the crude materiality of the body—has been increasingly confounded, in science and in popular thought, by a recognition of the inseparability of mind and body. A sometimes confused vacillation between the two perspectives—mind vs. body and mind/body (or, to use a term we define later, *embodied subjectivity*)—characterizes contemporary practices such as health and fitness regimes and forms of body modification such as tattooing, piercing, and plastic surgery, which view work on the body as a means of self-enhancement. The perception of the body as almost infinitely malleable to our individual specifications, a perception that is in line with broader beliefs about the role of choice in consumer society, is complicated by the recognition that the capacity to fashion ourselves and our bodies is not equally available to everyone. The persistence of categories of gender, sexual orientation, and race as markers of identity and social power highlights the complex relationship between culture and physicality, whereby material differences are invested with cultural meanings that in turn have material effects, in the form of unequal pressures and opportunities encountered by members of different groups in their quests for self-definition.

The relationship between identity and **agency**, or the capacity each of us has to shape our own life, is a critical problem that informs many of the concerns we explore in this chapter and the following one. Thus, while many of our discussions focus on the way identities function as stories or create meaning, of central importance is the way these meanings operate to produce particular kinds of power and pleasure.

Suggested Activity 6.1

As you read this chapter and the following one, think about the identities that define you—or that you choose to be defined by—and how these identities fit into the bigger symbolic and material networks that articulate the society you live in. When and how do these identities conflict with one another?

THE HISTORY OF IDENTITY—SOME DIFFERENT THEORIES

The seeming obviousness of the concept of individual identity belies the fact that, until relatively recently (up until the eighteenth century), nobody gave much thought to it. The idea of the individual as a unique self, with deep psychological needs and preferences, held no currency in a social context in which the meaning of an individual life was subordinate to the issue of the survival of society as a whole. Who you were was prescribed not by your own internal qualities or will, but by the role you occupied in the institutions of family, church, class hierarchy, and so on. So why has individual identity come to have such importance in contemporary society? One dominant explanation is that society simply evolved to a point at which people were liberated from tradition-bound structures, and the unique identities of individuals—which had been there all along—suddenly emerged from their straitjackets of class and religious conformity to claim their fundamental value and significance. It is certainly true that, from the late eighteenth century on, increasing attention was paid to the issue of identity and to debates over the role of nature or nurture in defining it. All of these debates were concerned with the meaning not just of individuals but also of society, as the issue of the role of birth or environment in shaping personality had critical implications for social policy relating to medicine, education, and the treatment of criminality.

Identity and the Unconscious

One of the first major bodies of work to concentrate on—and, ultimately, to unsettle—the grounds of identity was the field of psychoanalysis, pioneered by Sigmund Freud

(1856–1939) in the early part of the twentieth century. Through his work on adult psychiatric problems—essentially, identity disorders—Freud developed a theory, later elaborated upon by others, of the stages through which identity is formed as a critical precondition for the individual's integration into society. Significant to Freud's theory is the emphasis on the way in which identities are not pre-given, or natural, but rather *produced* in order to manage chaotic fears and desires whose expression is socially forbidden. Babies, psychoanalytic theory suggests, have no coherent identities to speak of. Their inner world is defined, rather, by an unorganized collection of primal drives and instincts, with no conscious sense of themselves as separate from the world around them. A baby's eventual realization that the world—most significantly his/her mother—is not merely an extension of him/herself but a separate being is both a traumatic break and the beginning of the process of socialization, marked by the management and containment of powerful, contradictory impulses toward "the other."

Freudian Theory of Psychosocial Development   Two key moments in the process of psychosocial development are 1) the recognition of sexual difference, which hinges on the presence or absence of a penis (symbolically expressed in Freud's theory as "the phallus"); this recognition imposes social meaning on our early desires, directing us, via fear of paternal authority, away from the forbidden love object of our mother's body, and 2) the acquisition of **language**. As a symbolic system that manages and mediates our relationship to the world, language is an important part of the social machinery that works to channel our desire into acceptable forms of adult sexual orientation and gender identity.

In Freud's formulation, these early moments in development, framed by the so-called Oedipal triangle of mother–father–child, lay the groundwork for two distinct ways of orienting the self in relation to others: the first, which comes later to be associated with sexual feeling, involves the desire to possess, or to *have* the other; the second—what Freud called identification—involves a recognition of a similarity between oneself and the other that inspires the desire to *be* the other. These two drives, which Freud suggests are biologically rooted, are organized, in the process of the resolution of the Oedipal conflict, to reflect "proper" gender identification and sexual orientation: the young boy learns to identify with males and to desire females, while girls, lacking phallic agency, learn to *be* desirable to males, and to identify with women. These patterns of desire and identification are reinforced culturally, by the dominant institutions of education and family as well as by popular culture (see our discussion of Laura Mulvey's theory of Hollywood cinema in Chapter Three).

However, sexual drives are by nature chaotic, and the initial Oedipal scene is fraught with unease: the boy's imperative to identify with the father is complicated both by his fear of punishment for desiring his mother in the first place, and by his aggressive desire to take his father's place. These fears and desires are repressed into the unconscious, inaccessible to our waking selves except through occasional chinks in our rational consciousness, where they appear in disguised form as dreams, fantasies, and verbal accidents (or "Freudian slips"). Because they cannot be articulated, these unconscious currents continue to create troubling ripples in our emotional lives, making the stability of both gender identification and heterosexual orientation precarious. The complex mix of love, fear, and aggression that characterizes our relations with others—particularly those closest to us—testifies to the impossibility of ever fully resolving the tensions enacted through the Oedipal conflict. The determination with which we cling to our identities—particularly gender and sexual orientation—is partly a reflection of an unconscious fear of the consequences of acknowledging the ambivalence that underlies them.

Identity and Ideology

The key lesson in Freud for understanding identity is not that it has no grounding in reality; rather, it is that the stable and coherent selves we articulate to the world and to ourselves are constructions, a bit like dams built to control and manage the torrent of chaotic drives and impulses that cannot be assimilated to society. Later psychoanalytic theorists, particularly feminist theorists, emphasize the importance of culture in defining psychosexual development, stressing that both the Oedipal complex and its resolution assume the shape they do in Freud's theory not because they represent natural or obvious stages in individual development but because they are already overdetermined by the values of a patriarchal, capitalist culture that lays stress on the nuclear family, on the possession of phallic authority, and on the development of the individual.

Marxist Theories of Identity   The suggestion that not just the shape but also the very concept of individual identity is determined in particular cultural, historical circumstances informs the theories of Karl Marx (1818–83), who, like Freud, understood the construction of identity as a response to underlying forces of which the individual is largely unconscious. For Marx, as for Freud, identity could be understood in one sense as a kind of mythical armour people assumed as a way of coping with the gap between their needs and desires and the social economy. While repression, for Freud, was the mechanism that shaped identity while concealing its own origins from it, for Marx the primary force in producing identity and consciousness as a kind of empty protective shell was **ideology** (see Close-Up 2.1). Ideology, you will recall from earlier chapters, is a form of knowledge or belief that is shaped by, while serving to conceal, powerful interests through its representation as natural or common sense. In the system of industrial capitalism that was gaining force during the time Marx wrote, ideology played a hugely significant role in securing the acceptance of an exploited working class by promoting a belief in the naturalness of the capitalist order and in the freedom of the individual within it.

In Marx's theory, ideology is the (disguised) expression of underlying economic relations. Later theorists, particularly the French theorist Louis Althusser, revised Marx's theory in order to emphasize the centrality of the social structures—what Althusser termed **ideological state apparatuses (ISAs),** through which ideology is reproduced. Rather than being absolutely determined by the economy, the realm of culture and ideology, as it is disseminated through institutions such as schools, universities, and the media, comes to have a semiautonomous or independent role in shaping individuals and society. The new importance accorded to culture means its effects are more pervasive than Marx suggested: while earlier concepts of ideology saw it as a kind of "false consciousness," which could be enlightened by seeing through it to the *real* economic conditions it concealed, Althusser's revised concept, which was strongly influenced by psychoanalysis, emphasized the impossibility of ever totally liberating identity from ideology.

In particular, Althusser focused on the process he termed "**interpellation,**" by which individuals are compelled, through a mix of individual psychological and social imperatives, to identify with social roles offered them. This happens in a variety of contexts: for example, in the university setting the architecture of the classroom, modes of academic discourse, and signs and ads around campus all combine to construct a set of relationships between different people. In order for the institution to function, it requires individuals to take up their assigned places in those already established relationships, not through a system of elaborate rules but through each individual's recognition of, and *identification with,* his or her role.

Suggested Activity 6.2

Think about how the educational institutions you have attended work to interpellate you into particular roles as a student and member of society. Elements you might consider include specific, material structures of authority, such as the arrangement of the classroom in which the professor sits or stands at the front while students sit together in a body, as well as the broader institutional structures that shape your expectations of what kind of social position your education, in conjunction with other social forces such as family and class, prepares you to assume.

Following psychoanalysis, particularly the work of the French theorist Jacques Lacan, Althusser locates the roots of this process of identification in the early stages of socialization, in particular the acquisition of language. Particularly critical in this process is the moment Lacan identifies as the *mirror stage,* which corresponds to the child's recognition of himself as a separate being. The mirror stage describes the moment in which the child sees his reflection in the mirror (which can also be read as a metaphor for the eyes of his mother and the world outside himself) and identifies with that image. What's particularly significant about that moment of recognition, Lacan suggests, is that it's actually a *misrecognition*: the stable, unified figure the child sees in the mirror—more stable and unified, in fact, than the child himself, whose body and its sensations are still relatively uncoordinated—is a reflection, a pleasing image of integrated selfhood that the child can never fully inhabit. The moment of identification, then, is actually a moment of splitting, in which the promise of wholeness is haunted by the impossibility of resolution: identity is always characterized by lack. This lack creates the potential for challenging the terms of identity, something we take up later in this chapter.

All Selves Are Not Created Equal

Of course, because the possibilities for identification are defined and limited through their production within unequal social systems, they hold out much more promising opportunities for some people than for others: in other words, identity may be an illusion, but it is an illusion that *works* for some people in a way that it doesn't for others. This inequality is highlighted explicitly in Marx's theory, which shows that the stakes of ideology are different depending on what position one occupies in the class structure, and more implicitly in psychoanalysis, where sexual difference determines what identities and authorities are available to whom, based on physiological sex characteristics.

According to both Freud and Marx, then, the process of socialization into a patriarchal, capitalist society not only establishes identity as a crucial focus of self-organization; it also prescribes and delimits what kinds of identities it is possible to adopt. Identity-formation is thus both enabling and disabling—*how* enabling or disabling depends largely on the place one is assigned in social hierarchies defined by gender and class.

Feminist Theories   Feminist theory has taken up the insights of Freud and Marx while also showing the limits of psychoanalysis and Marxism in understanding the mechanisms and the politics of gender identity. The concepts of the unconscious and ideology help to explain how gender identity is socially constructed, and why it is so firmly entrenched. They explain, in other words, both why it is important to challenge so-called "natural" patterns of identification and desire and why it is so difficult. Forged in an intricate amalgam of biology and culture, women's self-perception as the "other" of male desire can't be undone by a simple political assertion of equality. Neither is it possible to counter ideological constructions of femininity with some "real" essence of femaleness, since the very notion of gender is shot through with ideology, experienced by each of us at the most basic level of self-perception.

Paradoxically, it is through the essentially fractured nature of women's self-perception that it becomes possible to mount a challenge to conventional ideologies of gender. Assigned a role in culture that is defined not as autonomous or self-sufficient but as always in-relation-to—"other" than—the normative category of man, women do not inhabit the myth of identity as comfortably as men do. They are, in the words of feminist Luce Irigaray, "the sex which is not one"—a phrase that sums up the construction of women as negative, *less than* whole, desiring subjects, and as irreducible: not "one," but always split between the myth of stable identity and the reality of its fragmentation and flux. While this condition of always-incomplete self-affirmation can be seen as disempowering, it also arguably offers a lever through which to tear apart the whole fiction of identity on which patriarchy is based. That is, rather than aspiring to the ultimately empty idea of coherent selfhood—an idea that is always haunted by the shadow of the inferior, incoherent, other—female identity actually exposes the emptiness of the edifice that has served to shut women out.

One way of conceptualizing this challenge to the traditional terms of identity is through the idea of performance, or **performativity**. With its connotations of the theatre, in which actors play scripted roles, performativity, formulated most extensively in the work of cultural theorist Judith Butler, is an apt metaphor for the enactment of sex and gender identity. The script—which, in broad social terms, would refer to mythologized gender ideals (for a discussion of mythology see Chapter Three)—is naturalized through its repeated performance. At the same time, the whole concept of performance, which is based on re-presentation—*playing*, not being—throws into doubt the solidity of the identity on which it is supposedly based. While departing from the script is not an option—*all* selves reproduce to some extent socially prescribed roles—the recognition that it *is* a script disables its authority. For those whose identities have always been precarious—women, homosexuals, and, in a different way, racial minorities—the anti-authoritarian potential of performativity is always to some extent implicit. Their identities challenge the mythological norm whether they realize it or not, no matter how tightly they try to conform to their assigned roles. A more significant challenge is mounted by such self-conscious performances as the hyper-feminized display of drag queens or the assumption of typical "butch" or "femme" lesbian identities. These performances, by re-presenting gender norms to excess, draw spectacular attention to their artificiality.

As critics of Butler have suggested, it is easy to exaggerate the subversive power of performativity; the inevitable risk of parody is that the standard that one is playing with or trying to ironically undercut is actually reinforced through its repetition. Moreover, in a cultural context in which the manipulation of conventional gender *style*—in the form of clothes, accessories, hair, and so on—has become an element of high fashion, the political implications of gender–role playing can't be assumed in advance. This is particularly true given that the capacity to play around with sex and gender depends a lot on one's social position, including one's race, culture, and class. The stakes of "passing"—conforming convincingly to accepted ideals of beauty, behaviour, and belief—are not the same for everyone.

Identity and Power/Knowledge

A critical premise informing psychoanalytic and Marxist thought, foregrounded by feminism, is that identity is defined by and through power.

Michel Foucault   French philosopher and social critic Michel Foucault (1926–84) devoted particular attention to that relationship, showing how power both constrains and produces social meaning, especially that privileged site of meaning that is individual identity. One of the crucial ways Foucault's theory departs from Marx is in his understanding of how power operates in society. While traditional Marxist theory conceives of power as belonging to, or wielded by, a ruling class (similar to the assumption in early feminist theory that power rests primarily in the hands of men), Foucault saw its function in a much more nuanced way.

Moving beyond the obvious critiques that Marxists and feminists could direct at one another—that class is complicated by gender and vice versa, so power could never be said to rest in the hands of a single, identifiable group—Foucault suggested that power is not possessed at all; rather, it circulates continuously throughout society, concentrating in different places at different historical moments and constituting particular meanings and identities as it does so. Foucault's theory does not contest Marx's point that power is unequally distributed; rather, it questions the stability of that distribution, emphasizing its fluidity and the ambiguity of its effects. One of Foucault's most significant insights is his observation that power shapes society productively rather than repressively. This does not mean that all of the effects of power are good; it means, rather, that power takes the form not only of regulations restricting people's freedom to be, speak, or act a certain way, but also of **discourses**—whole systems of thought, speech, and knowledge-*production* that structure institutional and social practices (see Chapter Three).

Foucault was particularly interested in the period of the late eighteenth and early nineteenth centuries (the same period, not coincidentally, that Marx's work focused on), a period in which cultivation of the *self* took on a new urgency. As we have mentioned above, before the eighteenth century the idea of individuals possessing complex and meaningful interior lives did not hold much interest. The idea began to gain currency not because people were finally free to "be themselves," but because, in an industrial-capitalist society characterized by the fragmentation of old social hierarchy and the burgeoning of a middle class whose entrepreneurial energies translated into new forms of wealth and freedom for individuals, new forms of social discipline were required to maintain order. As Freud, Marx, and others had already clearly shown, discipline need not take the form of physical force or punishment, or even law; it works most effectively through the largely unconscious internalization of ideas, values, and modes of discrimination that are represented as natural, or "common sense." Thus "discipline," in Foucault's sense, combines what are usually seen as two separate meanings of the word, the first associated with methods of training or techniques designed to enforce obedience, and the second with branches of knowledge (e.g., science, modern languages, philosophy) characterized by particular rules or methods.

By highlighting the connection between forms of knowledge and the exercise of power (significantly, "discipline," when used in this second sense, can be either a noun or a verb), Foucault emphasizes the material consequences of knowledge as it becomes classified into different discourses—medicine, for example, or the law—that are enacted, or put into effect, through institutions such as hospitals, schools, and prisons. These institutions play a critical role in the reproduction of social hierarchies, and in the shaping of individuals through technologies of treatment, training, or punishment. Foucault's work on prisons in particular led to particular insights into the way technologies of discipline that were developed in the eighteenth century led to new forms of self-regulation and management.

An important architectural innovation in eighteenth-century prisons was the *panopticon,* a structure comprising a tower erected in the centre of a courtyard with cells arranged all around it (see Figure 6.1). All the cells were visible from the tower and—more importantly—the tower was visible from all the cells. The special disciplinary power of the panopticon lay not so much in the power it gave guards to keep an eye on the prisoners, but rather in the effect it had on the prisoners themselves, who had a sense

Figure 6.1 Panopticon

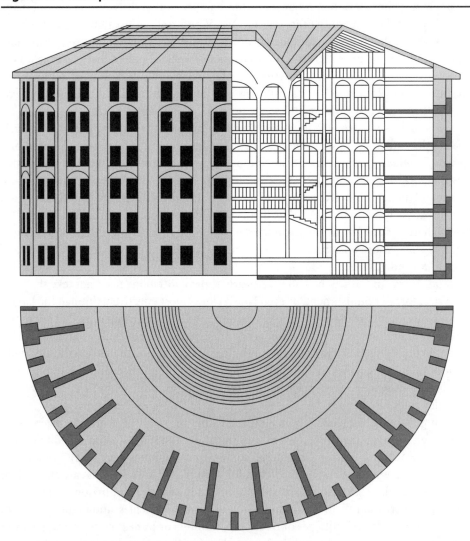

Jeremy Bentham's panopticon worked to maintain the effect of constant surveillance whether the central watch-tower was occupied or not.

of being constantly under surveillance whether there was anyone in the tower or not. The prisoners' internalization of the disciplinary gaze of the tower represents a concrete model of a more general process, intensified throughout the nineteenth century, in which individuals came to subject themselves to a kind of social scrutiny. They developed, in other words, what Foucault termed "technologies of the self," modes of conscious self-construction devised in response to naturalized systems of social power. Central to this process of self-construction was an awareness of the physical body, whose control and management is always the ultimate end of power.

The History of Sexuality

The need for a disciplined labour force in an industrial economy, combined with the unstable conditions of life in industrial society—crowded slums, the decline of traditional institutional checks on individual behaviour, along with new opportunities for leisure—led to a heightened focus on the body as a critical site of social regulation and discipline. Sexuality thus became a preoccupation in the latter half of the nineteenth century, with a host of moral codes, laws, medical theories, and treatments designed to investigate and manage it. The idea that the Victorians were obsessed with sex is, of course, nothing new. Where Foucault's theory departs from conventional assumptions is in his insistence that sexuality, as a unified collection of drives, fantasies, and behaviour, is not a natural foundation of human identity repressed in the nineteenth century and now liberated; rather, sexuality as a coherent idea emerged in the nineteenth century *at the same time, and as a product of* its construction as an object of discourse.

That does not, of course, mean that sex did not exist before the nineteenth century, only that it was not constituted as an object of knowledge in the way that it came to be in the nineteenth century and still is today. People obviously had feelings about sex and engaged in sexual activity; these feelings and acts were subject to discussion and representation in literature, popular media, and pornography, and, occasionally, to legislation. What differentiated this earlier view was the indistinguishability from other aspects of daily life of those behaviours and characteristics we now associate with sex. Only in connection with the production of "sexuality" as a subject of discourse did it come to assume its significance as a critical component of identity.

The historical production of "normal" sexuality as an idea does not precede, but actually coincides with, the emergence of the concept of *homo*sexuality as a way of classifying a form of sexual deviance. As with other forms of classification whose historical emergence Foucault traces (e.g., the concept of madness, along with its particularly gendered form of hysteria), homosexuality is not an actual condition or mode of being but rather what Foucault terms a "regulatory fiction," produced as part of a system of social control that works on the basis of drawing a distinction between "normal" and "deviant" identities. This key distinction, which is reproduced through the discourses mentioned above—medicine (particularly psychiatry) and law—underwrites a whole network of practices that work, through treatment, punishment, and exclusion, to enforce social conformity. The reasons for the production of homosexuality as an object of discourse at a particular juncture in history are complex, stemming in part from the need to secure the integrity of the newly emerging institution of the nuclear family as a place for the reproduction of bourgeois social values; thus, the regulatory fiction of sexuality is closely tied to the regulatory fiction of gender.

The critical point to emphasize here is the entanglement of identity—specifically, that highly charged component of identity that we have come to define as sexuality—with power. Power should be understood here not as a mechanism of repression or oppression, as the theories of Freud or Marx would seem to imply, but rather as a force whose impulse to control and regulate is facilitated by its productive capacity, its ability to bring into being new objects, new knowledges.

It is this productive, generative aspect of power that makes it so ambiguous and volatile. The concept of homosexuality, Foucault suggests, did not just underwrite the production of new systems of social control: "it also made possible the formation of a 'reverse' discourse: homosexuality began to speak on its own behalf, to demand that its legitimacy or 'naturality' be acknowledged, often in the same vocabulary, using the same categories by which it was medically disqualified" (*The History of Sexuality*, 101–102). In other words, while the "invention" of homosexuality serves institutional interests, embodying a new object of knowledge and by extension a new tool of social regulation, it also opens new possibilities for modes of identity formation and associated pleasures.

Summary of the Key Theories of Identity

Foucault's insights into the operation of power—that it is all-encompassing, circulating throughout the whole social body rather than remaining in the possession of particular groups, and that it works not by restriction but by the production of new meanings, new identities, new objects of knowledge—build on the insights of Freud and Marx to tell us some key things about identity: 1) it arises not from within individuals or groups, but from the complex social structures—and, in particular, the relations of power—in which those individuals and groups are situated; 2) it is historically specific, such that some aspects of identity—individualism, for example, or homo/heterosexuality—emerge as particularly significant in the context of particular social or economic arrangements; and 3) it is both imaginary and real: imaginary in the sense that its apparently essential qualities are ideologically or discursively constructed, and real in the sense that those constructions have material consequences in the form of laws and policies, beliefs and actions.

Ideologies of individualism are concretized in laws relating to private property, freedom of expression, and human rights, while discourses of sexuality are implicated in regulations and practices that seek to police or treat so-called deviant forms of sexual behaviour (regulations and practices that sometimes conflict with the laws designed to uphold the rights of the individual). The embodiment of the concept of identity in legal, educational, and medical institutions firmly entrenches it as a fundamental principle in Western society. It is not merely those institutional imperatives that make identity so compelling to us as individuals; rather, it is also the way in which our own needs and desires are interpellated, or addressed by those institutions, which leads us to internalize a sense of identity as something we simply cannot do without.

KEEPING THE STORY STRAIGHT? REPRESENTING HOMOSEXUALITY ON TV

Identity, says cultural theorist Iain Chambers, is "a labour of the imagination, a fiction, a particular story that makes sense" (25). We began this section by mentioning the role of television in telling stories of identity. Here, we will expand on those earlier comments by looking in more detail at an example of a television program that highlights some of the complexities and ambiguities of identity.

Sexuality is a particularly highly charged area for the production of identity. The strong feelings surrounding sexuality are especially evident in discussions of homosexuality, a concept which, Foucault has shown, emerged as the deviant "other" of a socially regulated (patriarchal, monogamous, married) heterosexuality. In the last few decades,

In the last decade of the twentieth century, homosexuality assumed an accepted and increasingly prominent place in shows like *Will & Grace, Oz,* and *Queer as Folk.* While some shows, like *Dawson's Creek,* took an explicitly didactic or moralistic tone, others, such as *Queer as Folk,* were hailed (or condemned) by critics for their out-and-out, often graphic, celebration of homosexual relationships.

great strides have been made in popular and political culture toward a more inclusive vision of sexuality. Changes in the laws regulating sexual behaviour, including the rights and privileges surrounding cohabitation and marriage, have been accompanied (and arguably influenced) by more positive representations of homosexuality in the media. Looking at an example of one such representation can help us to see some of the tensions and anxieties that still inform the construction of gay—and, by implicit extension, straight—identities.

Coming-Out on *Dawson's Creek* In 1999 *Dawson's Creek* aired a series of episodes that were remarkable for their unusually sensitive portrayal of a teenager's coming to terms with his homosexuality. One of the main elements in the episode, a feature inherent in the coming-out story, is an emphasis on affirming homosexuality as an *identity*, an essential part of a person's character that is repressed by a homophobic society. Drawing on the idea that truth is revealed through art, Jack's sexual orientation is first hinted at by a poem he reads aloud to his English class. Counselled by Dawson to "listen to yourself . . . I mean, poetry is your chance to give the world a peek at the innermost, private part of yourself that you'd otherwise stifle," Jack writes a poem describing a male figure and an "inner fear" ("To Be or Not to Be"). Before he can finish reading it, he bursts into tears and runs from the classroom. The poem sparks a fire of speculation amongst his friends—not least his girlfriend, Joey—about whether or not he is gay.

Besides Jack's strict and stereotypically patriarchal father, the character who reacts most intolerantly to his declaration is Ty, the Christian boyfriend of the much more liberal Jen. Ty's angry comments about the deviance of "the homosexual lifestyle" are strongly countered by Jen's defence of sexual freedom. The show clearly asks us to reject Ty's views—which, however sincerely motivated, spring from a lack of understanding compounded by guilt and confusion about his own sexuality. Interestingly, though, we are not encouraged to endorse the idea of absolute sexual freedom—not quite—as can be seen from the reaction of another character on the show.

Jen's friend, Abby, is the series' "bad girl," whose selfishness and sexual promiscuity stand in stark contrast to the more morally upright, thoughtful, and self-disciplined characters of Dawson and Joey. (Indeed, Joey inevitably turns to Dawson during the crisis over Jack's sexuality, telling Dawson that she doesn't know Jack half as well as she knows him, in part because she can't "read his eyes" the way she can Dawson's ["And That Is the Question"].) In a show that admits much moral murkiness, being honest and true to oneself is a primary virtue.

Given the questions the show casts on Abby's constancy and integrity, we inevitably respond with suspicion when she advises Jack (in classic *Dawson's Creek*–style academic-speak), "Gay . . . is just a name people came up with to persecute the normal inclination to go both ways. We're all bisexual, don't you think? We're all just sexual animals under God. This . . . society would make us think our natural impulses are something to be ashamed of, when really it's those kind of attitudes that are the embarrassment" ("Be Careful What You Wish For"). The moral dangerousness of her comments—highlighted by a quick cut to a scene in a bar in which Dawson and Jack's sister, Andie, are getting drunk—is confirmed by Abby later kissing a confused Jack, just as Joey walks in. The clear implication of an encounter that serves ultimately to convince Jack that he really *is* gay is to emphasize the importance of clear-cut, straightforward identities vs. a more fluid, uncertain terrain of desire that is shown to lead only to pain and social disorder.

The importance attached to the consistency of identity is highlighted by fans and critics who criticized Jack's coming-out as "unconvincing and insincere" (Nos4a2). Noting that "there wasn't a hint of his homosexuality before his secret was revealed during February sweeps" (Fretts), they dismiss the coming-out as "a plot device on a soap opera" (Nos4a2). There is no doubt truth to the charge that the timing of Jack's revelation of his homosexuality was prompted by a commercial drive for ratings; we might also speculate about whether an increase in audience viewership of the episodes in question reflects acceptance or prurient curiosity—that is, does it speak to a perception of homosexuality as normal or deviant? However the issue of whether the portrayal is convincing or not speaks to different concerns, about the failure of the show to convey "real life."

The constraints of the weekly television drama that require the simplification and concentration of dramatic situations so they can be presented and resolved within a forty-five-minute time slot make it easy to respond—as the fan quoted above does—by acknowledging "maybe I shouldn't take stupid TV shows seriously" (Nos4a2); however, dismissing *Dawson's Creek* and its portrayal of homosexuality ignores the role of television as part of a larger network of ideological state apparatuses that inform and *mediate* the way we understand ourselves and others. Rather than condemning the representation of Jack because it is less coherent and consistent than "real-life" homosexual identities, it is useful to think about television as one of the many resources that help to define who we are. Thinking about the production of stories on TV can prompt us to start thinking about the broader networks of production in which our own "stories," the building blocks of our identities, are implicated.

Current Debates on Homosexuality   *Dawson's Creek* illuminates some of the larger stories that define the meaning of homosexuality in North American culture. In particular, it self-consciously addresses a number of critical debates about the meaning of homosexuality, including the issues of whether homosexuality is a matter of nature or choice, and whether sexuality is defined by the binary poles of hetero- or homosexual orientation or operates on a continuum, with most people falling somewhere in between the two extremes in being attracted primarily to one sex or the other. With respect to the first debate, *Dawson's Creek*'s clear insistence on the biological basis of sexual preference, a thesis generally supported by the medical community, earned widespread approval from members of the gay community and other media commentators. By emphasizing the *naturalness* of homosexual attraction, the show effectively refuted the thesis, advanced by anti-gay crusaders, that homosexuality represents a deviant lifestyle *choice* that can be altered through faith and willpower. It further advanced the important goal of naming and claiming homosexual identity as a source of pride and personal fulfillment, not shame and alienation: later episodes depict Jack as a happy and well-balanced young adult, enjoying a loving sexual relationship.

In considering the implications of this representation of homosexuality, however, it is worth recalling Foucault's discussion of the historical production of a concept of identity centred around sexuality. Though sexual identity can offer a route to a positive sense of self and social integration, it also enables the operation of systems of discipline and social control. Significantly, these systems operate regardless of whether the characteristics they seek to classify and manage are seen as biological or learned. The perils of theories of biological essence emerge clearly in women's struggles to overcome stereotypes of "natural" feminine weakness or intellectual inferiority. Even more disturbingly, claims for the biological basis of certain aspects of identity do not preclude their regulation and control—just think about the technological and ethical debates surrounding the possibilities of genetic engineering.

In sum, looking at representations of identity, particularly those that focus on the fraught issue of sex, reveals the stakes of identity politics to be more confusing than they might initially seem. Affirming a minority identity can be an important way of bolstering a sense of worth that has been denied by mainstream society, as well as of asserting moral and legal rights. At the same time, by insisting on the qualities of individualism, binary categories ("you're either straight or you're gay, no two ways about it"), and consistent adherence to the conventions of a particular identity, such affirmations also work to preserve the status quo of a social order that is still defined by the regulation of self-expression and activity, particularly in the realm of sexuality. In Chapter Seven, we will explore the implications of upholding and challenging the concept of identity in relation to racial and cultural differences.

CHANGING OUR BODIES, CHANGING OURSELVES?

As the discussion of sexuality above makes clear, questions of identity cannot be pursued very far without reference to the body. The relationship between identities and bodies is the subject of this section, which looks at forms of body cultivation or modification in the context of such fundamental questions as: What role does the body play in the production of the self? Can we even define a "self" as distinct from the body? To what extent are our bodies the products of nature, and to what extent are they the products of our individual control? How are our bodies shaped or constrained by culture and vice versa? The answers to these questions all have significant bearing on the issue of *agency*: our power to act independently in the world, to determine our own meanings, our own actions, our own pleasures.

Embodied Selves

Descartes's famous formula, "I think therefore I am," informs the modern notion of identity as defined by the pre-eminence of mind (consciousness) over matter (the body).

Descartes's elevation of the rational mind as the faculty that gives meaning to human life, granting it supremacy over other, non-rational forms of life, informs a dualist philosophy characterized by a series of closely overlapping oppositions—spirit vs. matter, mind vs. body, reason vs. passion, nature vs. culture—that map out relations of being and, more significantly, relations of power. Besides laying the groundwork for laws surrounding the protection of private property, this framework has underwritten such dubious social practices as slavery and the subjugation of women on the grounds of a division of living beings into knowing subjects—"man"—and knowable (and possessable) objects.

Postmodernist thought has posed significant challenges to the dualisms that inform the modern concept of identity—and indeed much of modern Western philosophy (see Close-Up 6.1). In particular, postmodernism has blurred the scientific/philosophical certainty of distinctions between subjects and objects, consciousness and matter that allow us to know the world while remaining abstracted from, superior to it. The destabilization of philosophical dualisms associated with postmodernist thought is reflected by the more general breakdown of structure and hierarchy associated with contemporary social life. As old hierarchies dissolve—and with them any clear sense of identity based on birth, breeding, or old notions of class—the body becomes an increasingly important site for the negotiation of social meaning. In some ways, the new attention focused on the body reflects a move away from seeing bodies as simply containers for identity and toward recognition of the ways in which the self is embodied—at once natural and cultural, physical and psychological. This recognition is complicated, however, by the persistence of the modern notion of body and mind as somehow separate, with the latter being privileged as the home of substantial being.

This ambivalence about the relationship between self and body is highlighted in the 2001 movie *Shallow Hal*, a romantic comedy with a moral message about judging people by their inner qualities and not by outward appearance. With the help of a hypnotist, the hero, "Shallow Hal" (Jack Black), overcomes his obsession with beautiful women by losing his ability to perceive outward appearance entirely in favour of a focus on women's inner beauty. Thus, when he falls in love with Rosemary (Gwyneth Paltrow), he sees her not as she looks to others, and to herself—hugely overweight—but as a skinny goddess.

While the movie was cautiously praised for challenging stereotypes surrounding fatness—Rosemary is an extraordinarily (even unbelievably) energetic, selfless, and well-balanced person, despite insecurity about her weight—it inevitably upheld some problematic myths about body and identity. A critical component in the movie's success as a romantic comedy was the split between the images of Rosemary's outer and inner selves (unattractive vs. beautiful), conveyed by sporadic shots of Gwyneth Paltrow in a fat suit and much more frequent shots of Gwyneth Paltrow looking like, well, Gwyneth Paltrow. That Gwyneth Paltrow without the fat suit was meant to function as a metaphor for moral goodness is undercut by the overwhelming significance of her image as an icon of *physical* beauty. Our reading of Rosemary as a character is powerfully shaped by her embodiment as Paltrow.

The contradictory messages of *Shallow Hal*—that the physical body is irrelevant, and that it is the ultimate measure of the self—dodge uncomfortably around the complex relationship between mind and body.

Source: Glen Watson/MPTV.net.

Thus, the movie's overt message—that looks don't matter and that beauty is in the eye of the beholder—is compromised by the powerful myth of a correspondence between physical appearance and social and even moral worth. Moreover, to the extent that this myth is shaped by taboos against fatness—bodily excess—it expresses an ambivalent attachment to traditional ideas about the body, particularly the female body, as separate from, and essentially inferior to, the mind.

In spite of the contradictions just noted, it is tempting to take at least part of the message of *Shallow Hal* at face value, and to argue that, while we might sometimes confuse bodies and selves, we shouldn't. The relationship is purely a contingent one; there's no *natural* correlation between body weight and personality, or social value, only a culturally *constructed* one. It turns out, though, that it's not that easy to separate the two; not only do bodies shape identity, and vice versa, but the body itself is a complex amalgam of nature and culture.

The Human Body: Natural or Cultural?

Once we start to explore the entanglement of nature and culture in relation to the body, it becomes harder and harder to determine where one ends and the other begins. The body may be a material phenomenon, but the way we experience it is determined by culture. Concepts of health and disease are a case in point. Anthropologist Emily Martin has

Postmodernism

It has been said that postmodernism has come to have so many meanings that it is impossible to offer any simple definition. In the words of the critic Peter Brooker, postmodernism is "annoyingly elusive in its range of reference and attributions whether in academic debate or across the arts and culture" (174). Such variation in meaning has led many people to dismiss the term.

Generally, postmodernism refers to a phase in Western history that coincides with the information revolution and new forms of economic, social, and cultural life. Postmodernism names a period—the current era—and points to the fundamental differences of this era from even the recent past (i.e., modernism, ranging from roughly the mid nineteenth to the mid twentieth century).

One of the major changes in contemporary society lies in the character of the global economy. Rather than being based on the production of new things, economic transactions increasingly involve non-material commodities: stocks, information, the arts, and services (health care, fast food, tourism). The economy, then, is increasingly fuelled by culture, and culture, by extension, has become increasingly defined by economics. It is this development that Fredric Jameson refers to in his definition of postmodernism as "the cultural logic of late capitalism."

The economic circumstances Jameson highlights, along with recent historical developments such as decolonization, civil rights, and feminism (see Chapter Seven), have all contributed to intellectual and cultural changes now described under the heading of postmodernism. The concept is often used to describe a broad shift in approaches to truth and knowledge, away from the rationality and truth-seeking that emerged out of the Enlightenment. Since the late 1950s, the existence of such truths or laws has been challenged. Postmodernism views the search for truth as a project whose real aim is achieving social power and control, and is suspicious of any "grand narratives" or theories that seek to provide the single explanation for how human beings act (such as Freudian psychoanalysis) or how societies function (Marxism, for example).

The general public seems to share this skepticism to some degree: Where only a few decades ago people had faith in specialists (like doctors) and their political leaders, now there is widespread skepticism toward those who claim great expertise—as in Britain in February 2003, when the public simply did not believe what Prime Minister Tony Blair had to say about the threat posed by Iraq.

Postmodernism also refers to styles and movements in arts and culture that express this skeptical attitude, characterized by self-consciousness, formal and stylistic borrowing, irony, pastiche, parody, recycling, sampling, and a mixing of high and low culture. Films and novels today frequently highlight the fact that they are cultural constructions. For example, in the film *Adaptation* (2002) the screenwriter is also the film's main character. Cultural products today make self-conscious use of older forms to create new culture, such as Todd Haynes's film *Far From Heaven*, which mimics the Fifties melodramas of Douglas Sirk. Beginning with Andy Warhol, contemporary art has drawn on advertising (Jeff Wall), consumer culture (Jeff Koons), film (Cindy Sherman), and television. Irony and parody characterize the dominant modes of address on television (*Seinfeld, The Simpsons*).

For the French critic Jean Baudrillard, postmodernism is characterized by the culture of the "simulacrum"—a copy without an original, or a sign without a referent, defining a world in which representation quite simply is reality. Many find this disturbing, signalling the "emptying out" of history, the disappearance of nature, and the impossibility of defining a platform of belief from which to launch individual projects or political movement. For others, the erosion of traditional concepts of identity translates into exciting possibilities for the construction of new, multiply defined selves. In general, the way we respond to the breakdown of the old structures of meaning depends on whether our particular identities, defined by the traditional markers of class, gender, race, sexuality, and so on, were empowered or excluded by those structures.

investigated the role of myth and metaphor in the way science understands the human body—for example by looking at it as a kind of machine, or by employing metaphors of war to describe the operation of the immune system in maintaining health. Thus, we "fight" disease; our white blood cells "seek out and destroy" pathogens. The metaphorical construction of the body has especially interesting social implications in relation to the representation of reproductive processes. Think, for example, of what it might mean for conventional gender mythology if we were to replace the familiar, almost cartoonish image of eager sperm competing to *penetrate* the docile, receptive egg—an image comically rendered in Woody Allen's 1972 movie *Everything You Always Wanted to Know About Sex (But Were Afraid to Ask)*—with what some scientists suggest is a more accurate image of a tiny wiggling sperm being *enveloped* by the much larger egg (Martin). (See Figure 6.2.)

Some theorists suggest that the physiological category of sex itself is not a natural given, but determined by culture. This is not to say that the physiological differences we refer to in assigning sexual identity do not exist; rather, that they operate much more variably and diffusely than the division of humans and other animals into mutually exclusive categories of "male" and "female" suggests. For example, the designation of sex hormones as male (testosterone) or female (estrogen) does not account for the fact that both hormones are released by men *and* women (Shilling 75).

Moreover, the presence of those hormones—along with other secondary sex characteristics such as the size and function of reproductive organs, facial hair, voice, and physique—alters with age and in response to environmental factors such as nutrition and stress. Even the seemingly clear-cut genetic markers of XX (female) vs. XY (male) chromosomes are complicated by the presence of other genes influencing physique and behaviour, not to mention the range of conditions that can affect the "normal" correspondence of genes to physiological characteristics. In short, humans are characterized by biological variances relating to reproductive capacity; however, the reduction of those variances to fixed, bipolar categories "male" and "female" comes about not through nature but through *culture*. The cultural basis of fundamental sex differences is highlighted by the different values and meanings accorded those differences in different times and places. In pre–eighteenth-century Europe, for example, women were viewed as biologically inferior to, but not fundamentally different from, men. The view of sexual difference as one of kind rather than degree arose in conjunction with the need to reconcile the continued disenfranchisement of women with new views about the universal rights of "man" (Laqueur 19).

Learned "Body Techniques" But culture does not influence only the way we understand bodies; it also becomes inscribed on bodies themselves. As sociologist and anthropologist Marcel Mauss (1872–1950) noted, the way we conduct such basic activities as sleeping, eating, sitting, walking, having sex, and giving birth should be understood not as natural, but as a series of "body techniques" that are *learned* in particular social contexts and are hence culturally and historically specific. One of the most striking examples Mauss provides is French women's characteristic style (or technique) of walking, which changed in the 1930s with the arrival of American cinema: the movies carried with them a whole repertoire of fashion comprising ways not just of dressing, but also of comportment, of holding and carrying the body.

Figure 6.2 A Traditional Image of Conception

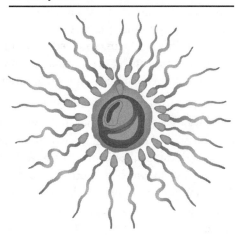

Traditional images of conception owe less to scientific accuracy than to metaphorical representations of gender stereotypes.

While French women's imitation of styles of movement associated with Hollywood film might be prompted by an association of the U.S. with images of energy and freedom, most body techniques serve a much more utilitarian function in relation to the demands of a smoothly running society. In most societies, this means that considerable effort is expended in what Mauss calls "education in composure . . . a mechanism inhibiting disorderly movements" (474). Thus we learn not only how to move, but also how and when to inhibit movement, techniques that differ significantly by age and gender.

The Self-Controlled Body   The idea that culture exerts a shaping and restraining effect on the body is carried further in the work of sociologist Norbert Elias (1897–1990), who documented the process by which centuries of Western civilization produced the modern, individualized, self-controlled body. Elias uses the concept of "civilization" not in the sense in which it is often used, to imply the progressive movement beyond the "backward" ways of the past, but rather to describe a series of specific historical changes in Europe, from the hardscrabble social world of the Middle Ages to the court society of the Renaissance, whose influence shapes our present-day culture. In particular, Elias focuses on the shift from a way of life in which physical strength, aggression, and indulgence of appetites were necessary to survival to one in which "polite society" defined by the court dictated increasingly complex social rituals, successful observance of which played a significant role in determining one's social status.

One of the critical aspects of this shift is a move toward interdependence, such that existence had to be negotiated with an increasing awareness of the effects of one's behaviour on others. Thus the civilized body is one that is subject to an expanding set of taboos and social codes, demarcating it sharply from the physical environment and from other bodies. Practices that were once widely tolerated, such as defecating in public or sharing beds with strangers, were subjected to increasingly strict social sanction as a new model of appropriate bodily conduct emerged. This new model was characterized by a broad repertoire of gestures—manners—that signified an observance of social relations, including an overall tendency toward self-restraint and a clear sense of separation between private and public.

Physical Capital and Social Status

Of course, body techniques and codes of civilized behaviour vary from social situation to social situation (for example, what's acceptable at a rave differs considerably from what's appropriate at your Great Aunt Ethel's tea party) and depending on what position one occupies in society (class, gender, etc.). Sociologist Pierre Bourdieu (1930–2002) sheds light on these differences by expanding Mauss's concept of the *habitus*. A term connoting both living space and habit, **habitus** describes the way in which particular social environments are internalized by individuals in the form of dispositions toward particular bodily orientations and behaviours.

The concept of habitus thus allows us to talk about the way in which social differences are reproduced at the level of the individual body. Class, Bourdieu suggests, plays a determining role in the development of bodies by influencing such factors as social location and taste (learned habits of discrimination influencing choice of lifestyle—discussed in Chapter Five), as well as more physical aspects of habitus. These differences in turn contribute to the production of different kinds and degrees of social value attached to different kinds of bodies. Value corresponds more or less closely to class, with working-class bodies possessing less value than dominant-class bodies—value here is determined principally by the ability to translate what Bourdieu terms physical capital into other forms of capital: economic (money), cultural (education), and social (networks of belonging).

Of course, the different kinds of capital don't map perfectly onto one another: professional sport has traditionally offered a venue for men from under-privileged circumstances to convert physical capital into economic capital in a fairly direct way. However, the heavy toll professional sport—like most forms of physical labour—exacts on the body, combined with its relatively restricted access as a career path, diminishes its significance as an exception to the rule that "white-collar" bodies tend to enjoy more privileged access to forms of economic, social, and cultural capital than do "blue-collar" bodies.

A somewhat crude example of the relationship between taste and habitus and social and economic capital can be seen in the 1988 film *Working Girl*, in which Tess (Melanie Griffith), a secretary, employs her brains and ambition to land an executive position and an attractive, financially successful husband (Harrison Ford). An important component of her social and economic advancement is her successful cultivation of her appearance, voice, and gestures in order first to impersonate, and then truly to embody the image of a female executive. One scene has her pedalling frantically on an exer-cycle while trying to imitate phrases and intonations of speech from a tape of her boss (Sigourney Weaver) giving a speech. Perhaps the clearest sign of her progress—besides her successful business negotiations with and seduction of Harrison Ford—is the increasingly striking contrast throughout the film of Tess to her best friend (Joan Cusack), whose permanently entrenched position in the secretarial rank is signalled by her big hair, caked-on blue eye-shadow, and vampish clothes.

Premised on outrageous class (and gender) stereotypes, *Working Girl* clearly can't be read as a sociological comment on how class mobility operates in "real life." However, its tremendous popularity, particularly among women, illustrates the pervasiveness of cultural myths about the role of physical appearance and behaviour in achieving—and, even more importantly, deserving—social and economic status.

In an interesting contrast with *Working Girl*, the 2002 movie *Maid in Manhattan* is much less conscious about the ways in which class and social position are articulated through bodily disposition or habitus. Unlike in *Working Girl*, where Tess has to unlearn her natural speech, gestures, and tastes to play the role of someone of a higher class, all it takes to transform Marisa (Jennifer Lopez) into a credible imitation of a rich socialite is a Dolce & Gabbana pantsuit. While both movies follow a fairytale format, *Working Girl* was arguably more realistic about the barriers to social mobility—barriers that are ingrained on the body.

Ingrained Habit—Culture Becoming Nature

One of the most obviously mythical elements of films like *Working Girl* and *Maid in Manhattan*—besides the stereotypes—is the assumption the films make that, through a combination of pluck and intelligence, it is possible for anyone to transform her or himself, mentally and physically, into whomever she or he wants to be. *Maid in Manhattan* was perhaps less wildly unrealistic in this respect: while Tess catapults from secretary to senior executive, Marisa just rises through the ranks of the service industry, from maid to manager. This difference may simply reflect a change in ideologies of identity and work, particularly with respect to gender, from the late 1980s to the early twenty-first century.

While the message conveyed by *Working Girl* was a strongly feminist one, inflected by the emphasis on individualism and corporate success in Ronald Reagan's America, *Maid in Manhattan* offers a view of ideal femininity that, depending on your perspective, is either less progressive (economic equality with men isn't really important so long as you're feisty, beautiful, and a good mom), or more so (identity is not defined by work). Both movies, however, arguably downplayed the physical consequences of occupying particular social categories—consequences measurable in terms not just of appearance, but also of one's biological capacities, including health and bodily function. In many instances, learned behaviours have real physical effects that come to actually conform to the stereotype on which the behaviour was initially based.

For example, in an essay titled "Throwing Like a Girl," Iris Marion Young identifies a tendency in Western industrial societies for girls to move in ways that are more limited and constrained than the ways in which boys move. In effect, responding to a learned physical orientation that Young calls "inhibited intentionality" (145), girls and women are not inclined to use their bodies' full potential range of strength and motion. Thus what is often regarded as women's "natural" lack of physical strength and coordination is at least partly attributable to the way in which their bodies are socialized to move (or not) in particular ways. These learned behaviours, ingrained into habit, contribute to the transformation of women's bodies into the stereotypically "weak vessels" they were already imagined to be.

Nature and culture, then, are inextricably connected in the production of the body as a site of identity-formation. Naturally occurring biological variances are simplified and reduced to signs of absolute cultural difference, which themselves come to take on the appearance of nature. The ways in which we conceive of the body influence the way we look at, treat, and inhabit it. Most significantly, cultural influences on the body come to assume physical significance, both at the level of the individual physical body and of the social structures in which individual bodies are placed. Possibilities for modifying and even transcending the body thus become a highly charged cultural and political issue.

ALTERED STATES

While people at all times and in all places have sought to change their bodies in different ways, advances in science combined with the unique pressures of a consumer culture highly biased toward the visual have contributed to a growing trend toward body-cultivation and modification. Body modification describes practices that include "piercing, tattooing, branding, cutting, binding and inserting implants," as well as less invasive practices such as exercise and diet, that seek to alter "the appearance and form of the body" (Featherstone 1). Whether these practices are motivated by health or by aesthetics, whether they uphold or challenge prevailing social norms, and whether they aim toward the accentuation or transcendence of the body—and few can be so simply classified—they demand examination in relation to the more fundamental questions of how they contribute to the production of individual and social meaning, identity, and power.

Enhancing/Producing the Healthy Body

At the beginning of the twenty-first century, Western cultures have come increasingly to see health as a matter of individual control and responsibility. This trend is reflected in such developments as the recent legislation passed in Canada on food labelling. The new law

Iodine, a shop on Toronto's trendy Queen Street West, exploits the blurring of medicine and aesthetics by selling beauty products in a clinic-like setting featuring a red-cross logo and sales assistants sporting nurses' uniforms.

requiring uniform labelling on all packaged food, listing information such as fat content and potential health benefits, makes the assumption that health and fitness are largely dependent on wise consumer choices. A variety of factors have contributed to this development: individuals tend to have much more knowledge and confidence about health-related matters than they did a generation ago, leading to a much more proactive stance in managing their own health. At the same time, both fuelling and responding to this trend, a massive consumer industry has sprung up around personal health care, promoting everything from so-called "nutraceuticals" (drug-enhanced foods) to fitness clubs.

Finally, the rising costs of an increasingly technology-based medical system have led governments and insurance companies to search for ways to encourage less reliance on the system and greater responsibility on the part of individuals in addressing their health needs. This pressure is particularly acute in countries, such as Canada, that have a public health care system. The idea that health is a human right that should be protected by the entire community through taxation is increasingly hard to sustain in the face of a growing emphasis on the individual as largely in control of, and responsible for, his or her own health. Thus questions about whether individuals who smoke or don't wear seatbelts should be entitled to free health care have begun to appear with some frequency in the media. Increasingly, then, issues surrounding health are being shaped by rhetoric about consumer choice, at the same time as they convey more moralistic messages about individual responsibility.

The ambiguity of these messages is reflected in practices surrounding diet and fitness, where the general goal of "health" is overlaid with the complex and often contradictory values of physical and sexual attractiveness (generally associated with pleasure) and moral well-being (frequently defined by discipline and self-denial). In these mixed motivations can be detected the ambivalence about the relationship between self and body discussed at the beginning of this section. While the pursuit of exercise as a form of self-improvement might imply on one hand a recognition of an integral connection between body and identity, many practices associated with exercise, including dieting (and its more extreme pathological form, anorexia) are inspired by the idea of the body as an alien thing, separate and requiring discipline from the self.

What's Natural/Normal?

Many health practices are founded on ideas about a natural physical state, which regimes of diet or exercise seek to enhance. These ideas are troubled by the burgeoning popularity of cosmetic surgery that clearly aims less to preserve a "natural" state of health than to produce a "cultural" convention of beauty. Crossing the line from medicine to aesthetics, cosmetic surgery sheds unexpected light on the reliance of both discourses on concepts of *normalization*. Celebrated by many as a technology of self-expression that allows them to convey an outer image that is more in tune with their inner selves (ditching the fat suit to become Gwyneth Paltrow), cosmetic surgery is condemned by others as a biotechnological reinforcement of oppressive gender norms (Balsamo).

The operation of such norms is most clearly evident in such forms of cosmetic surgery as liposuction and breast enlargement. While these procedures may be seen—and, more importantly, may actually *work*—to enhance the self-confidence of those who seek them, they do so at the expense of conscripting them more fully into the prescribed roles of a patriarchal social order.

Some forms of body enhancement work more ambiguously. For example, female bodybuilding seems in one sense to challenge conventional gender codes by rejecting a feminine ideal of almost-anorexic thinness. Maximizing instead of minimizing the body—replacing weakness with strength—bodybuilding represents a form of physical feminine empowerment. On the other hand, the maxed-out body is achieved at a cost of punishing discipline and "self"-denial that, at its extreme, actually compromises the goals of health and fitness.

Of course, bodybuilding is about more than health and fitness: like most fitness practices, it is also about display. For women, whose relationships to their bodies have always been mediated by social codes that define them as objects-to-be-looked-at (see Mulvey in Chapter Three), display is at best an ambiguous form of empowerment (Grosz 224). At the same time as it accentuates strength, the culture of bodybuilding still draws attention to the female body as the repository of female worth. As this example demonstrates, body-modification practices may challenge social norms, but they cannot avoid negotiating them. Most practices, like bodybuilding, take place in complicated conversations with our historically ambivalent conceptions about mind and body—conceptions that are inevitably tied to ideas about gender and power.

The Politics of Body Modification Body modification practices also raise other issues of power and agency. As with highly gendered forms of body modification, the practice of surgically altering black or Asian features to give them a more Caucasian cast can be understood in terms of its promotion of empowerment and/or subjugation. The practice of blepharoplasty, in which a fold is inserted to give the eyes a more rounded, open appearance, gained notoriety in Canada after the death of one patient from a botched, illicit operation. The incident sparked an unusual degree of media commentary on the powerful and damaging effect of myths of white normativity. A more nuanced perspective on the subject is expressed in Korean-Canadian Ann Shin's documentary *Western Eyes*, which mixes a critical analysis of racialized aesthetic conventions in pop culture with interviews with women who have undergone the procedure. The women emerge from the film neither as victims of the dominant culture nor as models of self-empowerment, but as individuals struggling to define their identities through conflicting codes of physical beauty/normality.

These codes are not "natural"; neither are they solely cosmetic. The complexity of the issues surrounding medical/surgical body modification is evident in relation to sex-change procedures, in which transsexual individuals—those whose gender *identity* (masculine or feminine) conflicts with their chromosomal and physiological characteristics—undergo a series of surgical and medical treatments to transform them from male to female or vice versa. While aspects of gender are largely culturally determined, they are sufficiently deep and pervasive that gender identity disorders are considered by the medical community to constitute threats to physical health. Sexual modification blurs the distinction between culture and nature in the determination of what constitutes a "normal" identity. It also demonstrates the ambiguous political significance of body modification: fuelled by dominant codes of sex and gender identity, sex reassignment surgery also throws those codes into confusion, challenging society's deepest prejudices about what counts as normal.

Transcending the Body?

The possibilities of body modification are taken to their extreme, at the same time as they are critically challenged, in the work of performance artist Orlan, who has subjected herself to nine plastic-surgery operations—including the implantation of horns in her forehead—in order to explore (and explode) classical notions of beauty. Orlan's is a self-conscious parody of more conventional versions of plastic surgery (which themselves assume an extreme form in the more than twenty operations undergone by American talk show celebrity Cindy Jackson in an eerily successful bid to look like Barbie). Declaring "I don't want to be the Barbie Doll" (qtd. in Goodall 160), Orlan seeks instead to expose the arbitrariness, the unnaturalness, of the standards of beauty that have come to define Western femininity. She does this not in defence of the so-called "real" body, but in order to expose its non-existence. The body, Orlan observes, "is obsolete. It is no longer adequate for the current situation. We mutate at the rate of cockroaches, but we are cockroaches whose memories are in computers, who pilot planes and drive cars that we have conceived, although our bodies are not conceived for these speeds" (qtd. in Goodall 151).

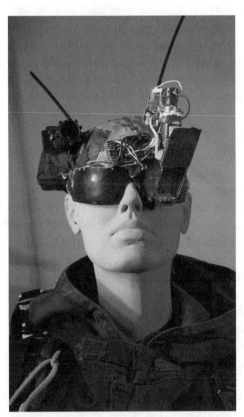

Designed by University of Toronto professor Steve Mann, "WearComp," the first wearable computer technology, blurs the line between human and machine.

Orlan's comment reflects the **posthumanist** position that the concepts "man," "self," and "body" that underwrite traditional ideas of human identity have become untenable as society confronts the inextricable entanglement of nature and technology, human and machine. This is not to say that the body *used* to exist in a more or less natural state that has been disrupted or corrupted by technology, but that the increasing difficulty of drawing distinctions between the human/natural and the technological highlights the inadequacy of the once-intelligible **myth** of an autonomous human identity.

Cyborgs The figure of the cyborg, an amalgam of human and animal and/or living organism and machine, is not simply the imaginary creation of the producers of cyber-punk novels and movies but an everyday reality, embodied in our use of computers and machines. In a significant way, we have not only come to inhabit technology, but technology has also come to inhabit us, as theorists such as Paul Virilio have pointed out; he cites as one example the medical use of micro-machines to view, diagnose, treat, and enhance the body. Such innovations have the potential to be socially useful, but also scarily invasive. University of Toronto professor and inventor Steve Mann highlights both the possibilities and the dangers of cyborg technology with wearable cameras and computers that turn the tables on such routine uses of surveillance as store security systems (see the photo on p. 196).

For many people, the prospect of an ever-closer relationship between humans and machines invokes utopian ideas of virtual reality, in which individuals and communities are able to transcend the limits of nature and their bodies to enjoy ever-greater freedoms. For others, the prospect of a progressive erosion of the integrity of principles like "humanity" and "nature" is deeply disturbing, heralding a nightmarish world like the one represented in *Blade Runner*, in which the complexity and beauty of our existence is transformed into a bunch of animate machines.

As artists such as Orlan and cultural theorists such as Donna Haraway and Steve Mann have shown, however, neither of these visions is ultimately viable. The techno-utopian dream, an extension of the Enlightenment project of harnessing the physical world to human need, relies, like the techno-pessimist vision, on the old idea of a separation between body and mind, nature and culture, that is simply not sustainable. Both the technological and the natural ideal are myths forged out of culture, whose ideological frames limit the possibilities for human liberation.

Contrary to the promises of technophiles and purveyors of cosmetic miracles, "identity has not turned into a free option for all subjects in all situations and all contexts" (Klesse 20). Prevailing structures of gender, class, racial, and sexual inequality mean that everyone does not enjoy the opportunities for self-fulfillment. The limitations on our freedom to define ourselves as we will is also compromised by the fact—of which we are periodically reminded, by environmental catastrophes (some of them human-caused) and by the inevitability of death—that we are not just *in*, but also *of*, nature. The critical issue, which we have tried to stress throughout this chapter, concerns not whether our identities are born or made, or whether they are defined through or against our bodies, but what they mean, in terms of our ability to enhance our own and others' power to act in a world not entirely of our own making.

SUMMARY

This chapter has advanced a number of arguments about the meaning and significance of individual identity, some of which are picked up and extended in the next chapter, which looks at the role of identity and difference in the construction of community. Key points to remember include the following:

- Identities do not precede or transcend social formations, but are defined through them. Rather than essential truths, identities can be usefully conceived of as stories that fulfill particular purposes at particular times.
- Dominant categories of identity, particularly those relating to gender and sexuality, operate to uphold ideologies that support existing social inequalities.
- As vehicles of social power, identities can work to restrict or enhance possibilities for individual self-definition.
- The meaning of identity is inseparable from the significance of the body as a natural and social fact.
- The growing trend toward body management and modification functions to enhance and to restrict possibilities for the development of identity and agency.

SUGGESTIONS FOR FURTHER READING

Bordo, Susan. *Unbearable Weight: Feminism, Western Culture and the Body*. Berkeley: University of California Press, 1993.

Butler, Judith. *Bodies that Matter: On the Discursive Limits of Sex*. London: Routledge, 1999.

Featherstone, Mike. *Body Modification*. London: Sage, 2000.

du Gay, Paul, Jessica Evans, and Peter Redman. *Identity: A Reader*. London: Sage, 2000.

Giddens, Anthony. *Modernity and Self-Identity*. Cambridge: Polity, 1991.

Shilling, Chris. *The Body and Social Theory*. London: Sage, 1993.

Woodward, Kathryn, ed. *Identity and Difference*. London: Sage, 2000.

Chapter 7

Identity and Community

INTRODUCTION: FOLLOW YOUR HEART OR HONOUR YOUR CULTURE?

The 2002 movie *My Big Fat Greek Wedding* is based on a premise that has become a popular cinematic formula: a woman from a tightly knit ethnic community falls in love with an outsider. Against the initial protests of her family and friends she decides to marry him, asserting the value of individual freedom and romance over the bonds of group allegiance and tradition. As with most movies in this genre, this one has a happy ending: the outsider, by the force of his essential good-guy qualities (and, in this case, by his conversion to their religion), wins over the family, who welcome him into their community with lots of food, music, and dancing—thus affirming the value of cultural tradition, or at least some aspects of it, within a broader notion of universal humanity.

A major source of tension in this movie is the contradiction between two compelling ideals: the ideal of collective belonging, defined by membership in a clearly defined community, and that of universal humanism, defined by the pre-eminence of the individual. This tension is one of the issues we will be exploring in this chapter, which focuses on how group (or collective) identities are formed, in conjunction and frequently in conflict with individual identities. We look in particular at the powerful significance of the concepts of **race, ethnicity,** and **nation** for the construction of group identity. Of course, the split between "individual" and "group" identity is really an artificial one, since *all* identities, individual and collective, come about through a dynamic of similarity and difference: there is no such thing as a unique individual identity, only different variations on the theme of identity that privilege the individual or the group to varying degrees. All of us, moreover, are defined at one time or another by different identities, some of which emphasize group belonging and some of which privilege individuality. Some identities assume greater importance than others at different times in our lives; less straightforwardly, we all occupy different identities simultaneously, and these—as in the example of Toula, the main character in *My Big Fat Greek Wedding*—can be a source of conflict.

The stakes involved in that conflict are clearly not the same for everyone, as the marriage crisis of this movie illustrates. While the comedy is enhanced by the reaction of Toula's boyfriend Ian's stuffy parents to her large, loud family, it is clearly *her* family, not his, who form the principal obstacle to their union. Where the clash for Ian's family is largely one of aesthetics or style, the problem for Toula's family goes much deeper; it is a question of fundamental identity. In most of the recent crop of marrying-outside-the-tribe movies (*Mississippi Masala, The Joy Luck Club, Jungle Fever*), the "tribe" is a cultural or racial **minority** in North American society, where "minority" is defined not by numbers but by relative cultural power. While comedies such as *My Big Fat Greek Wedding* speak cheerfully to the possibility of reconciling majority and minority values and identities, other films (and even this one in its darker moments) acknowledge the danger and loss, both perceived and actual, associated with assimilation. These dangers and losses are suffered almost exclusively by members of minority groups, who are invited to purchase admission to the dominant (i.e., white, middle-class) culture at the price of their own identity. Moreover, assimilation does not guarantee equal opportunity or treatment, since those signs of difference—hair, skin colour, language, speech—that underlay racist discourse to begin with persist, underlining the dominant group's claim to distinction and superiority. The liberal ideal of individualism that supports the policy of assimilation is not able, finally, to think through the problems of structural, institutional obstacles to equality that can't be overcome—in fact, these problems are arguably heightened by the emphasis on the individual as someone who transcends culture.

In tension with this liberal ideal, **identity politics**, or the strategic assertion of a racial or cultural unity, is one response to the marginalization and/or invisibility of minorities. Unlike the exclusivist identity claims of majority groups, which operate often invisibly to secure existing power imbalances, identity politics challenge the status quo in their explicit bid for recognition and the extension of majority rights to minority groups. However, identity politics carry certain risks; central among them is the way in which an emphasis on a singular group identity ignores differences within the group. Moreover, the positive stress on "community" tends to elide or gloss over the relations of power that define all communities. In the case of *My Big Fat Greek Wedding*, the community in question is one defined by strongly patriarchal values that work to entrench women in traditional roles as wives and mothers (Toula's mother puts a humorous face on this arrangement with her line "The man is the head but the woman is the neck . . . who chooses which way the head will move"). We will discuss the significance, and the limitations, of identity politics in more detail later in the chapter.

Rather than evaluating the merits and demerits of group vs. individual identities—as though it were possible to choose, finally, in favour of one or the other—our concern in this chapter is to explore how those identities are produced and reproduced, what function they serve, and, finally, how these identities help to shape, as they are themselves shaped by, specific political, economic, and cultural circumstances. Our investigation is also framed by more specific questions: What kinds of collective identities emerge or become important in different historical contexts? To whom are they important, and under what circumstances? How do particular identities conflict with and/or reinforce other identities, both individual and collective? How do they function to create communities of inclusion and exclusion? How do they work to reinforce and/or undermine structures of power? In this chapter, as in the last, our underlying concern in studying the question of collective identity is to explore the way in which identities function in society to help or hinder different people in their efforts to act autonomously or as self-conscious **agents**.

"THE PEOPLE WHO ARE OURS"

While all identities, whether collective or individual, are defined in relation to others, collective identities tend to be established in terms of a more self-conscious distinction between those who belong in the group and those who don't. This isn't surprising when we recall that among the other important key aspects of identity is its regulatory or disciplinary function: it serves to rein in impulses, ideas, and behaviour that might undermine a particular vision of social order—the prevailing social order and/or a threatened or emergent social order—that each of us has some vested interest in upholding. The social regulation of individuals is often hard to see because of the way we each internalize prevailing conventions and ideologies. With groups, the policing of identity tends to be more overt—particularly when identities are under threat. Thus, we can learn a lot about the production and function of collective identities by looking at how they are represented by members of different groups. (For a detailed examination of representation, see Chapter Three.)

Ordinary Human Beings and Others

In a 2002 survey commissioned by the Northern Ireland Community Relations Council, a sociologist interviewed Catholic and Protestant children between the ages of three and six to find out their views on the political situation there (see Close-Up 7.1).

When asked "What do you know about Catholics?" one Protestant child responded, "They're bad . . . Catholics are different from ordinary human beings because they are badder." In response to the question, "What do you know about Protestants?" Catholic children provided similar responses: "They want to kill all the Catholics. They're like Catholics. They do the same things only they're stronger."

These children's perspectives on Irish cultural identity are interesting for what they reveal about the politics of identity in general. First, they highlight the extent to which group membership, like all forms of identification, is defined by the terms of *sameness* and *difference*: Catholics are defined by virtue of their difference from Protestants, by their essential "otherness."

Bad and Badder

The following is excerpted from a report commissioned by the Northern Ireland Community Relations Council, published in June 2002, entitled "Too Young to Notice?" Paul Connolly, a sociologist at the University of Ulster, interviewed 352 Catholic and Protestant children from Northern Ireland about their attitudes toward the political situation there. All of the children were between three and six years of age.

WHAT DO YOU KNOW ABOUT CATHOLICS?

They rob.

They're bad. They batter Almond Drive people. Almond Drive—that's where I live.

Catholics are different from ordinary human beings because they are badder. The police come after them. They make petrol bombs, get petrol at garages, throw them, and they blow up.

WHAT DO YOU KNOW ABOUT PROTESTANTS?

They want to kill all the Catholics.

They're like Catholics. They do the same things only they're stronger. Protestants would take people hostage. The police give them their weapons and make a deal to get the hostages.

Catholics don't like Protestants, and that's why they don't like them. They're bad.

WHY DO YOU LIKE OR NOT LIKE THIS FLAG?

[After showing the Protestant children an Irish Tricolor flag.]

Northern Ireland flag. You put it up in July. It annoys people when it's waving. A Drumcree flag is the good one and that is the bad one.

It's the Fenian flag. It's only bad people that have that color of flag and that's all I know about that flag.

WHY DO YOU LIKE OR NOT LIKE THIS FLAG?

[After showing the Catholic children a Union Jack.]

I don't like that flag—a sad one—'cause it's bad.

It has red and blue and white. They burn them, down at a club. Put Union Jack on grass and burned it. All bigguns throw stones at British Police. Just don't like that one.

WHAT DO YOU KNOW ABOUT THE PEOPLE IN THIS PHOTOGRAPH? WHY DO YOU LIKE OR NOT LIKE THEM?

[After showing Catholic children a picture of a Protestant march.]

Sometimes they march when they're attacking other places and sometimes when somebody's dead.

They're holding up stuff. They're Orangemen. Because they're going to kill us. They wanted to kill us anyway.

They came to our road and my daddy said they're Orange bastards!

Because they're bad. They're police.

'Cause they be fighting.

Because they're not friendly.

They're Orangemen. People tried to kill the Orangemen because they don't like them. They're dangerous men. They're evil. They steal money.

They're not my favorite because they've got all the colors that I hate.

They're Protestants. They want to march so that they can get the Catholic area.

I like the people who are ours. I don't like those ones because they're Orangemen. They're bad people. Mummy told me they were bad.

Source: Community Relations Council, Belfast. Reprinted by permission of Paul Connolly.

What's particularly significant in the first example is the implied norm against which "Catholic" is defined: "Protestant" identity is not mentioned, but is assumed, in its absence, to be synonymous with "human beings." A key characteristic of group identity, particularly though not exclusively in the case of dominant groups, is the **ex-nomination**, or failure to acknowledge the distinguishing sign or particularity of that identity. Not mentioning a distinguishing characteristic—like whiteness, say, or, in the case of Northern Ireland, Protestantism—implies that it is just ordinary, the norm. Difference, within this framework, is never neutral; rather, it is conceived as deviation from a standard.

While this form of discrimination can sometimes seem relatively value-free (for example, the phrase "non-white" to describe blacks or Asians looks innocuous enough until we start to think about why we rarely hear whites described as "non-black"), it works implicitly—and sometimes explicitly—on the basis of hierarchy. Hence, the others are "badder" than we are. Critical to the operation of the hierarchy is the operation of **stereotype**, in which a group or individual is reduced to a few fixed, unchanging characteristics (again, in implicit opposition to the more complex and fluid "normal" identities we ascribe to ourselves and those identified by a child in the survey as "the people who are ours").

Like Us, Only . . . Worse

What's striking in the stereotypes that are used by the children in this interview—and what's true of stereotypes generally—is that, regardless of what group is being described, they tend to sound a lot alike. Though some allowance must be made in this example for the age of the interviewees—a four-year-old has a limited vocabulary to describe deviance—the terms in which they describe "otherness" resonate remarkably with the terms used by adults. "Badness," or treachery, an absence of morality, and a tendency toward the illegitimate use of violence (as opposed to the *legitimate* use of violence by one's own group) are standard terms of condemnation that establish the place of the other outside the bounds of civil society, while asserting, again by implicit comparison, the moral integrity of "us."

The children's comments also illustrate another interesting thing about stereotypes: one Catholic child's remark about Protestants—"*They're like Catholics. They do the same things* only they're stronger" (21, emphasis added)—points to the emergence of stereotypes through the tension between difference and *sameness*. Recall the discussion in Chapter Six of Freud's theory about the contradictory drives that inform relations between "self" and "other": the traumatic separation that marked our entry into the social world means that the stability of our identities always hinges on a tension between the desire for connection with the other and the fear of being consumed by the other. The ambivalent self-construction that underlies the production of stereotypes leads to a representation of the dominant group as simultaneously vulnerable and powerful in relation to an "other" who is both threatening and weak. Thus Protestants "do the same things [as Catholics] only they're stronger" because "the police give them their weapons." The moral superiority of the Catholics lies in their victimization at the hands of established power structures. On the other hand, claims to virtue frequently rest on *appeals* to traditional authorities—the law, God, or, in the case of children, parents: "Mummy told me they were bad" (21). The ambiguous positioning of authority as a site of identification (the thing that confirms our status) or source of victimization (the thing that shuts us out) again reveals the precarious foundations of the construction of the self.

Cultural Symbols, Material Contexts

Of course, frequently—as is the case in Northern Ireland—a tendency to ally oneself with or against established powers (and to construct those powers accordingly as legitimate or illegitimate) has a historical basis. As a consequence of centuries of British occupation, an occupation still rejected by many Irish Catholics in the North (the South became independent in 1922), most of the police force is English—that is, largely Protestant. However, the problems with using history as an absolute guide emerge in disagreements over what constitutes historical truth. Appeals to history that are framed in binary terms of power and vulnerability, strength and weakness are always suspect, particularly so in instances in which single groups vacillate strategically between identifications with power and powerlessness, authority and "ordinariness." Material circumstances do play a significant role in the construction of identity. However, the precise effect of that role is almost impossible to identify because of the mediating influence of culture.

The ambiguous role of the police in the stories of the children in the interview demonstrates the complex interplay between symbolism and society in the formation of the structures of power. The Protestant child infers the badness of the Catholics from the fact that "the police come after them" (21). As in most attempts to draw a link between race, culture or ethnicity, and criminality, this equation is confused in its attribution of cause and effect: the inference of guilt on the basis of pursuit or arrest is based on an assumption of the objectivity of the police. This objectivity is called into question by the Catholic children's reference to an alliance between the police and the Protestants. Regardless of its accuracy, the reference serves as a reminder of the **ideological** context in which power always operates. The role of ideology in determining identity is particularly clear to see in the case of children: we are not surprised when the shaping influence of "Mummy told me" appears behind the veil of personal conviction.

Nevertheless, it is important to resist the temptation to see children as the innocent victims of ideologies that are variously deployed and/or seen through by the rest of us who know better. As we argued in Chapter Three, no one, not even the supposedly impartial administrators of justice (nor, for that matter, the cultural critic!), escapes the discursive networks through which "truth"—including the "truth" of stereotypes—emerges as a function of power. The terms by which group identities are defined are always shot through with ideology, their mythological character highlighted in the arbitrariness of the symbols that convey their substance—for example, the Irish tricolour flag and the Union Jack, which Protestant and Catholic children characterized, not surprisingly, as "bad" and "the colors I hate." As empty of real significance as these symbols may be, however, we cannot dismiss their power, just as we cannot underestimate the material force of ideology as it is expressed in the beliefs and actions of individuals, police, and armies.

Collective Identity and Crisis

Within the context of what have come to be labelled "The Troubles" in Northern Ireland, it is easy to see how group identity comes to take on massive significance. As Kobena Mercer notes, "identity . . . becomes an issue when it is in crisis, when something assumed to be fixed, coherent and stable is displaced by the experience of doubt and uncertainty" (43). It would be a mistake, however, to assume that identities don't matter outside situations of obvious "trouble." The tendency for dominant groups to ex-nominate the signs or myths that designate their specialness means that it's possible for members of those groups to have, or at least to believe that they have, very little invested in belonging to a particular group. They are able to bracket questions of identity because the balance of social power allows *their* identity to pass as universal, unmarked. It is only when the balance of power shifts that it becomes necessary to haul out the symbols, to remind themselves and others what it is that makes them unique.

Particularism versus Universalism   Such a collective identity crisis arguably occurred in the wake of the September 11, 2001 terrorist attacks on the United States, when it suddenly became necessary to reassert the specific meaning of "America," all the while continuing to insist on the universality of that identity. The tension between particularism ("we are like this, we stand for these beliefs, ideas, practices") and universalism ("we are all human beings . . . except for those who don't do or believe as we do") underlies all definitions of group identity, with the fiction of universality being comfortably indulged in when times are good, and the defence of singularity being invoked when one's position of strength is threatened.

At these moments, as in the crisis following September 11th, people are generally more willing to surrender *individual* civil liberties, such as freedom of speech—liberties that under other circumstances are seen as natural—in order to gain the greater security perceived to be associated with the defence of the group. These defences take multiple forms, including the tightening of physical or territorial borders, the intensification of policing activity, and the dissemination of myths or ideologies that work to bind the group together and to enforce the exclusion of outsiders.

Looking at identities in crisis serves to remind us of conditions that are more or less critical to the maintenance of *all* identities. Designated through particular practices of representation in which differences are more or less highlighted, identities are always rooted, in the last instance, in relations of power and force. A recent *Globe and Mail* story about the arrest of a suspected terrorist carried the headline "Muslim Militant or Family Man: Terrorist Has Many Faces." At times of crisis, practices of racist stereotyping become more widespread, with boundaries between "us" and "them" expressed in the form of binary opposition.

Suggested Activity 7.1

Try to find recent media examples of the representation of *difference* defined by group identity. In what contexts do these representations occur? In what situations are the identities of specific groups promoted (and/or ex-nominated) or stereotyped?

MODERN IDENTITIES: NATION, EMPIRE, AND RACE

One of the principal ways of defining identity in the modern world has been through the idea of the **nation**. Historically connected to European practices of colonialism between the sixteenth and nineteenth centuries, nations and **nationalism** remain significant today, both as symbolic guarantees of identity and security and as obstacles to more global connections. Associated with such positive ideals as patriotism, loyalty, and collective strength, nations and nationalism also work—traditionally and today—on prin-

The success of Molson's 2000 "I Am Canadian" ad campaign can be measured by the range of pop cultural sites in which references to it—even mocking ones—continue to appear.

ciples of exclusion based on race, gender, and sexuality. Beginning with a specific example of how the nation functions in popular culture today, this section goes on to locate those contemporary resonances in a broader historical context.

I Am Canadian

In 2000, Molson produced an ad for its Molson Canadian brand of beer that came to be known as "The Rant," in which a young man in a plaid shirt—"Joe"—stands with a microphone in front of a huge crowd and offers a simple, powerful declaration of what it means to be Canadian (see Close-Up 7.2).

Introducing himself with a stereotypically Canadian, self-effacing "Hey," Joe begins his speech with a few negations of common American stereotypes of Canadians and concludes, positively and triumphantly, by proclaiming "My name is Joe and I AM CANADIAN! Thank you." The ad's instant popularity, measured by increased sales and a flurry of media and popular discussion, was widely attributed to its having expressed, simply and appealingly, the essence of Canadian national identity. Leaving aside the question of whether the ad was an accurate or positive representation of Canadianness (some people, including Ontario's Minister of Consumer and Commercial Affairs Bob Runciman, worried that it constituted "America-bashing" [see "I am. . . an asshole?"]), "The Rant" is useful to look at as a particularly powerful example of how **nationalist** discourse operates, both in the Canadian context and more generally.

Joe's Rant

"Hey.

I'm not a lumberjack or a fur trader.

I don't live in an igloo or eat blubber or own a dog sled.

And I don't know Jimmy, Sally, or Suzy from Canada, although I'm certain they're really, really nice.

I have a prime minister, not a president.

I speak English and French, not American.

And I pronounce it "about," not "a boot."

I can proudly sew my country's flag on my backpack.

I believe in peacekeeping, not policing.

Diversity, not assimilation.

And that the beaver is a truly proud and noble animal.

A tuque is a hat, a chesterfield is a couch,

and it IS pronounced zed, not zee, zed.

Canada is the second largest landmass, the first nation of hockey, and the best part of North America.

My name is Joe, and I AM CANADIAN!

Thank you."

On a general level, one of the first things the ad tells us is that the concept of national identity resists easy definition: is it subjective or objective? Does your national identity arise from within you, or is it imposed from outside? Is it inherent—something you just *are*—or is it an active concept, something that can be maintained only by *doing*? What kinds of relationships are assumed by claiming a national identity? What kinds of relationships are precluded? The answers to these questions, as evidenced by this ad, are contradictory.

One key component of national identity, Joe suggests, is its connection with a particular political body, a nation-*state*, which is defined, among other things, by a structure of governance—represented, for example, by a prime minister or a president. To cite this structure as critical to what it means to be Canadian or American suggests that national identity is predicated in part on a conscious acknowledgment of one's status as a *subject* of a particular political state. To the extent that one accepts that subject position, at least in a liberal democracy, it logically follows that one recognizes in a general way the legitimacy of the elected government and agrees—again, in a general way—to observe the obligations of citizenship such as voting, paying taxes, obeying the law, and so on.

If that were all that national identity amounted to, however—agreement to be represented and governed by a particular legal and political structure—it's hard to imagine how it could compel the kind of emotion and attachment that this ad obviously draws on. So, having a national identity is not just a matter of being a citizen of a particular state. It is also a strongly felt personal investment in being part of a special community— one defined by particular loves (hockey, beer, nature), and beliefs: in peace, for example, or in social justice. Belonging to a particular nation is not just a passive kind of subjection to an external, pre-determined, state structure, then, but a form of belief and action that is itself *constitutive*—a defining part of that nation.

This is not to say that national identity is entirely a product of conscious choice. Signalled by the language one speaks, and the way one speaks it ("I pronounce it *about*, not *a boot*"), national identity in part determines who we are, how we speak and act. It is something we are born or emerge into and is to that extent pre-conscious and non-negotiable. The pre-given or natural element of national identity is highlighted by its implicit association with territory: to be Canadian is to lay claim to—to be a part of— the land itself, which gives the nation and its inhabitants their character.

Identity as Difference   But at the same time as Canadianness, by Joe's reckoning, seems to be a rooted, essential quality, there is another sense in which being Canadian—or any nationality—doesn't mean anything in particular in and of itself. It signifies only insofar as it defines a particular *relationship*, one that is defined by connection with other Canadians and—equally importantly—by a *difference* from non-Canadians. The Canadian identity promoted by "The Rant" is one informed by self-conscious awareness of Canada's place in a world of other nations—nations toward which Canada assumes a particular political stance (peacekeeping vs. policing), and whose otherness is critical to the definition of the Canadian self.

Of course, the principal "other" in Joe's rant is the United States—or, more specifically, a mythical "America"—whose dominance, and implied aggressive indifference to Canada, is what turns this speech into a rant rather than a simple declaration of patriotism. Like all nationalist statements—indeed, more explicitly than most—Joe's rant is a deliberate act of boundary-drawing, establishing what, and more importantly who, belongs inside, and what belongs outside.

The urgency of defending what is often, as here seems to be the case, a fairly vulnerable boundary between "us" and "them" means that the arbitrary, or accidental, aspect of being a part of a particular national community needs to be played down in favour of an image of the nation as an organic whole. One of the chief ways this effect of incorporating all national citizens into a single coherent body is achieved in this ad, as in many nationalist statements, is by using the figure of a single individual to stand in for the nation as a whole.

Joe's status as a prototypical Canadian is highlighted by the series of images played on a screen behind him—the Parliament buildings, the flag, a set of individual faces of different races, and a waving crowd (Joe's audience?). By virtue of his placement on the stage, and his possession of a microphone, Joe is the spokesperson or representative of the community represented by these symbols. The choice of "Joe"—a good- but ordinary-looking guy in his late twenties who loves hockey and beer—as that individual is, of course, not accidental, since the target market for Molson Canadian beer is young men between the ages of 19 and 29. "Joe" is a subtler, more laid-back version of the composite identified on Molson's corporate Website in a section geared to the American export market: "Drinking Molson says you're a man's man, one who appreciates a premium Canadian import. It says you're a rugged, adventurous alpha male. You've been around the block. You know the score. But, you could still use a few tools to help you close the deal. Think of Molson as your wingman, the ultimate ice-breaker. Enter. Enjoy, Repeat" (Molson).

The question of what Joe represents (an alpha male with a sense of irony?) becomes much more interesting when framed in terms of his supposedly exemplary Canadianness, bolstered by the stereotypically masculine symbols of beer and hockey. Associated with a broader collection of **mythological** images of the nation as a rugged Northern climate, settled by bold pioneers who survived through teamwork and toughness, these symbols create an unmistakably gendered image of the representative Canadian. The picture of Canada and Canadians is also fleshed out in ways that are both more obvious and more subtle: Joe's proud declaration that he speaks "English *and* French," in contrast to implicitly monolingual Americans, draws on the idea of a bilingual and bicultural Canada—an idea that is supported, but also complicated, by his invocation of the idea of *multi*cultural diversity. Though the ad speaks powerfully to the values of inclusivity and difference as central components of Canadian identity, the voices in whom that symbolic "diversity" actually exists do not speak—except in disembodied and homogenized form, *spoken for* by Joe, as the generic (white, male, anglophone) Canadian.

Suggested Activity 7.2

Try to imagine how the ad "The Rant" might signify differently (more or less effectively, do you think?) if Joe's words were spoken by a teenaged girl, an old woman, a black man, an Asian woman, and so on.

Evoking an image of a vibrant national community, animated by values of peace, equality, and tolerance, "The Rant" simultaneously synthesizes and homogenizes that community into a single voice for the dominant culture. These contradictions are significant not just for what they illuminate about Canadian identity, but also for what they say about **nationalist** discourses in general.

One final point deserves mention about "The Rant" as a statement of national identity. In May 2000, federal Heritage Minister Sheila Copps aired the ad at an International Press Institute conference in Boston to demonstrate what culture means to Canadians. Some commentators were quick to condemn what they saw as the ludicrousness of Copps's presentation. One of the key problems, it was suggested, was her having mistaken a contrived image for real Canadian cultural identity. The gap between fiction and reality was starkly illustrated, as one writer noted, by proud Canadian Joe/struggling actor Jeff Thompson's departure for Hollywood following his appearance in the ad. Copps couldn't mention Thompson's departure, the writer suggested, because it would expose her government to critique for policies that make it hard to make a living in Canada: " 'I am Canadian' is fantasy. The reality is Copps's government is taxing Canadians out of the country" ("I Was Canadian").

Authentic versus Commercialized Culture   For some, even more troubling than Copps's substituting a fictional version of Canadian culture for the (absence of?) the real thing in order to score political points was her confusion of "authentic" culture with its corrupt *commercial* form. Interestingly, the distinction between deep and superficial, authentic and commercial was one that Copps herself insisted on in her statement to the conference that "for Canadians, culture is not just another good. It's not just entertainment. It's the expression of the soul and identity of who we are." Leaving aside for a moment the issue of whether/how "culture" differs from "entertainment" (an issue touched on in Chapters One, Two, and Four of this book), Copps's presentation, and the response to it, raises questions about the relationships between national identity, culture, politics, and economics.

The principal critiques directed at Copps's use of the Molson ad—that it invoked a contrived or made-up identity in place of a genuine one, that it exploited the theme of Canadian identity in order to achieve partisan political goals, and that it ignored *authentic* national culture in favour of a commercial substitute—all miss a critical fact about **nationalism**, which is that it is, by definition, informed by a combination of spontaneous feeling and conscious construction. Even more crucially, it is inextricably tied to political and economic concerns, which it helps to influence even as it is in turn shaped by them. These complex relationships are easy to see when we look at **nations** and **nationalism** in a historical context (see Close-Up 7.3).

Nations and Nationalism

The dynamics of nations and nationalism are important to understand in the context of discussions of identity, not only because the nation is one of the most globally significant forms of collective identity, but also because the very concept of modern identity, in its individual and collective forms, is in significant ways tied to the historical emergence of the nation in eighteenth-century Europe.

Much as contemporary economic, technological, and political changes are throwing old identities into confusion, changes in eighteenth-century Europe associated with the Industrial Revolution, developments in technology and communication, and political conflict had a powerful impact on traditional identities.

Simply put, the changes associated with modernity reconfigured strongly hierarchical or "vertical" medieval empires, framed by the ordering principles of dynasty and religion,

Nations and Nationalism

As a form of what Benedict Anderson terms "imagined community," the nation is both example and instigator of the process by which identities that are constructed or imagined come to assume the force of *nature*. One useful way to approach the significance of the nation as a source of modern identity is to think about the relationship between nations and nationalism.

Our usual, common-sense way of understanding the relationship is to see the nation—a people defined by collective belonging to an extensive community, usually defined in relation to a specific territory—as primary, with nationalism as a frequent though not inevitable byproduct. Recent theories of the development of nations (Anderson, Gellner) suggest that the relationship might best be understood as working the other way around: that is, nations are how the ideological impulse of nationalism is legitimated and given concrete shape.

into a more chaotic collection of "horizontal" states, characterized by their secular, more fluid political and economic organization. As a form of mythological solidarity that transforms a population into a "people," the nation was an important correlate of the modern state, brought into being by state force at the same time as it fleshed out the meaning of the state, giving it a sense of purpose and natural rightness. As sociologist Zygmunt Bauman puts it, "the state supplied the resources of nation building, while the postulated unity of the nation and shared national destiny offered legitimacy to the ambition of the state authority to command obedience" (683).

Imagined Community, Invented Tradition

Thus, nations can be defined in relation to the machinery of particular states and to the territories they command. This is not a necessary relationship, however, as can be seen by contemporary examples of stateless nations such as Palestinians or Kurds. In fact, the nation, as a concept, derives its historical significance not so much through its grounding in a specific material polity or place, but rather through its unprecedented power to command connections between people spread out over vast distances. Unlike traditional civic groupings defined by village or even city-state, the nation demanded an imagined relationship between a vast body of people, most of whom had never met.

In the eighteenth century, as today, popular culture functioned as an important vehicle of nationalism. The nation became possible in part, Benedict Anderson suggests, because new forms of media such as the daily newspaper helped to create a large group of readers, linked by their capacity to imagine themselves as part of a whole network of unknown others. These readers form the basis of a community, informed by a collection of stories that, through their assemblage in the form of a single text, contribute to the creation of a coherent narrative of the world—a *national* point of view. Language and literacy play critical roles here, too: the rise of print capitalism that spurred the growth of newspapers corresponded with a decline of the privileged status of Latin as the sacred *written* language, to which all vernacular or spoken languages were secondary. The production of written texts in the everyday languages spoken by people throughout Europe hastened the break-up of religious empires, while granting real and symbolic significance to the communities defined by distinct vernaculars. Of course, the "community" facilitated by print was strongly linked to literacy, and its contours therefore shaped by the social as well as the economic interests of educated elites. Nationalism, understood in this way, is inevitably a top-down phenomenon.

Like other modern structures of identification, the nation can be understood as both empowering and restrictive (see Chapter Six). Fuelled by the spirit of revolutionary movements against absolutist regimes, expressed most dramatically in the French Revolution of 1789–99, nationalism was based partly on the idea of the rights of "the people" to govern themselves. This ideal became a defining principle in the French and American constitutions. Its democratic appeal masks the function of the nation as the legitimating ideology of the *state*, whose territorial boundaries are regulated internally and externally by instruments of force—police and military agencies, legal and educational institutions, and political organizations. The two meanings of the nation—as an expression of the ideal of equal citizenship, and as an alibi for state power—function simultaneously, the never fully realized promise of popular democracy working to justify the disciplinary force of the state while concealing the gaps in social and economic power that separate the mass of "the people" from the ruling elites. The compelling symbolism of "we" operates only to the extent that it is supported by forgetting that some of "us" own greater stakes in our collective project than others.

The nation's capacity to *work* as a collective project depends in large part on its ability to **interpellate** its members as citizens, enlisting their active and voluntary submission to the greater community. To this end, the idea of the nation must be embodied in a powerful narrative that grounds the present in the past. The principal mechanism for this grounding is what historian Eric Hobsbawm calls "invented tradition": "a set of practices, normally governed by overtly or tacitly accepted rules of a ritual or symbolic nature, which seek to inculcate certain values and norms of behaviour by repetition, which automatically implies continuity with the past" (2). National conflicts are often mediated by the struggle over *competing* invented traditions, whether "tradition" is defined by religion or by the much looser concept of "culture." Whether it signifies Matthew Arnold's version of high culture as "the best that has been thought and said" (see Chapter Two), or a more grassroots **folk culture**—and often it's a combination of the two—"culture" works within nationalist **discourse** as a powerful emblem of belonging. Both high and folk culture myths of nation work through principles of exclusion, the former by stressing qualities of taste, discrimination, and linguistic competence or "breeding," and the latter through birth, or indigenous attachment to the land.

The Nation and Its Others

Culture plays an important role in mediating one of the fundamental functions of the nation, which is its capacity to draw clear distinctions between who belongs and who doesn't. One of the nation's defining features is that its unity is marked off by specific boundaries and borders: "The nation is imagined as *limited* because even the largest of them, encompassing perhaps a billion living human beings, has finite, if elastic boundaries, beyond which lie other nations. No nation imagines itself coterminous with mankind" (Anderson 7). The corollary of this imagined limit to the nation's reach is that some parts of humankind are excluded from the nation; indeed, their exclusion is fundamental to the way the nation defines itself.

The first step towards lightening

The White Man's Burden

is through teaching the virtues of cleanliness.

Pears' Soap

is a potent factor in brightening the dark corners of the earth as civilization advances, while amongst the cultured of all nations it holds the highest place—it is the ideal toilet soap.

Nineteenth-century British ideologies of race and nation are reflected in advertising of the time. While messages like this one would never appear today, advertisements continue to be a potent site for the reproduction of mythologies of collective identity.

The critical role of difference and exclusion in establishing the meaning of the nation can be understood by thinking of nations in purely structuralist terms (see Chapter Three). " 'Nation' is a relational term; like any sign, one nation consists in being what the others are not. . . . Nations have no essential or intrinsic properties; each is a discursive construct whose identity consists in its difference from others" (O'Sullivan et al.). This definition helps to remind us of the signifying function of the nation; however, to understand *how* it comes to have such a powerful function as a signifier of identity and difference, we need to consider more material issues. First, the critical role of borders in defining the nation can be understood in *political* terms by considering the constitution of states as battles for territory and resources. It can also be understood in psychic terms if we recall from Chapter Six psychoanalytic explanations for how we come to define ourselves around the crucial poles of "self" and "other."

The Narcissism of Minor Difference   Historian Michael Ignatieff employs Freud's concept of "the narcissism of minor difference" to explain why seemingly small differences between nations come to take on such enormous significance in the process of self-definition. The narcissist defends the integrity of his or her own sense of self by projecting all the negative or unruly elements onto the other. The precariousness of this sense of self can be guarded only through the most vigilant policing of the boundaries between self and other. The most crucial boundaries in this respect are not those that mark obvious differences, but those that separate the self from the not-quite-self. A clear example of the mobilization of those distinctions was the persecution of the Jews in Nazi Germany. At a time of deep economic crisis, Germans took refuge in a hysterical defence of national identity whose unity could be maintained only by the purging of "foreign" elements within. Ignatieff notes:

> [Hitler's] language of purity and cleansing, so widely echoed today, is the most elemental language of narcissism: the reduction of all difference to the distinction between cleanliness and dirt. Cleanliness distinguishes the human from the non-human, the valued from the despised. This is the trajectory, the path toward moral abjection to which the narcissism of minor difference can (though it need not always) lead. (50)

Nationalism is not always based on, nor does it inevitably lead to, fascism or the violent elimination of those deemed "impure." However, it does rest on an assumption of unity, maintained not only by the accentuation of minor differences that are seen to separate the nation from other nations, but also by the *suppression* of the more significant differences and inequalities that shape the lives of its individual citizens. One relatively common way to express national integrity is through the metaphorical representation of the nation as a body: this image consolidates the *naturalness* of the nation along with its organic unity; made up of different parts, it is nevertheless more than the sum of those parts, which work naturally in conjunction with one another.

Suggested Activity 7.3

Try to think of other metaphors by which nations are represented (e.g., as a melting pot or mosaic). What different kinds of nationalist mythologies do these metaphors convey? What do they have in common?

The metaphor of the individual body serves to smooth over the differences and inequalities that define the nation, inviting all of its members to subordinate their particular interests—defined by class, say, or gender—to an identification with the greater unity. The "greater unity" is, of course, defined by the ruling interests in society—interests whose class and gender specificity are ex-nominated through the image of the exemplary national citizen as one who transcends particularity.

Nation and Gender

As the contemporary example of "The Rant" suggests, the exemplary national citizen has traditionally been gendered male. Not surprisingly, then, the language of nationalist discourse tends, implicitly if not explicitly, to reflect a **patriarchal** ideology. However, the privileging of male interests does not mean that women have no place in nationalist discourse. On the contrary, the relationship between essentialized notions of masculinity and femininity are critical to the construction of the nation (see McClintock).

As with other aspects of nationalist discourse, this emphasis on gender operates both as a reflection of, and an influence on, the role of the state as regulator of economic and social relations. With the rise of industrial capitalism, the family was a critical site for the reproduction—both physical and cultural—of a society dominated by bourgeois interests. As the linchpin of the family, female sexuality was subject to vigilant oversight and discipline, both through regulation and law (in relation to marriage and ownership of property, for example) and through ideology. The myth that the health of the nation hinged on the moral propriety of its women is a typical example of the way in which the discourse of patriotism aided in the suppression of female sexuality. This myth assumed even greater significance in relation to issues of nation and **race**, discussed further below.

The enlistment of women as emblems of the nation's integrity produces an interesting iconography in which, while the exemplary citizen is always male, the nation itself is often figured as female. The personification of the nation as woman has both political and quasi-spiritual resonances that emerge particularly clearly through the connection that is often made between women and the land. As in many other national anthems, the land in "O Canada" is personified: "True patriot love, in all thy sons' command." While the gender of Canada is unstated, conventional codes of national iconography invite us to read the nation as a maternal rather than a paternal figure. Regarded as territory to be conquered and possessed, the land (like "woman") also signifies the embodiment of Nature. This almost sacred designation works, bizarrely, to *naturalize* the masculine conquerors' claims to nationhood, while consigning the land, along with women, to the status of property. The gendered and sexualized image of nation as a male soldier guarding (or cultivator ploughing) the female earth strongly contradicts the mythology of a community defined by "deep, horizontal comradeship" (Anderson 7). It also shapes the material operations of the state, contributing to a long delay in women's—and others'—achievement of equal civil rights.

NATION AND EMPIRE

We have tried so far to show how, while identity in a general sense is predicated on difference—the community of "us" dependent on an excluded "them"—this is particularly true for nations, as a consequence of the historical circumstances in which they emerged. Both nationalism and nation-*states* are products of the Industrial Revolution, as discussed above. The Industrial Revolution was itself dependent on the resources of distant regions of the world, which supplied it with raw materials as well as capital in the form of gold and silver. These regions were not themselves industrialized, and were not to enjoy the benefits of industrialization for a long time, even though they came to assume a crucial role as markets for the products of industry. The economic development of European nation-states, in other words, was fuelled by the *under*development of other parts of the world—Asian, African, and American colonies, exploited for their resources and their labour while they were prevented, through trade regulations backed up by military force, from becoming full partners in the generation of wealth (see Blaut).

The construction of European national *identities* was similarly dependent on the non-European world. The process of secularization and scientific enlightenment that contributed to the break-up of the old religious dynasties was strongly connected to the voyages of exploration undertaken by Spain, Portugal, England, France, and the Netherlands during the fifteenth and sixteenth centuries. As much as these travels were undertaken in search of wealth, they were also driven by a quest for knowledge, and ultimately served to shape an understanding of the physical world and its human inhabitants as more vast and complicated than had previously been imagined. As Europeans came into contact with other, previously unknown peoples, two things happened: on the one hand, other places and cultures were translated and distorted—made to fit, positively or, more often, negatively into categories of the already-known, thus consolidating the universality of European ideas and values. On the other hand, contact with otherness led, in innumerable local circumstances as well as more generally, to a recognition of a multitude of radically different worlds that could not—indeed should not—be reduced to a version of the same. National identities were shaped by both of these responses to difference: the recognition of **cultural relativism**, whereby in contrast to the religious view of a single universal truth differences in belief and practice were seen to be inevitable and perhaps even desirable, and the consolidation of singular **sovereign** identities characterized by an imperative to safeguard and even to extend their sovereignty, by force if necessary.

The West and the Rest

Colonialism was not just an economic and political undertaking, in which European nations competed for dominance through the exploitation and settlement of overseas colonies. It was also, importantly, a **cultural** project, in which these nations sought to extend throughout the world their concept of civilization, defined by the Enlightenment values of scientific rationalism and liberal humanism: the imperative to conquer the non-European world was tempered (but, importantly, not contradicted) by the will to save it.

Refining and complicating the explicit *universality* of the colonial vision, according to which all of humanity was marching in the same direction along a single, historically determined road to progress, was its grounding in principles of identity and difference. The humanistic thrust of colonialism, which sought to impart the idea of the natural sovereignty and brotherhood of man, was more seriously undermined by the fundamental principle of *in*equality that structured the whole colonial and civilizing project. Like the mission of the "rational recreationists" (see Chapter Two), which sought to improve the working classes of England by enlisting them in middle-class programs of education and recreation, the colonial project reflected two connected but irreconcilable assumptions: that of a fundamental equality between humans that could be advanced through education, and that of a fundamental and hierarchical difference between groups that justified the material and ideological domination of the inferior group by the superior one.

The ambivalence that motivated the cultural mission of colonialism is clearly summed up in the words of British civil servant Thomas Babington Macaulay, who argued in his 1835 "Minute on Indian Education" that teaching English literature in India would accomplish the critical goal of forming "a class who may be interpreters between us and the millions we govern; a class of persons, Indian in blood and colour, but English in tastes, in opinions, in morals, and in intellect" (Macaulay).

The Minute is part of an argument about colonial policy, about the way best to control and manage India. It is also an interesting statement about identity, informed by conflicting assumptions about the boundaries of "civilized" community: on the one hand, the suggestion of a possible, if not yet realized, moral equivalency between Indians and English speaks to the ideals of a universal humanism, embodied in certain forms of capital-C Culture such as literature. On the other hand, Macaulay's statement is based on a firm sense of natural and unchanging differences defined by class ("governors" vs. "masses"); by race ("colour and blood"); and by culture (he argues for the teaching of English literature on the grounds that nothing worthwhile has been produced in the Indian languages).

His argument is a logical paradox that highlights the contradictions in the allegedly humanist character of English "tastes, opinions, morals and intellect" by exposing their racist foundations. At the same time, it undermines the supposed singularity and superiority of Englishness by drawing attention to the fragmentation of identity that colonialism entails. Like the Indian class of "interpreters" who assume English tastes, opinions, and morals, the colonial settlers who take up residence in the colonies become a little bit less English as they are exposed to the corrupting influences of native culture and environment. As the boundaries between the community of "us" and "them" start to look more and more porous, it becomes increasingly necessary to reiterate them.

Orientalism—Then and Now

That process of anxious drawing and redrawing of boundaries impels the operation of colonial discourse, which produces forms of knowledge and ways of talking about "the other" as a way of securing the identity of the imperial "self." Edward Said uses the term **orientalism** to describe a dominant form of colonial discourse in which a mythologized East, or "Orient," becomes a site for the projection of Western fantasies of otherness as well as a mechanism for Western domination of actual non-Western cultures.

Based on Foucault's formulation of a nexus between knowledge and power, orientalism consists of a repertoire of images and ideas that *produce* "the Orient" as an object of Western knowledge and control. Disseminated through a variety of institutionalized forms (travel writing, civil service briefs, government policy documents, journalism, and even so-called "innocent" forms of culture such as art and literature), orientalism played a critical role in European—particularly British—domination of non-Western cultures. It draws on a bank of stereotypical (and frequently inconsistent) qualities—inscrutability, deviousness and treachery, religious fundamentalism and immorality, violence, and excessive delicacy and effeminacy—in order to construct the oriental as a fixed, unchanging other, lacking subjectivity or internal variation and condensed in binary opposition to Western consciousness and culture. At the same time as orientalism serves to mark the absolute otherness of Eastern people, thus shoring up the integrity of Western identity, it is also a way of making the foreign familiar, of turning other cultures into objects of Western knowledge

Like all discourses, orientalism emerged out of particular historical circumstances, in which it served a number of specific functions. The term can seem somewhat confusing to us today, because the term "Orient" has come to refer specifically to the Asian Pacific (China, Taiwan, Japan, Korea), whereas its eighteenth-century meaning was much broader, covering the areas now referred to as the Middle East (Turkey, Iraq, Iran) and South Asia (India, Pakistan, Bangladesh, etc.). In part, the change in terminology can be seen as the product of a more sophisticated understanding of global cultures: the West has come to recognize critical differences between and within non-Western societies.

Contemporary Orientalism   It's easy to dismiss both nationalism and orientalism as products of unsophisticated cultures or bygone eras remote from our contemporary world. However, both persist in Western popular culture in forms that, like other myths of collective belonging, show up more obviously in times of crisis. While the term "orientalism" may not signify precisely what it used to, however, the discursive practices it refers to continue in different forms. Long after it became unacceptable to typecast black or Native characters as the bad guys, films and TV shows ranging from Disney's *Aladdin* to the TV series *24* continue to draw on stereotypes of the Middle East and/or Arabs as evil and barbarous. Orientalist stereotyping became particularly acute in conjunction with the 1990 Gulf War and subsequent conflicts in Afghanistan and Iraq. Most obviously, the September 11th terrorist attacks were followed by an upsurge in racist violence, in which "Middle Eastern–looking" people were targeted for attack. Instances of the crudest kind of stereotyping occurred, such as the torching of a Hindu temple in Hamilton, Ontario, which the arsonists presumably mistook for a mosque (Clairmont).

Accompanying the rapid circulation of racist stereotypes and ensuing violence in the present context, a new academic and popular-knowledge industry for the production of knowledge about Eastern, specifically Islamic, cultures has grown up seemingly overnight. Like the eighteenth-century European scholars of the East (actually called "orientalists"), a host of Western experts began appearing on talk shows, producing new books and articles and reviving old ones that purported to explain the "essential" qualities of Islamic culture (see for example Huntington, and, in a more sympathetic vein, Lewis).

Like their eighteenth-century forebears, these new forms of "knowledge" homogenized a number of vastly different, complex cultures into a single, static classifiable entity, defined by implicit contrast with a more variegated, fluid West. Read in the context of a generalized Western anxiety about the non-West in general, and Islam in particular, the bulk of these studies reinforced an image of Muslim culture as fundamentally different from, and threatening to, Western culture, while also serving to legitimate Western initiatives to *contain* and *manage* the threat. While they might seem remote from acts of racist violence, these discursive forms of "cultural profiling" assume material significance in the form of new customs and immigration, policing, and legal regulations in the United States and Canada that make it easier to detain and deport, arrest and imprison people on the basis of race or national origin.

Race and Identity

Lurking in the background of much of the preceding discussion is the significance of **race** (see Close-Up 7.4), which, for the last two hundred years, has been a particularly highly charged means of defining collective identity.

When it first appeared in English around the beginning of the sixteenth century, the word "race" had a fairly neutral meaning, referring simply to different kinds of people or things. By the late eighteenth century, the term was used increasingly to designate fixed, biological, and hierarchical differences between groups of people. It became, in other words, caught up in the currency of power.

A number of historical circumstances combined to ignite the charge around the concept of race. First, the European Romantic movement stressed, among other things, the idea of natural, essential qualities of beings that defined distinct peoples and established

---

Close-Up 7.4

Race

Simply defined, race is a concept that delineates categories of human beings based on physically, biologically, and genetically distinct types. Linked implicitly or explicitly to psychological and intellectual characteristics, these "types" become the basis for drawing hierarchical distinctions between groups. Race, then, is inextricably linked to **racism**—to the extent that, as with **nations** and **nationalism**, we can gain a clearer understanding of both terms if we think of them as developing in a direction that is opposite to how we usually think of them. By this reckoning, " 'racism' is not so much a product of the concept of race as the very reason for its existence. Without the underlying desire for hierarchical categorization implicit in racism, 'race' would not exist" (Ashcroft et al., 1999). One of the critical premises this statement illustrates is that "race" is not a natural, pre-given category, but one that assumes significance in particular historical circumstances to suit particular purposes.

---

their primordial claim to particular places. Though not itself based on an idea of race, this foundation of popular nationalism drew on the ideas of "blood and soil" that were to become fundamental to racist theories. Second, the development of biological science, proceeding from a very narrow reading of Darwin, tipped the balance of heredity vs. environment debates in favour of a new preoccupation with genetic inheritance. Specific branches of (what is now recognized to be) "pseudo-science"—such as phrenology, which added more precise quantifiers such as skull measurement to crude delineations of race based on skin colour—contributed to a growing consensus on the significance of a correlation between specific categories of physical characteristics and moral and intellectual qualities.

Put together with the political and social missions of colonialism, these developments contributed to the development of the modern sense of race as a critical marker of essential human differences and inequalities. The metaphorical appropriation of Darwin's theory of natural selection (evolution) into a model of social *progress* legitimated the domination of certain groups on the basis of their alleged genetic "backwardness." It also paved the way for programs of social and biological "improvement," whereby those inferior races might be raised up or cultivated to a higher level, while at the same time fuelling fears about the possibility of the degeneration of the dominant, white race through miscegenation (interracial sexual intercourse).

Manifested, among other ways, in the obsessive myth of a vulnerable white woman being threatened by a predatory black man, this fear highlights the way in which categories of power and identity such as race and gender are inevitably mixed up with one another. It also shows how the construction of race, like other identity-formations, is shaped by the confused tangle of fear and desire that defines the interface between "self" and "other."

Race-based Identity   The concept of race was challenged first in the debates that led, finally, to the abolition of slavery at the end of the nineteenth century, and again following the Second World War (which confirmed the alarming congruence of the ideas of nationalism and racism) and the decolonization movements of the Fifties and Sixties. Scientific debate continues over the existence of significant genetic differences corresponding to traditionally defined race, with the majority of scholars agreeing that genetic differences *within* racial groups outweigh the differences *between* groups. Whether or not it exists in a natural, biological sense, it is inarguable that race, like other markers of identity, *matters* in a cultural, political, and economic sense, affecting not just the way different people are represented based on the group they allegedly "belong" to by virtue of skin colour, but also economic opportunities, social freedoms, and even mortality. Besides influencing how others see us, race also partly determines the way we see ourselves, shaping our identities in both positive and negative ways.

In the cultural context of colonialism and its aftermath, racial minorities are driven to define their identities in split and fractured forms. Where fully human identity is characterized by the "unmarked" race of whiteness, being black presents an untenable choice: become fully human by identifying with what you are not and never can be, or be your "self"—in effect a non-self, defined only by difference and negation. At best, this dilemma leads to a strongly conflicted sense of self and community; at worst, it can lead to forms of mental illness (see Fanon, *Black Skin, White Masks*). *Post*colonial culture offers new forms of racial identification, in which the hierarchies are, if not absent, then at least more flexible.

POSTCOLONIAL IDENTITIES

Beginning with India/Pakistan in 1947, most of Britain's former colonies became independent in the three decades following the Second World War. In a technical way, then, the period from approximately 1950 through the end of the twentieth century can be referred to as **postcolonial**. Once we start to think about that concept in more detail, however, it becomes apparent that many of the structures of power and identity that characterized the colonial period still have a firm grip on us today. Not only do forms of colonialism and **imperialism** persist (take, for example, the situation of First Nations groups in Canada, the United States, and Australia), but the terms in which formerly colonized groups shape their demands for *post*colonial autonomy inevitably also bear the mark of those earlier signs of European dominance: nation and race. Rather than see the hangover of colonial vocabularies and structures simply as signs of a colossal failure on the part of contemporary society to free itself from oppressive tradition, we can look at postcolonial reformulations of nation and race as evidence for the continuing attraction and danger of forms of collective identity that inevitably signify both more and less than what they claim.

Postcolonial Nationalism

In one of the more infamous events of the last age of empire, representatives of the dominant European powers met—in the spirit of cooperation—over a period of a couple of months in 1884–85 to divvy up the territory of Africa amongst themselves. As a result of what became known as the Berlin Conference, more than thirty newly created states, "superimposed over the one thousand indigenous cultures and regions of Africa," were parcelled out amongst France, Germany, England, Italy, Spain, and Portugal (Rosenberg). There were no African representatives at the conference. Some seventy-five years later, much of Africa successfully won liberation from Europe, via independence movements mounted in the name of the "nations" that had so recently and arbitrarily been imposed *by* Europe. This situation illustrates the paradox of postcolonial nationalism, whereby the discourse former colonies take up to defend their own unique identities and right to sovereignty is freighted with the legacy of colonialism from which the modern nation was born.

New Players, Same Game   African and other colonial subjects face the challenge of framing their calls for liberation in the language of a project from which they have been excluded by definition. Postcolonial nationalists in Africa faced this challenge in a couple of ways: first, by calling up an image of a mythic African past around which the idea of a present nation might be articulated. This project of reviving the pre-colonial past played a critical role in refuting colonialist assertions that Africa had no history, nothing that might be deemed a **culture**, before the arrival of the Europeans.

There were, however, at least two problems with this model of African nationalism. First, while the ancient traditions (on whose revival the contemporary identity of the nation hung) often drew on actually existing practices, these practices were never as uniform or as stable or as widespread as nationalists claimed. Moreover, since the European invention of African states carved up societies along arbitrary boundaries, separating groups that had once functioned as coherent communities and forcing together others with no common traditions or even languages, the project of defining "authentic" national cultures was especially daunting.

Thus, what was implicit in European nation-building was in African and other post-colonial nations more obvious: traditions were, to a large degree, invented, reflecting not a past, unified culture but current nationalist ideology, framed by the interests of the dominant group. In Africa, that group consisted of largely European-trained intellectuals and civil servants—like Macaulay's class of "interpreters," who attempted to give their imported ideas legitimacy by dressing them up in the language of the people. Once again, the contradictions inherent in the very idea of the nation, as it first evolved in Europe, emerged with particularly painful clarity in the postcolonial context: the dependence of nationalist discourse on the concept of *identity*—an unchanging, homogeneous essence—denies the possibility of fulfilling the nation's promise to reflect the living will of the people, in all their diversity.

The revival/invention of the past was not the only trajectory of postcolonial nationalism. Many nationalists, including Fanon, tried to define a vision of nationhood in which the European myth of *universal* and *equal* humanism might truly be realized. Such a nation would be the ultimate realization of the natural rights of man. This ideology of nation—embodied most explicitly in the dominant nationalist tradition of the United States—emphasized not roots but mobility and liberty, through which national belonging could be imagined to be something freely chosen.

As with other postcolonial nationalisms, however, American nationalism was influenced and ultimately constrained by its reliance on the Enlightenment ideal of humanism, with its inherent tensions between universalism and binarism such that the human was defined by what it excluded (rational vs. irrational, civilized vs. primitive, etc.). Thus, at the same time as the idea of "nature's nation" tends naturally toward imperial expansion (formalized in American policy in the idea of Manifest Destiny, by which it was deemed to be the natural right of the United States to control the whole continent), it also sanctions the "natural" restriction of rights to those seen to embody the characteristics of rational man—a category that, until comparatively recently, excluded women and blacks.

Finally, to the extent that nations work to legitimize the political boundaries of particular states, their universalist myths are necessarily grounded in specific territorial claims. In settler–invader societies like the United States and Canada, in which colonizing populations displaced indigenous cultures, these myths inevitably involve the justification and/or erasure of their violent origins. This is often accomplished by the transformation of a history of conquest by force into a story of natural inheritance or romantic conjoinment. Such is the case in Walt Disney's *Pocahontas*, in which the violence of colonialism (translated, in the film, into an unfortunate instance of cultural misunderstanding), is ultimately overshadowed by a love story that signals the possibility of a new race of "Americans" defined by the harmonious blending of (masculine) Europe and (feminine) Indian (see *Mickey Mouse Monopoly*).

As Canadian As...   Because their "founding" populations are the direct descendents of colonizing groups, settler–invader societies expose the contradictions of national identity in particularly obvious ways—which takes us back to "The Rant." In the absence of a revolutionary mythology of freedom like that of the United States, Canada—due in part to its Loyalist heritage and in part to the presence of two founding/invading groups, French and English—assumes a national identity that has been described as peculiarly postmodern (Hutcheon *Canadian Postmodern*).

The dilemma is represented in a 1988 *Canadian Forum* article that asked readers to think about how they might complete the phrase "As Canadian as. . .," the idea being to come up with a simile comparable to "as American as apple pie" to capture Canadian identity. The most appropriate answer, the article suggested, would be that given by a woman in response to a recent survey: "As Canadian as . . . possible under the circumstances" (qtd. in Hutcheon *As Canadian as Possible* 9).

The assertion of Canadianness as something definable only in the negative—an assertion that is echoed in Joe's articulation of Canadian identity as, above all, not American (and not what Americans think it is)—reflects a sense of the provisionality and constructedness of all founding mythologies. Identity in this context becomes ironic, expressed in terms that are more or less false, not quite right. Joe's rant is rife with irony, including the playing of the British imperialist "Pomp and Circumstance" in the background of the humble performance of a guy in a lumberjack shirt, the assertion and negation of indigenizing mythologies ("I don't live in an igloo, I don't eat blubber"), and finally the tension between arrogance and humility ("I AM CANADIAN. Thank you.") that characterizes Joe's speech.

Some Canadians lament what they see as the uncertainty and impotence of what amounts to a national identity defined by non-identity. Given the problems inherent in strong and monolithic nationalisms, this concern would seem to be misguided. However, it is also a mistake to idealize the self-conscious slipperiness of Canadian national identity as a model of pluralistic tolerance. As "The Rant" reveals, the foregrounding of "difference" does not make nationalist discourse immune to the dangers of speaking for, or over, other groups. It can, rather, exacerbate those dangers by appearing to have recognized and dealt with them, and/or disguising cultural chauvinism with an ironic, self-deprecating demeanour.

As anthropologist Eva Mackey has observed, "the project of Canadian nation-building has not been based on the erasure of difference but on controlling and managing it" (148). Differences are allowed—even celebrated—to the extent that they conform to a *singular* vision of happy pluralism, defined by the "ordinary" voice of Joe Canadian. As one self-consciously "ordinary" Canadian woman put it in an interview: "How can you stand strong if you're all separate, right? It's almost like we're all these different little countries within a country. But . . . you can't expect to be a strong country as far as unity. It'd be great if Canada was first and then you still keep your culture" (qtd. in Mackey 144).

In sum, postcolonial claims to national identity and autonomy can appear to be more or less legitimate (the "more or less" determined in part by what role the dominant national force played in the history of colonization). They are, however, prone to the pitfalls of European nationalism, which they expose and magnify. Partly for this reason, it is easy today to dismiss the validity of *all* nationalism, particularly if one happens to be part of a strong nation-state such as the United States. The nation remains viable as an idea, however, because the ideals of political sovereignty and cultural autonomy that it embodies—ideals that many still strive for— don't seem to be attainable in any other form. For indigenous groups in particular, who remain subject to forces of formal colonialism, the framework of nationhood remains a powerful cultural and legal mechanism for securing basic rights to self-determination.

Diaspora and Cultural Hybridity

Most obviously in relation to the indigenous cultures defined as First Nations, connection to place remains an important determinant in national identity. One of the most powerful forces shaping contemporary identities, however, is the unprecedented *movement* of people throughout the globe sparked by colonialism and more recent forces of globalization (see Chapter Nine). The term **diaspora** refers to the dispersal or scattering of a people, by choice or by force (and often those motives are blurred), from their homeland to diverse geographical regions. Colonialism itself was a diasporic process, as it involved the movement of millions of Europeans across the globe. For some, such as the convicts transported to Australian penal colonies, the trip was far from voluntary. In the case of many of the colonial settlers, comprising largely poor, marginalized members of their respective societies, relocation to the colonies in search of opportunities was a choice only in the most technical sense.

Arguably the most traumatic process of migration, and one that has become central to contemporary theorizations of diaspora (see Gilroy, *The Black Atlantic*), was the forced exile of thousands of Africans as slaves, who constituted the primary labour force in the American colonies. The new cultural forms that evolved out of that massive uprooting had a profound effect on postcolonial society, particularly in the Caribbean where indigenous populations had been virtually wiped out. The abolition of slavery in the beginning of the nineteenth century brought a new wave of settlers to the colonies in the form of mostly Indian and Chinese indentured labourers—workers, generally farmers, who paid off the costs of their passage through decades of servitude. The process of global migration initiated by colonialism has accelerated in the years following decolonization, as people from the former colonies have migrated to metropolitan centres, including the settler–invader societies of the United States, Australia, and Canada.

These movements have fragmented traditional place-bound communities at the same time as they have created new ones, shaped by complex dynamics of memory, movement, and encounters with new places and cultures. These new cultural forms demand new ways of understanding identity beyond the traditional singular markers of class, race, and nation. In *The Black Atlantic*, Paul Gilroy suggests that the metaphor of "roots" by which identity—particularly black identity—has traditionally been understood might usefully be replaced with "routes"—the lines of movement and exchange that connect Africa, England, and America, historically by slave ships and more recently by the migrations of people, money, and culture across the Atlantic. The identities that emerge from these movements cannot be easily located; they exist, rather, between cultures, and even between contrary impulses, toward return on the one hand (even if the "homeland" is largely imaginary, as it is for the descendents of African slaves) and assimilation on the other (Gilroy "Diaspora" 329–330).

The image of diasporic identities as "in between" cultures—suggesting a kind of entrapment in the "Middle Passage" of slave routes—is inadequate, however, both in its characterization of diaspora and in its suggestion of the existence of static, stable cultural poles between which diasporic peoples vacillate. In addition to being defined by conditions of loss and longing, diasporic identities can also be experienced as exhilarating and enriching forms of multiple attachment. For individuals, moving between cultures can translate into an advanced form of cultural literacy, often enhanced by knowing more than one language, and a healthy sense of tolerance for others.

The Musical Diaspora   On a broader scale, the dynamics of diaspora have produced new and powerful forms of cultural expression, nowhere more evident, perhaps, than in the realm of music. The dominance of musical forms rooted in ex–African slave culture—jazz, blues, rock and roll—leads one critic to take note of the remarkable situation in which "an utterly exploited and dominated group managed to colonize not European music, which is henceforth relegated to the outermost margins of 'high' culture, but Music itself" (Brown). Whether or not the evidence supports such a global claim, one need only look at the contemporary examples of rap and hip-hop as forms that developed not out of only black, but specifically diasporic, culture. "Rap," as Paul Gilroy notes:

> is a hybrid form rooted in the syncretic social relations of the South Bronx where Jamaican sound-system culture, transplanted during the 1970s, put down new roots and in conjunction with specific technological innovations, set in train a process that was to transform black America's sense of itself and a large proportion of the popular music industry as well. (*Small Acts* 125)

Rap has, of course, long transcended the borders of the United States, shaping music throughout the world. In Canada, groups such as War Party and 7th Generation use rap and hip-hop as a way to define Aboriginal identity, drawing on the social history of those styles to stress similarities between life in the ghetto and the conditions on reserves. The dynamics of diasporic culture, especially when they are embodied in forms such as music, which is boundary-crossing by its very nature, move beyond identities defined by race to illuminate and create wider, more **hybrid** communities.

A buzzword just now, *hybridity* is often used to describe a condition of multicultural plurality, a happy blend of cultures thrown together in a gigantic global jam session (see the discussion of a Bell Sympatico ad in Chapter Nine). As theorized by contemporary critics such as Homi Bhabha, however, hybridity describes not just a movement between identities, but also an agitation *within* the notion of identity itself whereby, through cultural exchange, we are forced to recognize the "other" within ourselves. That is, contemporary movements of cultural exchange don't just break down singular identities into multiple and conflicted forms; rather, they reveal that identities were multiple and conflicted all along. At the same time, it would be a mistake to extend the concept of diaspora so far that it becomes simply a loose metaphor to describe contemporary cultural identity *in general*. To suggest, as some theorists have done, that we are all more or less diasporic now risks glossing over the important differences between degrees and kinds of movement, as well as the importance of place in shaping identities, particularly in the context of indigenous cultures.

Suggested Activity 7.4

Think about how your own identity is constructed in relation to place. To what extent is your sense of self and/or belonging in a particular community determined by particular social or physical environments? How has your (or your family's) location in, or movement between, different places affected your sense of self and community?

Old Allegiences, New Alliances   It is also important to avoid the temptation to idealize the material conditions of diaspora as necessarily leading to greater tolerance, equality, or political progressiveness. Celebratory accounts of hybridity often gloss over the dynamics of power that shape contemporary cross-cultural relations. Those conditions, and responses to them, can serve to entrench rather than dissolve identities. Benedict Anderson notes the rise of new "long-distance" nationalisms, "whereby well-off immigrants to the rich, advanced countries (and their children) are becoming key sources of money, guns, and extremist propaganda in their distant, putative countries of origin—in perfect safety and without any form of accountability" (qtd. in Robbins 11). Even where diasporic identities are translated into more hybrid forms, the results are not always positive.

Rap has produced controversial forms of community, in part because its politics are so ambiguous. At the same time as it expresses a sense of collective anger and alienation at the racist structures of dominant society, rap also has a strong affinity with mainstream cultural aspirations of individualism and material success, along with extreme forms of patriarchy and homophobia. This politics has produced some odd alliances across race and class—demonstrated, for example, by the huge success of white rapper Eminem, who is popular not just amongst white youth, but also with blacks, who respect both his talent and his (often ironic) self-consciousness about race, and also identify with the themes of suffering and resistance in his music. Less positively, Eminem has been characterized as drawing a community of fans, black and white, united by a generalized anger against "society" that is stoked by songs that evoke fantasies of violent revenge (Holloway).

Thus, the forces of diaspora, and the forms of cultural hybridity they enhance, powerfully influence the formation of contemporary group identity. As well as reconfiguring the identities of those who have experienced migration in a direct way, the politics of diaspora has shaped the production of community more generally, creating greater fluidity—and sometimes conflict—between collectivities defined by race, class, and cultural tradition. We need to be cautious, however, not to read the story of identity and community as a tidy linear narrative that moves from enclaves of race and nation to a more open and cosmopolitan global culture shaped by diaspora and hybridity. Identity/community formations in the contemporary world are characterized by strong foundations in traditional models of belonging that are constantly being broken, modified, and in some cases reinforced in response to the pressures of **globalization** (see Chapter Nine).

POSTNATIONAL IDENTITIES: MELTED, FROZEN, RECONSTITUTED

"Can we build a new kind of politics? Can we construct a more civil society with our powerful technologies? Are we extending the evolution of freedom among human beings?" (Katz 68). These stirring questions (a sharp contrast to the ironic tone of Joe's rant!) provide the lead-in to an article in the December 1997 issue of *Wired* magazine describing the emergence of a new kind of community—the digital nation. Based on a Merrill Lynch–*Wired* survey of the attitudes and beliefs of users of communications technology— cell phone, beeper, laptop, and home computer—the article set about to describe (and celebrate) the possibilities of digital citizen- or *netizen*-ship, a new form of belonging unconstrained by place, gender, race, sexual orientation, or national origin (see Figure 7.1).

Defined in the survey as falling within the categories of "connected" or "superconnected" according to their level of technology use, netizens were found to share a number of traits in common: in general they are "knowledgeable, tolerant, civic-minded, and radically committed to change. Profoundly optimistic about the future, they're convinced that technology is a force for good and that [the] free-market economy functions as a powerful engine of progress" (Katz 71). They also constitute a powerful new force in society, able to assert considerable influence over traditional political processes but, more significantly, embodying possibilities for new forms of democratic politics.

Figure 7.1 A Growing Slice

The *Wired*/Merrill Lynch Forum Digital Citizen Survey, conducted by Luntz Research Companies, polled 1,444 Americans to examine their views on technology and society. The survey divided respondents into four categories:

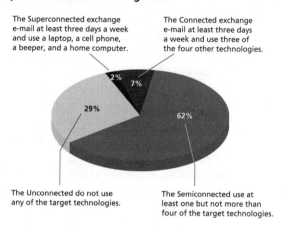

The Superconnected exchange e-mail at least three days a week and use a laptop, a cell phone, a beeper, and a home computer.

The Connected exchange e-mail at least three days a week and use three of the four other technologies.

The Unconnected do not use any of the target technologies.

The Semiconnected use at least one but not more than four of the target technologies.

They Believe in Democracy...

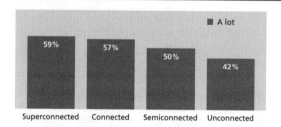

How much confidence do you have in democracy?

...and Worship Free Markets

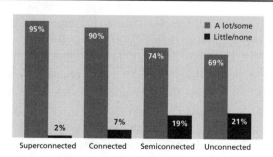

How much confidence do you have in the free-market system?

While articles like this one lost some currency after the decline of the high-tech boom in the late Nineties, they do speak to a common belief, usually though not always framed in optimistic terms, about the possibilities for new identities and communities created by economic, technological, and cultural processes of globalization. To some extent, as we discuss in Chapter Nine, this belief is a reasonable one: the weakening of traditional borders obstructing the flow of information, goods, money, and, to a lesser extent, people has created new forms of community and made it possible to imagine the fulfillment of Marshall McLuhan's idea of a truly "global village." At the same time, the economic and social inequalities that define current global relations—inequalities that are, by most estimates, growing—seriously undercut the utopian ideas presented in articles such as Katz's. That the constituency of the "netizens" in Katz's article was exclusively American—a fact not commented on in the article—suggests the extent to which the dominant vision of global society is still confined, culturally and geographically, to a specific segment of the world's population.

The things not mentioned in Katz's article—economic inequalities, fears (whether real or imagined) of Americanization, and the existence of vast numbers of the "unconnected"—all complicate the possibilities for the achievement of a global wired community, let alone a genuinely democratic one. These factors, in combination with concerns about loss of cultural heritage, a form of historical belonging that is often grounded in the ecology of particular places, give rise to new forms of nationalism and other models of local community that rival the placeless world of the netizen. While some of these new identities clearly serve to advance the autonomy of their members, others, often in paradoxical cooperation with the *dis*identifying forces of global capitalism that they in principle oppose, serve to further entrench inequality and conflict.

Deterritorialization/Reterritorialization

One of the major cultural symptoms of globalization, at least in the "wired" West, is a decline in the importance of place in determining identity. In conjunction with this geophysical shift, nationalism has receded throughout much of the world. This is a consequence of the economic and technological shifts we have already discussed, but it is also a consequence of post-1960s politics, in which decolonization movements and women's and civil rights groups called attention to the oppressive foundations of dominant ideas of nation and identity. The academic legacies of these challenges are clearly evident in the rise of feminist, postcolonial, and poststructuralist theory in the university, all developments that contributed to the flourishing of the field of cultural studies (see Chapter Ten).

The political legacies are less clear-cut, and not just because, as with earlier revolutionary moments, the potential for genuine transformation was defused by a combination of conservative backlash and compromise. The deconstruction of identity was also resisted by radical groups themselves, who recognized its ambiguous political connotations. On the one hand, by exposing the historical constructedness of concepts such as "man," "woman," "black," and "white," feminist and anti-racist groups can challenge the justification of laws or beliefs that seem to legitimate unequal treatment based on race or gender.

On the other hand, the destruction of the grounds of identity also undercuts the foundations of meaning by which marginalized groups can marshal their own political positions. Thus, the breaking up of traditional identity categories has been accompanied by the resurgence of new forms of nation and identity politics. Many of these movements are informed by strong histories of marginalization that cannot be addressed by a new rhetoric of inclusivity and the erasure of distinct identities. As with all such collective identity projects, they are also beset by problems of exclusions and the suppression of internal differences.

Quebec Nationalism   The nationalist movement in Quebec offers an example of some of the contradictions that plague the definition of contemporary imagined communities. Based on the concept of a distinct French culture whose legitimate drive for autonomy has been oppressed politically, culturally, and especially linguistically by the English majority, the sovereignty movement has mounted a longstanding campaign for Quebec to become its own nation. Some of the problems with the sovereignty claims arise when its leaders have been forced to define exactly what constitutes an authentic *Québécois* identity. While the French language is an obvious marker of cultural belonging, the case becomes murkier, and less credible, when the politics of *language* begin to merge into claims for essential cultural identities.

Some theorists (see for example Balibar, Bauman) argue that "culture" and "ethnicity" have come to stand in for race as legitimate forms of discrimination. Less essentialist than race, **ethnicity** identifies differences between groups on the basis of a shared constellation of traits, including tradition, language, national origin, and shared memory. Its affinity with race as a tool for hierarchical boundary-drawing is revealed, in the case of Quebec nationalism, by the occasional slip-up in official sovereigntist discourse, such as then-Premier Jacques Parizeau's off-the-cuff remark blaming the defeat of a 1995 referendum on sovereignty on "money and the ethnic vote." The legitimacy of Quebec's nationalist claim is further complicated by sovereigntists' insistence that "Quebec" also includes the territories of indigenous groups such as the Cree. As with more traditional nations, new forms of anti-globalist nationalism—even those constructed as self-consciously postcolonial—function through the suppression of the cultural and political aspirations of minorities within their borders.

Identity Politics   Identity politics, mentioned earlier in this chapter in relation to the film *My Big Fat Greek Wedding*, is another mode of contemporary identity-formation that resists traditional social structures not by radically deconstructing them, but by reclaiming their devalued terms. The prototypical model of identity politics is the Civil Rights movement that emerged in the United States in the Fifties and Sixties along with the Black Power movement. Although these movements had different political thrusts—the Civil Rights movement called for racial integration, while the Black Power movement embraced a more radical, nationalist agenda—both countered the negative constructions of blackness by reasserting black identity in powerfully positive terms. Aspects of physical appearance like the afro, which had been the target of negative racial stereotyping, became new focal points of black pride, and, inspired by the Caribbean and African *Négritude* movement, African Americans sought to articulate a distinct black cultural identity defined by a pre-colonial, pan-African solidarity.

Black identity politics found popular media expression in the development of a new kind of black cinema that grew up in the late Sixties, characterized most notoriously by so-called "blaxploitation" films like *Sweet Sweetback's Baadasssss Song* (1971) and *Shaft* (1971), which took white stereotypes of black men—sexual promiscuity, aggressiveness, and unscrupulousness—and fashioned them into heroes. Blaxploitation cinema was successful in drawing in black audiences, not just because for the first time it featured blacks in leading roles, but, arguably, also because its parodic form licensed a kind of savage and defiant laughter at racism.

The strong note of moral disapproval of blaxploitation cinema (inherent in the name of the genre itself) might speak, on the one hand, to a general discomfort with the slippery form of parody. It also expresses, however, some of the principal problems of identity politics. Most obviously, identity politics, particularly as they are employed in blaxploitation cinema, inevitably reinforce the rigid, binary categories of identity that functioned to categorize and disenfranchise minorities in the first place. By employing stereotypes as a weapon, not a stigma (saying "sure, we're *baaad*, but we're strong"), or recasting them in a more positive light, hierarchies might be provisionally overturned but the discriminatory categories on which they're based are only reinforced. Moreover, any attempt to represent group identities through individuals—whether those representations seek to highlight the negative, the positive, or even just the truth—inevitably distort and gloss over crucial differences within the group. Black feminists criticized blaxploitation cinema, as well as elements of the Black Power movement, for defining "blackness" according to a crudely masculinist code that ignored female experience and branded as traitors any women who dissented from the "majority" black position. These feminist critiques—in conjunction with those launched against *feminist* identity politics by black women who felt co-opted into a white liberal agenda—highlight the key problem of identity politics: that it imposes a singular collective identity on individuals who hold multiple affiliations.

Consumerism, Identity, and Resistance

An additional problem with the assertion of more or less homogeneous group identities rests in the danger of commodifying difference—that is, of turning it into an exotic spectacle that not only lacks political agency, but also further disenfranchises minority groups by objectifying them for consumption by the majority. This danger is accentuated in our intensely visual culture, which tends to operate through the *aestheticization* of difference, in which meaning is reduced to pure visual effect. This form of signification is more or less harmful depending on the power of the group whose identity is being portrayed, the context in which that portrayal occurs—how it is represented—and how and by whom it has been produced.

My Big Fat Greek Wedding, the film discussed in the opening of this chapter, raises some interesting questions about this process. On the face of it, this film is a largely positive representation of Greek-American identity. Its gently mocking use of ethnic stereotypes (e.g., kinky hair, food fetishes, odd taste in clothes and architecture) is more than compensated for by its emphasis on the hospitality, emotional honesty, and loving loyalty of Toula's family. It is possible to argue, however, that the essential "Greekness" of the film is an aesthetic overlay—like the columns and fountains adorning the Portokalos's house—on what is ultimately a celebration of *American* culture.

This argument finds support in the film's treatment of Ian's conversion to the Greek Orthodox Church—a conversion made easy by the fact that, as Ian explains to his parents, neither he nor Toula are at all religious. The paradoxical presentation of religion as operating not despite, but precisely *through* the absence of deep religious feeling is enhanced by the scene of Ian's baptism, in which he is dunked into a plastic wading pool in a ritual he clearly doesn't understand and which is played largely for comic effect.

One of the many messages this scene conveys is that difference, as conveyed by cultural traditions—among which religion is arguably the most deeply rooted—is not disturbing because we're all really the same: secular Americans, living in a consumer culture (of which weddings are a particularly spectacular example), with others who are just like us though their clothes, music, and food might initially seem strange. Through the commodification of culture, "objects and images are torn free of their original referents and their meanings become a spectacle open to almost infinite translation. Difference ceases to threaten, or to signify power relations. Otherness is sought after for its exchange value, its exoticism and the pleasures thrills and adventures it can offer" (Rutherford 11).

The Marketing of Difference   Difference has become a major marketing tool, functioning not just to increase profits by appealing to increasingly narrow market segments, but also to reproduce a particular ideological vision that harnesses the happy image of unity-through-diversity to an individualist ethic of consumerism. Represented most famously in 1980s Benetton ads, which promoted an idealized racial diversity through the presentation of stereotypically white, black, and Asian models dressed in different-coloured sweaters, the strategy of difference also defines more recent ad campaigns by companies such as Gap and Nike. These ads convey a message of corporate social responsibility, while carefully abstracting the images they present from any complicating historical contexts. Thus, "difference is stripped of all social and political antagonisms and becomes a commercial symbol for what is youthfully chic, hip, and fashionable" (Giroux 15).

These representations of difference interact in complicated ways with actual group identity. On the one hand, advertising depends on extensive research, in which consumers are polled in an attempt to identify genuine group identities, which then become the basis for the images portrayed in ads. As our discussion of **consumption** in Chapter Five emphasizes, however, marketers ultimately do not find so much as they *create* their ideal consumers, appropriating forms of identity, meaning, and pleasure that are based on memory and lived experience into superficial categories of "lifestyle"—in which being

With their in-your-face violation of cultural taboos surrounding race and sexuality, Benetton ads have been read as both socially progressive and crassly exploitative of the minority groups represented in them.

part of a particular tribe (or switching from one tribe to another) is as simple as changing one's shirt or listening to a different band.

This is not to suggest that there is a simple distinction between "real," lived identities and those produced through commercial media; indeed, as Benedict Anderson shows, modern identities are inseparable from the structures of the media and the capitalist economy. Just as forms of early print media such as the newspaper played an instrumental role in the creation of national identities, more recent forms of electronic media have helped to shape postmodern identities. The so-called 500-channel universe of television, with its abundance of specialty channels, has arguably helped to reinforce identities based on age, religion, culture, and ethnicity, while facilitating the production of new, increasingly narrow identities based on taste and lifestyle. The development of more interactive television, in addition to the much greater capacity of Internet technology to increase user autonomy, has further served as a means for new and flexible constructions of community.

That many of these communities are initially constructed as fan groups, brought together by their participants' love for a particular celebrity or media form, does not mean we should dismiss them as shallow or insignificant. The collective mourning by members of an opera e-group for a woman in the group who died in the Sept. 11 attacks, for example, demonstrates that the pleasures of fandom can be a catalyst for more substantial forms of emotional investment (Wiltse). Interpellated as consumers, the members of these groups frequently translate the pleasure and emotional connection they derive from a particular manifestation of celebrity or entertainment culture into deeper forms of belonging.

In sum, commercial culture has been instrumental in defining a new model of society that moves far beyond the construction of a "mass" audience/imagined community to the production and accentuation of diversity. To a large degree, this represented diversity functions to smooth over substantial social differences with the end of fostering a universal consumer culture. Commercial media also work to ends not entirely anticipated or managed by their producers, however, producing new forms of imagined community—some of which define themselves in explicit opposition to the culture of consumerism.

With the massive demonstrations that were launched against meetings of world financial and political leaders in Seattle, Washington D.C., and Quebec City (2000, 2001) new and unexpected collective identities emerged, defined by coalitions of farmers, environmentalists, students, socialists, and anarchists. Significantly, these were groups that previously had little to do with one another, and that differed radically in demographics, geographical base, and even politics. They came together, however, in new and powerful coalitions, united through their critical resistance to economic globalization. These alliances were enabled in large part through technologies such as the Internet, which, while they may not have realized the utopian dreams of some users discussed at the beginning of this section on postnational identities, have clearly been taken up to democratic ends far different from their initial commercial and military applications.

Significantly, these coalitions work by harnessing the engines of global capitalism to more or less anti-capitalist ends. They thus point to the power of collectivities to enact substantial political change. They also point to a significant shift in the dynamics of collective identity from the relatively fixed markers of class, nation, and race to more fluid and multiple forms of definition. These activist groups both reflect and influence the generation of identities in the realm of popular culture—identities that may not be explicitly political, but that have concrete political *effects* in the way people imagine their places in the world and capacities to effect change.

SUMMARY

In this chapter we have explored the phenomenon of collective identity from its distinctly modern incarnation in *nation* and *race* through the formation of ambivalently resistant *postcolonial* identities to the production of postmodern identities that depart in some significant ways from their traditional foundations, while maintaining—and sometimes reviving—strong connections. Among the significant points this chapter has stressed are that:

- Collective identities, like individual ones, are not natural, but constructed—the products of particular historical and social circumstances.

- Again, like individual identities, they are structured around principles of difference and exclusion, in which internal contradictions and tensions are projected outward, onto an (also constructed) other. These differences are not neutral but value-laden, such that the collective identity of "us" is elevated hierarchically over "them."
- Collective identities are often signalled not by emphasizing the particularity of the group, but through an explicit denial or ex-nomination of specific traits in favour of an implied universality—hence "we" are ordinary; "they" are defined by race, ethnicity, gender, and so on.
- The dynamics of group identity production—markers such as race, class, and gender—do not operate independently, but in complex (context-dependent) interaction with one another
- Over the last five hundred years, colonialism has played a key role in defining collective identities, from those based on *nation* and *race* to new identities defined by different forms of *diasporic* belonging.
- As the social manifestation of forces of *globalization*, postmodern culture features a general movement away from group identities fixed by place or ideology toward more flexible identities defined by contradiction and movement. At the same time, these de-territorializing currents have been met by the (re)construction of more fixed, resistant identity formations.
- Commercial culture and media play a major role in the construction of collective identity, strengthening consumer culture while fostering different, non-commercial forms of belonging along with politicized resistance to consumerism.

SUGGESTIONS FOR FURTHER READING

Anderson, Benedict. *Imagined Communities.* London: Verso, 1983.

Bhabha, Homi. *Nation and Narration.* London: Routledge, 1990.

Giddens, Anthony. *Modernity and Self-Identity.* Cambridge: Polity, 1991.

Hall, Stuart, and Paul du Gay, eds. *Questions of Cultural Identity.* London: Sage, 1996.

Hooks, Bell. *Yearning: The Cultural Politics of Race and Gender.* Toronto: Between the Lines, 1990.

Mackey, Eva. *The House of Difference: Cultural Politics and National Identity in Canada.* Toronto: University of Toronto Press, 2002.

Said, Edward. *Culture and Imperialism.* London: Chatto and Windus, 1993.

———. *Orientalism.* New York: Vintage, 1979.

Chapter 8

Subcultures and Countercultures

Not a moment passes without each one of us experiencing, on every level of reality, the contradiction between oppression and freedom; without each one of us being caught up and weirdly twisted by two antagonistic perspectives simultaneously.

—Raoul Vaneigem

INTRODUCTION: THE MAINSTREAM AND OTHER STREAMS

To a large degree, the way that we have been addressing popular culture in this book has been to focus on the dominant or most prevalent forms of culture in the Western world today. By "dominant" we mean what is usually described as **mass culture**—forms of culture that are accessible, widely available, and intended for consumption by as many people as possible. There is no real mystery about the forms of popular culture that one might consider to be dominant: Hollywood blockbusters, pop music on the Billboard Top 40, broadcast television, video games, and so on.

There are two ways in which such things might be seen as dominant. First, if we measure the prevalence of this or that form of culture by the sheer number of people that listen to it, watch it, or otherwise participate in it (whether this is measured by attendance, sales, or revenue figures), James Cameron's *Titanic* is dominant in ways that Canadian films like Gary Burns's *Waydowntown* (2000) or Michael Dowse's *Fubar* (2002) can only hope to be. Second, dominance can refer to the core set of beliefs, ideas, and identities that are circulated through forms of popular culture. In this respect, *Waydowntown* might be seen as an expression of dominant culture, too. Though made on a small budget and shot in Calgary, the critique of dead-end business culture articulated in *Waydowntown* shares a great deal with other much more popular films, such as *American Beauty*. Even though *Waydowntown* is an indie film, financed outside of the major studio system, formally and structurally it shares a great deal with the most common forms of movie making. In this second, wider understanding of dominance, a small or limited audience isn't in and of itself a guarantee that a film or any other form of popular culture advocates or expresses views and ideas contrary to mainstream, dominant culture.

While we have tended to focus on the meaning and impact of dominant forms of popular culture, some of the ideas that we have been discussing in the preceding chapters cannot help but cast doubt on the existence of this very fact—that is, that there is anything like a single, dominant culture. In Chapter Four, we challenged Horkheimer and Adorno's culture industry thesis, which imagines people as little more than consumers who are completely duped by the nature of the capitalist world in which they live; in our discussion of consumption in Chapter Five, we drew attention to the multiple ways in which people make meaning through their varied practices of consumption; and in our discussion of groups and identities in the previous two chapters, it is clear that identity-formation, too, is more complicated than might be suggested by the idea of dominant forms of popular culture.

In the context of these discussions, "mainstream" culture looks a lot less mainstream than we generally tend to imagine when we employ this term. Or to put this another way: one of the things that becomes clear when studying popular culture is that our idea of the

Gary Burns's *Waydowntown* exposes the sterility of contemporary life through an investigation of the arid spaces of work and consumption.

mainstream is sometimes less a reality than it is a cultural construction that regulates our activities through the establishment of very powerful cultural norms—norms that everyone adheres to in some ways, but that everyone also contravenes or goes against in numerous others. No one is purely mainstream, not even the characters on *Friends* (who, for instance, revel in free pornography, engage in sexual relationships outside of marriage, and engage in other forms of behaviour that belie their otherwise straight, clean-cut image). As popular culture itself has pointed out over and over again, there is an infinity of strange and unusual things happening behind the "normal," everyday façade of white picket fences and suburban garage doors. Who would have thought, for instance, that so many Canadians would support the legalization of marijuana—and even have tried it themselves?

But to say that the idea of the mainstream is a creation is not to say that there is no such thing. There *do* seem to be general, widespread patterns of social behaviour present within societies that guide both individual and group activity. As we have seen throughout this book, one of the main reasons why scholars have become interested in the study of popular culture is because of the powerful role it plays in generating and regulating social behaviour. Scholars are also interested in how popular culture has been used to work *against* dominant ways of behaving and acting, in both the minor ways in which (as we suggested above) everyone goes against the grain of the mainstream in some way, but also in more extreme or direct ways. In this chapter, we will be focusing on groups that challenge the values, ideas, and structures of mainstream culture consciously and directly through their actions and practices: **subcultures** and **countercultures**. In their actions and practices, subcultures and countercultures oppose dominant structures that they see as limiting, repressive, and/or problematic. Subcultures and countercultures are engaged in the struggle to create new and different forms of social reality. In many cases, but especially since the Second World War, this struggle has often been directed against popular or mass culture itself; paradoxically, this attack on popular culture has often come through the creation of new forms of popular culture, which are themselves often absorbed into mainstream culture in a perpetual back-and-forth that has shaped contemporary experience profoundly.

Minority/Majority Relationships

In the next section, we will establish some preliminary distinctions between these two kinds of groups. But first, we need to note that the very idea of subcultures and counter-cultures immediately re-invokes the idea of a dominant culture that we challenged above. The prefixes "sub" and "counter" each imply a number of things, as we will see below. One of the main things that they signify, however, is the relationship of a smaller "culture," however understood, to the larger, defining culture of a given society at a given moment. In other words, whatever else they might signal, the concepts of subcultures and countercultures opposes a minority group to the majority: it makes no sense to speak of a subculture or a counterculture that is "dominant."

Furthermore, this minority–majority relationship is generally an antagonistic one. While it has become common to use the term "subculture" to refer to all kinds of practices and activities that might be considered strange or unusual, we will try to use these concepts somewhat more precisely. For example, people who play Scrabble seriously enough to attend tournaments and vie for national (and even global!) championships might be interesting or unusual. But these Scrabble players do not constitute a genuine subculture. Why not? First, players of Scrabble—no matter how attentively or religiously—are, in the end, playing a popular game by its prescribed rules. This stands in contrast to, for instance, writers of "slash fiction," who express their own desires and fantasies by writing original (and often erotically charged) stories that borrow characters from popular televisions shows such as *Star Trek*. Similarly, Scrabble players don't bend a popular cultural form into a different shape—like, for example, the numerous fans who produced and distributed online "improved" versions of George Lucas's *Star Wars Episode I: The Phantom Menace*. Through their actions, writers of slash fiction and the creators of the "phantom edits" express dissatisfaction with the limits and constraints of popular culture; the same cannot be said of serious Scrabble players, who can easily indulge their passion for the game while being otherwise upstanding, productive citizens.

Of course, the same could be said for our other two examples: a phantom-editor by night could well be a university professor by day. What we want to draw attention to here is that a practice shouldn't be considered subcultural unless its aim is to draw attention to the limits of majority practices and to offer new practices or cultural forms as an alternative. Subcultures and countercultures are both antagonistic; one of the ways of distinguishing between subcultures and countercultures is by looking at the precise nature of their antagonism toward mainstream culture and at the kinds of new forms that they propose as an alternative to mainstream or dominant culture.

After making some general distinctions between subcultures and countercultures, the remainder of this chapter will examine the relationship between popular culture and these groups in two ways. First, it will consider the ways in which sub- and countercultures have been *represented* in popular culture, specifically popular film. There are a few reasons why we have chosen to begin with representations of these antagonist cultures. One of the main ways in which sub- and countercultures are brought into contact with the "dominant," mainstream culture is through popular cultural representations of these practices. Our sense of the possibilities and limits of these groups—a sense that tends to be very different from what these groups themselves believe their aims and goals to be—is often staged within popular cultural forms. While analyzing representations of sub- and countercultures does not give us an accurate account of the practices of these groups, it does help us to understand one of the ways in which these practices become meaningful within popular culture. Starting out with representations also reminds us of the proximity of subcultures to mainstream culture. All too commonly, sub- and countercultures are imagined as being absolutely separate from and unaffected by popular culture. The opposite is in fact the case: often, popular culture has an impact on how subcultural groups stylize or represent themselves. To offer just one small snapshot: the roots of the "gangsta" tough-guy pose that emerges in hip-hop culture can be found in part in the gangster tough-guy pose of *The Godfather* films. In the mid-Nineties, rapper Snoop Dogg styled himself as "Tha Doggfather," striking a very *Godfather*-esque pose on an album cover. The writers of *The Sopranos* have whimsically depicted its contemporary New Jersey hoods, also making use of Coppola's filmic trilogy as a source for their own gangster poses; "authentic" roots sometimes have representations at their base.

Following this look at representations of sub- and countercultures, the second emphasis of this chapter is on the politics of subcultures in particular. As we will see below, countercultures are usually imagined as explicitly political; it's harder (at first) to see how a subcultural practice like skateboarding might also be political, if in a different way than an organized march down the streets of a capital city might be. For this reason, we have chosen to focus to a greater degree here on subcultures as opposed to countercultures.

Investigating the practices of subcultures and countercultures offers rich insights into the ways in which culture, especially popular culture, operates in the world today. From culture jamming (see Close-Up 8.1 later in this chapter) to the practices of religious countercultures (a category in which one might be able to include everything from Mormonism to the Raelians), from the peace movements of the 1960s to the contemporary techno-music-infused Love Parades that fill the streets of Berlin and other European cities each summer, there are numerous groups in which "culture is deeply political" and "can be used as means of resistance" (Duncombe). In the words of Stephen Duncombe, "In order to strive for change, you first have to imagine it, and culture is the repository of the imagination" (35).

SUBCULTURES AND COUNTERCULTURES: WHAT'S THE DIFFERENCE?

In what way do subcultures differ from countercultures? Are they fundamentally different, or do these two terms point to the same groups, activities, and practices, though in slightly different ways?

To some degree, the distinction between subcultures and countercultures is artificial. Subcultures and countercultures flow fluidly into one another: their boundaries are permeable. As the cultural critic George McKay puts it, "subcultures feed the counterculture—the range of subcultural movements from hippy through punk through rave and others contributes to the increasingly resistant lifestyle or perspective of counterculture" (6). Even so, it is both possible and necessary to draw a distinction between subcultures and countercultures, especially if we want to understand both the relationship that each has to popular culture *and* their impact and influence on mainstream culture. While their aims and activities are often congruent, these terms do point to different kinds of practices and activities, and should not be seen as simply interchangeable terms designating the exact same thing.

One way of gauging this difference is by considering the use of the terms in scholarly studies. A quick library search will show that the term "subculture" is used to describe things as diverse as science-fiction fans, communities in Appalachia, gay and lesbian communities, the lifestyle of singles, the practices of minority religious groups, cults, squatters, Japanese-Americans, body-builders, and food co-operatives. A search under the term "counterculture" pulls up a much more limited range of topics: communes, the Sixties, and what have been described as "new social movements"—groups that are engaged in politics outside the boundaries of traditional political parties (e.g., environmental groups, women's rights, the Civil Rights movement, etc.).

Even this first, cursory attempt to separate sub- and countercultures highlights a key difference between the two terms: while subcultures may be political in their aims and activities, countercultures are *explicitly* so. The goal of countercultures is to replace with their own social and political values and beliefs the values of the majority, which they see as unjust, discriminatory, limiting, and regressive. For example, the heterogeneous groups and activities that are commonly referred to by the term "the Sixties," from the hippie movement to drug culture, from the struggle for civil rights to the movement against the Vietnam War, were motivated by a common dissatisfaction with dominant social and political institutions and a desire to fundamentally alter these values. The energies that fuel countercultures come from the possibility (and hope) of radically altering the way things are. On the other hand, the power of subcultures comes from the tensions created by the relationship between subcultural practices and the practices of majority culture. Subcultures draw strength from the fact that their practices *are not* those of the rest of the society of which they are a part. As Sue Thornton has put it, "the defining attribute of 'subcultures'... lies with the way the accent is put on the distinction between a particular cultural/social group and the larger culture/society" (5).

Subcultures

The concept of "subcultures" is a relatively recent one, developed first in the 1940s by a group of sociologists associated with the University of Chicago. These sociologists wanted to better understand the complex dynamics of contemporary Western societies. All large societies are made up of numerous smaller groups of people. While we might belong abstractly to a national-defined society (Canadians, Americans, Slovenians, etc.), we do so through our participation with concrete groups of people with whom we have something in common. Such groups might include political organizations, churches, ethnic groups, sports teams, and work communities. Subcultures are also groups of people who share something in common. What makes subcultures different than other groups or communities in society is that they are (most commonly) groups that deviate or differ from existing social norms.

Subcultures are typically conceived of as "disenfranchised, disaffected and unofficial" (Thornton 2). They exist "underground," outside of the mainstream of society in hidden tributaries and out-of-the-way spaces that they try to secure as their own. Furthermore, subcultures are often identified with youth groups, and youth culture in particular. In contemporary societies, youth have creatively expressed their dissatisfaction with the social norms that they encounter as they enter adulthood by adopting unconventional practices, lifestyles, and attitudes. Space is also an essential component of subcultures: space within which to meet, to act, to form a community, to forge common bonds. Such spaces can range from underground clubs in semi-abandoned parts of large urban centres (CBGB in the Bowery section of New York, Yorkville coffee houses in Sixties Toronto) to open-air festivals (the numerous large concerts held in the U.K. in the Seventies, outdoor rave events in Europe and Canada in the Nineties); from the use of public spaces by skateboarders (for example, the poured concrete ramps and stairs that make up the Art Gallery of Hamilton's sculpture garden) to the "space" that the Internet has made available for the creation of a wide range of virtual subcultures (for example, *Buffy* fans, those who want to do away with copyright, and video gamers).

Countercultures

The concept of a counterculture is equally recent, though as with the concept of subcultures the term has since its invention been used to refer to groups and activities prior to the second half of the twentieth century. "Counterculture" is a term still most commonly used in reference to the politics of the 1960s, especially with respect to the art, culture, and politics generated around the protests against the U.S. war in Vietnam.

Countercultures pose an explicit challenge to the existing order of things. Put bluntly: their goal is to change the world. While this is an explicitly political goal, countercultures cannot be reduced to their political activity alone. There is an important cultural aspect to the activities of countercultures, which distinguishes them from (for example) the actions of non-governmental political organizations (NGOs) or even most contemporary activist groups. Countercultures have their own privileged set of cultural objects (especially, forms of countercultural music), through which they express, articulate, and consolidate their political views (think of the link between some forms of popular music in the Sixties and the activism of the period).

The anti-globalization movement, which has held protests in Quebec City and other urban centres, constitutes one of the major countercultural forces today.

To perhaps an even greater degree than subcultures, countercultures express their politics culturally, through a demand for a fundamental revision of lifestyle practices. After all, what makes a culture a *counter*culture is its contravention and contradiction of not just mainstream politics, but also the culture that produces these politics, which can be located in the daily, lived practices of the mainstream. If we use as an example Sixties youth culture (in the U.S. as well as in much of the rest of the world), this reform of lifestyle was expressed in the adoption of communal living (group living in response to the alienation and individualism of capitalist culture, expressed spatially by the suburbs), vegetarianism (animal rights and healthy lifestyles), drug use (in opposition to the mainstream demands that everyone spend their lives engaged in productive labour), and open sexuality (a challenge to the restrictions of "normal" sexuality and the marriage bond). This list could easily be expanded.

Both subcultures and countercultures take culture seriously. They understand not only that culture can be a way of articulating political views and perspectives, but also that in contemporary society culture plays a crucial role in political expression. In general, both have a tendency to view popular culture through the lens of Horkheimer and Adorno's cultural industry thesis (see Chapter Four). One of the things that subcultures and countercultures react to is what they see as the dearth of genuine cultural expression and experience in the age of mass culture. In response, they produce their own forms of culture—their own clothing styles, music, and cultural practices—and articulate new ways of living and behaving.

Differences of Scale   The emergence of the concepts of subcultures and countercultures following the Second World War can be linked to the decline of genuine public spaces for political debate and a sense that mainstream political groups were no longer accountable to the public. With so many similarities, what distinguishes sub- from countercultures more than anything else is perhaps the *scale* of their reaction to the gradual impoverishment of contemporary political and social life, which seemed to go hand in hand with the fiscal improvement of life in Western countries; even while most people were better off financially, they felt more and more unhappy socially. Countercultures presume to act on a bigger social canvas than subcultures and are limited neither spatially to specific "scenes" or locales, nor by the dominance of youth within them.

It is important to emphasize that this difference of scale should not by itself be seen as valorizing the politics of countercultures over subcultures. That is, one conclusion that could be reached quickly is that because countercultures work out their political commitments more explicitly and engage them more directly, they accomplish more than subcultures. Indeed, while countercultures have not been immune to criticism from any number of vantage points, it has been subcultures that are more commonly viewed (by the mainstream media, for example) as little more than self-indulgent practices engaged in by spoiled youth who will "grow out of it" soon enough. This view of subcultures tends to reduce them to something like fashion trends, which youth engage in energetically only to forget about when another trend arises. One of the main things that scholars who have studied subcultures over the past two decades have shown is that this view is mistaken. If subcultures aren't always explicit in their politics, their very existence stands as an implicit rejection of the practices and ways of life of majority culture. As we'll see below, subcultures have complex politics, too, even if these are expressed in different ways than in countercultures.

We want to stress two points before continuing. First, the goal here is not to lay out strict definitions for the purpose of setting up a taxonomic or classificatory system into which we would then place various resistant, minority groups. The aim of these distinctions is to offer a broad initial framework within which to consider the specifics of sub- and countercultural practices and actions; simply dividing groups into one or another category is only the first step in trying to understand what is going on. Second, as we already suggested above, there is considerable slippage in these categories. As McKay points out, the counterculture draws on subcultures for elements of its own cultural practices. This slippage will be evident in our discussion in this chapter, and, indeed, is endemic to the study of these groups and their practices.

Artistic Manifestoes   As an example of this slippage, it is has become common to treat artists' movements and avant-garde manifestoes as expressions of countercultural sentiments. In terms of the rough distinctions that we have drawn here, however, artistic avant-gardes seem more like subcultures. Though artist manifestoes gesture to wholesale revolutions in sensibility (as in Tristan Tzara's "Dada Manifesto" of 1918: "I am against action; for continuous contradiction, for affirmation too, I am neither for nor against..." [249]), they do so within a relatively restricted social sphere (elite forms of artistic production) and do not always demand a complete lifestyle revolution. (That is, being both for and against contradiction does not mean that one has to give up smoking, or one's sports utility vehicle, and so on; one can be bourgeois and a dadaist at the same time.)

However, the gesture made to a total social revolution is not insignificant. In a way common to countercultures, a shift in the form and style of artistic production is imagined as having large-scale political effects. A similar categorical ambiguity can be seen in the case of punk. While punk is almost always treated as a paradigmatic example of a contemporary subculture, the depths of its critique of contemporary culture, which draws on a wide array of political and countercultural currents and theories, suggests that there is more at work than might be indicated by the term subculture.

One final note: As we have stressed elsewhere, it is unproductive to simply dismiss the activities of subcultures and countercultures on the basis of what we know about (for example) the incorporation of punk or Sixties culture into our present-day mainstream. As we said in Chapter Four, the phrase "Resistance is futile!" doesn't turn out to be true— even for the Borg in *Star Trek*, who tried and failed repeatedly to assimilate Captain Picard and his crew into their mechanized world (a perfect allegory for how many of us see the world of contemporary popular culture: as an unfeeling mechanism intent on absorbing everything organic into its metallic confines). Why, then, should it constitute an adequate way of considering the nature of our responses to popular culture? It doesn't—which is not to say that the practices of subcultures and countercultures aren't often contradictory or that they do not have problems. They do, but so does everything else: we shouldn't demand purity of aims or authenticity of intent from subcultures and countercultures—in the contemporary world, it is best to imagine that everything is already contaminated, and go from there.

Suggested Activity 8.1

Given the discussion above, is it possible to identify a counterculture (or counter-cultures) today? Are the various political groups that oppose capitalist culture today linked by common goals and/or ideas about appropriate counter-lifestyles? Make a list of subcultures and countercultures and try to think about how and why we refer to these groups with these different terms.

POPULAR REPRESENTATIONS OF SUBCULTURES AND COUNTERCULTURES

How do we come to understand or know about groups that lie outside the mainstream? Unless we happen to be an active part of a particular subculture or counterculture, our knowledge of it comes to us secondhand, through studies, reports, newspaper articles, and, of course, popular culture. Representation plays a crucial role in how we conceive of these sub- and countercultures. For example, for most of us, our sense of what the Sixties counterculture was like and what its lasting significance has been is based on an accumulated sludge of television and film representations, *Behind the Music* documentaries, and experience with bits and pieces of Sixties "classic" rock. It is just as difficult to think about punk, except through the lens of films like *Repo Man* and *Sid and Nancy*; the music of more recent "punk" bands, such as Green Day and blink-182; and perhaps through reading the obituaries of punk luminaries like Dee Dee Ramone and Joe Strummer (lead singer of The Clash). These popular representations influence our sense of what subcultures and countercultures are about. We need to be conscious of this not because it is possible to get the accurate, authentic "truth" about sub- or countercultures, but because we should be aware of the way that such representations shade our perceptions and interpretations.

The issue of representation raises another important point, one that we alluded to earlier and that we will discuss in more detail below. In a complex way, popular representations of subcultures and countercultures play an important part not only in how they function, but also in how we understand popular culture. Our sense of subcultures is that they are hidden from view or that their activities take place entirely unnoticed, in the dark. The truth is somewhat different, as Chuck Klosterman makes clear in his discussion of the very different reactions to the almost simultaneous deaths of two American rock musicians: Robin

Crosby, lead guitarist for the early-1980s heavy-metal band Ratt, and Dee Dee Ramone, bassist for the punk band The Ramones. Klosterman writes:

> The reason that Crosby's June 6 death was mostly ignored is that his band seemed corporate and fake and pedestrian; the reason Ramone's June 5 death will be remembered is that his band was seen as representative of a counterculture that lacked a voice. But the contradiction is that countercultures get endless media attention: the only American perspectives thought to have any meaningful impact are those that come from the fringes. (25)

Though millions and millions of people bought Ratt albums, the band is now "forgotten" in a way that The Ramones (whom no one listened to) are not. In popular culture, subcultures tend to be viewed in two dichotomous ways: either as threatening and dangerous, or as the conscience of mainstream—that is, as the "real" cultural expression of a culture that is otherwise dominated by "bad" commercial culture. There is another division built into this first one. When subcultures are represented as dangerous, they are often also characterized as lacking substance: as mere style that constantly changes. Part of what is dangerous about subcultures, then, is that they attract people to engage in activities that have far less substance and meaning than mainstream culture. This is the exact opposite of what the public (or at least the media) reaction to Dee Dee Ramone's death suggests: that it is the practices of subculture that leave the permanent record for an otherwise insubstantial mainstream culture, which is defined by shifts in styles or fashion in music, film, and so on that are driven not by art but by the market. We will consider these conflicted ways of representing subcultures and countercultures by looking briefly at three recent films: *Forrest Gump* (1994), *Fight Club* (1999), and *Ghost World* (2001).

Forrest Gump: Subcultural Deviance

The goal of the film *Forrest Gump* is to offer an overview of the American experience following the Second World War. It accomplishes this by a fairly typical cinematic and novelist procedure, using the life of one individual, the eponymous Forrest Gump (Tom Hanks), to both highlight important events and milestones in U.S history during this period and to explore related shifts in culture and sensibility. Forrest, a fatherless, intellectually challenged Southerner, manages over the course of the film to successfully navigate his way through the real and metaphoric landmines of the past forty years. His life passes through all of the major events of post–Second World War history, and Forrest comes into direct contact with some of the period's important historical figures. Elvis, a boarder in Forrest's home, adopts his performance style by imitating the inhibited gait that Forrest possesses as an adolescent. Forrest wins a national football championship with Alabama on a team coached by the legendary Bear Bryant; plays a crucial role in the struggle to racially integrate schools in the U.S. South; becomes an inadvertent hero as a soldier in Vietnam; becomes a champion ping-pong player; guests on Dick Cavett's TV show (where he appears alongside John Lennon); single-handedly invents the running craze; and makes a bundle on Apple stock—just to name a few of the symbolically charged things he accomplishes.

Forrest represents the adventure that America undergoes during this era and he navigates it bluntly, pragmatically, and successfully. For the most part, then, even as the film examines many of the difficult moments in post–Second World War American social and cultural life, it celebrates American drive and initiative and suggests that more good things are coming in the future. Forrest's life ends in that most typical place in American cinema: back at home, folded into the comforts and security of family life.

No account of the U.S. experience after the Second World War would be complete, however, without some attention to the roles played the subcultures and countercultures in creating this history. In *Forrest Gump*, the activity of subcultures is typified through the life history of the other major character in the film: the love of Forrest's life, Jenny. Through the opposition of Jenny and Forrest, it becomes clear that Forrest represents not *all* of American experience, but merely the experience of mainstream culture; Jenny represents an alternative path through recent U.S. history—the dark side of Forrest's generally blissful (or at least, blissed out) experience. The film is unambiguous in its portrayal of American counterculture. If Jenny is unable to follow Forrest's path through the major institutions of American life—college, the military, small business, sports, and so on—it is because she has been sexually abused by her father. Her immersion in the counterculture is treated less as a conscious choice than the consequences of a psychic trauma that she never gets to adequately address. Countercultures and subcultures, the film seems to tell us, are for damaged souls. Jenny drifts through the American underworld: she appears in *Playboy*, while Forrest is in the mud of Vietnam, she gets involved with hippies and peaceniks (who drive a VW van painted with rainbow colours); she becomes involved with the SDS (Students' Democratic Society) in Berkeley, which is led by her physically abusive boyfriend; she becomes suicidal after doing lines of coke as part of the early-1980s "me" generation; and, when she finally shows up again in Forrest's life to introduce him to their son, she tells him: "I have some kind of virus and the doctors don't know what it is and there isn't anything they can do about it." If Jenny's trauma leads her into the U.S. counterculture, it is her involvement with the latter that leads to her death.

It is not difficult to see that the film suggests that subcultures and countercultures are dangerous, destructive, and misguided, especially for those involved in them. In the world narrated by Forrest Gump, happiness and fulfillment are achieved only by following the path of the straight and narrow (which in Forrest's case has the added advantage of putting him into contact with important people, like Presidents Kennedy and Nixon). Forrest's own happiness is impeded only by the fact of Jenny's death, which is the direct consequence of her alternative lifestyle. Forrest's son, who represents the future of American society, is in some respects the product of both the mainstream and the counterculture, of Forrest and Jenny. But what the film actually seems to argue is that America has a future *despite* the presence of the subculture. It is up to Forrest, after all, to raise Forrest Jr. It is not accidental that Forrest Jr. is raised in the same place as his father; for all the things that have happened, the real America perseveres, unchanged by the challenges that the counterculture and history seemed to have posed to it. Near the end of the film, Jenny suggests: "I was messed up for a long time." *Forrest Gump* exemplifies very clearly one of the dominant ways in which subcultures are represented—simply as the actions of misguided, messed-up people.

And yet, there are elements of the film that make us question its representation of American counterculture. Most obviously, it is the character of Forrest himself who causes us to wonder about the narrative we are being sold. Jenny is far more intelligent and self-conscious than Forrest; if Forrest represents the mainstream, then the mainstream is shown to be unthinking—emotional and intuitive rather than reasoned and reflective. Forrest suggests that "for some reason I fit in the army like a round peg." His successes come out of his ability to slide into pre-existing systems and institutions; he challenges nothing and accepts everything. In *Forrest Gump*, the options in post–Second World War American society come down to two equally problematic positions: *either* one joins the counterculture and challenges norms and limits, but at the price of one's own happiness, health, and life; *or* one unthinkingly accepts "what is," even if this means participating in an imperialist war or raping the environment (as recorded by Forrest's enormous haul of shrimp in the Gulf of Mexico). This is a false choice, of course; we need not acquiesce to the *either/or* that the film constructs for us. Nor need we accept its stereotypes of the counterculture, even if we should note that it is precisely such representations of sub- and countercultures that inform the way in which we view their activities, as well as the people who participate in them.

Fight Club: Fight the Power?

A very different, if equally troubling view of subcultures is presented in David Fincher's cult hit *Fight Club*. What made the film attractive to critics and audiences when it was first released was that it appeared to offer a unique, critical perspective on the values of capitalist society—in particular, the way in which consumption has come to constitute the main goal and purpose of contemporary society. While criticisms of contemporary reality are actually a quite common theme of American cinema, what made *Fight Club* appear to be different from films like *The Cable Guy* (1996), *The Truman Show* (1998), *The Matrix* (1999), or *Series 7: The Contenders* (2001), was that it translated critique into action through the creation of an anti-capitalist subcultural movement whose ultimate goal is the violent destruction of the system of global consumer credit.

Based on the 1996 first novel by Chuck Palahniuk, *Fight Club* narrates the story of Jack (Edward Norton), an insomniac, bored, corporate drone who finds meaning in his life through his newly formed relationship with Tyler Durden (Brad Pitt), a thrill-seeking everyman. In a number of memorable set pieces, both Jack and Tyler rail against the limits of consumer society. In order to make some connection with people in an unfeeling, individuate society, Jack begins to attend group meetings for people struggling with various diseases and ailments—none of which he has. Jack's job, which is to calculate the cost-effectiveness of consumer recalls (that is, if the cumulative cost of the lawsuits brought against the company as a result of the malfunction of a product would be

Brad Pitt gets tough on consumer culture in *Fight Club*.

Source: Merrick Morton/MPTV.net.

less than a recall, they cynically decide against it), is depicted in all its existential horror as a brain-deadening series of unfulfilling routines.

It is only when Jack meets Tyler that he begins to "feel" again. A spontaneous fight in the parking lot of a bar leads to the creation of an underground bare-knuckles club where men can beat their sufferings out of each other and learn to feel something (even if it is pain) in a world that has crushed their sensibilities under the weight of consumerism. This "fight club" forms the genesis for an anti-consumerist army that is assembled by Jack and Tyler; it engages in a campaign that adopts the stratagems of culture jamming (see Close-Up 8.1) but also moves to more violent and direct assaults on computer stores and coffee shops, and, finally, on the corporate headquarters of credit-card companies, which are destroyed in the final frames of the film.

The film and book contain many rich (though problematic) strands that could be followed up and teased out, but perhaps the defining element of the narrative is the connection that it makes between consumerism and the decline of masculinity in contemporary society. The fight clubs are an exclusively male domain: it is not just that men need to be awakened out of their consumerist lassitude, but also that by beating each other up they are re-asserting a supposedly essential masculine identity that contemporary culture has stripped from them. For Tyler, the real trauma in contemporary life is that men can no longer be "real" men: virile, physical, and firmly in charge of both the family and the culture at large. Contemporary experience has emasculated men and rendered them impotent. What has brought about this situation is nothing other than consumerism itself,

Culture Jamming

Culture jamming is the practice of turning manifestations of consumer culture—in particular, advertising images—against themselves for political ends. By parodying targeted ad images, culture jamming recontextualizes them and offers a different set of associations through which they can be read.

Culture jamming has a double aim: to draw attention both to the problems of specific activities and practices (driving environmentally damaging SUVs, exporting the practice of smoking to the developing world, watching television, subscribing to the damaging beauty ideals promoted by the fashion industry) *and* to the limits and dangers of the larger consumerist and capitalist system that legitimates and promotes these activities and practices. One of the most well-known forms of culture jamming is the annual "Buy Nothing Day," held worldwide on the day after American Thanksgiving, which is one of the largest shopping days each and every year. Culture jammers take to the street not only to dissuade people from shopping, but also to remind them of the troubling link that has been developed between the celebration of family and belonging (everyone gathering together for Thanksgiving) and the orgy of consumerism that follows.

The Canadian magazine *Adbusters* has played an integral role in promoting and celebrating various forms of culture jamming. Examples of their campaigns and ads, as well as those of jammers from around the world, can be found at www.adbusters.org.

which the film repeatedly identifies as a specifically feminine realm, in line with the long-established ideologies of consumerism that we discussed in Chapter Five.

In many respects, the critique of consumerism in *Fight Club* becomes an alibi for an attack on the feminine, especially of the rise of women (and minorities) to positions of power and influence in Western society. The film claims that in a world in which women have at least the potential to be equal to men, men cannot be real men. Instead of working with their bodies in factories, they have to drag themselves to "soft" office jobs and dream of the furniture in Ikea catalogues, instead of the supine female bodies one finds in pornography. Changing the world for the better seems to mean putting women back in their place—hardly an instance of progressive politics or a successful criticism of consumerism, which should presumably create a situation in which men *and* women could engage in consumption differently.

Unlike *Forrest Gump*, which demonizes sub- or countercultural resistance even as it highlights its lack of importance to the main script of historical development, *Fight Club* takes the activities and possibilities of subcultures seriously. Only a group outside the mainstream could shake up a world lost in consumerist dogmatic slumbers: Jack and Tyler cannot change things on their own, nor is it likely that mainstream society will change of its own accord. Nevertheless, this representation of a subculture reinforces mainstream ideologies concerning gender roles in a way that makes us question their aims and goals. Of course, in one respect, this is indeed an "accurate" portrayal of the very real limits of an engagement with gender stereotypes in many subcultures. For example, women skateboarders have had to struggle with the dominance of this practice by men, while women in punk faced similar limits and problems: even as the punks fought against the capitalist world, women punks had to fight for recognition and respect within the subculture itself. However, representational accuracy is hardly the aim of *Fight Club*: if an engagement with the politics of gender in subcultures emerges as a moral of the film, it is only by reading against the grain of its otherwise deeply patriarchal logic.

Ghost World: Being Ghostly

Terry Zwigoff's *Ghost World* (2001) offers one of the most compelling and original representations of subcultural practices and activities in recent film. The film's title is quite literal; it explores the ghostly world of alternative lives and practices that exist parallel to and overlap with what we generally imagine as mainstream culture. In doing so, the film also offers an incisive look at the assumptions and presumptions that constitute the mainstream, probing the very real limits that it places on individuals and groups to express their differences.

Ghost World tracks the entry of two high-school friends, Enid (Thora Birch) and Rebecca (Scarlett Johansson), into adulthood in the summer following their graduation from high school. The film begins with Enid and Rebecca's graduation ceremony and the reception that follows. Both are by-the-numbers affairs, with the valedictorian mouthing platitudes (she describes high school as "the training wheels for the bicycle of life") and the reception being typically amenable to the cool kids and torture for the geeks and nerds. From the way that Enid and Rebecca snarl and quip their way through their graduation day, it is clear that they are outsiders. For them, the utter kitschiness and predictability of the graduation exercises are a source of amusement.

Unlike typical depictions of those who do not conform to accepted models, both Enid and Rebecca are remarkably self-confident. Being at right angles to the mainstream and its expectations does not isolate them, but rather it gives them a feeling of power as they navigate their way through the clichés and stereotypes of contemporary culture. They are critical of faux enthusiasms and false emotions, without being cynical or dismissive; indeed, the falsehoods with which contemporary society surrounds itself are for them a continual source of interest and amusement. While dining in Wowsville, an "authentic Fifties diner," Rebecca turns on the tabletop jukebox and out pours rap music. "Who could forget this greatest hit from the Fifties!" she remarks, to the delight of both women.

Can the friends sustain this joyous, devil-may-care attitude as they make the transition from adolescence to an adult world in which there is a price to be paid for nonconformity? This is the key question around which the plot of the film revolves. Following high school, the women endeavour to find their own apartment, which immediately introduces them to a world that demands compromise and shifts in their priorities. To get an apartment Enid and Rebecca need money, which means that they need to find jobs. Rebecca gets a job in a coffee shop, and as soon as she does her sarcasm seems to become tempered by the pragmatic demands of making money and getting through the week. However, Enid's entry into the adult world is delayed by the need to make up an art class that she, a talented artist in her own right, nevertheless failed in her last term. More significantly, over the course of the summer she gets to see deep into the "ghost world" of the film's title, by coming into contact with Seymour (Steve Buscemi), whom she describes at one point as "such a clueless dork, he's almost cool."

Seymour is a lonely, middle-aged man whom life seems to have beaten down. He is equally dismissive of a world made up of, at best, people Enid refers to as "extroverted obnoxious pseudo-bohemian losers." Seymour seems to have enthusiasm for only one thing: collecting rare 78-rpm records, especially of early blues music. His skill and enthusiasm for collecting music that others do not care about defines him against the mainstream, who express open admiration for the rock-band Blues Hammer while ignoring the aging blues legend who opens the show that Enid and Seymour go to see.

At the same time, Seymour's interests also confine him to the ghostly, half-real world that he exists in. When Enid first sees Seymour's room, she stands in complete awe: "This is like my dream room," she says, "I would kill to have stuff like this." Seymour is dismissive: he says that he hates his collection, and suggests that collecting is unhealthy, a problem that one would be better off without.

Enid and Seymour develop a strong relationship, based as much on their common attitude toward what is supposedly the "real" world as it is on any physical attraction or emotional involvement. Up to the final sections of the film, *Ghost World* presents us with a remarkable view of the ghost world that subcultures occupy. Zwigoff successfully showed us, in his earlier filmic depiction of the life of the comic book legend R. Crumb, the world and views of outsiders in a sympathetic, though not celebratory light. Occupying the real world's ghost world does not come without consequences: Enid and Rebecca's relationship erodes, Enid squanders a chance at a college scholarship by producing a controversial work of art, and Seymour's loneliness and isolation seems to be exacerbated rather than improved when he starts dating Dana, a real-estate agent, who buys him his first pair of designer jeans.

In the end, the film seems to imply that no matter how much power Enid's unique attitude yields over the faux–real world she inhabits, it is not enough. Abandoned by all of the people who could have constituted the community of individuals that together produce a sub- or counterculture, Enid leaves town alone on the bus that supposedly never comes. Even in this film, as surely as in *Forrest Gump*, the "real" world appears to have an ultimately irresistible power over all those who try to exist at right angles to it. There is never a firm community of dissenters established, and even where one might expect to find such a community—at Zone-O-Phobia, the comic book store Enid frequents—she and the manager are in constant conflict. "If you really want to fuck up the system," he says, "go to business school. Join a big corporation and fuck up stuff from the inside."

The goal of this section has been to emphasize the various ways in which sub- and countercultures have been represented in dominant forms of popular culture. What we can see from these three very different examples is that while subcultures are celebrated as playing an essential role in history and in social transformation, they are also almost always represented as a problem for society. Sub- and countercultures tend to be represented in relation to dominant culture either as the fringes occupied by those who just can't make it within the mainstream (which is then correspondingly valorized as the domain of "real" values, morals, and beliefs), or as the space in which genuine social discontent is voiced, but in the wrong way (violently in *Fight Club*, individualistically in *Ghost World*).

Whatever position different films or television programs take on sub- and counter-cultures, we can see from these examples that what they in fact highlight are the views of mainstream groups on subcultures—whether dismissive or sympathetic—as opposed to the views and needs expressed in and through sub- and countercultural practices. In other words, these representations tend to present subcultures predominantly as an issue or problem for the mainstream; insofar as these groups also always make use of the discourses and representations of mainstream culture, this has an impact on the nature and shape of sub- and countercultural practices as well. There are two things that we should take away from our analysis of these films: first, our understanding of subcultures is affected by representations of them; second, popular cultural representation plays an important (if seemingly contradictory) role in how sub- and countercultures imagine their own role and engage in their own practices, as we will see in more detail below.

THE POLITICS OF SUBCULTURES

There is no society, only individuals.

—Former British Prime Minister Margaret Thatcher

Earlier in this chapter, we suggested that even if subcultures are not explicitly political, their activities and practices always contain an *implicit* political stance—a position or attitude toward gaps and absences in the mainstream culture that individuals seek to redress through their involvement in subcultures. At a very general level, the fragmentation of contemporary societies into an enormous range of active subcultures after the Second World War points to a lack of genuine opportunities for communal or group relations *within* the mainstream. Perhaps a better way of putting this is that, since mainstream North American values tend to celebrate individuality above all else, communal forms of relation outside of the typical markers of group identity (such as race, ethnicity, or religion) couldn't exist except on the outsides or the margins of mainstream culture. There are, of course, always groups and sub-groups that make up each and every society;

but subcultures are something new whose very existence points to problems and contradictions in the way reality is constituted by the powers that be.

For instance, it is no surprise that the contradictory demands and stresses that contemporary society has placed on youth in particular would produce a flourishing range of youth subcultures. These subcultures aim to escape the controlling attentions of an adult society that simultaneously infantilizes youth (wants them to remain children) and encourages them to take on adult behaviours and responsibilities earlier and earlier in life. Participating in a subculture is a way of establishing one's own form of social life, with its own rules that may be very different from or even directly opposed to mainstream adult rules and values. While it may be true, as Sarah Thornton has argued, that "the vast majority of British youth subcultures, past and present, do not espouse overt political projects" (177), it nevertheless seems clear that even if their politics are implicit, such politics constitute an essential and important reason for the creation of subcultures to begin with. George McKay has described it in this way: "One of the things hippy and punk had in common ... was an oppositional impulse, an idealism or rhetoric of idealism. For both, politics and culture were, or could be, or should be, the same thing" (5). If we are to properly understand subcultures, separating forms of cultural expression from politics proper would be a mistake.

Hiding in the Light

What are the forms that this politics takes? There are many, of course: it is both difficult and dangerous to generalize across the wide range of activities and practices that have been characterized as subcultural. However, there does seem to be one mode of politics that many subcultures have adopted—though, again, they have adopted it in many different ways. In his influential book *Subculture: The Meaning of Style*, Dick Hebdige deftly explores the dual, apparently contradictory relationship that subcultures adopt toward mainstream culture.

The effect of subcultures—both with respect to those "within" them and the majority of members of society "without"—is produced through the adoption of both invisibility *and* visibility. Subcultures hide in the shadows, where one can do whatever one likes away from prying eyes, specifically the eyes of the authorities. But insofar as it also seems essential for subcultures to be able both to mark their difference from mainstream culture *and* to engage critically with the limits of that culture, it is also important for the mainstream to be able to sit up and take notice—to be shocked, in other words, whether by the harsh social reality depicted in rap songs or by the graffiti left on the walls of their garages. Hebdige explains that

> The subcultural *milieu* has been constructed underneath the authorised discourses, in the face of multiple disciplines of the family, the school and the workplace. Subculture forms up in the space between surveillance and the evasion of surveillance, it translates the fact of being under scrutiny into the pleasure of being watched. It is hiding in the light. (35)

The Arrival of Punk   We've already seen one of the strange consequences of the way subcultures "hide in the light." The death in June 2002 of Dee Dee Ramone, bassist for seminal New York punk band The Ramones, was widely interpreted as the passing of a significant cultural era. And yet, relatively few people ever heard him play, either live or on record, and it would be difficult to make a case that The Ramones had a major impact on the popular music that followed them. How could a supposedly minor cultural practice, hidden out of sight in dank clubs in the Bowery and in the rougher streets of London, end up as a pop culture era or touchstone? The answer: by hiding in the light of mainstream attention. For Hebdige, "subcultures are both a play for attention and a refusal, once attention has been granted, to be read according to the Book" (35). There is no better example of this than the one he himself draws on: punk music and style, which flourished ever so briefly in the mid-Seventies, and which has since given birth to numerous other "punk" styles.

As might be suggested by the title of Penelope Spheeris's documentary on the L.A. punk scene, *The Decline of Western Civilization*, punk represented an all-out assault on the values of mainstream "civilization." One would expect the public to recoil from punk and to respond to its challenge with diatribes against it. This is indeed what happened. In the United Kingdom, punk was treated as a pariah subculture, a dangerous movement that was colonizing the minds of some British youth and that thus had to be brought to a rapid end. But how, then, could one explain the incredible popularity and success of the group that became the whipping boy of anti-punk sentiment, the Sex Pistols? At the height of anti-punk fervour (such as it was), the Sex Pistols's "God Save the Queen" reached number two on the British pop charts, and their album *Never Mind the Bollocks* hit the top of the charts. The anti-establishment Sex Pistols and their ilk were tabloid celebrities throughout the late 1970s; by the 1980s, punk had become such a fixture of the London landscape that popular tourist postcards featured pictures of green-haired punks with ripped clothing to send back to the folks in Saskatchewan ("Greetings from London!").

As we will see in the next section, this is commonly seen as evidence of punk's *lack* of politics. But Hebdige's formula lets us see things differently: it is precisely by being available and open for display to the mainstream that the minority culture of punk was able to draw attention to the very real sources of its discontent with both the values of mainstream culture and their relationship to it. "Hiding in the light" allows subcultures to create, maintain, and nurture their own communities of belonging (by "hiding" in clubs, squats, and even the streets), while also engaging with the culture at large (exposing themselves to the "light" of public opinion by displaying their unique styles on the streets, and their music on the airwaves).

Not all subcultures engage in the same forms of display or do so to the same degree. Many subcultures prefer to remain more hidden than punk. However, secret societies, of the kind featured in Stanley Kubrick's *Eyes Wide Shut* and much beloved by scenarists for James Bond films, do not a subculture make.

Avant-Garde Punk

All that punk singers can bring to the presentations of their songs is the gesture of sexual obscenity or of impotent rage. There is a lot of caged simian gibber....

—Anthony Burgess, author of *A Clockwork Orange*

You don't sing about love to people on the dole.

— Johnny Rotten (cited in Szatmary 220)

Punk has been the subject of numerous scholarly studies, popular books (Greil Marcus's *Lipstick Traces*), films (*Sid and Nancy*), and documentaries (*The Great Rock'n'Roll Swindle, The Filth and the Fury*). As perhaps the first instance of a popular cultural form that seemed to be explicitly political (to a higher and more intense degree than the music of the 1960s), punk continues to fascinate and inspire musicians, audiences, and scholars. Yet for all its influence, the era of punk was remarkably short. Less than a year passed between the British début of the New York band The Ramones on July 4, 1976 (the event widely heralded for kick-starting punk in the U.K.) and the emergence of high-end copies of punk fashion, such as the gold safety pins sold at Saks on Fifth Avenue and the stylized rips and safety pins in the gowns designed by Zandra Rhodes for Bloomingdale's, which were already on the market by June 1977 (Szatmary 236).

As we have seen above, the way in which punk (and other subcultures) "hides in the light" makes it political in many more ways than by its subcultural "form" alone. But there are other ways in which punk is political above and beyond this form—the anti-establishment lyrics of punk music, and the anti-establishment disposition and demeanour of punks themselves. In a way that is too seldom appreciated, subcultures of all stripes draw heavily on a stew of political and cultural ideas and ideals, especially those that have been constructed by other oppositional or subcultural groups of cultures in the past.

The Marxist Influence   One of most important of these has been the tradition of socialist and communist thought. However partially or incompletely, Marx's insistence on seeing the history of society as a "history of class struggles" has remained a core element of the way in which many subcultures understand their social status (34): as minority cultures in permanent conflict with the wealthy and their duped middle-class supporters. Subcultures need not take up explicit class-based politics in order to see themselves as belonging to those groups who are systematically disadvantaged by capitalism, nor to make use of the kinds of cultural analysis and forms of cultural practice that such political identification opens up. And socialism is just the beginning. As the example of punk shows us, there is a great deal more going on in subcultures than angry youth spontaneously rebelling against their seniors.

Hamilton's Warsawpack combines fierce music with astute, intelligent analysis of the ills of society.

The familiar story told about punk is a cautionary tale that traces the rapid rise of a genuine subculture and its equally rapid co-optation by consumer culture (see Chapter Four for a discussion of co-optation in popular culture). The threat that punk posed seemed real enough to bring the wrath of the state down on the paradigmatic punk band the Sex Pistols, even before the release of their anti-monarchist anthem "God Save the Queen" in June 1976. Denounced by Members of Parliament, attacked by the Anglican Church, banned from playing live almost anywhere in England and from having their songs played on British radio, the Sex Pistols nearly brought about the conditions that they sang about in "Anarchy in the U.K." Yet by 1980, Linda Ronstadt, Billy Joel, and even Cher were posing in punk regalia on the covers of their albums.

The quick rise and fall of punk is real enough. But what this version of the events misses is the complex political roots of punk culture. The anarchy and chaos of punk music—its fearsome, angry, and terrifically loud sound and its utter rejection of "civilized" values—have tended to reinforce a sense of its spontaneous origins and generally unfocused politics. Punk is now often treated, as it was by a number of its detractors during the punk era itself, as little more than another blip in a long tradition of youthful rebellion expressed through pop music (falling temporally between the threatening sexuality of Elvis and the angst of Nirvana and Eminem).

But if we were to pull apart any of these forms of rebellion, we would find an enormously rich reservoir of ideas and concepts. Like Dadaism and Surrealism before it, punk understood itself quite self-consciously as a cultural form (in both its music and its style) whose aim was to *épater les bourgeois*—to pierce through the sterile drone of bloated Seventies art rock (epitomized by the band Yes) and the flabby corporate culture that was increasingly coming to stand for culture as such. The New York precursors of U.K. punk music, artists such as the Velvet Underground, Patti Smith, and Tom Verlaine, drew inspiration for their lyrics from the Beat Generation (epitomized by writers such as Jack Kerouac and Allan Ginsberg); from the avant-garde centred around Andy Warhol; and, in the case of Verlaine (a.k.a. Tom Miller), from French Symbolist poetry. Though the Sex Pistols famously rejected Patti Smith's literary, avant-garde leanings, the transition of punk from New York to London interjected new political dimensions into punk even as it stripped away others.

Situationism   Malcolm McLaren, the infamous manager and midwife of the Sex Pistols, wanted to use the band to explore the "politics of boredom" first expressed in Situationism, a political movement that explored the new kinds of politics required in a society crushed not by a lack of things (i.e., too little food to feed everyone), but by an abundance of material goods. Situationism played an important role in the May 1968 Student Revolution in France, which began in reaction to the U.S. war on Vietnam but turned into a more general assault on the banality of a post–Second World War capitalist culture that promised so much (less work and more leisure!) and delivered so little (boring work and boring leisure!).

The philosophy of Situationism can be summarized by one of the popular slogans of May 1968: "The more you consume, the less you live." Punk carries on the tradition of Situationism, both in spirit and (as Greil Marcus shows in his history of punk) in substance, but in a political situation in which there is *neither* work *nor* leisure. If nothing else, punk responds directly to the economic chaos and high unemployment that enveloped Britain in the mid-1970s. It was civilization that was in decline and punk that was trying to save it from itself. In other words, punk was not the problem but the solution.

It would be possible to continue in this vein for some time. For instance, we have yet to mention the political roots of punk art, which was featured on album covers and posters advertising band performances. Again, the slapdash quality of this art might suggest unfocused, youthful spontaneity. But in reality, punk art drew heavily on the slogans and art of the May 1968 student revolution in Paris, as well as from the tradition of agitational-propaganda (agitprop) aesthetics created by the artists of the Soviet Revolution. Punk was also an importantly hybrid musical form, which drew inspiration (as well as licks) from Jamaican reggae and ska music that "lambasted the racism and capitalism that Britain had imposed on Jamaica" (Szatmary 232). In April and June 1978, The Clash and other bands played to audiences of 80,000 and 50,000 young punks respectively, who came out to show their solidarity with their black brethren against the organization of the racist National Front in Britain. It is clear that there was a whole lot going on in punk—even if most punk musicians relied on only three chords to express themselves.

The Invention of Skateboarding

So, punk is political. But what about other kinds of subcultural practices? Haven't we stacked the deck in our favour? What about a practice whose politics is somewhat more obscure, if it exists at all? What about, say … skateboarding?

Even though skateboarding has now become a staple of popular culture, it wasn't always a recognized sport with its own stars (like Tony Hawk), brand names, specialist magazines, and the like. Skateboarding first emerged as a post-surfing pastime in the late 1950s and briefly surged to popularity in 1963, when the national championships were aired on television. It then died out—seemingly just another fad kids' pastime, like the hula hoop. The conditions that saw its revival in the early to mid-1970s highlights the politics that continue to be played out through this seemingly innocuous pastime.

Dogtown and Z-Boys Stacy Peralta's documentary *Dogtown and Z-Boys* (2002) provides not only an exceptional account of the second birth of skateboarding, but also a compelling narrative of the politics that emerges out of the sport. The film explores the birth of the famous Zephyr Skateboard Team, which would later produce many of the most successful of the first wave of professional skateboarders. The Zephyr team hailed from Dogtown, a decrepit, run-down area of West Los Angeles that was quite literally built on the ruins of the American dream: the area had once sported one of the most famous of the many amusement-park piers that lined the California coast. After the park closed in 1967 the area fell into economic decline, leaving the abandoned amusement park and the area around it to "pyromaniacs, junkies and surfers." The team members grew up in this area, mostly in broken families that were never far from bottoming out. Yet, far from describing Dogtown as an urban wasteland, they describe it as a "dirty, filthy paradise."

What made Dogtown a paradise was the degree of control that the youth could exert over their space, both as surfers and then later as skaters. Dogtown was covered with graffitied signs warning outsiders to stay away: "Locals only!" "Go home!" As the Zephyr team began to develop and build skateboards to "surf" their mostly abandoned streets, they also began to stretch their claim over public space to other parts of the city. Because much of California is built on hills or in valleys, many schoolyards in the area had a landscaping quirk: in order to level out school playgrounds, landscapers had to build in walls of banked asphalt. Though these were fenced off from the public, they became the first rudimentary skate parks, which the Dogtown kids would, on weekends, bike miles and miles to get to in order to practise their new craft. During the mid-1970s, another off-limits space opened up to skateboarding. The prolonged drought in California during this time meant that the numerous swimming pools in the L.A. area were left empty. Dogtowners began to covertly enter private property in order to skate the abandoned swimming pools, and in so doing risked arrest and imprisonment.

The documentary is careful to highlight the fact that the kids who pioneered contemporary skateboarding were motivated by nothing more than having fun. There was "no promise in it," and they had "no goals, no aspirations." None of them knew what skateboarding would become or what it was accomplishing. Nor did they have a sense that by skating the streets, pools, and hidden and sealed-off spaces of the city, they were doing something more than having a good time. Of course, the consequences of one's actions can easily exceed what one believes one is doing. In a series of influential articles published in *Skateboarder* magazine in 1975, Craig Stecyk made explicit what the Zephyr team had been doing as a matter of course: making new use of the dead spaces created by contemporary culture. "Skaters by their very nature are urban guerrillas: they make everyday use of the useless artifacts of the technological burden, and employ the handiwork of the government/corporate structure in a thousand ways that the original architects could never dream of.... Two hundred years of American technology has unwittingly created a massive cement playground of unlimited potential," Stecyk writes, "but it was the minds of 11-year-olds that could see that potential."

The disputes that continue to arise throughout North America over the uses that skateboarders try to make of public and private space for a bit of simple recreation suggests that there is something larger at stake in these practices. It might seem a stretch to equate kids interested in doing grinds and flipping their boards with anti-globalization demonstrators who take over the spaces of the city, but in a way both are making the same fundamental demand: "Whose streets? Our streets!" Skateboarding has a politics, too.

SUMMARY

The activities and practices of subcultures and countercultures play an important role in popular culture. Given space constraints, we have been able to offer only the barest overview of the range of subcultural and countercultural practices that intersect with popular culture today. This chapter has explored some general issues with respect to subcultures and countercultures by first assessing how we understand these groups and then considering some of the ways in which they challenge mainstream values and practices. Key points to remember include:

- Sub- and countercultures are defined against a dominant, mainstream culture; they necessarily involve minority rather than majority practice. While the idea of the "mainstream" is a useful one, it is important to recognize that this names a concept rather than an actual group of people who partake in all of the prescribed majority practices.
- All minority practices should not be considered to be subcultural.
- Subcultures and countercultures share many things in common; what distinguishes them is the degree to which they emphasize politics as part of their practices and activities.
- Popular representations of subcultures and countercultures inform how we view these groups, as well as (to some degree) how these groups understand themselves. Generally, such representations tend to simultaneously (and in contradictory ways) downplay the substance of these groups and suggest that they play an important role in defining social practices.
- Even if they are not explicitly political, subcultures articulate a complex politics through the ways in which they make demands on the attention of the mainstream, through their connections to other modes and forms of politics, and by the way that they engage with contemporary social spaces and everyday reality.

SUGGESTIONS FOR FURTHER READING

Austin, Joe, and Michael Nevin Willard. *Generations of Youth: Youth Cultures and History in Twentieth-Century America*. New York: New York University Press, 1996.
Debord, Guy. *Society of the Spectacle*. New York: Verso, 1996.

Hall, Stuart, and Tony Jefferson, eds. *Resistance Through Rituals: Youth Subcultures in Post-War Britain.* New York: Routledge, 1993.

Hebdige, Dick. *Subculture: The Meaning of Style.* London: Methuen, 1979.

Lasn, Kalle. *Culture Jam: How to Reverse America's Suicidal Consumer Binge—And Why We Must.* New York: Quill, 1999.

Marcus, Greil. *Lipstick Traces: A Secret History of the 20th Century.* Cambridge, MA: Harvard University Press, 1989.

Muggleton, David. *Inside Subculture: The Postmodern Meaning of Style.* New York: Berg, 2000.

Redhead, Steve, D. Wynne, and J. O'Connor, eds. *The Clubcultures Reader: Readings in Popular Cultural Studies.* Oxford: Blackwell, 1997.

Ross, Andrew, and Tricia Rose, eds. *Microphone Fiends: Youth Music and Youth Culture.* New York: Routledge, 1994.

Roszak, Theodore. *The Making of a Counter Culture: Reflections on the Technocratic Society and Its Youthful Opposition.* London: Faber and Faber, 1970.

Chapter 9

Globalization and Popular Culture

INTRODUCTION: WHAT IS GLOBALIZATION?

Globalization is a term that has gained increasing prominence over the past decade. It has been discussed with equal fervour in the halls of the academy, in the pages of business magazines, on the front pages of newspapers around the world, and on the Websites and Internet discussion groups of organizations and individuals dedicated to fighting global corporate dominance. At the beginning of the 1990s, globalization was a term most commonly associated with the decline of industrial manufacturing in the "Rust Belt" of the U.S. and in Eastern Canada. Unlike typical recessions connected to the cyclical downturns characteristic of capitalist economies, the loss of blue-collar jobs was seen in these cases as the result of an unprecedented migration of North American industries to lower-wage countries, especially to the **maquiladoras** along the U.S.–Mexico border. By the end of the decade, globalization was linked to an ever-expanding range of political, economic, social, and cultural phenomena, from public demonstrations against multilateral trade and economic agreements to the potential dangers of genetically modified foods to worries over what Britney Spears is doing to the Philippines.

Though globalization is primarily the name of a *process* (just like modern*ization* and industrial*ization*), the increasing use and visibility of the term in both the media and in public debates has sometimes made it seem as if it is the name for the particular moment in history we are now living through. Just as the **Cold War** was the name for the entire set of events and processes that made up the international order between the end of the Second World War and the fall of the Berlin Wall in 1989, globalization is sometimes taken to be synonymous with the "**New World Order**" announced by President George Bush and described by the author Francis Fukuyama as "the end of history." While it does seem to be the case that the term "globalization" begins to be used with frequency only *after* the end of the Cold War and the dissolution of the Soviet Union, the claims made for and against globalization can be understood only if we treat it as an ongoing historical process. Indeed, much of the debate surrounding globalization concerns questions of just what kind of processes it names and how far back these processes can be traced.

What kinds of processes are associated with globalization? At its most basic level, globalization is the name for the social, political, cultural, economic, and technological processes that together have created the changed conditions of contemporary existence. At the centre of these altered conditions is an enormous change in both the physical and psychological experience of time and space. Globalization has brought previously distant parts of the world together. Instead of being composed of distant and distinct places, we have begun to imagine the world as a single, global space in which peoples and communities are connected to one another as never before. New communications technologies, such as the Internet, cell phones, and satellite transmissions, have made it possible for people (or at least some people) to communicate with one another instantaneously across huge distances, and to receive immediate information about political and social developments in other parts of the world. The communications revolution has also helped to produce greater integration of the national economies, particularly with respect to financial markets. Multinational agreements that have been ratified by most countries on the globe, such as the General Agreement on Tariffs and Trade (GATT), have changed the nature of the world economy. Today, there is more than $1.5 trillion (U.S.) in foreign-exchange transactions, an increase of 2,100 percent between 1980 and 1995 (Anderson and Cavanaugh 33, 16). As recent financial crises in Mexico (1994), Southeast Asia (1997), Russia and Brazil (1998), and Argentina (2002) have shown, economic developments in one country have an increasingly large impact on every other country in the world.

Culturally, globalization is experienced as the increased knowledge of and access to the culture and cultural products of peoples around the world, as well as the often-unwanted imposition of one especially powerful culture's values and products on nearly all the others. In the first instance, globalization can be witnessed in the popularity of world music (such as the Buena Vista Social Club), the global interest in Japanese *manga* and *anime*, and the fascination in Eastern Europe (and elsewhere) with *telenovelas* produced in Mexico and other parts of South America. On the other hand, the overwhelming, ubiquitous global presence of films, television programs, and fast-food franchises from the United States has been seen by many as one of the negative results of a smaller and faster world.

As this chapter will show, there is an almost endless number of phenomena associated with globalization. As a result, a strict definition of globalization cannot help but reduce the complexity that discussions of it deserve. Nevertheless, all of the processes associated with globalization can generally be related to the historically unprecedented compression of time and space (Harvey). Many of the most prominent scholars who have written about globalization have described it in similar terms. The sociologist Anthony

Giddens has described it as "the intensification of world-wide relations which link distant localities in such a way that local happenings are shaped by events occurring many miles away" (64), while the geographer Doreen Massey characterizes globalization as "the stretching out of social relations." Malcolm Waters has described it as "the receding constraints of geography on social and cultural arrangements" (5), and for Roland Robertson, one of the leading scholars of globalization, it is "the compression of the world and intensification of the consciousness of the world as a whole" (8).

Popular culture today in every part of the world exists in some relationship to globalization. Indeed, as John Tomlinson suggests at the beginning of his book *Globalization and Culture*, "globalization lies at the heart of modern culture; cultural practices lie at the heart of globalization" (1). In exploring contemporary popular culture, it is thus essential to understand the reciprocal relationship between globalization and culture. As a way of examining this relationship, we need to consider a perhaps surprising question that impacts greatly on how we perceive the effects of globalization. We need to ask: Is globalization *real*? While no one disputes the fact that there have been significant changes in every sphere of human life over the past several decades, there are disagreements over just how *new* globalization is. Whether globalization is a genuinely new development in human life or whether it is merely the acceleration of much longer-term developments, it has a significant impact on how we understand its relationship to cultural practices around the world.

IS GLOBALIZATION REAL?

It is sometimes easy to forget just what life was like in North America only a few decades ago. For the few households with cable television, only a few dozen channels (comprised primarily of different local stations of the major broadcast networks) were available. Personal computers had only just been introduced and could barely manage to generate text on their screens, much less the complicated graphical interfaces that we are accustomed to today. There was no Internet, no cell phones, no personal handheld assistants, no laptops. Most of the world's stock exchanges were still populated with people (with the exception of a few exchanges, most trading now takes place electronically). Mutual funds were not a mainstream investment vehicle and few people paid much attention to the daily fluctuations of the stock market. The threat of nuclear war hung over the world, as the chill of the Cold War deepened during President Ronald Reagan's bellicose administration. And if you forgot to take money out of your bank account for the weekend, you were stuck: there was virtually no such thing as a bank machine that could bail you out, and even credit-card use was restricted by today's standards.

The Digital Revolution

Of course, there are numerous other differences between 1983 and 2003 that one could point to. Why these? What has made today so different than even the recent past is not the changes in the clothes we wear, the music we listen to, or the films we watch (though these too have changed), but the explosion in computer and communications technologies that has affected every part of our lives. The increasing presence of these technologies throughout North American society has changed how we work and enjoy ourselves. There are professions today that didn't exist two decades ago (from Web design to network maintenance to day trading), and new modes of labouring (such as working from home, or *telecommuting*). The market for video games, both on home console systems and on computers, will soon exceed the annual revenue generated by Hollywood film production. Digitalization has enabled a convergence of media forms (music stations available on television, the presence of music and video on the Internet), as well as the creation of entirely new forms of popular culture (electronica, raves, "surfing the 'net"). At the same time, it has also led to the decline of some long-established cultural products (digital cameras have threatened the very existence of traditional film cameras).

Additionally, these technologies have made it easier to for North Americans to access people, products, and places around the globe. Tourism, for instance, has grown exponentially over the past several decades, becoming one of the major industries in the world today; there are no longer parts of the world that seem inaccessible by phone or air travel. At least, this is true in theory: the impact of globalization is clearly not the same for everyone everywhere, a point we will return to later.

Of course, focusing only on what has changed in contemporary culture tends to obscure not just all of the things that have stayed the same, but also the long developments that have led up to these changes. As we saw in Chapter Four, a continual emphasis on the new or "hip" is itself a feature of contemporary culture and of the practices that we associate with **consumerism**. One of the most powerful engines of consumerism is our fascination with the "new." Along with each year's new car models and fashion styles, announcements of upcoming movie blockbusters and a new season's worth of television shows fuel the purchase of items that seem entirely original, but which are in fact more of the same. When we take a longer view of many of the products that make up contemporary popular culture, we can see that things change much more slowly than each fashion season might suggest. Not only do older fashions (and even car styles) return, but underneath all the evidence of change the function of cars and clothes remains the same, as has their structural role in North American society. This is not to say that the increased use of the automobile since the Second World War, or even the increasingly popularity of particular kinds of automobiles (in particular, over the past ten years, sports utility vehicles or SUVs), haven't had a broader social or cultural impact. But this impact has to be assessed and understood in the context of longer trends: suburbanization and environmental damage have accompanied the automobile since its advent.

While globalization is far from being just a passing fashion or style, our sense of how the world has changed also needs to be tempered by considering (for example) the computer and communications revolution in a historical context. In other words, rather than conceding that a *revolution* has happened, it is important to understand the *evolution* that has brought about globalization. The compression of time and space that has made it possible to imagine the globe as a single space didn't occur overnight: it is the outcome of a long and complicated history. While not all parts of this history impact directly on contemporary popular culture, understanding the historical process by which globalization has come about does allow us to better comprehend the reciprocal relationship between globalization and popular culture, and to understand the broader context within which popular culture is experienced and analyzed.

NOT JUST ONE THING, BUT A COLLECTION OF PROCESSES

Claims about the "newness" of globalization have been raised in a number of related areas, including economics, politics, and technology. Though we take each of these areas up separately below, it is important to recognize that these areas are in fact connected in important ways. As we shall see in the discussion that ends this chapter, one of the things that globalization has meant is that it is no longer possible to even make such divisions *heuristically*—that is, as a simplified model that limits the range of events and concepts that we need to investigate in order to make sense of specific phenomena.

Economic Globalization

Globalization is a term that has perhaps been most frequently discussed in corporate boardrooms and on the pages of the business press. Globalization is understood as presenting both new challenges and fresh opportunities in the never-ending quest to generate ever-greater corporate profits and to maximize shareholder value. In the eyes of the general public, too, globalization is linked to new forms of business practice. Businesses and economies were once linked to definite, national spaces, which meant that they could be controlled and regulated by the governments and citizens of nation-states. However, in the era of globalization many businesses have become **transnational**: able to relocate to whatever jurisdiction has the most favourable climate for business, and sometimes able to exist outside of any jurisdiction whatsoever. The former CEO of General Electric, the largest company in the world, described the ideal location of his company as a gigantic barge that could be moved around the world as needed to take advantage of changes in economic climate (Welch). Similarly, shipping companies have increasingly registered their fleets in small protectorates such as the Marshall Islands in order to avoid taxation in the countries from which they really originate.

The ability of corporations to shift production around the world, often in order to take advantage of cheap wages and loose environmental and labour regulations in less developed countries (LDCs), has been accompanied by two other factors associated with globalization. First, many companies have become global enterprises in order to expand the range of consumer markets that they can reach. Several fast-food chains based in the United States operate in almost 100 countries worldwide, while cell phone and consumer electronics giants have established consumer outlets and the production facilities to support them on virtually every continent. Second, globalization has enabled unprecedented flows of financial goods and services. The world's stock markets are integrated as never before, with a small fluctuation in capital markets in one country able to produce major financial shifts and swings in others. Today, the equivalent of the combined global **gross domestic product (GDP)** flows across borders in the form of foreign-exchange transactions in roughly eight days.

The Roots of Globalization The contemporary world economy is truly global in scope. But in many respects, it has been "global" for hundreds of years, even if we haven't used the term "globalization" to describe this fact. While prior to the time of Christopher Columbus's journey to the Americas most food and goods originated close to where people lived and worked, even in the ancient world there was a great deal of cross-cultural contact. This contact came about through military conquest (from Alexander the Great to the Roman Empire to the Crusades), travel along established trading routes between regions and even continents, and through journeys of exploration—such as Marco Polo's travels to Asia and the voyages of the Vikings, who, five hundred years prior to Columbus, had already established a settlement in the Americas at *L'Anse aux Meadows*, in what is today known as Newfoundland.

The "discovery" of the Americas by Europeans initiated a process of ever-accelerating, truly global trade in and production of goods. The establishment of far-sprung colonial empires by Spain, Portugal, England, Germany, Belgium, France, the Netherlands, and Italy (followed later by Japan and the United States) produced a market in Europe for goods produced abroad (bananas, oranges, coffee, tobacco, sugar, etc.). These empires also established a global division of labour that remains with us to this day. The colonies

THE FINAL MERGER

in South America, Africa, and Asia became sites of resource extraction and agriculture production for the European market. In turn, value-added manufacturing took place in Europe, with these goods often being exported back to the colonies in an effort to maximize the size of the markets (and thus of the profits) for European goods. The powerful textile industries of India and the Philippines (e.g., cotton) were devastated by the cheaper textiles exported from England.

This global division of labour exists in very much the same form today, with an ever-increasing range of local economies (and, thus, local ways of life) feeling the impact of new global economic arrangements. In particular, the agriculture sector of many countries has been threatened by the availability of Western agricultural products that, due to protectionist tariffs and subsidies, can be sold much more cheaply than locally produced goods.

Globalization is imagined as the era in which corporations have developed global reach and achieved newfound power. But here, too, the story is a much longer and more complicated one than many debates and discussions about globalization might lead us to believe. During the Cold War, a number of companies were already described as having operations that were **multinational** in scope. For example, Japanese automobile manufacturers such as Toyota and Nissan sold *and* produced cars in many countries outside of Japan during the Sixties, Seventies, and Eighties; the same holds true for all of the major corporations in the world.

A little farther back, by the end of the nineteenth century a number of U.S. corporations had developed not just national but global **monopolies** (or "trusts"), which led to the passage of "anti-trust" legislation to limit the control of trade by a few large companies. The global might of Standard Oil, Carnegie Steel, American Tobacco, and other large corporations was reined in under this legislation, which has been used subsequently to challenge the power of corporations such as AT&T and Microsoft. Even farther back, enormous corporations developed alongside the creation of the European colonies. The insurance giant Lloyd's of London has been underwriting corporations and colonial expeditions since 1688; in Canada, the Hudson's Bay Company, which has been in existence since 1670, organized trade from the new world to Great Britain and Europe.

Corporations as "Persons"   In many ways, then, the world economy functions very similarly to the way it has over the past century (if not even longer). Nevertheless, there are significant differences, due to both developments in technology and geopolitical shifts, which have a direct impact on the shape and character of contemporary popular culture. Due in part to fears about the possibility that large corporations might relocate to other countries, the past decade has witnessed an unprecedented relaxation of government legal and economic controls on corporations worldwide.

This, too, is part of a longer history that extends back to 1886, when corporations in the United States were granted full legal rights as "natural persons," far in advance of women and minorities. Prior to this date, corporations were extended short-term charters, which gave the public the ability to limit a company's profits and debt (among other things), and provided procedures for full public accounting of the company's books.

Today, nation-states around the world have less legal recourse than ever in controlling the actions of corporations, which now exist to some degree outside of the laws of nation-states altogether. This has been one of the major consequences of the international trade agreements pursued by states over the past two decades. These agreements have the effect of spreading the U.S. legal definition of corporations, as well as other aspects of corporate law (such as definitions regarding **intellectual copyright**), into other countries around the world.

As a result, the balance of power between corporations and states has shifted considerably. For example, under the provisions of Chapter 11 of the North American Free Trade Agreement (NAFTA), corporations are able to file suit against governments for infringing on "investor rights." United Parcel Services (UPS), the world's largest package delivery company, has filed a US$230-million suit against Canada Post (a public corporation), alleging that the Canadian federal government is involved in a service already provided by a private corporation in violation of NAFTA. Similarly, citing NAFTA's fair and equitable treatment rules, Vancouver-based Methanex Corp. has sued the U.S. government as a result of a California decision to phase out the use of a gasoline additive produced by the company due to environmental concerns. While NAFTA and other trade agreements have included provisions to limit their applicability to cultural issues, this has in reality done very little to limit the erosion of state control over corporate activities.

The shift in the relationship between states and corporations has taken two other forms as well. First, as a way of attracting and retaining business, governments have committed significant public monies (through tax breaks, loan guarantees, or direct transfers) to entice companies to their countries, cities, and regions. This transfer of tax revenue, which is now generated predominantly by taxes on individual income rather than on corporate profit, has occurred in almost every sector of the business world. Its most public face in North America, however, has been seen in the debates over public financing of sports franchises and stadiums (see Chapter Two).

Second, though the U.S. federal government is currently challenging the monopoly status of Microsoft, the world's largest producer of computer software, for the most part there has been a loosening of restrictions on the size and power of corporations. In order to gain and maintain their competitive advantage globally, corporations from across the world have been merging into larger and larger entities. In 2000 alone, according to the consulting firm KPMG, the value of cross-border mergers was $643 billion. To put this in perspective, the value of cross-border mergers in 2000 was about the same as Canada's GDP for that year.

Integration and Convergence   The effects of these mergers have been especially pronounced in the culture industries. Changes in legislation regulating telecommunications in Canada and the United States have permitted the development of enormous multimedia conglomerates over the past decade. Giant media corporations such as AOL Time Warner, Bertelsmann, Viacom, and Vivendi Universal have an enormous global reach. Contemporary media conglomerates not only are **vertically integrated,** like the early–twentieth-century film industry (see Chapters Two and Four), but also are **horizontally integrated,** owning several record labels, television channels, or film studios. Technological changes (especially digitalization) have also made it possible for these conglomerations to make use of programming or content produced for one medium in several others. For example, a movie produced by Warner Brothers' film studio can receive positive press in *People* magazine, be publicized on the Internet via America Online, and be screened later on television on TNT, a television "superstation" that broadcasts across North America.

A look at just some of the companies owned by Disney Corp. shows the endless possibilities that such **media convergence** provides for corporations. In addition to its famous theme parks, Disney owns

- publishing houses, including Hyperion and Miramax Books;
- magazines, including *Jane, Discover*, and *ESPN Magazine*;
- the ABC Television Network;
- community radio and TV stations across the U.S.;
- a range of specialty cable channels, including Disney, A&E, ESPN, The History Channel, and Lifetime;
- movie production and distribution companies, including Touchstone Pictures and Miramax Films;
- various Websites;
- Disney Interactive, which produces computer games (often based on Disney movies or television shows);
- record labels, including the indie label Mammoth;
- sports franchises (the NHL's Mighty Ducks of Anaheim and Major League Baseball's Anaheim Angels);
- Walt Disney Theatrical Productions, which produces stage versions of Disney films;
- travel agencies and tourist resorts, including a cruise line and an island in the Caribbean;
- and, finally—for those who prefer to stay home—the planned community of Celebration Village, Florida.

(Note that the most up-to-date source for media ownership is the list maintained by the *Columbia Journalism Review* on its Website: www.cjr.org/owners/index.asp.)

While none can boast of a portfolio like Disney's, Canadian media corporations have also pursued more or less successful strategies of convergence. With its recent acquisition of media properties formerly owned by Hollinger, CanWest Global Communications Corp. now owns television stations, a national television network, and an enormous number of newspapers in Canada; in Vancouver, it owns both daily newspapers and two television stations. Bell Globemedia owns CTV, *The Globe and Mail*, and the Internet service provider Sympatico. In Quebec, two corporations, Power Corp and Quebecor Inc., control virtually all media outlets in the province.

The increasing control by fewer and fewer corporations of much of what we understand as contemporary popular culture has important effects and repercussions (which we will discuss in more detail below). The most obvious impact is on our very sense of what constitutes popular culture. To some degree, the concentration of media power has meant a restriction in the range of cultural objects (in form if not in quantity) produced by these culture industries, which has consequently had a significant impact on what is represented and signified in the films, television programs, books, and magazines produced today.

The culture industries belong to the sector of the economy known as *service industries,* which now constitute almost 30 percent of the total exports of the United States (World Bank 190, 198). As culture becomes more closely identified with global economics, popular culture undergoes a shift. For example, the popularity of the action-film genre has much to do with the ease with which these films can be exported to countries outside the United States: dialogue is minimal and easily translated, and costly Hollywood special effects offer a spectacle that few indigenous cinemas can match. In other words, because they are able to generate enormous revenues in the global film market, movies starring action stars Jean-Claude Van Damme and Steven Seagal represent an increasingly large proportion of Hollywood productions. They are hugely popular international stars, without doing particularly well in North America.

Contemporary cultural industries require costly infrastructural investments in production facilities and distribution networks. They also require a high degree of technological innovation and expertise. Unsurprisingly, in a world in which the division of wealth has increased both among and within countries, only a very small number of countries have been able to participate actively in the production and export of some forms of popular culture. While the United States is the most visible of these, Canada has also aggressively marketed its cultural products abroad. This has sometimes placed the Canadian government in the awkward position of defending Canadian culture from outside influence through various cultural policies (such as Canadian content rules on television and radio), while simultaneously pushing for greater exports of Canadian-produced culture.

The global economy has developed over several hundred years, and is in many respects structurally similar today to what it was like at the end of the nineteenth century. There are, however, differences—especially with respect to the production and export of culture—that are an essential aspect of popular culture in globalization.

Suggested Activity 9.1

In what contexts have you heard the concept of globalization discussed (e.g., newspaper and television stories, books, etc.)? In these contexts, is globalization presented as an opportunity or a cost? How do different groups and organizations view globalization? What do these differences (between, for example, Fortune 500 companies and environmental groups) suggest about the general public's understanding of the meaning of globalization, and how does this differ from what we've outlined so far (and what we go on to say in the rest of the chapter)?

Globalization and Politics

Many of the points made about the economic realities of globalization apply equally to its political aspects. Politically, discussions about globalization have tended to focus on two things: (1) the decline of the power of nation-states and the rise in power corporations and international agencies such as the International Monetary Fund (IMF) and the World Trade Organization (WTO), and (2) the increasing privatization of public services and public spaces.

There is some truth to both of these claims. Especially with respect to economic decision making, nation-states face considerable pressure from foreign economic developments and are forced to act reactively rather than proactively to current events. At the same time, the massive privatization of the economy and culture offers evidence to the contrary. Though the decisions of governments to outsource services they once provided as a public good—everything from state-run utilities, to prisons, to the education system—are often presented to the public as matters of rational logic (i.e., the private sector can do things more efficiently that the government) or of external compulsion (i.e., global competitiveness demands it), it is in fact only a strong state that could bring about such a massive change in the structure of Western politics and economics.

In other words, the claim that the power of the state has declined is in many respects little more than a ruse that has disguised a massive transfer of publicly accumulated wealth into private hands. In many cases, state spending has in fact increased more quickly than corporate growth over the past two decades, though this new spending has been directed toward different ends than in the past—policing, prisons, anti-immigrant spending, enforcement of drug politics, militarization, and transfers to business and infrastructural development that tends to benefit private corporations rather than the public at large. Nation-states continue to control the major institutions through which laws are enforced and legitimate force is exerted (armies, police, intelligence agencies, etc.).

National Identity   Not only has the decline of the power of the nation-state been exaggerated, but so too has the claim that globalization signals a decline in feelings of national identity or pride in national culture (see Chapter Seven). Feelings of national belonging now compete with other forms of identification, which can range from various kinds of consumer identity (e.g., patterns of belonging derived *from* your belongings, such as occurs with Harley-Davidson or Saturn owners) to identities based on ethnicity, sexual orientation, and political affiliations, all of which exceed the boundaries of individual nation-states. While it is true that national identity constantly interacts and competes with other forms of identification, this is true of the *entire* history of the nation, and not just during the period of globalization.

Even where new nationalities (if not nation-states) are not in the process of being formed, national identity remains an extremely powerful force. Pride in national identity is still reinforced by schooling (through the playing of the national anthem and the teaching of national histories and cultures), revived during the Olympics, and crystallized during times of tension and conflict—as the reaction of the citizens of the United States to the terrorist attacks on the World Trade Center and the Pentagon showed all too clearly.

The politics of globalization are complex and multifaceted. There are new political agents and institutions involved in shaping global politics, including a wide variety of non-governmental organizations (NGOs) and institutions, such as the European Union, developed to manage international agreements of various kinds. Once again, however, it is best to stress continuities as opposed to a sudden, massive discontinuity in the nature of politics in the era of globalization.

The Technological Dimensions of Globalization

In 2001, Bell Canada produced a TV ad it called "Online Jam." Designed to promote its high-speed Internet connection service, the ad featured a guitarist and musician who log onto an Internet server in Toronto and start playing. In quick succession, a series of other musicians join in spontaneously, including a Rasta group in Jamaica and an accordion player in Austria, creating an amazingly eclectic but harmonious world-beat sound. Whether or not such a technological feat was actually possible (some of the ad's critics claimed it wasn't), "Online Jam" offers a nice, if clichéd, image of the cultural benefits to be realized through technological globalization.

The possibility of imagining the world as one interconnected space can certainly be attributed to the global revolution in telecommunications. As with other developments we've traced so far, this "revolution" isn't all that new. The ability to reach virtually any part of the globe with phone calls, television images, and computer-based information can be traced back to the launch of the first communications satellites in the early 1960s. The ability of these satellites to change the way in which we get information about the world became clear by the summer of 1964, when parts of the Tokyo Olympics were broadcast live on television.

Development of a global satellite communications network proceeded very rapidly. By the summer of 1969, an estimated 500 million people were able to witness the landing of *Apollo 11* on the moon. The rest, as they say, is history. In North America today, millions of individuals own tiny dishes that provide them with television images beamed from orbiting satellites; the use of cellular phones is ubiquitous, especially among young people; and live, continuous news coverage has become the norm since CNN covered the first cruise missile strikes live from Baghdad during the Gulf War in 1991. The widespread global mourning that accompanied the death of Princess Diana in 1997 and the terrorist attacks on the United States in 2001 was in some sense the product of contemporary telecommunications technologies: without these technologies, the reaction to these events would likely have been very different in character and scope.

New Communication Technologies The growth and spread of new modes of communication have had an impact on popular culture in a large number of ways. Cell phones have changed the nature of work and family life, and have introduced new cultural practices—such as the use of text messaging by teens to communicate with one another in secret. In many parts of the world, including parts of Eastern Europe, the advent of cell phones introduced phone communication for the very first time: the high infrastructural cost of traditional phones means that in these places cell phones are the primary means of interpersonal electronic communication. As the case of the Zapatistas shows, new communication technologies have also changed the nature of political struggles in the contemporary world (see Close-Up 9.1).

Close-Up 9.1

The Zapatistas and the Internet

Though new communications technologies have had an impact on the cultural and political sovereignty of nation-states, they have also been used in innovative and unexpected ways in various political struggles over the past decade. The online availability of multiple perspectives on political issues has re-shaped public opinion worldwide, has enabled political groups to keep up-to-date about each others' activities, and has created new forms of political action and expression.

Perhaps the best example of this is the revolutionary struggle of the ELZN in Mexico (the Spanish acronym for the Zapatista Army of National Liberation), more commonly known as the Zapatistas. At its most basic level, the Zapatista movement is a grassroots struggle for greater social, cultural, and political autonomy for the indigenous people of Chiapas, the most resource-rich Mexican state. However, the Zapatista movement has had more far-reaching consequences than other grassroots or local struggles around the world. The subject of songs and videos by the U.S. rock band Rage Against the Machine and an inspiration for the worldwide anti-globalization movement, the Zapatistas were among the very first political movements to effectively use online discussion groups, listservs, mail lists, and Websites to report on their efforts and to rally international support for their struggle.

The Zapatista struggle is rooted in local circumstances that are repeated in different ways across the world. With abundant agriculture, ranching, timber, and significant oil reserves the state of Chiapas should be one of the richest in Mexico. The exact opposite is the case. Due to endemic political corruption and the actions of powerful corporations, the wealth of Chiapas has benefited a few at the expense of the people who live there, especially the large population of indigenous Mayan Indians. The Zapatista movement was formed in order to challenge the disenfranchisement of local peoples under the existing political order in Mexico. From the outset, this "local" movement was engaged with global politics in a way that connected their struggle with other struggles against neo-liberalism around the world.

The Zapatistas first came to global consciousness on January 1, 1994, when they declared war against the Mexican government on the first day that the North American Free Trade Agreement took effect. For the Zapatistas, NAFTA signalled a continuation of the attack on the autonomy of indigenous peoples that began with the repeal of the article of the Mexican constitution that protected communal lands from privatization—a precondition of Mexico's entry into NAFTA. This was part of a broader global trend that has seen the transference of public goods into private hands over the past two decades or more. Beginning with their declaration of war, the Zapatistas have challenged stereotypes that have cast Natives and peasants as technologically backward peoples, by keeping up a constant stream of communiqués and information explaining their situation to Mexicans and to the rest of the world and thereby bypassing the indifference or propaganda of state-controlled media (such as the Mexican TV network Televisa).

"Zapatistas in Cyberspace" offers a comprehensive guide to the activities of the Zapatistas on the Web. It can be found at www.eco.utexas.edu/homepages/faculty/Cleaver/zapsincyber.html.

The Internet has introduced new modes of consumerism and interpersonal interaction, greater flows of official and non-official information, and an astonishing number of new cultural practices, from online interactive gaming to Internet dating to the transnational bride market. The impact of these technologies has been so dramatic that globalization is often associated with these developments alone. Once again, however, current developments are the product of a process dating back at least a century: the invention of the telegraph in the mid-nineteenth century (see Chapter Two) and the laying of an underwater phone cable across the Pacific in 1902 were just two early instances of the long process of what Armand Mattelart has described as "networking the world."

It is certainly the case that contemporary technologies are both more intensive and more extensive in ways that do suggest the world has become networked in a very different way than before. For our purposes, what is perhaps most significant are the possibilities that **digitalization** has introduced for the dissemination of information and cultural products across the globe. Music, images, and printed text can now all be transmitted, distributed, and consumed electronically. The digitalization of popular culture has also made it increasingly inexpensive for individuals to produce and distribute to a global audience the movies and songs that they make.

Connected to this process of digitalization has been a remarkable convergence of cultural forms and products: digital music can be played on cell phones, movie clips can be downloaded to personal digital assistants (PDAs), and so on. Nevertheless, a sense of the longer history of developments in communications technologies is essential in order to temper some of the more exaggerated claims about the communications revolution espoused by magazines like *Wired* and companies like Microsoft and Oracle.

Globalization *is* real. The intent of this section has been to put globalization in a larger context so that we can see past the hype that often surrounds it. In order to understand contemporary popular culture, we will need to keep the influence and importance of all of these levels in mind—a complex but necessary procedure to make sense of the already complicated set of positions and issues that has surrounded popular culture in the second half of the twentieth century.

GLOBALIZATION AND POPULAR CULTURE

Given the long history of economic, political, and technological developments that have led up to globalization, it should come as no surprise that there have been all kinds of cultural exchanges between peoples and cultures for thousands of years. When we speak about globalization with respect to culture, what we often imagine is not just an acceleration of these exchanges, but a whole new set of cultural practices produced as a result of them. Inevitably, the conjunction of globalization and culture also evokes the promise and/or threat of a single global culture, a culture that would be shared by everyone on the earth for better and/or worse.

One of the most important things about all the various processes associated with globalization is that they have forced us to rethink long-held assumptions that continue to inform our understanding of culture. Our changing experience of time and space opens up new ways of looking at the past as much as it offers up rich opportunities to speculate about the future. The impact of globalization on culture is thus both empirical (effecting real changes in the real world) and theoretical (producing a change in our very understanding of just what culture is). In this section, we will look at these changes and discuss the various ways in which culture has been perceived with respect to globalization.

Culture and Space

As we have seen throughout this book, there are so many definitions of culture that it is difficult to keep them apart: folk culture, mass culture, popular culture—culture as the name for a whole set of practices that people engage in, or as the word that describes particular kinds of artifacts and events that people produce to express themselves. It is hard to imagine that all of these very different ways of thinking about culture might have anything in common. But there is (at least) one thing that all of these senses of culture share: the idea that culture comes from some *place*. We usually think of culture—whether as practices or products—as having a definite and unambiguous point of origin. Today, we usually think of this place as being a nation or regions; either within a nation, or regions that are collections of nations (e.g., the Middle East, Southeast Asia, etc.).

Without thinking about it, and almost without being able to help it, we attribute attitudes and behaviour to people based on their point of origin: Italians are loud and argumentative, Americans are brash, and so on (see the discussion of **stereotypes** in Chapter Seven). This is done not only with people, but also with the ideas and culture that they produce. While we sometime realize that these attributions are oversimplifications, when they come from experts in the study of these nations or regions we are often ready to believe that the unique characteristics that make one people different from another have in fact been discovered.

There are several problems with this way of locating culture in specific places—in this case, the space of the nation. First, as we discussed above and in Chapter Seven, while it continues to produce pride, along with ethnic and racial tensions, the seemingly "natural" space of the nation is a recent political invention. Second, it is very difficult to isolate distinct cultural practices or products in the contemporary world. Every culture has felt the impact and influence of other cultures. In Japan and other parts of the world, rock'n'roll is often taken to be typically American. The origins of rock music are, however, quite complicated—a mix of indigenized African music (as in blues) combined with musical influences from various parts of Europe. Musical forms such as Jamaican dance hall music show even greater degrees of cultural migration: rock'n'roll begets Jamaican reggae, which has an influence on American hip-hop, which in turn comes back to Jamaica as dance hall music (see Chapter Seven for a more detailed discussion of the role of **diaspora** in shaping hip-hop). As the sociologist Mel van Elteren has put it, "national and other cultural identities are best grasped when seen as being constituted in and through their relation to each other, rather than analyzing cultural (or national) identities one by one and then subsequently thinking about how they are related to one another" (51–2).

Specific cultures are now connected with specific spaces so closely that it is very difficult to speak about cultural migration without using the reductive vocabulary of national cultures. By allowing us to see these migrations and movements much more rapidly—occurring not just in the space of one lifetime but within a matter of years or months—globalization has made it possible for us to question these links as never before. This is not to say that there aren't still vast "cultural" differences between, for example, Canada and Hong Kong. At the same time, as peoples and cultural practices move around the globe, we might also want to think about the connections as opposed to the disconnections among these spaces.

For example, with more than 300 stores, Market Village and Pacific Mall in the affluent suburb of Markham, Ontario constitutes the largest indoor Chinese mall in North America. Given its location and the patterns of consumption that it structures and produces, it is worth considering the ways in which this mall is as Canadian as it is Chinese—just as many of the new affluent suburban houses being built in China borrow heavily from the new North American housing styles exhibited in Markham.

Gu Xiong's photographs depict a world in which the comfort of traditional categories is increasingly blurred and placed into doubt.

Global Culture and Cultural Imperialism

These points are well worth keeping in mind as we shift to the other extreme. For many, globalization represents that birth of a truly global culture, a single culture shared to varying (if ever-increasing) degrees by everyone in the world. This global culture may not yet be in existence, but its arrival seems to be only a matter of time.

The effect of globalization's acceleration of time and collapse of space is to eliminate cultural distinctions—already more plural and complex than previously imagined—that might have once existed. Coincident with this process is the simultaneous decline of the world's languages and the establishment of a few major *lingua franca*: English, Mandarin, Spanish, Hindi-Urdu, and so on. Soon we will all be sharing a wide, but common, set of beliefs and practices that are reflected in a variety of international agreements, such as the United Nations' Universal Declaration of Human Rights (available in more than 300 different languages) or, indeed, the General Agreement on Tariffs and Trade (128 signatory countries as of the 1994 Uruguay Round). We'll also soon all be reading the same comic books, watching the same movies, drinking coffee from the same outlets … or so the story goes.

In its most general outlines, this *does* sound like a description of our world today—or, at least, our world as it sometimes looks like from Europe and North America. There are in fact practices that seem already to have made their way to all corners of the world, the most significant being the practice of industrial management famously codified by Frederick Winslow Taylor in 1911. But if the links between space and culture were in the past overly determinate, the belief in the possibility of a global culture overestimates the degree to which culture has or can be severed not just from space, but also from specificities of history, economics, and politics that intersect in unique ways in different parts of the globe.

Class Issues   One of these, for instance, is class. Visions of global culture are more often than not an expression of the viewpoint of a group that the sociologist Zygmunt Bauman has described as "tourists": a relatively wealthy, socially mobile middle class, which exists to varying extents in different parts of the world, that is able to travel to remote locations where they interact with others like themselves in conference hotels or tourist resorts that are more or less indistinguishable from one another. For these people, the degree of global cultural convergence might seem to be startling enough to warrant belief in a truly global culture.

For the vast majority of the people in the world, however, mobility is greatly limited—and, when movement does become a necessity, it is usually due to terrible economic, natural, or political circumstances that have generated refugee crises around the world. The UN has estimated that there are currently more than 30 million "internally displaced people" worldwide.

The *possibility* of a global culture has to be clearly distinguished from questions of its *desirability*. Interestingly, with the exception of a few American commentators who positively equate global culture with the worldwide dominance of U.S. values and beliefs (e.g., *New York Times* columnist Thomas Friedman), very few critics, scholars, or citizens see global culture as an end worth achieving. Abstractly, the possibility of the universalization of certain "cultural" beliefs—such as human rights and freedom of the press—seems desirable to most people. At the same time, everyone seems to be aware that a global culture can be achieved only through the globalization of **mass culture**—a form of culture in which the central motive of cultural production is profit and in which culture is produced primarily by "experts" (film directors, professional musicians, etc.).

One of the things that no doubt dismays Bauman's tourists even as it comforts them is the widespread diffusion of North American, European, and Japanese brand-name appliances, food franchises, clothing stores, and automobiles. One of the reasons to travel is, after all, to experience "difference" (in however problematic a form), and if every place looks like "home" the thrill of encountering "exotic" peoples and places begins to lose its appeal. Westerners have an enormous amount invested in the idea of cultural diversity. The intrinsic desirability of cultural diversity seems to be one of the "facts" of contemporary human life that can't be challenged. Nevertheless, it is something that we should consider before rushing to judgment in open condemnation of the rapid "massification" of culture worldwide.

Suggested Activity 9.2

Globalization names the increased flow of ideas, goods, and cultural products around the world. But while borders may have become more porous to images, ideas, and products, the mobility of people has in many cases become more controlled than ever. Zygmunt Bauman suggests that globalization has divided the world into two new classes of people: "tourists," for whom globalization has meant increased mobility and for whom the world is almost entirely open to exploration; and "vagabonds," those who either can't move outside of fixed boundaries (for a variety of reasons) or who are forced to move by circumstances beyond their control (civil war, famines, etc.). Make a list of groups and individuals that would fit into these two categories and consider the implications of a world divided by degree of mobility. Do tourists exist only in the First World and vagabonds only in the Third World? What roles do race and gender play in the politics of mobility?

Cultural Imperialism   The *undesirability* of global culture (and desirability of cultural diversity) is usually expressed as part of broader worries about **cultural imperialism**. The concept of cultural imperialism has come to mean many things since it was first articulated in the 1960s. However, there are two elements that seem to belong to any usable definition of the concept. First, most generally, cultural imperialism refers to the process by which political and economic power is used by a foreign culture to spread its culture and values to the detriment of cultures that it comes into contact with. Second, cultural imperialism also points to the important role that culture played in the process of colonialism and imperialism in the nineteenth and early twentieth centuries.

The second use of culture has been investigated extensively in **postcolonial** criticism and literature. The first definition has been used more frequently to characterize the unequal power relations—economic, political, *and* cultural—that continue to exist between developed and developing countries even after the official end of European colonial rule in most parts of the world. In the absence of direct political control, culture, especially mass culture, is seen as one of the forms through which these unequal power relations are maintained.

In what ways can culture be seen to maintain (and indeed, to produce) this situation? John Tomlinson has identified four main ways in which culture has been seen as abetting imperialist relations: 1) through foreign ("American") mass media, whose global diffusion manages to produce the other three conditions; 2) through the imposition of the values and beliefs of one nation on another; 3) through the imposition of consumerism and capitalism as *the* "way of life"; and 4) through the imposition of modernity on parts of the world that might be interested in developing historically along a very different path than that taken by the West. These four senses are very often confused and folded into one another.

This has certainly been the case in discussions of the relationship of Canadian culture to the United States. The massive presence of U.S. mass media in Canada has produced continual worries about the possibility that U.S. national values will subsume Canadian ones. This in turn has led Canadians to overestimate the degree to which they stand outside of capitalism, consumerism, and modernity, which has tended to be far too exclusively associated with the United States alone.

From our discussions of the discourse of the nation and of the relationship between culture and space, one should be able to see quickly that—despite its intuitive power—the concept of cultural imperialism is problematic. First, as we have emphasized throughout this book, it is difficult to speculate about *any* particular outcome of an audience's encounter with mass media. Foreign audiences make sense of foreign mass media in their own contexts and for their own purposes; foreign audiences are also hardly uniform in their composition, with different segments of the audience reacting in different ways. Tomlinson suggests that "the simple notion of an immediate ideological effect arising from exposure to the imperialist text" is both "naïve and improbable" (*Imperialism* 47).

Second, the idea that cultures are neatly divided into national units and possess characteristics that can be communicated in any easy way is one that can no longer be sustained, for all of the reasons we outlined earlier in this chapter. The third and fourth claims about cultural imperialism are more interesting to consider, and we take these up in the following sections.

The Noble Savage vs. Ronald McDonald

For many, the most alarming aspect of globalization is the potential it represents of imposing the Western values of consumerism, capitalism, and modernity on cultures to whom these values are not only foreign, but also hostile. In one sense, fears of the dilution of cultural diversity are real—borne out, for example, in the accelerated extinction of hundreds of indigenous languages in the face of the dominance of English. But it is also important to note that many of these fears do not actually arise out of the problem of cultural imperialism as it is normally framed: the imposition of one culture's forms and values on another. Rather, what is being expressed here is a more general worry about the value and viability of mass culture, not so much in foreign contexts but in North America itself. Until the past decade or so, such worries didn't seem to have too much applicability to the rest of the world.

In addition to making North American mass culture more globally available, what contemporary communications technologies have done is to allow North Americans to take note of the shape of the rest of the world—a world with skyscrapers, freeways, and shopping malls on every continent (except Antarctica, of course). For a significant part of the group who fit the description of Bauman's "tourists," this vision is both comforting and depressing: comforting in that it attests to the universality of our culture, and depressing in that it fails to offer the temporary escape that the tourist craves. However, it is important to remember that what seems like a threat to Westerners may look very different in other parts of the world. As Tomlinson points out, the "the Kazakhstani tribesman who has no knowledge of (and, perhaps, no interest in) America or Europe is unlikely to see his cassette player as emblematic of creeping capitalist domination" (*Imperialism* 109).

The Western concern with preserving the cultural uniqueness of non-Western cultures has effects on those cultures that are in some cases more damaging than the imagined effects of global mass culture. For example, New Age celebrations of a romanticized Native American tradition have the effect of freezing real, living Native cultures outside of time, thus denying them the agency and opportunity to negotiate their way in the global economy. Ironically, the fantasy that there is something outside that economy is a luxury that is really available only to those who are firmly inside it.

But just because there are no insides or outsides to the global economy, just as there are no purely local, **authentic** cultures outside the network of global culture, does not validate the darkest visions of cultural imperialism. That global culture is both more fluid and more uneven in its effects than is represented either by its champions or its critics is clear if we look at an example that is often cited by both: McDonald's. For many people, the fast-food giant McDonald's has become a powerful cultural symbol of globalization. With more than 20,000 restaurants in more than 100 countries worldwide, McDonald's is a truly global company whose products represent more than quick meals at low prices.

The first appearance of a McDonald's in small towns across North America is seen by some as a sign not only of a community's economic development and growth potential (since McDonald's is careful to build its restaurants only in places where it is certain to make a profit), but also its emergence into the mainstream of contemporary culture. News of openings of new McDonald's restaurants in Moscow and Beijing made headlines in the United States, as it was taken as an indication of the global victory of free-market values. Some commentators have gone even further, to see McDonald's as an ambassador of world peace: as *New York Times* columnist Thomas Friedman notes, no two countries possessing a McDonald's outlet have ever gone to war against each other (qtd. in Burkeman).

McDonald's as a Target   In contrast to these positive views of McDonald's, the ubiquitous golden arches that make up the restaurant's logo have also been seen as a symbol of the dangers of the globalization of culture. The attacks on McDonald's storefronts during anti-globalization protests around the world, the dismantling of a McDonald's in Millau, France, by the Peasant Confederation (headed by activist José Bové) as a protest against genetically modified foods and corporate globalization, and the protests that greeted the announcement of a plan to build a McDonald's in Niagara-on-the-Lake, a small, well-preserved nineteenth-century tourist town in Ontario, all share the same commonly held view of the restaurant as a symbol of a global **monoculture**. The way in which the prefix "Mc" has come to be used suggests the same thing: "McWorld," "McAmerica," "McDonaldization"—these labels have become synonymous with the dark side of globalization that it seems everyone wishes to avoid.

When we speak about globalization as cultural imperialism, McDonald's immediately comes to mind. As anyone who has taken a long-distance trip can attest, the ubiquity with which McDonald's restaurants (and other franchise stores and services) dot the landscape at highway interchanges can seem depressing, especially because travel is often undertaken precisely to discover different places and ways of living. In part because McDonald's spread to other countries so early (to Japan, Germany, and Australia in 1971), it has come to be seen as the leading-edge and primary example of a much larger trend in which U.S. popular culture is exported to other parts of the world, to the detriment of local cultures and practices.

McDonald's is symbolic of the larger worry expressed by the cultural imperialism thesis that it is not just the choice of purchasing hamburgers that is being made available to peoples outside of the United States, but also the export of a whole way of life: American consumer society and the fantasies of the good life that accompanies it. Gaining a McDonald's franchise means losing local dietary habits, patterns of daily behaviour, and even norms of work and consumption—in other words, a whole range of the life activities that make cultures distinct from one another.

However, this view of McDonald's as a force that is inevitably corrosive to cultural difference is one that fails to account for the genuine complexities of culture and globalization. There is no country or culture that has not experienced influences from other cultures and nations. Even in the case of contemporary popular or mass culture, McDonald's is hardly the only form to have had an impact worldwide, though it is per-

McDonald's restaurants are now at "home" around the world, including countries such as Egypt.

haps often the most visible symbol of foreignness to many people around the world. Worries about the influence of the kinds of popular cultural practices that are at least symbolically associated with McDonald's—consumerism, the consumption of mass-produced food, branding, and so on—also always underestimate or fail to account for the interests of local peoples and cultures, casting them in the role of helpless "victims" who are unable to resist the allure of the golden arches. In fact, there are some suggestions that customers are beginning to do just that: after years of unchecked expansion, the chain is considering closing 175 outlets in ten countries.

Among the culprits cited for a loss of appetite amongst Big Mac eaters are the BSE (mad cow disease) scare in the U.K., concerns about the effects of a fatty diet, and political resistance to McDonald's as a symbol—like Starbucks—of all the negative effects of globalization, both real and imagined, that we have discussed above. (See Chapter One for more on the symbolism of Starbucks.)

Both the recent losses in McDonald's stock-market share prices and its surprising ability to rally in the face of changing fashion and politics suggest that we need to develop a more complex account of the global role of popular culture than that expressed by worries over a coming "McWorld."

The Impact of McDonald's   To answer the question of whether the spread of fast-food chains around the world is helping to create a homogenous, global culture, a group of anthropologists set out to study the impact of McDonald's in five different locales in East Asia: Beijing, Hong Kong, Taipei, Seoul, and Tokyo (Watson). What they discovered was that, while the introduction of McDonald's in these countries *was* having an impact on local customs and practices, the precise nature of this impact was very different in each context. For example, before McDonald's came to their country, Japanese consumers very rarely ate with their hands; in Hong Kong, the restaurant has replaced tea houses as the most popular place to have breakfast.

At the same time, McDonald's has been adapted to local circumstances in ways that differ not only amongst the different countries examined, but also in relation to the role that McDonald's plays in North America. In North America, McDonald's is generally a site to pass through for a quick meal on the way to doing something else. But it is also used for other purposes: a place for seniors to meet and talk in the mornings (most restaurants offer seniors discounts on coffee); a place for small children to play, especially in winter months; and, in the evenings, a place for teens to hang out. In East Asia, too, McDonald's has been transformed, often more forcefully, into a space serving local purposes. In Beijing, Seoul, and Taipei, McDonald's functions as a retreat from urban stresses; in Hong Kong, it is a place where middle-school students spend large amounts of time studying and gossiping—the function that coffeehouses sometimes assume in North America. Throughout the region, it is a place where women go to avoid other social spaces (such as bars) that are havens for men.

What even these few examples should suggest is that it is through the constant interaction of the global and the local that contemporary culture is produced. Even this distinction is misleading, however, since both of these terms suggest that there is something identifiably "global" (usually imagined as transnational corporations) and "local" (small communities across the globe).

Corporations like McDonald's have global reach, but at the same time the company has shareholders from many localities and, like other corporations working on a global scale, its managers and investors tend to come from the localities in which McDonald's has a presence. The anthropologists examining McDonald's in East Asia discovered that virtually all of the managers came from Korea, Japan, China, and so on. The raw materials used to produce fast food tend to originate within geographic proximity of the restaurants, and McDonald's has generally adapted its menus to suit customers and cultures across the globe (though recently it has faced enormous problems as a result of concealing the use of beef fat in products created for the global Hindu community). Though it has been often (and deservedly) criticized, in many respects McDonald's has been a far more responsible and responsive transnational corporation than many others.

The point here is not to absolve McDonald's or other transnational corporations from criticism, or to suggest that their power and cultural influence is benign. As much as it sells a set of products, like so much else in contemporary popular culture McDonald's also sells an *experience* that has had noticeable effects around the world. With its hamburgers and fries, McDonald's sells friendly service, predictability, speed, cleanliness and hygiene, and toys and cultural symbols (e.g., Ronald McDonald) to its young customers. The experience of eating at McDonald's has had an impact on the experience of eating out almost everywhere the restaurant has been introduced. These are often subtle changes, but because dietary patterns and attitudes toward food are so important to everyday life, their impact is widely felt. Almost without exception, fast food is extremely unhealthy. There is no reason to celebrate the increase in consumption of mass-produced fast food around the world.

At the same time, the typical narratives that we use to imagine the impact of companies like McDonald's on the shape of global popular culture have to be seen as far too simplistic. The idea that globalization leads to the production of a single "bad" global culture is not supported by more careful attention to the networks and processes through which cultural products and cultural experiences are produced in the world. Large, global corporations play an important role in this, but to see them as having almost omnipotent powers over the shape of contemporary culture tends to negate the need to produce more complex accounts of culture in globalization that might in fact yield a better understanding of where we all stand today.

Defending Cultural Sovereignty: The Case of Canada

As we have suggested above, many of the fears surrounding globalization arise more from a **mythologized** image of cultural imperialism than from cultural or economic realities. However, one undeniable consequence of the expansion of the powers of global financial bodies like the IMF has been a decrease in the power of nations and local regions to determine the direction of their own economic development. For poor nations these concerns are often directed at the policies of powerful nations like the U.S., whose trade policies are, ironically, still not global enough in their maintenance of powerful tariffs protecting American agriculture and industry. For those countries just slightly off the crest of the wave of globalization—countries like Canada and France—concern is more likely to take the form of vigorous assertions of cultural **sovereignty.** (This is not to say that culture is not a concern for poorer countries; only that rapidly growing material inequities have placed cultural worries lower on the agenda than they once were.)

By way of concluding this chapter, we look at a particular example of Canadian cultural policy as a way of illustrating some of the complex, and perhaps unexpected, ways that globalization shapes not just specific cultures, but also the notion of culture as a whole.

For almost its entire history, Canada's citizens and the Canadian government have worried about the cultural, political, and economic implications that flow out of the particularities of Canada's geographic place in the world. Proximity to the United States, a country with which Canada shares a great deal of history and culture, but that possesses a much larger population and economy, has been both a blessing and a curse. The late Pierre Elliott Trudeau described Canada's relationship with the United States as like being a mouse in bed with an elephant: while the elephant barely notices the mouse, the mouse has to be aware of the elephant's every shift and move lest it be crushed to death.

Smaller countries around the world have been able to maintain their sovereignty in the shadow of larger, more powerful ones. What makes Canada's relationship to the United States different than, for example, the relationship of Hungary to the Soviet Union is that Canada and the U.S. share common origins and even (with the exception of Quebec) a common language. The Canadian economy is also dependent on exports to the United States, so much so that its performance mirrors the ebb and swell of the U.S. economy almost perfectly.

The constant threat (real and imagined) that the United States poses to Canadian sovereignty has resulted in an almost obsessive worry about the distinctiveness of Canadian culture and Canadian identity. One of the most important places in which this worry has been played out has been in the field of popular culture. The size of the United States has made it able to produce popular culture in large quantities, and to commit major economic resources to its production. For example, while the average budget of a U.S. feature film today (including marketing) is $76 million, Canadian films are generally produced for 2 percent of this amount—about $1.5 million.

Canada is not the only country to feel the impact of the power of the U.S. cultural industries. In other countries, too, U.S. films dominate at the box office, and have done so since the First World War, when production by European studios fell to a trickle. However, Canada is in a unique situation. Radio and television transmissions can easily make their way across the border, and the availability of an enormous amount of easily accessible English-language programming, music, and films has meant that even Canadian broadcast networks rely heavily on programs imported from the United States.

Government Regulation   As we saw in our discussion of cultural imperialism, this reliance on foreign or imported culture is almost always perceived as a threat to national sovereignty and to the very existence of a nation-state. Just as in other countries, the government of Canada has intervened in a variety of ways to lend support to Canadian cultural producers and to limit the amount of foreign cultural imports. Over the course of the twentieth century, the Canadian government has established agencies such as the Canada Council (1957), which allocates financial resources to cultural groups and individual cultural producers and which also provides insight into the state of Canadian culture through reports and commission findings; the Canadian Radio-television and Telecommunications Commission (CRTC; 1968, though existing in earlier forms since the 1930s), which regulates all forms of telecommunications and broadcasting in Canada; and the Canadian Broadcasting Corporation (CBC; 1936), which supports the production and dissemination of Canadian culture through its radio and television networks. Though there is substantial debate over the function of these agencies and the overall effects of their policies, they have had a role in creating and supporting Canadian popular culture. The relative vibrancy of Canadian popular music (from The Guess Who to The Tragically Hip to newer artists like The Weakerthans and Nelly Furtado) has been aided by policies that require radio stations and music TV stations (such as MuchMusic) to include specified amounts of Canadian content; without the CBC, there would likely be very little television production in Canada other than programs produced in Canada for broadcast on U.S. networks.

Globalization has produced new challenges for attempts to regulate Canadian culture, and has also exposed some problematic assumptions that have formed the basis of Canadian cultural policy to date. For example, while the CRTC has made modest attempts to consider the possibility of regulating Canadian content on the Internet, the very nature of this new medium would seem to make it almost impossible to regulate what Canadian companies can display on their Websites, much less where Canadians choose to go as they surf the Web. The deterritorialized nature of contemporary culture might be nowhere so evident as on the Internet. But the current problem of regulating the "Canadianness" of the Internet should also draw our attention to the fact that, as we discussed above, cultural forms have *always* crossed borders from one country to another, mixing with indigenous forms in order to produce new ones, which themselves travel to other places on the globe, and so on.

Canadian Culture Goes International   Canadian literature is enjoying a period of remarkable worldwide success, with authors including Michael Ondaatje, Margaret Atwood, and Carol Shields winning major literary prizes over the last ten years. Canadian pop music has been similarly successful: from Shania Twain to godspeed you black emperor! to Nickelback to Kid Koala, Canadian artists have staked a claim on virtually every genre of contemporary music. However, if we consider the form of Canadian literature or music, we notice two things immediately: first, while there might be some distinctly Canadian styles, the overall form of popular culture in Canada shares broad characteristics with that of other countries and traditions: pop songs are generally four to five minutes long and use predictable instrumentation. Similarly, novels are written in well-known genres, such as literary fiction, mystery, and science fiction.

The fact that Canadian popular culture belongs to a broader Western cultural tradition doesn't mean that it isn't valuable or significant to Canadians in particular ways. Our intention here is simply to point out that what the Canadian government has tried to defend as *Canadian* culture is already the product of many different cultural influences and traditions—as every culture is, for that matter. Policies to defend Canadian culture are about the need for the nation-state to legitimize its political role as much as a question of economic policy—of producing the conditions for Canadians to be able to participate in the cultural industries, an increasingly important and highly competitive industry worldwide.

Split-Run Magazines   In Canada, the new conditions for the production and regulation of popular culture in the era of globalization can be seen in the recent controversy over the government's support of magazine publishing. In an effort to support the development of the Canadian magazine industry, in the 1960s the government introduced measures designed to limit the distribution of "split runs" of American magazines in Canada. This was done on both financial and cultural grounds. Split runs are magazines that combine the editorial content of a "parent" issue of a magazine—for instance, the version of *Time* produced in the U.S.—with advertising solicited from Canadian companies.

For the publisher, split runs are a way of generating new advertising revenues while acquiring few or no additional editorial costs. The articles have already been written anyway, so they might as well try to sell the magazine in as many national markets as possible. Since the ad revenue of a split-run magazine constitutes a source of "extra" (or unanticipated) profit, U.S. publishers are able to compete for Canadian advertising dollars by offering ad space at a lower cost than comparable Canadian magazines (in the case of *Time*, a news magazine like *Maclean's*). Without sufficient ad revenue, Canadian magazines would be unable to generate enough money to publish, which is an economic and cultural loss since the publishers of split runs are under no pressure to deal with issues of particular interest or relevance to Canadians.

In 1965, the federal government passed legislation that (among other things) introduced tax penalties intended to dissuade Canadian companies from advertising in split-run magazines (*Time* and *Reader's Digest* were granted an exemption from these rules because they were already distributed in Canada). These policies made it possible for a Canadian magazine industry to develop. Over the past ten years or so, the legitimacy of these policies has been challenged by the United States. There is a long and complicated history of Canada–U.S. disputes over Canadian cultural policy, and over magazine policy in particular. The most recent of these offers us perhaps the best insight into the challenges that globalization has introduced into attempts to regulate cultural policy.

Trade Agreements   Over the past decade or so, a wide range of Canadian government policies have been reassessed as a result of Canada's involvement in a number of new international agreements. The most important of these are the North American Free Trade Agreement (NAFTA) and the General Agreement on Tariffs and Trades (GATT). Globalization is often identified with the concerted global push to establish rules governing trade that will result in the elimination of tariffs and other trade barriers and lead eventually to the establishment of global free trade.

What this has meant is that all policies that provide protection or support to local industries against foreign competition have come under increasing scrutiny. Though both the original Free Trade Agreement between Canada and the U.S. and NAFTA have clauses that are intended to exempt culture from this scrutiny, in practice cultural policies, too, have been subjected to pressure.

In the case of Canadian magazine policy, the U.S. government challenged Canadian legislation on two different occasions in front of a World Trade Organization dispute panel. The WTO agreed with the U.S. argument that Canadian policies unfairly affected the ability of U.S. publishers to compete in Canada. The final outcome was new Canadian magazine legislation that permitted increasing levels (up to 18 percent) of Canadian ad content in U.S. magazines to be phased in over several years. The impact of this decision on the Canadian magazine industry is expected to be disastrous enough that in 2001 the Canadian Heritage Ministry announced plans for $150 million in aid to Canadian publishers.

In one respect, this is the latest in a long story of the challenges faced by Canadian culture. However, the details of the WTO case offer insights into some of the significant changes that popular culture has undergone as a result of globalization. As much as the U.S. case was about unfair trade practices, it was also about what constitutes culture today. The Canadian government argued that Canadian magazines and U.S. split-runs were not "like products," and so should not be governed by the same laws:

> Magazines are distinct from ordinary articles of trade. Magazines are intended, by their very nature, for intellectual consumption as opposed to physical use (like a bicycle) or physical consumption (like food). It follows that the intellectual content of a cultural good such as a magazine must be considered its prime characteristic. ... Editorial material developed for the Canadian market reflects a Canadian perspective and contains specific information of interest to Canadians. The content is qualitatively different from editorial material copied from foreign publications. What has been said of the essential properties of magazines is equally applicable to their end-use. The end-use of a magazine is not simply reading: it is transmission and acquisition of specific information. (World para 3.6.1, 3.6.3)

For most of us, this sense of what constitutes a "cultural good" sounds right: the most important thing about a Canadian magazine lies in what it communicates to Canadians about the Canadian experience. The United States presented a very different argument about what a magazine "is":

> The type, texture, color, thickness, and even the perfume of the paper can be important factors to market appeal. The dimensions of a magazine, the manner in which its pages are bound, the typesetting, and the appearance of the ink, can also be significant. The type, appearance, and frequency of advertisements may be a factor in a consumer's purchasing decisions as well. All of these attributes— including editorial content—combine to form an *overall package.. . .* For the

Canadian and U.S. magazine industries, editorial content generally represents substantially less than 20 percent of the cost of producing a consumer magazine. (World para 3.7.8)

The WTO's ruling in favour of the U.S. position does not mean that we should now see culture as being just like every other commodity. It does, however, point to larger structural and institutional forces that are reshaping our sense of what culture is and what we expect it to do. This offers us perhaps the clearest way of understanding what globalization has meant for popular culture.

Globalization is the moment that mass culture becomes globalized. The cultural theorist Richard Ohmann has defined mass culture as "voluntary experiences, produced by a relatively small number of specialists, for millions across the nation to share, in similar or identical form, either simultaneously or nearly so; with dependable frequency; mass culture shapes habitual audiences, around common needs or interests, and it is made for profit" (14). The collapse of time and space has resulted in new forms of culture and new countercultures—and, in the midst of the new, residual forms of culture (for example, cultural practices related to religious practices) continue to exert an important influence.

Even so, and even though the effects of globalization have been unevenly distributed, it is increasingly difficult to understand contemporary popular culture except as a mass culture that has been distributed across the face of the globe in increasingly intensive and extensive ways.

MASS CULTURE AND NEW CULTURAL FORMS

Globalization has produced many new forms of culture and has changed older forms in significant ways as well. The fact of globalization has also changed *how* we talk about culture. The recent collapse of time and space that we associate with globalization has led to a reconsideration of the ways in which we once imagined that time and space kept cultures and people apart; while the discourses of nationalism may have in fact done so, there has been considerable cultural interchange for a very long time. Globalization has also led to a re-examination of the divisions that we have used to study contemporary societies—divisions established initially for heuristic purposes, but which have since come to seem as if they were formed in response to actually existing divisions in the real world. The discussion in this chapter is an example of how globalization has made it impossible to discuss economics without politics, politics without culture, culture without economics, and so on.

What globalization hasn't produced (at least not thus far) is a comparably new way to think about both the mass culture that we now experience (unevenly) at a global scale *and* the new cultural forms, events, and movements that have appeared in the last decade of the twentieth century and the beginning of the twenty-first. Our attempt to make sense of the complexities of a mass culture that has become globalized seems to be arrested in the discourse of cultural imperialism. Attempts to understand the political and cultural significance of the coalitions of groups that make up the anti-globalization movement also seem to be confined by the terms of older discourses that don't properly describe them. Policy-makers appear particularly out of step with historical developments. Through its involvement in the International Network on Cultural Policy (whose aim is "to facilitate dialogue on issues related to cultural diversity in the context of globalization, and suggest leads for solutions") and other similar organizations, the Canadian government has been leading the attempt to re-establish strong national cultures in the context of globalization. That national culture is by its nature an exclusionary idea seems to have escaped the forty-five governments involved in this quixotic task, as has the real source of their discontent: a mass culture that is identified confusingly with American national culture alone.

SUMMARY

In this chapter we have attempted to analyze the contemporary phenomenon of globalization in a way that acknowledges its material significance while challenging some prevailing myths about its effect on popular culture. Some of the principal ideas advanced in this chapter are that:

- Globalization is a multi-faceted process involving interdependent economic, political, technological, and cultural dimensions. It is characterized most clearly by the image of a "shrinking" globe in which social relations are less and less restricted by geography.
- Though the changes associated with globalization—the expansion of global trade, revolutions in communication technology, the unprecedented movement of people—are seen as, and in some ways are, unique to the present moment, globalization can be understood only as part of an ongoing historical process.
- Globalization is often associated with the severing of identity and community from place, and with the weakening of the concept of the nation-state. However, the extent and the nature of globalization's effects remain strongly determined by local material circumstances as well as by culture and class. In some cases, the pressures of globalization have led to a strengthening rather than a weakening of nationalism.
- In opposition to the rosy picture painted by many CEOs, politicians, and cyberculture enthusiasts, a growing number of critics offer a darker view of globalization, articulated particularly around fears of cultural imperialism. The reality of globalization's cultural impact is more complex than either of these views would suggest. While it poses a threat to cultural diversity, globalization also opens up new cultural possibilities, ultimately demanding a fundamental reconceptualization of what culture is and why it matters.

SUGGESTIONS FOR FURTHER READING

Appadurai, Arjun, ed. *Modernity at Large: Cultural Dimensions of Globalization.* Minneapolis: University of Minnesota Press, 1996.

Barlow, Maude, and Tony Clarke. *Global Showdown.* Toronto: Stoddart, 2001.

Bauman, Zygmunt. *Globalization: The Human Consequences.* New York: Columbia University Press, 1998.

Giddens, Anthony. *Runaway World: How Globalization Is Reshaping Our Lives.* New York: Routledge, 2000.

Gray, John. *False Dawn: The Delusions of Global Capitalism.* New York: New Press, 1999.

Hardt, Michael, and Antonio Negri. *Empire.* Cambridge, MA: Harvard University Press, 2000.

Held, David, Anthony McGrew, David Goldblatt, and Jonathan Perraton. *Global Transformations: Politics, Economics and Culture.* Stanford: Stanford University Press, 1999.

Jameson, Fredric, and Masao Miyoshi, eds., *The Cultures of Globalization.* Durham, NC: Duke University Press, 1998.

Klein, Naomi. *No Logo.* New York: Picador, 2000.

Robertson, Roland. *Globalization: Social Theory and Global Culture.* London: Sage, 1992.

Scholte, Jan Aart. *Globalization: A Critical Introduction.* Basingstoke, UK: Macmillan, 2000.

Zemans, Joyce. "Canadian Cultural Policy in a Globalized World." *Canadian Review of American Studies 27*.3 (1997): 111–25. ch 1997.

Chapter 10

Why Study Popular Culture? A Brief History of Cultural Studies

INTRODUCTION: WHY THIS? WHY NOW? WHY ME?

Every year, a couple of reports appear in the media about some new and outrageous course that has made it onto the curriculum of some university or college. In the Eighties it was a sprinkling of courses on Madonna and feminism; now they are more likely to be on reality TV or the J.Lo phenomenon. Less remarkable than the appearance of these courses is the fact that they still raise eyebrows. Only a few decades ago, the idea of a course on popular culture in general would have been unthinkable—the equivalent of bringing a case of beer into class and asking students to contemplate the meaning of drinking in their lives while tossing back a few. The fact that popular culture is more or less comfortably entrenched in the halls of higher learning while some aspects of it—certain celebrities, particular practices—are still excluded raises questions that are relevant for our discussion in this book: What counts as worthwhile knowledge in our culture? What is the relationship between popular culture and education? How has this relationship changed? Why has it changed? This chapter attempts to answer these questions by outlining a brief history of cultural studies (see Close-Up 10.1). In the process it will, we hope, also lead you to think about why you're studying popular culture, and what it means in terms of the larger process of your "higher" education.

The focus of this book so far has been on giving you a set of tools that will help you in a practical way to make sense of your experience as a consumer, creator, or "user" of popular culture. Here we take a step back to look at some of the theory behind the methods. This chapter offers a bridge to the more advanced study of popular culture: it is also an important complement to the skills you have learned in this book. One of the

Cultural Studies

Looser in its parameters than conventional disciplines such as psychology or history, cultural studies is, as one practitioner puts it, "a term of convenience for a fairly dispersed array of theoretical and political positions which, however widely divergent they might be in other respects, share a commitment to examining cultural practices from the point of view of their intrication with, and within, relations of power" (Bennett 33). It embraces a definition of culture that includes—in addition to conventional "texts" such as books—television shows, music and advertising, and ways of life (in the sense of concrete practices such as shopping, eating, drinking, fashion, etc.), as well as more abstract structures such as language, beliefs, "the contradictory forms of 'common sense' which have taken root in and helped to shape popular life," and the institutions that surround them (Hall "Gramsci" 26).

This broad definition of culture obviously contains a complex mix of elements—social, linguistic, political, economic; indeed, the study of popular culture might be described in one sense as the study of the interrelationships among what were once seen as discrete fields of existence. As such, cultural studies embraces a number of different disciplines, including literary studies, film studies, political science, anthropology, sociology, and communications studies, and employs a variety of methodologies: close reading, ethnography, content analysis, population surveys, and historical research.

fascinating but tricky things about studying culture is the recognition that we can never actually get outside the thing we're looking at to get an objective picture. For that reason self-consciousness, or a constant awareness of the knowledges, beliefs, and experiences we bring to bear on our study, is a mandatory element of cultural studies. We are offering this brief history of cultural studies, then, not to trace an evolution of ideas toward a *truer* contemporary perspective; if anything, we want to highlight the impossibility of arriving at a "true" perspective on popular culture given the embeddedness of our vision in the subject we're studying. That is to say that cultural studies is a product of a particular history—it is itself **ideological**.

POPULAR CULTURE INVADES THE CLASSROOM

In our survey of the development of popular culture in Chapter Two, we talked about the development in the mid to late nineteenth century of a distinction between high, or capital-C Culture and popular culture. Among the engineers of this divide were the rational recreationists—religious and charitable groups bent on "improving" the lower classes—and education experts like Matthew Arnold, who saw in "culture" a way to knit society together and soften the edges of the materialism infecting, in different ways, the middle and lower classes. Strangely, it was from this clearly hostile move against popular culture that the impulse to understand it—an impulse that informs this book—was first born.

Sneaking in Through the Back Door

Matthew Arnold and his followers saw mass media (understood in the form of such things as popular novels) as leading to social disintegration, through the replacement of spiritual with commercial values. They were particularly concerned with what they saw as the crass materialism of the new middle class and the degeneration of working-class morals. Behind this critique lay a powerful resistance to industrialization and nostalgia for an organic agrarian society in which people knew one another (and, not incidentally, knew their own place). As people moved away from the supporting structures of church and community into the alienating and anonymous environment of the city, it was argued, they became vulnerable to all sorts of corrupting influences. Implicit in this position is a view of the masses as childlike in their ability to be easily led. The problem, as cultural conservatives saw it, was that they were being led by the wrong forces. The beneficial influences of the classic works of Culture, which discouraged the pursuits of materialism by offering more spiritual forms of sustenance, were being replaced by commodities that, in their form (cheap paperback novels, pop songs played on the gramophone) as in their content, seemed to celebrate values of easy pleasure and instant gratification.

These critiques grew throughout the early decades of the twentieth century, as new cultural technologies and modes of production facilitated easier distribution of forms of popular culture such as fiction, movies, music, and eventually TV. Recognizing that it was impossible to shield impressionable minds from this trash, early twentieth-century educators like F.R. and Q.D. Leavis suggested that schools should focus on training students' tastes, to help them discriminate between true culture and its "multitudinous counter-influences—films, newspapers, advertising—indeed the whole world outside the classroom" (Leavis and Thompson 1). Such discrimination, they argued, was essential to the development of a sensitive moral character.

The course of study they proposed featured such inspiring study questions as "'Modern Publicity debases the currency of spiritual and emotional life generally': Discuss and illustrate." Another question lists a number of popular media clichés, such as "clean-cut executive type," "good mixer," "short-haired executive," "'regular guy' (Americanism)," and asks "Why do we wince at the mentality that uses this idiom?" (121). The target of these "discussion" questions (which don't leave a whole lot of room for discussion!) is both the products of popular media culture and the ignorant masses who consume them. Education in taste, then, is, as Pierre Bourdieu was later to point out (see Chapter Five), an education in class discrimination. That many of the students

Why Study Popular Culture? A Brief History of Cultural Studies **297** themselves came from the class they were now being taught to despise was something not taken up by the Leavises or other educators of the time.

In the Leavises' educational program, popular culture made it onto the curriculum as an example of a social problem—like alcohol, say, or bad hygiene—that could, with the proper techniques of discipline and avoidance, be successfully banished. In a way, though, these efforts were defeated by their own intentions: bringing popular culture into the classroom both acknowledged and promoted its legitimacy as a powerful social force.

The Democratization of Culture

The Leavises' approach to culture was unashamedly elitist. F.R. Leavis's 1930 work *Mass Civilization and Minority Culture* painted a picture of a society clearly divided, in which the cultured minority on the inside, the world of "*us*," fought valiantly to preserve itself from the degenerate civilization on the outside—the world of "them." These certainties began to break down after the Second World War, when an increasingly diverse university student body started to challenge the boundary between "us" and "them." Most significant was the arrival of a large number of working-class students. Many of these were adults who, because of the war or for economic reasons, had deferred their education. They brought along with them a whole raft of knowledge and experiences that did not conform to elite conceptions of Culture.

Williams, Hoggart, and Thompson   From this group, three figures emerged as particularly influential in the development of the more inclusive vision of "culture" that would come to define cultural studies. Raymond Williams and Richard Hoggart, scholars of English literature, and E.P. Thompson, a historian, all began their university careers as scholarship students from working-class backgrounds. Williams and Hoggart's later experiences working as adult-education tutors confirmed their sense that the prevailing scholarly understanding of culture was far too narrow and exclusive to encompass the rich and complex fabric of their students' lives.

While the work of these three theorists is characterized by important differences of disciplinary perspective, approach, and argument, some of the central general implications of their work can be summarized here. First, all three established the legitimacy of working-class life as a subject of academic study, expanding the prevailing definition not just of culture but also of history to include experiences traditionally dismissed as insignificant. In the process, they also refined the definition of culture, moving away from "a literary-moral" to a more anthropological understanding of it as "the 'whole process' by means of which meanings and definitions are socially constructed and historically transformed." In this new definition, "literature and art count as only one, specially privileged, kind of social communication" (Williams qtd. in Hall "Cultural Studies and the Centre" 19).

For Hoggart and Williams in particular, literature and art retained their significance as embodiments of important human values. Part of their projects recalled the efforts of Leavis in their determination to expose students to classic works of literature in order to enhance their literacy and, by extension, their understanding of the broader cultural contexts that shaped their lives. They all shared, to a certain extent, Leavis's elitist disdain for the products of the culture industry, enhanced by nostalgia for an earlier, more innocent (and partly imaginary) time, when culture had yet to be totally corrupted by commerce. Hoggart and Williams extended Leavis's focus, however, in their extension of the principles of literary criticism, especially the techniques of close reading, to a wide range of popular texts—songs, magazines, newspapers—and in their emphasis on the connections between these texts and other aspects of everyday life: leisure activities, family relationships, gender roles, and so on. They also differ from Leavis in the crucial respect that, while Leavis wanted to preserve the terrain of minority culture against the threat of "mass" civilization, they sought to enhance democracy by understanding the substance of ordinary people's lives.

One important area of conflict between, and even within, the works of these theorists concerns the relationship between the individual and broader institutional and social structures. While histories "from below" such as Thompson's tried not only to foreground working-class experience but also to highlight the *agency* of working-class people in shaping their own lives, his work was also characterized by a recognition of the way agency is shaped and constrained by broader economic and cultural conditions. Debates about the relative power of individuals and the structures that constrain them became increasingly urgent in the context of a rapidly expanding culture industry.

These debates shaped the 1960 National Union of Teachers (NUT) conference, titled "Popular Culture and Responsibility," which marked the recognition by British teachers of an increasing gap between the high culture they sought to cultivate in their students and the commercial culture those students were consuming. Rather than issuing a blanket condemnation of media culture, however, the majority of the participants in the conference agreed that it needed to be understood not as a degraded form of high culture, but as a different kind of expression that had to be approached on its own terms. While their efforts to rescue "serious" popular culture from the "pre-digested" **mass culture** of Hollywood still bore traces of Leavisite elitism, the conference marked a growing willingness to extend the boundaries of what counted (and what was worth studying) as "culture." It was also a recognition that the hierarchy of value that distinguished high from low culture was informed as much by **ideology** as by anything inherent to the cultural forms themselves. The establishment of the new Centre for Contemporary Cultural Studies at the University of Birmingham in 1964 (headed by Richard Hoggart) began to apply these insights to the study of media and youth subcultures—a diversity of subjects that marked the ambiguity of popular culture as defined simultaneously from above and below.

THE AMERICANIZATION OF POPULAR CULTURE

The changes that were occurring in Britain in the years following the Second World War were part of broader, global upheavals. One significant change resulted from Britain's shift from a dominant to a subordinate political and economic power in relation to the

United States as the new leader of the "free" (i.e., non-communist) world. Combined with the position of media dominance that the U.S. had occupied since the early twentieth century (see Chapter Two), the new configuration of global power meant that, from the 1950s onward, global popular culture increasingly had an American face.

The reaction amongst British cultural critics was, predictably, mixed. In the 1950s, art critics working at the Institute of Contemporary Arts (ICA) established a working group to study contemporary trends in architecture, visual culture, and other forms of popular art. They were particularly interested in—and, generally, excited by—the growing influence of American popular culture on British culture. Their approach was different from most of the other critical responses to the culture industry, which were just that: critical. In the U.S. itself, serious interest in popular culture was motivated by an unlikely source: the Cold War. The contest between communism and capitalism spurred a push in American universities to study, and thereby promote, the liberal democratic values that represented the American way of life. American studies programs sprang up that were at first mostly committed to the teaching of American "high" culture—literature and art, along with the triumphant narrative of American history.

Soon these programs began to acknowledge the importance of the media in communicating democratic values through popular culture. The tendency to view the new media culture in a celebratory mode, as the embodiment of America's democratic spirit (as opposed to the culture of censorship and repression that was seen to exist in Russia), competed with concerns about the capacity of the commercial media to lure audiences into habits of unthinking consumerism. Concerns about subliminal advertising (e.g., ads that implanted ideas into the subconscious—by incorporating a shadowy image of a naked women into a glass of soda, for instance) played a large part in the move to incorporate media studies into university curricula.

While worries about the capacity of the media to weaken society's moral fibre by bombarding it with images promoting sex and shopping preoccupied many American educators, the explicit *American*-ness of the media also concerned many critics outside the United States. This vaguely defined quality was seen to shape not just the content of a popular culture that promoted values of liberalism, individualism, and consumerism, but also the way it was produced and distributed. Improvement in communications technology, in conjunction with American economic and cultural expansionism, granted the products of the American culture industry unprecedented access to the rest of the world, a development that spawned fears about cultural imperialism (see Chapter Nine) as well as the growth of critical media studies in Britain and elsewhere. The presence of an extremely powerful, linguistically identical culture on its southern border also led to the development of a unique form of communications theory in Canada. Major early figures in the establishment of both communications studies and Canadian studies, such as Harold Innis and Marshall McLuhan, have paved the way for a wide range of contemporary work in cultural studies in Canada by scholars such as Jody Berland, Will Straw, and Arthur Kroker.

THE DECOLONIZATION OF CULTURE

Challenges to the comfortable dominance of the model of British Culture advanced by Matthew Arnold and the Leavises came not just from a shift in power away from Britain toward the United States, but also from more widely dispersed challenges to the world order associated with decolonization (see Chapter Seven). The challenge was not only from the renaissance of other traditions, such as the African and South Asian cultures that had been submerged during the colonial period, but also the necessity—highlighted by anti-colonial activists such as Mohandas Gandhi and Frantz Fanon—for European culture to confront the contradictions that lay at the heart of its cherished ideals of freedom and progress. Around the same time, women's and labour groups, along with the Civil Rights movement in the United States, had begun to highlight the faultlines of race and gender that defined the supposedly universal norms and values of liberal democracy.

What's an Education For?

In addition to their broad consequences for society as a whole, these social justice movements, which came to a head in the massive protests launched in the U.S. and France in 1968, had an enormous impact on higher education. Among the strongest participants in the protests, which included anti-colonial and labour rights activists, were students calling for changes inside and outside their universities. Underpinning their demand for a greater role in determining the shape of their education was a sense of anger about the detachment of the world inside the university from what was going on outside it: lectures celebrating the values of freedom, civilization, and the dignity of man did not accord with the realities of violent conflict such as the Vietnam War, human rights abuses, and environmental destruction. If academic institutions were to serve any useful role in advancing human understanding they needed to acknowledge the bankruptcy of many of their foundational principles.

The crisis of higher education sparked by the social movements of the 1960s had an intellectual as well as an institutional dimension; indeed, it highlighted the connection between those dimensions by revealing the ways in which privileged forms of knowledge were bound up with structures of power. This is one of the key insights of the cultural moment known as postmodernism (see Close-Up 6.1), which brought about what one theorist described as a "crisis of legitimation" (Lyotard): once the most fundamental beliefs of Western culture are shown to be the product not of timeless truth but of particular social arrangements, they and the structures of authority that uphold them crumble, taking with them the possibility of *any* universal, objective truth.

Feminism and Cultural Studies

Feminism played a particularly significant role in challenging not just the prevailing social order, but also the new discipline of cultural studies. In 1978, the Women's Study

Group at the Birmingham Centre for Contemporary Cultural Studies published a collection of essays called *Women Take Issue*. In it, they challenged the strongly masculine bias that had characterized the field of cultural studies from the time of the "forefathers" Hoggart, Williams, and Thompson. They pointed out that Williams' account of popular culture as a "whole way of life" did not acknowledge tensions between dominant and subordinate cultures. In particular, it completely ignored the one sphere of life that women inhabited most fully, if not necessarily by choice: the sphere of home and family.

Beginning with the Women's Study Group, a succession of feminist critics throughout the Seventies and Eighties radically challenged the mythologies that had unconsciously underpinned the study of culture at the Birmingham Centre and elsewhere. In particular, they noted that the categories through which cultural theorists looked at life in capitalist society—"production/consumption; work/leisure; work/personal life; work/everyday life"—represented a split "which operates for *men* but which is dependent on women's patriarchal subordination—their confinement to family, home, personal and everyday life" (Winship 136–37). One of the biggest myths of cultural studies, they pointed out, was its assumption of a binary opposition between production and consumption, in which production was essentially seen as *good*, associated with masculine strength and creative energy, and consumption as *bad*, associated with feminine weakness and passive self-indulgence. In a cultural context in which women were largely barred from the workforce (housework and childcare didn't count as work), their roles couldn't be comfortably accommodated within the categories of production and consumption; in fact, in addition to their work as (re)producers and consumers, women had also traditionally functioned as commodities, or objects of exchange. In order to speak to the experiences of women as well as men, the new field of cultural studies needed to be significantly reconfigured to take account of these conflicted identities and relationships.

Even though cultural studies might have seemed in some ways hostile, or at least indifferent, to women's experience, in other ways it offered an ideal arena for discussing issues of concern to women. Three key aspects of cultural studies fit particularly well with the principles of feminist criticism: an insistence on the relationship between culture and economics, a concern with the importance of ideology in shaping consciousness, and a rejection of a firm line between the political and the personal—or, in the case of academic work, between objective knowledge and subjective experience. Finally, the determination of cultural studies scholars to investigate not just high or capital-C Culture, but also those practices and texts that lurked in its shadows—mass media, subcultures, the practices of everyday life—echoed feminists' commitment to making visible the unacknowledged cultural lives of women. In cultural studies, Sue Thornham suggests, the primarily *political* movement of feminism found a theoretical vocabulary as well as an "academic and institutional context" that, for all the limitations noted by its early female occupants, provided a place where "feminist research could explore all the complexities of women's positioning in culture" (8).

Culture Wars

The somewhat grandiose term "culture wars" refers to fights that took place in humanities departments of American universities in the 1980s—fights that spilled over into the arenas of media and public policy—between a traditional idea of Culture, in Matthew Arnold's sense of "the best that has been thought and said," and the forces of postcolonialism, feminism, and postmodernism that sought to undermine it. While the move was sometimes characterized as a campaign to simply replace the Western canon—the preserve of Dead White Males—with a new and eclectic selection of texts, from works by women of colour to Hollywood films, what was actually at issue was not so much the works themselves but the structures of authority that sanctioned some forms of culture while dismissing others.

One important challenge to those structures was a shift in emphasis from "Culture" to "cultures"—a rhetorical shift that expressed more substantial changes in focus. First, and most generally, it marked a move away from the humanities/literary critical definition of culture toward a more anthropological one (see Chapter One). This entailed both an extension of the term from its traditional focus on works of art to embrace the practices of everyday life and a recognition of the existence of multiple cultures, existing within and between societies. The idea of culture was thus transformed from something timeless and universal to a historically determined, and thus constantly changing, phenomenon with local and global dimensions. The myth of a unified *English* culture, which frequently lurked behind the "universal" label, disintegrated in the face of the recognition of the many *sub*cultures—youth culture, for example, or gay culture—on whose exclusion it was based. At the same time, the invisible lines of race (white) and gender (male) that marked traditional definitions of culture—including the more inclusivist, working-class definitions proposed by Williams and Hoggart—began to emerge through the pointed critiques of women and minorities, who had been stuck somewhere on its margins.

The opening-out of the idea of culture in response to the claims of its excluded others occurred in conjunction with the arrival in Britain and North America of successive waves of immigrants from the former colonies, including many who ended up working and studying in universities. Some, like the Jamaican-born Stuart Hall, who succeeded Richard Hoggart as director of the Birmingham Centre for Contemporary Cultural Studies, helped to define new directions in cultural studies by, among other things, giving the discipline international focus and by insisting on the necessary connectedness between intellectual work and politics.

Who won the culture wars, then? The persistence of English undergraduate programs that still require majors to take a course in Shakespeare suggests that the ideological magic of "Culture" has not entirely been exorcised. However, the enormous growth in cultural studies programs would seem to suggest that history is on the side of the culture critics. This might look like a victory for feminism and postcolonialism against conservatism—but, as should be clear by now, the relationship between culture and power is never that simple.

CULTURE AND ECONOMICS—THE POSTINDUSTRIAL REVOLUTION

As in the late eighteenth and nineteenth centuries, the social and political upheavals that marked the late twentieth century were accompanied by economic and technological changes. The growth in communications technology, and the development of a "post-industrial" economy—characterized by trade liberalization and more flexible structures of production and distribution, along with the increasing commercialization of communications itself through the entertainment and information technology industries—has made culture today a very different thing than it was a hundred or even thirty years ago. Just as industrialization brought about not just huge gains in economic productivity but also new kinds of social mobility, the new economy played a large part in facilitating the global cultural movements discussed above. As with the Industrial Revolution, the weakening of old regulations in conjunction with the decline in traditional structures of authority created new freedoms. However, they also eroded structures that had served not only to suppress the development of diverse forms of popular culture but also to nurture them.

The extension and intensification of market forces, while granting greater powers to private interests, weakened the imaginary and actual power of public institutions. The university, one of the key sites for the distribution of what Pierre Bourdieu calls *cultural capital*, is affected particularly strongly by these shifts, in terms not just of the way its resources are allocated, but also of the role it is seen to play in society. While that role was traditionally conceived as one of nurturing future citizens—a goal facilitated by ensuring students had a solid grounding in the humanities, English (or American) literature in particular—the idea of university is now more likely to conform to the much less romantic vision of a factory for the production of workers in the global knowledge economy. Students, according to this model, are seen not as junior members of an academic community to which they are bound by an idealized commitment to learning or becoming "cultured," but as consumers—and, ultimately, products—to be bought up by the corporations that play an increasing role in funding, and thereby shaping, the universities' basic operations.

According to the essentially commercial logic of this model of education, resources cannot be wasted on those departments or faculties that are concerned with abstract values like citizenship or critical thought. These departments—English, for example, or philosophy—are forced to rationalize their budgets, and to modify their course offerings to favour those that can be taught by a few faculty members to large numbers of students from a variety of different disciplines. Here, then, is one institutional explanation for why courses in popular culture are quietly popping up alongside (and sometimes in place of) more traditional courses in subjects like, say, medieval history: they're popular in the same commercial sense that *Baywatch* is popular, which is to say they are profitable.

This poses a challenge for cultural studies scholars, whose aim, as we have suggested throughout this book, is not simply to affirm the value of commercial culture, nor—equally simply—to denounce it, but to map its place within a constellation of signifying practices that correspond to underlying relations of power. That constellation is constantly shifting, which means that we need to remain constantly alert to the social and political significance of *all* our cultural roles, including the roles of students and teachers of popular culture. Why—personally, institutionally—are we doing what we are doing? What other subjects *might* we be studying if we were not studying popular culture? What are the educational implications of the growing popularity of popular culture courses?

A COUPLE OF FINAL ARGUMENTS FOR THE IMPORTANCE OF STUDYING POPULAR CULTURE

To sum up the last few sections: There are lots of reasons why you are reading a textbook on popular culture instead of Chaucer's *Canterbury Tales*. First and foremost are the political and social changes that, over the course of the last century, have demanded a radical rethinking of the intellectual foundations of "culture" and its connection to other areas of life. These changes have shaped society in general and education in particular. On a more pragmatic level, schools, colleges, and universities have changed their curricula in response to economic pressures so that what is considered valuable in educational terms is increasingly determined by what is profitable. Those are large, impersonal, and, in the latter case, cynical reasons for why popular culture is suddenly a popular thing to study.

We would also encourage you to think about it in more personal terms. One compelling reason to study popular culture, mentioned in Chapter One, is that it is everywhere. To borrow an expression from T.S. Eliot, if most academic study is about helping to make the strange familiar, studying popular culture is a process of making the familiar strange. This can be a pretty uncomfortable experience, since it involves taking what feels most natural and pleasurable and subjecting it to detached inquiry. Actually *studying* popular culture helps us to move beyond a range of typical reactions to it: a) unconscious consumption (which is of course a theoretical position, since most consumers have achieved some level of critical consciousness); b) contemptuous dismissal—"popular culture is trash, so I avoid it" (an equally mythical position, since it is virtually impossible to live entirely outside commercial culture); and c) cynical consumption ("I *know* this is garbage, but I like it anyway"—or, stranger, "I like this *because* I know it is garbage"). Most of us probably respond to culture in a way that is something like position c. A variation on this position is the belief that, while other people are vulnerable to the messages of popular culture, *we* are smart enough to see through its manipulations.

Studying popular culture, while it might seem to make this position appear even more valid, usually leads to a different conclusion, revealing the culture industry to be both less and more powerful than we initially imagined. Cultural studies unmasks and to a certain extent disables the power of commercial culture, by helping us to recognize the narratives, genres, myths, and discourses through which its meanings are encoded— meanings that tap into fundamental beliefs about ourselves, our relationships with others, and society at large.

But, as cultural studies also emphasizes, culture is not just about texts, about how the products of the commercial media are put together, and how certain meanings are produced, but also about how we consume those products, what we actually *do* with them. The title of this book, *Popular Culture: A User's Guide*, reflects our belief that not only is it possible for all of us to learn to *use* popular culture more effectively, in the sense of actually shaping it in productive ways, but also that it is vitally important we do so. As Stuart Hall puts it, "there is something *at stake* in Cultural Studies, in a way that I think, and hope, is not exactly true of many other very important intellectual and critical practices" (Hall "Theoretical Legacies" 278).

Many cultural studies practitioners go further, stressing a key connection between doing cultural studies and engaging in political activism—as distinct from other kinds of study, which stress mere "technocratic competence" (Freccero 5). The study of popular culture is necessarily political, in the sense of being concerned with the distribution of social and economic power in society. It's important to recognize, however—in spite of the prescriptivist tone of what we've just said about why you *should* want to do cultural studies—that each of us approaches the study of culture in different ways, and that students and teachers of popular culture are often situated quite differently in relation to the subject, based on factors such as age, class, experience, and temperament. For students, what often proves most illuminating (or, for some, simply irritating) about taking a course in cultural studies is its revelation of the connection between popular culture and power. For teachers, one of the insights that proves most strangely elusive—one that they often need to be reminded of by students—is that popular culture is about pleasure. Figuring out what happens at the intersection of those forces of power and pleasure is perhaps the principal value of studying popular culture.

SUMMARY

This chapter, which functions as a kind of conclusion and postscript to discussions in the earlier chapters, takes a step back from the practical analysis of culture to look at cultural studies in more theoretical and historical terms. Some of the critical ideas/questions you should take away with you are that:

- Cultural studies, broadly defined as a collection of approaches to the analysis of culture, looks at a range of practices, texts, and ideas in the context of broader structures of power and social relations.
- A basic premise of cultural studies is the assumption that the student is embedded in the subject s/he is studying. Cultural studies therefore resists the subjective/objective binary that characterizes many academic disciplines in favour of an emphasis on critical self-consciousness.
- Initially rooted in the determination of conservative critics' determination to root *out* popular culture from educated minds, cultural studies flourished in the twentieth

century along with the democratization of higher education and the work of broad political movements such as anti-colonialism, civil rights, and feminism.

- Challenged by the "culture wars" of the 1980s, popular culture still occupies a politically precarious place in the classroom, raising questions that extend beyond its particular significance as a subject of worthwhile knowledge to the whole meaning and purpose of "higher" education.

- Perhaps more than any other subject, cultural studies asks students to examine their own practices, pleasures, experiences, and beliefs in light of broader social structures.

What have you learned from reading this book? How might it change the way you consume and construct the popular culture you inhabit?

SUGGESTIONS FOR FURTHER READING

During, Simon. *The Cultural Studies Reader.* London: Routledge, 1999.

Fiske, John. *Understanding Popular Culture.* London: Routledge, 1989.

Freccero, Carla. *Popular Culture: An Introduction.* New York: New York University Press, 1999.

Grossberg, Lawrence, Cary Nelson, and Paula Treichler. *Cultural Studies.* London: Routledge, 1992.

McRobbie, Angela. *Postmodernism and Popular Culture.* London: Routledge, 1994.

Naremore, James, and Patrick Brantlinger, ed. *Modernity and Mass Culture.* Bloomington, IN: Indiana University Press, 1991.

Niedzviecki, Hal. *We Want Some Too: Underground Desire and the Reinvention of Mass Culture.* Toronto: Penguin, 2000.

O'Sullivan, Tim, John Hartley, Danny Saunders, Martin Montgomery, and John Fiske. *Key Concepts in Communication and Cultural Studies.* London: Routledge, 1994.

Thornham, Sue. *Feminist Theory and Cultural Studies: Stories of Unsettled Relations.* London: Arnold, 2000.

Glossary

Compiled by Carolyn Veldstra and Tim Walters

Agency: The ability of individuals to act as self-conscious, willful social actors, and to exert their will through involvement in social practices, relationships, and decision-making.

Appropriation: The process by which often innovative or resistant cultural forms are taken up, incorporated, and commodified by the culture industry. One of the most frequently cited examples is that of punk, which, though it developed as a dissident movement in working-class England, was quickly marketed by major fashion designers, music labels, and other producers of mass youth culture. In analysis of popular cultural forms, appropriation is often viewed pessimistically as evidence of the power of late capitalism to absorb dissent into itself and turn it around for a profit; however, it is important to remember that resistance continues to circulate and change in form, even as its products are co-opted by a dominant culture.

Assimilation: Also known as *acculturation*, this term refers to the sometimes forced integration of an immigrant or subordinate group into the perceived "dominant" culture of the host community through the absorption of the host's cultural practices and history. This stands in opposition to the idea of **multiculturalism**, which suggests that different groups can co-exist on an equal basis.

Authenticity: A positive quality of genuineness and originality attributed to objects, practices, or ideas, often in order to demonstrate the extent to which an initially authentic phenomenon has been compromised or drained of its value. The notion of authenticity has been critiqued for its **ideological** grounding in a nostalgic vision of a more "real" cultural past now sullied by rank commercialism.

Binary Opposition: An analytical system that uses specific examples of symmetrically opposed pairs, or mirror opposites, which, although mutually exclusive, generate meaning through their difference and describe a complete, if extreme, system of understanding. For example: "us:them"—in forming group identities, people are categorized either as part of the group ("us"), or outside of it ("them"). Binary oppositions can be dangerous in that they work to repress the ambiguities that exist between the two terms by positioning the binary as natural and any other forms of identification as deviant. In addition, binary terms often carry a positive:negative value assumption; for example, "we" are "safe, good, blameless," while "they" are "dangerous, bad, evil."

Branding: A recent phenomenon in economics wherein a company shifts its resources from producing goods or services to producing a corporate image defined by abstract emotional or spiritual qualities. Critics of this process have suggested that the reallocation of resources and the marketing strategies it entails contributes to trends such as the rise of child and sweatshop labour in developing nations, a decline in the number and quality of available jobs, and a disturbing new invasiveness on the part of corporations into our lives and minds.

Capitalism: See Close-Up 1.1 on page 10.

Cold War: A phrase that popularly refers to the tense, hostile relationship between the communist (U.S.S.R.) and capitalist (U.S.) superpowers and their respective allies from the end of the Second World War until the collapse of the Berlin Wall in 1989. Although marked by bitter animosities fuelled by ideological differences, a similarly voracious desire for world domination, and numerous moments of near-disastrous military escalation (for instance, the Cuban Missile Crisis), the Cold War was known as such because it was fought largely by diplomatic and economic means rather than by sustained and overt acts of aggression. Though the Cold War spawned numerous proxy wars in Third World countries, the U.S.S.R. and the United States never came to blows directly.

Colonialism: The historical process through which dominant groups have assimilated, dominated, and subjugated less powerful ones. Distinct from **imperialism**, which can also be used to describe non-territorial kinds of control, colonialism involves physical settlement along with the military, political, and economic conquest of a people.

Commodification: Rendering any artifact, action, object, or idea into something that can be bought or sold. Popular culture is often maligned for its commodification of formerly more **authentic** cultural forms, with the assumption that through commodification things lose their implicit value.

Commodities: Objects and services produced for consumption or exchange by someone other than their producers. Although humans have always exchanged the goods that they produced for other goods, in the nineteenth century a new focus on the consumption of an increasingly diverse array of commodities by greater numbers of consumers was partly responsible for the gradual shift to a consumer culture. Marx employed the term **commodity fetishism** to describe the almost magical value attributed to objects in a capitalist economy—value derived not from how they are used or the labour that produced them, but from the price they command on the market. The most significant, and most damaging, aspect of commodity culture from a Marxist perspective is its tendency to attribute value to things and the relations between them rather than to people and human relationships.

Commodity Fetishism: See **Commodities**.

Conspicuous Consumption: A pattern of behaviour, initially observed by Thorstein Veblen, that began in the nineteenth century as a result of increased incomes and leisure time along with the growth of marketing. "Wasted" consumption (that which exceeds what is strictly necessary for life) began to be *used* by members of different classes in a way that was "conspicuous"—obvious, noticeable, visible—in order to signal or symbolize social distinction.

Consumerism: The name for the complex set of dominant values and practices produced by and arising from life in a consumer society: a historically unique form of society in which consumption plays an important, if not central role. Central to consumerism is the (generally implicit) belief that the organization of life around the purchase of commodities is the optimal way to address the needs and wants of individuals, and even to allocate social goods.

Consumption: See **Conspicuous Consumption.**

Copyright: See **Intellectual Property.**

Counterculture: Groups that express antagonism toward the existing social and political order, and propose alternative ways of organizing society. The term counterculture is most commonly used to refer collectively to the alternative politics expressed by a variety of groups in the 1960s (feminists, civil rights and anti-war activists, etc.). More generally, "the" counterculture describes all those groups that challenge and contradict the "common sense" of everyday life with the aim of creating a better society.

Cultural Imperialism: A term describing the ideological infiltration of the cultural products of dominant nations (typically, the United States) into less globally powerful ones, at the expense of some aspects of indigenous culture. Globalization theorists have cast some doubt on the concept of cultural imperialism, pointing to its problematic assumption of a passive, colonized global audience, as well as its simplistic reading of actual processes of global production and consumption.

Cultural Relativism: The acceptance of difference across a range of cultural activities, with the understanding that different cultures, individuals, and groups hold different values, all of which are of equal merit. This idea often works together with a postmodern refusal to accept fixed meanings or explanations and opposes **essentialist** assumptions about culture, race, gender, and so on.

Cultural Studies: See Close-Up 10.1 on page 296.

Culture: Culture has been described by critic Raymond Williams as "one of the two or three most complicated words in the English language." The term has a wide and diverse range of meanings and associations that cannot easily be reduced to a single definition. In contemporary usage, the term carries three main significations: (1) a description of a whole way of social life (as in the idea that humanity is comprised of numerous, distinct cultures); (2) the name for "serious" works of literature, music, fine arts, film, and so on, and the activities involved in producing these kinds of works; and, finally, (3) as an extension of the latter definition, culture can be used to refer to a wide range of signifying and symbolic works and activities, whether these involve everyday social practices (e.g., **folk culture**) or the objects and practices of popular culture (e.g., detective novels as well as serious literature, television as well as film, etc.).

Deconstruction: A method of analysis initially articulated in the work of Jacques Derrida which involves exposing the submerged philosophical assumptions that underpin texts and concepts. Derrida asserted that all Western thought is founded upon countless sets of **binary oppositions** (black and white, speech and writing, man and woman, etc.) wherein one term is invariably considered to be superior to its "opposite," a valuation with vast cultural consequences. Deconstructionist readings attempt to discover how such unarticulated ideologies underpin seemingly straightforward surface meanings.

Diaspora: From the Greek word for "to disperse," diaspora refers to the voluntary or forced migration of peoples from their homelands to new regions. In areas that are greatly affected by large diasporic movements (i.e., in the West Indies via colonization and the slave trade) distinct, or creolized, cultures have developed, which blend indigenous with homeland cultures. These unique diasporic cultures challenge **essentialist** models of culture or the **nation**.

Digitalization: The translation of any kind of data (text, images, sounds, etc.) into an electronic language that can be used by a computer or other digital system for purposes of storage, distribution, or manipulation. Depending on one's perspective, digitalization is either an empowering tool with which to create and share diverse forms of information more democratically, or a practice that threatens more authentic (or "real") forms of cultural production and challenges **copyright** protection laws. Because it offers unprecedented possibilities for the manipulation of sounds and images, digitalization also raises important issues for practices of **representation.**

Discourse: A concept articulated by Michel Foucault to describe the way speech and writing work in conjunction with specific structures and institutions to shape social reality. Discourse refers to distinct areas of social knowledge (typically, broad subjects such as law, science, or medicine) and the linguistic practices that are associated with them, but also establishes rules about the context of this speech or writing, such as who is permitted and authorized to address these subjects. Knowledge, according to the concept of discourse, *is* power, since it comes into being through the operations of power and also exercises power by determining what truths will be endorsed. Discourses thus have immediate, material effects on the way a culture operates.

Distinction: The condition of being set apart and considered different or special, usually through the achievement of a specific honour, and connected to value. In the study of popular culture, distinction is often linked to consumption, with the implicit idea of a capitalist system being that one can achieve distinction through one's purchases.

Essentialism(ist): The belief that categories, or individuals and groups of human beings have innate, defining features exclusive to their category (e.g., the belief that different races have inherent characteristics that differentiate them from other races). Essentialism has been challenged by **social constructivist** theories that point to the ways in which identity and meaning are culturally produced.

Ethnicity: Ethnicity is a broad social category that addresses one's perceived membership in a larger group based on characteristics such as religious, cultural, or national background. Whereas one's **race** is generally "determined" by specific physical traits, ethnicity typically implies a somewhat more conscious and flexible affiliation with a particular group. Like race, however, the concept of ethnicity has often been used to discriminate against groups based on **stereotypical** perceptions of their common attitudes or attributes.

Ex-nomination: A term used by Roland Barthes to identify one of the ways in which the dominance of the ruling class goes unexamined precisely because *it is not named as such*: the process of ex-nomination ensures that we see the values or attributes of dominant groups not as the product of particular class interests, but simply as apolitical, intrinsic *human* values that are, therefore, as unsuitable for critique as a grapefruit or any other "real thing." Ex-nomination also works to legitimate the dominance of specific racial and cultural groups by failing to acknowledge or "mark" their distinctive qualities (e.g., white, heterosexual), thereby assuming their universality.

Folk Culture: Those cultural products and practices that have developed over time within a particular community or socially identifiable group, and that are communicated from generation to generation and amongst people who tend to be known to one another.

Fordism: A highly mechanized and standardized manner of production, pioneered on the assembly lines of auto-maker Henry Ford in order to improve worker efficiency by duplicating the specialized precision of a machine. Fordism now refers not only to a seminal development in the history of industrialization that enabled hitherto unimaginable levels of mass production/consumption, but also to a type of culture (or a particular aspect of a culture) that displays similar—generally negative—qualities of uniformity and conformity. Fordism has been supplanted in much of the North American economy by **post-Fordism**, a mode of production characterized by smaller, more flexible decentralized networks of labour and work organization, catering to more specialized ranges of consumer demands (though not necessarily a freer workforce).

Frankfurt School: See Close-Up 4.1 on page 102.

Globalization: An (arguably) recent, complex shift in the relationship between the world's many cultures fuelled by complex economic, political, and technological factors. Its central effect is that temporal and geographic distances are no longer as divisive as they once were. Although seeming to possess enormous potential for improving the conditions of some of the world's poorest regions, globalization is increasingly seen as being primarily profit-driven, and is closely allied with the remarkable ascension to power of massive transnational corporations and with the connected phenomenon of cultural imperialism. Some critics of globalization argue that it is little more than a process of further concentrating wealth and power in the hands of those who already have it, and that its effect on the indigenous cultures of developing nations is devastatingly corrosive. Others distinguish between different aspects of globalization (economic, political, technological, cultural, etc.) and point to the potential for new forms of cultural expression and new democratic alliances that are facilitated by a more globally connected world.

Gross Domestic Product (GDP): The total monetary value of all the goods and services produced within a nation's economy during a one-year period, a figure often used as an indicator of a nation's financial well-being. The GDP's value as a diagnostic tool to measure the health of a country is often critiqued because it fails to account for a host of relevant social transactions as diverse as domestic work, volunteering, and criminal activities.

Habitus: Concept outlined by Marcel Mauss connoting both living space and habitat that describes the way in which particular social environments are internalized by individuals in the form of dispositions toward particular bodily orientations and behaviours. The habitus we occupy radically affects such basic activities as sleeping, eating, sitting, walking, having sex, and giving birth, all of which should be understood not as natural, but as a series of "body techniques" that are *learned* in particular social contexts, and are therefore culturally and historically specific. Pierre Bourdieu extended this concept to talk about the relationship between habitus and social class.

Hegemony: See Close-Up 2.2 on page 40.

"Highbrow"/ "Lowbrow": A colloquial reference to "high" and "low" culture—a distinction that is made on the assumption that high culture holds some sort of greater innate intellectual or moral worth, while low culture is base and degrading to those who partake in it. The distinctions between these two groups become unclear with, for example, pop art, which borrows images from "low culture" (i.e., Campbell's soup cans) and displays them in a venue for "high culture"—the museum. The term "nobrow" has been used recently to describe images, objects, or experiences that can't easily be classified into high or low. In fact, the quotation marks that often surround mentions of "high" or "low" culture suggest that these categories are not only constantly shifting, but also arbitrary, often deployed as a means of legitimating class hierarchy.

Horizontal Integration: A **synergistic** venture wherein one company acquires (and integrates with) another company that is making the same kind of product or providing the same kind of service, in order to increase the purchasing company's presence in (and power over) a given market.

Hybridity: In horticulture a term that means to graft two different plant types together in order to create a third, unique plant; in cultural studies a term, generally associated with **diaspora** and **postcolonialism,** that refers to the blending of two or more cultures. The "third culture" that results from this interaction is not simply a combination of the two, but a space of possibility in which differences both between and within individual cultures express themselves.

Identity: An individual's unique personality or self (i.e., "who we are inside"). The concept of individual identity is complicated by the fact that, rather than inhabiting a single identity, we all assume multiple identities that are defined by particular circumstances and relationships. Marxist and psychoanalytic theories further challenge the concept of identity, showing how it is constructed by largely unconscious processes of **interpellation**. More recent theories of **performativity** offer possibilities for challenging the rigidity of the traditional identities on offer—identities that are founded in **essentialist** notions of gender, race, and sexuality.

Identity Politics: The strategic assertion of unity, defined by characteristics such as race, culture, ethnicity, or sexuality. Identity politics challenge prevailing power structures by demanding recognition and the extension of majority rights to minority groups.

Ideology: See Close-Up 2.1 on page 32.

Ideological State Apparatuses (ISAs): Term coined by French Marxist Louis Althusser to describe those social structures/organizations that indirectly (i.e., not by direct coercion) ensure that individuals subscribe to the ideology of the state or ruling class. Unlike repressive state apparatuses (for instance, the police or the military), which explicitly enforce the laws of a culture, ISAs work via the process of **interpellation** to compel individuals to conform to particular, class-specific, social roles.

Imperialism: Imperialism refers to the extension of rule over different countries, territories, or peoples, usually by force, for the purposes of economic gain. Imperialism continues today through trade regulations that inhibit development in poor countries, or that tie the course of their development to the economic agendas of wealthier nations. See also **cultural imperialism**.

Industrialization: The movement within a culture or economic system toward an increased emphasis on large-scale/mechanized industry rather than agricultural/small-scale commercial activity. Although initially conceived as a primarily economic process in its broadest sense of organization, capitalization, and mechanization, industrialization has sweeping social and cultural implications. As well as determining the manner in which things are produced (and, therefore, what kinds of products are available), the process of industrialization also affects the way labour and other resources are divided up within a culture.

Instrumental Rationality: See Close-Up 4.2 on page 105.

Intellectual Property/Copyright: Intellectual property refers to one's legal ownership of an idea or any other kind of original creative work. This ownership may be protected by trademarks, patents, and copyright. Largely as a result of recent sweeping advances in technologies that can be used to reproduce or disseminate digital information, converting even the genetic material of living things into readable "code," intellectual property has become a hotly disputed issue.

Interpellation: A term coined by the French Marxist Louis Althusser to describe the process by which an individual is addressed, or "called on," by ideology to assume a certain identity. Critical to the success of interpellation is the degree to which an individual recognizes and identifies with the roles s/he is assigned by the dominant culture.

Language: A term that in cultural studies refers to more than literal words, language can be broadly applied to describe all forms of communication (or **sign** systems)—visual, oral, aural, physical. In the study of culture, the units of any type of language are a focus for study, as societal values, relations, and power distribution are reproduced through a culture's language(s).

Maquiladoras: Spanish term describing the thousands of factories that have sprung up along the U.S.–Mexico border in the wake of NAFTA (the North American Free Trade Agreement). An inexpensive source of labour for **multinational** corporations, maquiladoras are known for meagre wages, brutal management practices, dangerous working conditions, and widespread environmental violations.

Market Segmentation: Beginning in the latter half of the twentieth century, a paradigm shift in the marketing world that involves gearing cultural production toward increasingly narrow segments of the public with the express goal of better catering to a consumer's specific tastes.

Mass Culture: A form of culture produced for profit by a vertically integrated factory system, for a large and diverse audience. Mass culture, though in some ways more pervasive than ever, is also breaking down as a result of economic processes of **market segmentation,** cultural developments such as **identity politics,** and the growing accessibility of technologies that allow "the masses" to produce culture for themselves.

Media Convergence: The combination of "new media" (primarily, cable and the Internet) with older media forms (radio, television, film, and newspapers and books), primarily by large corporations, with an intent to realize greater profits through the **synergistic** sharing of resources.

Minority: In cultural terms, any relatively small and/or powerless group of people who differ from the majority, or dominant, culture in ethnicity, religion, language, political persuasion, and so on. Minority politics are linked to movements by groups to gain certain political, economic, or social rights that they have been denied because of their minority status. In cultural studies, minority culture may also refer to **highbrow** (serious, intellectual) culture, as opposed to **lowbrow** (mass) culture.

Monoculture: From the agricultural term for the cultivation of a single crop, in cultural studies the idea of monoculture is linked to **globalization** and refers to the concept of a single world culture shared by all. This term has negative implications in that it suggests the destruction of local and cultural diversity. It is often implied that monoculture is synonymous with American or consumer culture.

Monopoly: An economic situation in which a single supplier controls the market for a particular product or service. This situation puts the producer in a position of unchallenged dominance from which it can inflate price to cover more than just necessary costs (including a return on capital). Governments often legislate to restrict the emergence of monopolies, since they are usually detrimental to the consumer and the economy.

Moral Panic: See Close-Up 3.2 on page 69.

Multiculturalism: A sociopolitical concept (and, in some countries, a government policy) that describes the coexistence of many different cultures in one place. As it is linked to national politics, multiculturalism recognizes that there is no essential or unified definition of a national culture, but rather emphasizes an idea of the nation as one of cultural freedom (i.e., Canada). Nominally a celebration of all cultures as equal, multiculturalist policies can often gloss over substantial power inequalities within a nation.

Multinational (Corporation): Any firm that extends itself outside of national boundaries by operating branches in many different countries simultaneously.

Myth(ology): A term coined by Roland Barthes to describe the ways in which sign systems work ideologically to reproduce and legitimate particular social relations. Myth is a mode of signification that works to express and surreptitiously to justify the dominant values of a given historical period. Unlike the relatively simple level of denotative or literal meaning, in which a word or image corresponds to a single, straightforward definition, myth brings into play a whole chain of associated concepts (e.g., tree–nature–goodness) by which members of a culture understand certain topics, and which help to shape their collective identities.

Nation/Nationalism: See Close-Up 7.3 on page 212.

New World Order: A phrase associated with the **postcolonial,** post–**Cold War** configuration of world power, which remains dominated by the West, and particularly by the United States. Coined by former U.S. President George H. Bush, the phrase describes genuine shifts in the geopolitical order, but also covers up long-term continuities in the global power and capitalism (i.e., not everything is "new" in the New World Order).

Orientalism: Refers to the way in which "The Orient" was and is constructed by the West as a means to claim authority and exercise control over Eastern cultures. The Orient is not a fact, or a specific geographical place; rather, it is the complex layers of knowledge and **mythology** that have been constructed around Western ideas about the non-West. For example, the way in which North American media characterize the "Middle East" as a place of repressive government regimes and fundamentalist religion glosses over the vast cultural differences between different groups of the region and contributes to the Western assumption that domination of these "backward" nations is legitimate and necessary.

Patriarchy (Patriarchal): A social system in which men hold power in the family and in the social structure. Patriarchy has more recently been used as a term in feminist criticism to describe the total system of gender relations in which male dominance has historically worked to dominate and disempower women. The challenge in trying to dismantle this system is that it has been historically naturalized to seem as though the social position of both genders has been biologically determined.

Performativity: Developed most extensively in the theory of Judith Butler, performativity refers to the process by which identities are enacted through repeated performance rather than inherently possessed or inhabited. The idea of performativity works on the premise that roles such as sex and gender are produced within an **ideologically** determined social script. While it's not possible to throw away the script—to be "oneself" instead of playing one's assigned role—the theory of performativity, by highlighting the tension between the scripted ideal and its embodied performance, offers possibilities for resisting the straitjacket of traditionally defined identities.

Postcolonial(ism): *Postcolonial* refers to the period after the formal retraction of colonial rule in the developing world. This period varies considerably, but in the case of the former British colonies, it refers to the period after the Second World War. *Postcolonialism* is a term that refers to the working through of the effects of colonization on a society or culture. The study of postcolonial culture examines the various mechanisms of **colonialism** (e.g., political rule, economic exploitation, colonial education systems) and their long-term, embedded cultural and social implications. While many former colonies are now independent states, postcolonial studies insists on the need to recognize and understand the ways in which colonialism's effects persist in the social, cultural, and political life of former colonial states today.

Posthumanism: A philosophy that questions concepts that underpin the tradition of humanism, such as identity, subjectivity, consciousness, and the soul. While humanism is based on ideas of human beings as unique individuals, and of humanity as a clearly defined, superior life form, posthumanism rejects the autonomy of "the human" in favour of the cyborg—a being defined by a combination of human and machine and/or animal characteristics. Posthumanism has been taken up in different ways by feminists, for whom it represents a way of challenging biologically essentialist views of sex and gender, and by proponents of genetic engineering, who support the idea of designing "better," more powerful humans through technological enhancement.

Postmodernism: See Close-Up 6.1 on page 187.

Preferred Reading: Any given text (be it a novel, film, image, or song) can be interpreted in a theoretically infinite number of ways depending on the perspective and experiences of the reader. However, the preferred reading is the particular interpretation that emerges as the most obvious to the greatest number of people based on prevalent and culturally specific modes of understanding (e.g., it is the reading that in many cases strikes interpreters as being "common sense").

Pseudo-individualization: Along with standardization (which it facilitates), one of the primary characteristics of the products of the culture industry, as described by Max Horkheimer and Theodor Adorno. Pseudo-individualization refers to a mode of capitalist production wherein, although virtually identical, cultural products are superficially varied to enable them to seemingly speak directly to a consumer's sense of individuality, their unique taste, and apparent freedom to choose.

Race: A constructed category that is widely used to distinguish among various groups of human beings based on inherited biological or physical characteristics (such as skin colour or facial features). Although seemingly a neutral descriptive tool, race has functioned historically as a way to draw spurious connections between specific physical characteristics and the possession of certain behavioural traits assumed to be shared by all members of the race. The idea of *race* is therefore inseparable from the discriminatory attitude and practices of *racism*.

Racism: The systematic practice of stereotyping and persecuting people on the basis of their race. Racism remains a central form of ideology today. Cultural studies has focused on the ways in which racist attitudes and stereotypes are both reinforced by and challenged in popular representations, and institutionalized in a variety of popular cultural practices.

Realism: See Close-Up 3.3 on page 74.

Representation: The social production of meaning through sign systems (i.e., words, images, gestures, etc.). Involves making meaning by creating links between conceptual and linguistic or signifying levels of meaning, links that are established through codes shared by members of a culture. Inseparable from the socially specific processes of **ideology** and **mythology**, representation constructs the world in particular ways that have significant bearing on the organization of society.

Semiotics: See Close-Up 3.1 on page 61.

Sign: The smallest unit (such as a word, image, or sound) of communication to which meaning is attached. In order to be a sign, the unit must meet three criteria: it must possess a physical form, it must refer to something else, and it must do so in a way that is recognizable to others. The sustained and large-scale interconnection of signs facilitates the construction of shared sign systems that enables individuals to communicate with other members of their culture in a comprehensible manner.

Social Constructivism: One of two general ways (the other is **essentialist**) in which meaning and identity formation is often understood. Social constructivists believe that identity is not inherent within an individual, group, or thing, but is instead largely a creation of cultural, political, and historical forces.

Sovereignty: The possession of legal control and governance over a specific geographic territory. Sovereignty once rested in the body of the monarch, who possessed supreme power over his or her kingdom. In the modern context, sovereignty has been located in nation-states. Globalization has been understood by many scholars as having complicated and undermined the sovereignty of nation-states. The growth in the political power of international organizations (e.g., United Nations, World Trade Organization) and the rise of non-governmental organizations has redistributed nation-state sovereignty to a multiplicity of sites and political levels (from local to global).

Standardization: Along with **pseudo-individualization,** one of the primary characteristics of the products of the culture industry, as formulated by Max Horkheimer and Theodor Adorno. Standardization refers to a widespread similarity between cultural products. Both a method of production and a manner of consumption, standardization not only dictates the kind of cultural products that will be manufactured but also inscribes in the consumer a shared mode of passive, apolitical, and disengaged reception.

Stereotypes: A form of representation that reduces people to a few simple, essential characteristics that are represented as fixed by nature. Stereotyping is predicated on the simplistic notion that an individual's membership within any given social group (based on, for instance, class, gender, race, age, or sexuality) invariably predisposes him or her to possess certain personality characteristics, attitudes, or behaviours.

Structuralism: An analytical approach characterized largely by a shift in focus from interpreting a text in order to unveil its hidden meaning to identifying and interrogating the ways in which meaning is brought into being *structurally*. Structuralism is a diverse approach encompassing numerous methodologies, connected by this concern with the ways in which the structure of any given text is implicated in the production of its meaning. Although it has been subject to intensive critique (focusing, for example, on its inability to take account of historical change), structuralism's once-radical emphasis on of the role of relationship and context in determining meaning has been enormously influential in many disciplines.

Subculture: A term that describes groups or communities that deviate or differ from existing social norms. Subcultures are typically conceived of as groups of individuals who come together around shared practices and ideas that are rejected or treated with suspicion by official, mainstream culture. By creatively expressing their dissatisfaction with existing social norms and practices, subcultures challenge and modify what counts as normal, everyday life. Subcultures are often identified with youth and youth culture in particular.

Synergy: A strategy of synchronizing and actively forging connections between directly related areas of entertainment. For example, the merger of media giant Time Warner with Internet giant AOL was intended to allow content developed for one communication medium (e.g., television) to be re-used, recycled, and reinforced in different media (e.g., film, Internet, etc.).

Transnational (Corporation): A firm that operates on a global scale and works, to a greater or lesser extent, outside of national jurisdictions. For example, former General Electric CEO Jack Welch's fantasy of operating the company from a permanently floating barge in order to avoid all national trade regulations and laws would be an example of a completely transnational company—it operates worldwide without operating from within any specific country.

Urbanization: The long-term but increasingly intensifying shift of human populations from the country to the city. In nineteenth-century Britain, urbanization contributed significantly to the reduction of open spaces available for recreation as land was expropriated for the building of industrial infrastructure. As fields disappeared with no new playgrounds to replace them, it became harder to find places to hold outdoor sports, festivals, and other forms of public gathering, which shaped the development of popular culture in significant ways.

Vertical Integration: A **synergistic** venture wherein one company acquires the means by which a particular product or service is manufactured, distributed, *and* sold. Its aim is to increase a corporation's control over its own products by diminishing its reliance on other companies. Vertical integration is considered by some to be responsible for a reduction in the diversity of available cultural products.

Works Cited

Adorno, Theodor. "Excerpt from 'On Popular Music.'" *A Critical and Cultural Theory Reader*. Ed. Anthony Easthope and Kate McGowan. Toronto: University of Toronto Press, 1992. 11–23.

———. "The Culture Industry Reconsidered." *The Adorno Reader*. Ed. Brian O'Connor. Oxford: Blackwell, 2000. 230–38.

Akin, David. "From Igloo to Internet: First Nations Gain Entrée to the Electronic Age." *Hamilton Spectator* 22 Sept. 1997: B1.

Althusser, Louis. *Lenin and Philosophy and Other Essays*. Trans. Ben Brewster. London: New Left, 1971.

"And That Is the Question." *Dawson's Creek*. The WB, Global, Toronto. 17 Feb. 1999.

Anderson, Benedict. *Imagined Communities*. London: Verso, 1983.

Anderson, Sarah, and John Cavanagh. *Field Guide to the Global Economy*. New York: The New Press, 2000.

Arnold, Matthew. *Culture and Anarchy*. 1875. Ed. J. Dover Wilson. Cambridge, UK: Cambridge University Press, 1990.

———. "Sweetness and Light." *A Cultural Studies Reader: History, Theory, Practice*. Ed. Jessica Munns and Gita Rajan. New York: Longman, 1995. 19–32.

Ashcroft, Bill, Gareth Griffiths, and Helen Tiffin. *Key Concepts in Post-Colonial Studies*. London: Routledge, 1998.

"Bad and Badder." [Q & A]. *Harper's Magazine* Sept. 2002: 21–22.

Bailey, Peter. *Leisure and Class in Victorian England: Rational Recreation and the Contest for Control, 1830–1885*. London: Methuen, 1978.

Balibar, Etienne. "Racism and Nationalism." *Ambiguous Identities*. London: Verso, 1991. 37–67.

Balsamo, Anne. "On the Cutting Edge: Cosmetic Surgery and the Technological Production of the Gendered Body." *The Visual Culture Reader*. Ed. Nicholas Mirzoeff. London: Routledge, 1998. 228–233.

Barthes, Roland. *Mythologies*. Trans. Annette Lavers. London: Granada, 1973.

Baudelaire, Charles. *The Painter of Modern Life*. New York: De Capo, 1964.

Baudrillard, Jean. *Simulations*. Trans. Paul Foss, Paul Patton, and Philip Beitchman. New York: Semiotext(e), 1983.

Bauman, Zygmunt. "Soil, Blood and Identity." *The Sociological Review* (1992): 675–701.

"Be Careful What You Wish For." *Dawson's Creek.* The WB, Global, Toronto. 7 Mar. 1999.

Benjamin, Walter. *Charles Baudelaire: A Lyric Poet in the Era of High Capitalism.* Trans. Harry Zohn. London: New Left, 1973.

———. *Illuminations.* Trans. Harry Zohn. New York: Schocken, 1968.

Bennett, Tony. "Putting Policy into Cultural Studies." *Cultural Studies.* Ed. Lawrence Grossberg, Cary Nelson, and Paula Treichler. London: Routledge, 1992. 23–37.

Berger, John. *About Looking.* New York: Pantheon, 1980.

Best, Geoffrey Francis Andrew. *Mid-Victorian Britain, 1851–1875.* London: Weidenfeld and Nicolson, 1971.

Bhabha, Homi. *The Location of Culture.* London: Routledge, 1994.

Blaut, James M. *The Colonizer's Model of the World: Geographical Diffusionism and Eurocentric History.* New York: Guilford, 1993.

Bourdieu, Pierre. *Distinction.* Trans. Richard Nice. Cambridge: Harvard University Press, 1987.

Branston, Gill. *Cinema and Cultural Modernity.* Philadelphia: Open University Press, 2000.

Briggs, Asa. *Mass Entertainment: The Origins of a Modern Industry.* Adelaide: Griffin, 1960.

Brooker, Peter. *A Concise Glossary of Cultural Theory.* London: Arnold, 1999.

Brown, Nicholas. "The Music of the Sphere." *Globalization and the Human Condition Working Paper Series.* Hamilton: McMaster University Institute on Globalization and the Human Condition, 2003: 23–28. Available online at <http://www.humanities.mcmaster.ca/~global/wp/Content.pdf>.

Burke, Peter. "The 'Discovery' of Popular Culture." *People's History and Socialist Theory.* Ed. Raphael Samuel. London: Routledge, 1981. 216–226.

Burkeman, Oliver. "Not So Big, Mac." *The Guardian Unlimited* 22 Nov. 2002.

Carey, James W. *Communication as Culture: Essays on Media and Society.* Boston: Unwin Hyman, 1989.

"The Case for War." Editorial. *The Economist* 3–9 Aug. 2002: 9–10.

Chambers, Iain. *Migrancy, Culture, Identity.* New York: Routledge, 1994.

Clairmont, Susan. "Road Hockey Sparks Conflict." *The Hamilton Spectator* 4 Jan. 2002 <http://www.hamiltonspectator.com/clairmont/516812.html>.

———. "We Should Have Done More to Stop Hate Crimes." *The Hamilton Spectator* online edition. 20 Sept. 2001 <http://www.hamiltonspectator.com/clairmont/471523.html>.

Cohen, Leah Hager. *Glass, Paper, Beans: Revelations on the Nature and Value of Ordinary Things.* New York: Doubleday, 1997.

Cohen, Stan. *Folk Devils and Moral Panics: The Creation of the Mods and Rockers.* London: MacGibbon and Kee, 1972.

Coupland, Douglas. *Generation X.* New York: St. Martin's Press, 1991.

Crime Statistics. *The Daily* 17 July, 2002. <http://www.statcan.ca/Daily/English/020717/d020717b.htm>.

Cunningham, Hugh. *Leisure in the Industrial Revolution.* London: Croom Helm, 1980.

"The Daily." *Statscan* <http://www.statcan.ca/Daily/English/020830/d020830a.htm>.

Darnton, Robert. *The Forbidden Best-Sellers of Pre-Revolutionary France*. New York: W.W. Norton & Co., 1995.

DeMott, Benjamin. "Put on a Happy Face: Masking the Differences Between Blacks and Whites." *Harper's Magazine* Sept. 1995: 31–38.

Denning, Michael. "The End of Mass Culture." *Modernity and Mass Culture*. Ed. James Naremore and Patrick Brantlinger. Bloomington IN: Indiana UP, 1991. 253–268.

Dogtown and Z Boys. Dir. Stacy Peralta. Prod. Agi Orsi and Jay Wilson. Sony, 2002: USA.

du Gay, Paul, and Michael Pryke, eds. *Cultural Economy*. London: Sage, 2002.

du Gay, Paul, ed. *Production of Culture/Cultures of Production*. London: Sage, 1997.

du Gay, Paul, et. al. *Doing Cultural Studies: The Story of the Sony Walkman*. London: Sage, 1997.

Duncombe, Stephen. *Cultural Resistance Reader*. New York: Verso, 2002.

During, Simon. "Towards the Global Popular? Knowledge, Strength and Magic." *Cultural Studies: Pluralism and Theory*. Ed. David Bennett. Melbourne: University of Melbourne Literary and Cultural Studies, 1993. 133–155.

———, ed. *The Cultural Studies Reader*. New York: Routledge, 1993.

Elias, Norbert. *The Civilizing Process, Volume 1: The History of Manners*. New York: Pantheon, 1982.

Engels, Friedrich. *The Condition of the Working Class in England*. Trans. and ed. W.O. Henderson and W.H. Chaloner. Oxford: Basil Blackwell, 1958.

Evans, Caroline, and Minna Thornton. *Women and Fashion: A New Look*. New York: Quartet, 1989.

Fanon, Frantz. *Black Skin, White Masks*. Trans. Charles Lam Markmann. New York: Grove, 1967.

———. *The Wretched of the Earth*. Trans. Constance Farrington. New York: Grove, 1963.

Featherstone, Mike. "Body Modification: An Introduction." *Body Modification*. Ed. Mike Featherstone. London: Sage, 2000. 1–14.

Fight Club. Dir. David Fincher. Prod. Ross Bell, et al. 20th Century Fox. 1999: USA.

"Fighting for the Right to Play Road Hockey in Hamilton." CBC Sunday Report. *The National* Transcripts. Host Alison Smith. 6 Jan. 2002 <http://tv.cbc.ca/national/trans/T020106.html>.

Fiske, John. *Reading the Popular*. London: Routledge, 1989.

———. *Understanding Popular Culture*. London: Routledge, 1989.

Forrest Gump. Dir. Robert Zemekis. Prod. Wendy Finerman. MGM, 1997.

Foucault, Michel. *History of Sexuality* Vol. 1. Trans. Robert Hurley. Harmondsmith: Penguin, 1984.

Frank, Thomas. *The Conquest of Cool*. Chicago: University of Chicago Press, 1997.

Freccero, Carla. *Popular Culture: An Introduction*. New York: New York University Press, 1999. New York: Basic, 1974.

Fretts, Bruce. "Remote Patrol." *Entertainment Weekly* 476 12 March, 1999 <http://members.tripod.com/~Lilybunny/magazines/articles/ewmarch99.html>.

Galt, Virginia. "Precautions No Guarantee of Safety, Officials Concede." *The Globe and Mail* 12 Feb. 2000: A30.

"Game On! Road Hockey Charges Dismissed." CBC News Toronto. 8 Jan. 2002 <http://toronto.cbc.ca/template/servlet/View?filename=hockey_010802>.

Garnham, Nicholas. "Concepts of Culture: Public Policy and the Cultural Industries." *Cultural Studies* 1.1 (1987).

Garratt, Cheryl. "Wake Up. . ." *The Observer* 8 Sept. 2002: Food Section: 14–15.

Gellner, Ernest. *Nations and Nationalism.* Oxford: Blackwell, 1983.

Gendron, Bernie. "Theodor Adorno Meets the Cadillacs." *Studies in Entertainment.* Ed. Tania Modleski. Bloomington: Indiana University Press, 1986. 18–36.

George, Jane. "Montreal Carving Factory Churns Out the Soapstone." *Nunatsiaq News* 30 Dec. 1998. <http://www.nunatsiaq.com/archives/nunavut981231/nvt81231_12.html>.

Gerry. Dir. Gus Van Sant. Prod. Danny Wolf. Thinkfilm, 1991: USA.

Ghost World. Dir. Terry Zwigoff. Prod. Mr. Mudd. MGM/UA, 2001: USA.

Giddens, Anthony. *Consequences of Modernity.* Palo Alto: Stanford University Press, 1990.

Gilbert, Matthew. "Fox's 'John Doe' has Identity Crisis." *The Boston Globe* 20 Sept. 2002 <http://www.boston.com/dailyglobe2/263/living/Fox_s_John_Doe_has_identity_crisi+.shtml>.

Gilman, Charlotte Perkins. *Women and Economies.* 1898. Mineola, NY: Dover, 1998.

Gilroy, Paul. *The Black Atlantic: Modernity and Double Consciousness.* London: Verso, 1993.

———. "Diaspora and the Detours of Identity." *Identity and Difference.* Ed. Kathryn Woodward. London: Sage, 1997. 301–349.

———. *Small Acts: Thoughts on the Politics of Black Cultures.* London: Serpent's Tale, 1993.

Giroux, Henry. *Disturbing Pleasures.* New York: Routledge, 1994.

Goodall, Jane. "An Order of Pure Decision: Un-Natural Selection in the Work of Stelarc and Orlan." *Body Modification.* Ed. Mike Featherstone. London: Sage, 2000. 149–170.

Grierson, Bruce. "Headrush." *Adbusters* 25 Spring 1999: 23–29.

Grossberg, Lawrence, Ellen Wartella, and D. Charles Whitney. *Media Making: Mass Media in a Popular Culture.* Thousand Oaks, CA: Sage, 1998.

Grosz, Elizabeth. *Volatile Bodies.* Bloomington: Indiana University Press, 1994.

Hall, Ann, Trevor Slack, Garry Smith, and David Whitson. *Sport in Canadian Society.* Toronto: McClelland & Stewart, 1991.

Hall, Stuart. "Cultural Studies and the Centre: Some Problematics and Problems." *Culture, Media, Language.* Ed. Stuart Hall, Dorothy Hobson, Andrew Lowe, and Paul Willis. London: Hutchinson, 1980. 15–47.

———. "Cultural Studies and Its Theoretical Legacies." *Cultural Studies.* Ed. Lawrence Grossberg, Cary Nelson, and Paula Treichler. London: Routledge, 1992. 277–294.

———. "Encoding, Decoding." *The Cultural Studies Reader.* Ed. Simon During. London: Routledge, 1993. 90–103.

———. "Gramsci's Relevance for the Study of Race and Ethnicity." *Journal of Communication Inquiry* 10.2 (1986): 5–27.

———. "Notes on Deconstructing the Popular." *People's History and Socialist Theory.* Ed. R. Samuel. London: Routledge & Kegan Paul, 1981. 227–240.

Hall, Stuart, Chas Critcher, Tony Jefferson, John Clarke, and Brian Roberts. *Policing the Crisis: Mugging, the State, and Law and Order.* New York: Holmes & Meier, 1978.

Harmon, Amy. 2001. In an Online Colloquy, an Absent Voice. *New York Times* 4 Oct. 2001: G1.

Harvey, David. *The Condition of Postmodernity.* Cambridge, UK: Blackwell, 1989.

Hebdige, Dick. *Hiding in the Light: On Images and Things.* New York: Routledge, 1994.

Hegde, Raksha. "KBC May Topple *Baywatch* as Most Popular TV Show." <http://www.rediff.com/money/2001/may/07kbc.htm>.

Hirschberg, Lynn. "The Thinking Inside the Box." *New York Times Magazine* 3 Nov. 2002.

Hobsbawm, Eric. *The Age of Extremes: A History of the World, 1914–1991.* New York: Vintage, 1996.

———. *Industry and Empire: An Economic History of Britain Since 1750.* London: Weidenfeld and Nicolson, 1968.

Holloway, Lynnette. "The Angry Appeal of Eminem Cuts Across Racial Lines." *New York Times* 28 Oct. 2002 <http://www.nytimes.com/2002/10/28/business/media/28RAP.html?ex=1036838360&ei=1&en=aec9e21c86415ad0>.

Horkheimer, Max, and Theodor Adorno. *Dialectic of Enlightenment.* New York: Continuum, 1971.

Hutcheon, Linda. *As Canadian as Possible . . . Under the Circumstances!* Toronto: Robarts Centre for Canadian Studies, 1988.

———. *The Canadian Postmodern: A Study of Contemporary English-Canadian Fiction.* Oxford: Oxford University Press, 1988.

"I Am . . . an Asshole?" *wwwegulphy.com* 16 April 2000 <http://www.angelfire.com/rock/cpar/p2k/2kapr16paperless.html>.

Ibbitson, John. "Harris Vows to Rid Streets of Pushy Beggars, Squeegees." *The National Post* 20 May 1999: A1, A8.

Ignatieff, Michael. "The Narcissism of Minor Difference." *Clash of Identities: Essays on Media, Manipulation, and Politics of the Self.* Ed. James Littleton. Toronto: CBC, 1996. 41–54.

"I Was Canadian." *BC Free Press* June 2000 <http://www.bcfreepress.bc.ca/page129.html>.

Jameson, Fredric. *Postmodernism, or the Cultural Logic of Late Capitalism.* Durham, NC: Duke University Press, 1991.

Jenkins, Henry. "Professor Jenkins Goes to Washington." *Harper's Magazine* July 1999: 19–23.

Jhally, Sut. *The Codes of Advertising: Fetishism and the Political Economy of Meaning in the Consumer Economy.* New York: St. Martins P, 1987.

John Howard Society. "Youth Crime in Canada: Public Perception vs. Statistical Information." 1998 <http://www.johnhoward.ab.ca/PUB/C16.htm#exe>.

Jones, Gareth Stedman. "Working-Class Culture and Working-Class Politics in London, 1870–1900: Notes on the Remaking of a Working Class." *Journal of Social History* 7.4 (1974): 460–508.

Katz, Jon. "The Digital Citizen." *Wired* Dec. 1997: 68+.

Klesse, Christian. "'Modern Primitivism': Non-Mainstream Body Modification and Racialized Representation." *Body & Society* 5 2/3 (1999): 16–38.

Klosterman, Chuck. "The Ratt Trap." *New York Times Magazine* 29 Dec. 2002: 24–25.

Lacan, Jacques. *Ecrits: A Selection.* Trans. Alan Sheridan. London: Tavistock, 1977.

Lacayo, Richard. "Violent Reaction: Bob Dole's Broadside Against Sex and Violence in Popular Culture Sets Off a Furious Debate About Responsibility." *Time* 145–24 12 June 1995 <http://www.time.com/time/magazine/archive/1995/950612/950612.cover.html>.

Laqueur, Thomas. *Making Sex: Body and Gender from the Greeks to Freud.* Cambridge, MA: Harvard University Press, 1990.

Lasn, Kalle. *Culture Jam: How to Reverse America's Suicidal Consumer Binge—And Why We Must.* New York: HarperCollins, 1999.

Law & Order. Prod. Dick Wolf et al. NBC.

Leavis, F.R., and Denys Thompson. *Culture and Environment.* Westport CT: Greenwood, 1977.

Levine, Lawrence W. *Highbrow/Lowbrow: The Emergence of Cultural Hierarchy in America.* Cambridge MA: Harvard University Press, 1988.

Lewis, Bernard. *What Went Wrong? Western Impact and Middle Eastern Response.* Oxford: Oxford University Press, 2002.

Lury, Celia. *Consumer Culture.* New Brunswick, NJ: Rutgers University Press, 1996.

Lütticken, Sven. "The Art of Theft." *New Left Review* 13 (2002): 89–104.

Lyman, Rick. "Black Actors Are Still Keeping Their Eyes on the Prize." *New York Times* 27 Feb. 2002 <http://www.nytimes.com/2002/02/27/movies/oscars/27OSCA. html?ex=1015827477&ei=1&en=cc19dc5fb5ed0083>.

Lyotard, Jean-François. *The Postmodern Condition: A Report on Knowledge.* Minneapolis: Minnesota University Press, 1984.

Macaulay, Lord Thomas Babington. "Indian Education: Minute of the 2nd February, 1835." *Selected Writings.* Ed. John Clive and Thomas Pinney. Chicago: University of Chicago Press, 1972. 235–51.

MacGregor, Roy. "Here's the Skinny on Shinny: It's Starting to Pick Up Again, But Shame About Those Rinks." *The Globe and Mail* 2 Jan. 2003: A2.

Mackey, Eva. *The House of Difference: Cultural Politics and National Identity in Canada.* Toronto: University of Toronto Press, 2002.

Malcomson, Robert W. *Popular Recreations in English Society 1700–1850.* Cambridge, UK: Cambridge University Press, 1973.

Mallick, Heather. "Ready, Aim, Swipe." *The Globe and Mail* 14 Dec. 2002: L5.

Martin, Emily. "Body Narratives, Body Boundaries." *Cultural Studies.* Eds. Lawrence Grossberg, Cary Nelson, and Paula Treichler. New York: Routledge, 1992. 409–423.

Martin, Randy. "Introduction: Globalization? The Dependencies of a Question." *Social Text* 60 (1999).

Marx, Karl. "Excerpt from the Preface to 'A Contribution to a Critique of Political Economy.' *A Critical and Cultural Theory Reader.* Ed. Anthony Easthope and Kate McGowan. Toronto: University of Toronto Press, 1992. 45–46.

Marx, Karl, and Friedrich Engels. *The Communist Manifesto: A Modern Edition*. New York: Verso, 1998.

Massey, Doreen. "Problems with Globalization." *Soundings* 7 (1997).

Mauss, Marcel. "Techniques of the Body." *Incorporations*. Ed. Jonathan Crary and Sanford Kwinter. New York: Zone, 1992. 455–477.

McClintock, Anne. *Imperial Leather: Race, Gender and Sexuality in the Colonial Context*. New York: Routledge, 1995.

McKay, George. *Senseless Acts of Beauty: Cultures of Resistance Since the Sixties*. New York: Verso, 1996.

McLuhan, Marshall. *Understanding Media: The Extensions of Man*. New York: McGraw-Hill, 1964.

McRobbie, Angela. *Postmodernism and Popular Culture*. London: Routledge, 1994.

Mercer, Kobena. "Welcome to the Jungle: Identity and Diversity in Postmodern Politics." *Identity: Community, Culture, Difference*. Ed. Jonathan Rutherford. London: Lawrence and Wishart, 1990. 43–71.

Metcalfe, Alan. *Canada Learns to Play: The Emergence of Organized Sport, 1807–1914*. Toronto: McClelland & Stewart, 1987.

Mickey Mouse Monopoly: Disney, Childhood and Corporate Power. Dir. Miguel Picker. Prod. Chyng Sun. Artmedia, 2001.

Miller, Daniel. *A Theory of Shopping*. Ithaca, NY: Cornell University Press, 1999.

Mulvey, Laura. "Visual Pleasure and Narrative Cinema." *A Cultural Studies Reader*. Ed. Jessica Munns and Gita Rajan. New York: Longman, 1995. 322–332.

My Big Fat Greek Wedding. Dir. Joel Zwick. Prod. Tom Hanks, Gary Goetzman, Rita Wilson. IFC Films, 2002.

Nachbar, Jack, and Kevin Lause. "Getting to Know Us: An Introduction to the Study of Popular Culture: What Is this Stuff that Dreams Are Made Of?" Ed. Jack Nachbar and Kevin Lause. 1–36. In Jack Nachbar and Kevin Lause, eds. *Popular Culture: An Introductory Text*. Bowling Green, OH: Bowling Green State University Popular Press, 1992.

Naremore, James, and Patrick Brantlinger, eds. *Modernity and Mass Culture*. Bloomington, IN: Indiana University Press, 1991.

Negus, Keith. "The Production of Culture." *Production of Culture/Cultures of Production*. Ed. Paul du Gay. 67–118.

Nos4a2. "*EW* Questions *DC*" <http://www.geocities.com/Hollywood/Guild/ 5740/dcbb/ gayjack.html>.

Ohmann, Richard. *Selling Culture: Magazines, Markets and Class*. New York: Verso, 1996.

O'Sullivan, Tim, John Hartley, Danny Saunders, Martin Montgomery, and John Fiske. *Key Concepts in Communication and Cultural Studies*. London: Routledge, 1994.

Page, Don. "A View from the South." *Coast to Coast* 5.3 (1999) <http://www.stleonards.ca/ docs/coast/5-3/5-3.html>.

Pocohantas. Dir. Mike Gabriel and Eric Goldberg. Prod. James Pentecost. Walt Disney Films. 1995.

Radway, Janice. *Reading the Romance: Women, Patriarchy and Popular Literature*. Chapel Hill, NC: University of North Carolina Press, 1984.

Rankin, Jim, Jennifer Quinn, Michelle Shephar, John Duncanson, and Scott Simmie. "Black Arrest Rates Highest." *Toronto Star* 26 Oct. 2002 <http://www.thestar.com/ NASApp/cs/ContentServer?pagename=thestar/Layout/Article_Type1&c=Article&cid =1026146837542&call_page=TS_RaceAndCrime&call_pageid=1034935301156&call_ pagepath=GTA/Race_and_Crime&col=1034935301113>.

Reynolds, Joshua. *Discourses on Art*. 1797. Ed. Robert Wark. New Haven, CT: Yale University Press, 1975.

Robbins, Bruce. "Introduction Part I: Actually Existing Cosmopolitanisms." *Cosmopolitics: Thinking and Feeling Beyond the Nation*. Ed. Bruce Robbins and Pheng Cheah. Minneapolis: University of Minnesota Press, 1998. 1–19.

Robbins, Richard. *Global Problems and the Culture of Capitalism*. Second Edition. Boston: Allyn and Bacon, 2002.

Robertson, Roland. *Globalization: Social Theory and Global Culture*. London: Sage, 1992.

Robinson, Laura. "Girls Should Take to the Streets." *The Globe and Mail* 11 Jan. 2002: A15.

Rosenberg, "Berlin Conference of 1884–1885 to Divide Africa." <http://geography. about.com/ library/weekly/aa021601a.htm>.

Rutherford, Jonathan. "Identity and the Cultural Politics of Difference." *Identity: Community, Culture, Difference*. Ed. Jonathan Rutherford. London: Lawrence and Wishart, 1990. 9–27.

Said, Edward. *Culture and Imperialism*. London: Chatto and Windus, 1993.

———. *Orientalism*. New York: Vintage, 1979.

Schivelbusch, Wolfgang. *Tastes of Paradise: A Social History of Spices, Stimulants, and Intoxicants*. New York: Pantheon, 1992.

Schnellner, Johanna. "Only Money Breaks the Colour Barrier." *The Globe and Mail* 21 Dec. 2001: R3.

Schor, Juliet. "Towards a New Politics of Consumption." *The Consumer Society Reader*. Ed. Juliet B. Schor and Douglas Holt. New York: The New Press, 2000. 446–62.

Shallow Hall. Dir. Bobby Farrelly, Peter Farrelly. Twentieth Century Fox. 2001

Shears, Mary Deanne. "Our Duty: Examine All Issues." *Toronto Star* 19 Oct. 2002 <http://www.thestar.com/NASApp/cs/ContentServer?pagename=thestar/Layout/ Article_Type1&c=Article&cid=1026146584089&call_page=TS_RaceAndCrime&call_ pageid=1034935301156&call_pagepath=GTA/Race_and_Crime&col=1034935301113>.

Shilling, Chris. "The Body and Difference." *Identity and Difference*. Ed. Kathryn Woodward. London: Sage, 1997. 63–120.

Shohat, Ella, and Robert Stam. *Unthinking Eurocentrism: Multiculturalism and the Media*. London: Routledge, 1994.

Stackhouse, John. *Timbit Nation*. Toronto: Random House, 1993.

Stallabrass, Julian. "Digital Commons." *New Left Review* 15 (2002): 141–46.

Stevenson, Seth. "I'd Like to Buy the World a Shelf-Stable Children's Lactic Drink." *New York Times Magazine* 10 Mar. 2002: 38–43.

Strasser, Susan. *Satisfaction Guaranteed: The Making of the American Mass Market.* New York: Pantheon, 1989.

Szatmary, David P. *Rockin' in Time: A Social History of Rock-and-Roll.* Upper Saddle River, NJ: Prentice Hall, 2000.

"A Talk with the Producers of 'The Merchants of Cool'" <http://www.pbs.prg/wgbh/pages/frontline/shows/cool/etc/producers.html>. Accessed 3 Oct. 2002.

Taubin, Amy. Review of *Gerry*. *Woodstock Film Festival Feature Films.* 2002 <http://www.woodstockfilmfestival.com/Schedule/features2002.htm>.

Thompson, E.P. *The Making of the English Working Class.* Harmondsworth: Penguin, 1963.

Thornham, Sue. *Feminist Theory and Cultural Studies: Stories of Unsettled Relations.* London: Arnold, 2000.

Thornton, Sarah. *Club Cultures: Music, Media and Subcultural Capital.* Cambridge: Polity, 1995.

"To Be or Not To Be. . ." *Dawson's Creek.* The WB, Global, Toronto. 10 Feb. 1999.

Tomlinson, John. *Cultural Imperialism: A Critical Introduction.* Baltimore: The Johns Hopkins University Press, 1991.

———. *Globalization and Culture.* Chicago: University of Chicago Press, 1999.

True Lies. Dir. James Cameron. Twentieth Century Fox, 1994.

Twitchell, James. *AdCult USA: The Triumph of Advertising in American Culture.* New York: Columbia University Press, 1996.

Tzara, Tristan. "Dada Manifesto 1918." *The Dada Painters and Poets.* Ed. Robert Motherwell. New York: G. Wittenborn, 1951.

Van Elteren, Mel. "Conceptualizing the Impact of US Popular Culture Globally." *Journal of Popular Culture* 30.1 (1996).

Veblen, Thorstein. *The Theory of the Leisure Class.* New York: New American Library, 1953.

Victoria's Secret. Prod. Marleen Trotter. Rep. Wei Chen. 10 Mar. 1992. Vancouver: CTV.

Virilio, Paul. *Open Sky.* London: Verso, 1997.

Wallace, Amy. "True Thighs." *More.* Sept. 2002.

Waters, Malcolm. *Globalization.* London: Routledge, 1995.

Watson, James, ed. *Golden Arches East: McDonald's in East Asia.* Stanford: Stanford University Press, 1997.

Weber, Max. *The Protestant Ethic and the Spirit of Capitalism.* Trans. Talcott Parsons. New York: Charles Scribner and Sons.

Weiss, Brad. "Coffee Breaks and Coffee Connections: The Lived Experience of a Commodity in Tanzanian and European Worlds." *Cross-Cultural Consumption: Global Market, Local Realities.* Ed. David Howes. London: Routledge, 1996. 93–105

Welch, Jack. Interview on CNN *Moneyline.* 8 Dec. 1998.

Wente, Margaret. "It's Okay to Hate Hockey." *The Globe and Mail* 10 Jan. 2002: A21.

——. "Today We Are All Americans." *The Globe and Mail* 13 Sept. 2001: A6.

——. "We are all Australians Now." *The Globe and Mail* 19 Oct. 2002: A23.

Western Eyes. Writ. and Dir. Ann Shin. *Rough Cuts.* CBC, Toronto. 16 Apr. 2002.

Whorf, Benjamin Lee. *Language, Thought and Reality.* Cambridge, MA: MIT Press, 1963.

Williams, Raymond. "Advertising: The Magic System." *The Cultural Studies Reader.* Ed. Simon During. London: Routledge, 1993. 320–336.

——. "British Film History: New Perspectives." In *British Cinema History.* Ed. J. Curran and V. Porter. London: Weidenfeld and Nicolson, 1983.

——. *Culture and Society 1780–1950.* New York: Columbia University Press, 1983.

Williamson, Judith. *Consuming Passions: The Dynamics of Popular Culture.* London: Boyars, 1986.

Wilson, Elizabeth. "The Invisible *Flâneur.*" *New Left Review* 191 (1992): 90–110.

Wiltse, Ed. "Globalization, Fandom and Cyber-solidarity." In Susie O"Brien and Imre Szeman, ed. *Content Providers of the World Unite!* Institute on Globalization and the Human Condition Working Paper Series. Hamilton: McMaster University. Available at <http://www.humanities.mcmaster.ca/~global/wp/Content.pdf>.

Winship, Janice. "A Woman's World: *Woman*—An Ideology of Femininity." *Women Take Issue: Aspects of Women's Subordination.* Women's Studies Group, Centre for Contemporary Cultural Studies. London: Hutchinson, 1978. 133–54.

Wise, S.F., and Douglas Fisher. *Canada's Sporting Heroes.* Don Mills, ON: General, 1974.

Wolff, Janet. "The Invisible *Flâneuse*: Women in the Literature of Modernity." *Theory, Culture & Society* 2 (1985): 37–46.

Wong, Jan. "Shootout at School Prompts an Eerie Attitude." *The Globe and Mail* 12 Feb. 2000: A1, A30.

Working Girl. Dir. Mike Nichols. Twentieth Century Fox. 1988.

World Bank. *World Development Indicators 1998.* Washington, D.C.: World Bank, 1998.

World Trade Organization. "Canada—Certain Measures Concerning Periodicals." Dispute Resolution Panel Report WT/DS31/R, 14 Mar. 1997.

Young, Iris Marion. "Throwing Like a Girl: A Phenomenology of Feminine Body Comportment, Motility and Spatiality." *Human Studies* 3 (1980): 137–156.

de Zengotita, Thomas. "The Gunfire Dialogues: Notes on the Reality of Virtuality." *Harper's Magazine* July 1999: 55–58.

Index

authenticity, 9
blockbuster shows, 5
capitalism, 9, 10
coffee, 12–21
commercial mass culture, 39–47
commercial value, 9
consumerism, 146
defining concepts, 2, 9, 25
definition of popular, 5–6
dominant forms of, 237–239
and everyday life, 2, 9
evolution of, 24–56
examples of popular, 5–6
folk culture, 7–8
and globalization, 277–291
impact of new technology, 131–132
importance of studying, 305–306
mass culture, 7–8
McDonald's, 286
meanings of, 7
media culture, 39–47
money as measure of success, 98–99
politics of, 9, 38–39
popular recreation, 23, 34–39
and power, 9
pub and music hall, 44–46
subcultures, 108
visual representation, 79–80
Popular recreation, 23, 34–39
    before 1830, 25–26
    protection of, 37–38
Postcolonial identities, 222–228
Postcolonial nationalism, 222–225
Posthumanist position, 196–197
Postindustrial revolution 304–305
Postmodern capitalism, 10
Postmodernism, 185, 187–188, 301
Poverty, 30
Power Corp, 271
Power, 9
    in coffee industry, 17
    discourse, 65, 177
    economic, 54
    identity, 176–179, 195–196
    of photographic representation, 72–73
    relationships, 11–12
    of representation, 78–83
    social, 54
Printing press, 41–42
Prisons, 177, 178
Privacy, 29
Prizefighting, 37–38
Procter & Gamble, 17, 114
Product packaging, 124, 142, 143
Production, 7, 12

assembly-line labour, 30
digital, 130–132
economy, 9, 18, 95–97
Hollywood film, 116–122
Industrial Revolution, 29–30
Prostitution, 45
Protestants, 201, 202, 203, 204
Pseudo-individualization, 107, 108
Psychoanalytic theory
    identity, 272
    identity formation, 79
Psychosocial development theory, 172–173
Public space, 23
    Enclosure Acts, 27
    limitation of, 25, 52
    management of, 25
    pubs, 28–29
    redefined, 25, 27–29
Public transit, 42
Pubs, 28–29, 35, 38
    music hall, 44–46
Pulp Fiction, 81
Punk, 245, 255, 256
    avant-garde punk, 257–259
    Ramone, Dee Dee, 247, 256
    Sex Pistols, 256, 258, 259
    The Decline of Western Civilization, 256
    The Ramones, 247, 256, 257

Quebec nationalism, 231
Quebecor Inc., 271

Race, 199, 216, 220
    and identity, 220–222
    and racism, 220
Racial minority, 200
Racial profiling, 92
Racism, 220
    contributing factors, 220–221
    stereotypes, 219
Radiohead, 108
Radway, Janice, 88
Railroads, 42
Ramone, Dee Dee, 247, 256
Rap music, 8, 226–227, 228
Rational recreation, 34–35, 218, 297
    main goal of, 35
Ratt, 247
Reader's Digest, 289
Reading the Romance: Women, Patriarchy and Popular Literature, 88
Reagan, Ronald, 265
Realism, 73, 74
Recording industry, 11

Credits

Pg. 3: Used by permission of ROM and Hudson's Bay Company; 13 Tracy Carbert; 15 Used by permission of New Scientist; 19 Tracy Carbert; 24 Dick Hemingway; 37 Reproduced by permission of National Trust of Scotland; 49 Hulton Archive by Getty Images; 50 Hulton Archive by Getty Images; 51 CP (Domenico Stinellis); 59 Source: "Rates of Youth Criminal Code Incidents, 1983–1999," http://www.statcan.ca/ english/freepub/89F0123XIE/29.htm, Statistics Canada; 57 Courtesy W-Five and CTV; 68 © Anton Vengo/SuperStock; 73 Peter Redman/National Post; 80 Everett Collection/Magma; 89 Reprinted by permission of Stuart Hall; 104 Image by Abrupt, 1996. http://www.abrupt.org; 109 © Jeff Koons. Used by permission; 130 Courtesy Copyleft.net; 144 Used by permission of Procter & Gamble; 151 Courtesy of Diesel Canada; 163 Christopher Anderson/VII; 181 Everett Collection/Magma; 186 Glenn Watson/MPTV.net; 193 Duncan O'Brien; 196 Courtesy of Steve Mann; 202–203 Connolly, P., Smith A., and Kelly, B. (2002) "Too Young to Notice? The Cultural and Political Awareness of 3–6 Year Olds in Northern Ireland," Belfast: Community Relations Council. Reprinted by permission of Paul Connolly; 207–208 Used by permission of Molson Canada; 214 The PEARS name is a trademark of A&F Pears Limited. By permission of the British Library; 229 Used by permission of Luntz Research; 234 © Copyright 1991 Benetton Group S.p.A. Photo: O. Toscani. Used by permission of Benetton; 238 Courtesy of Burns Film Ltd.; 243 Caleb Huntington; 250 Merrick Morton/MPTV.net; 258 Courtesy of Warsawpack; 279 "Ikea" photography 13″ × 19″, 2001. Artist: Gu Xiong. Reproduced by permission of Gu Xiong; 284 © Thomas Hartwell/CORBIS SABA/MAGMA

Statistics Canada information is used with the permission of the Minister of Industry, as Minister responsible for Statistics Canada. Information on the availability of the wide range of data from Statistics Canada can be obtained from Statistics Canada's Regional Offices, its World Wide Web site at http://www.statcan.ca, and its toll-free access number 1-800-263-1136.